Following God

LIFE PRINCIPLES FOR Worship FROM THE FEASTS OF ISRAEL

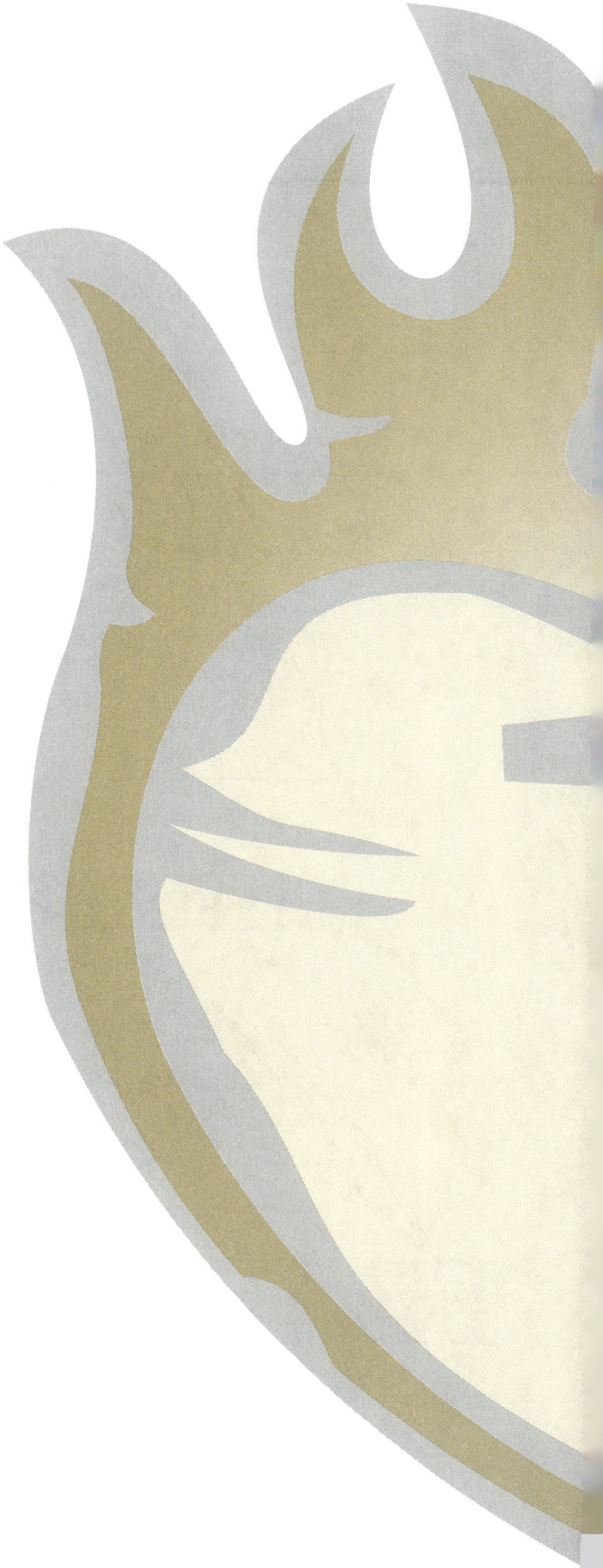

Following God

LIFE PRINCIPLES FOR Worship FROM THE FEASTS OF ISRAEL

RICK SHEPHERD

AMG Publishers
Advancing the Ministries of the Gospel
God's Word to you is our highest calling.

Following God

Life Principles for Worship from the Feasts of Isreal

© 2011 by Richard L. Shepherd

Published by AMG Publishers. All Rights Reserved.
No part of this publication, including the artwork, may be reproduced, stored in a retrieval system, or transmitted in any form or by any means, electronic, mechanical, photocopying, recording, or otherwise—except for brief quotations in printed reviews, without the prior written permission of the publisher.

First Printing, 2011

ISBN 13: 978-0-89957-345-8

Unless otherwise noted,
Scripture is taken from the *New American Standard Bible*®. Copyright © 1960, 1962, 1963, 1968, 1971, 1972, 1973, 1975, 1977 by The Lockman Foundation. Used by permission. (www.Lockman.org)

Scripture quotations marked (NKJV) are taken from the New King James Version, Copyright ©1982 by Thomas Nelson, Inc. Used by permission. All rights reserved.

Scripture quotations marked "AMPLIFIED" taken from the Amplified® Bible, Copyright © 1954, 1958, 1962, 1964, 1965, 1987 by The Lockman Foundation
Used by permission. (www.Lockman.org)

Editing by Rick Steele
Layout by Jennifer Ross and Rick Steele
Cover design by Michael Largent at InView Graphics, Chattanooga, Tennessee

Printed in Canada
16 15 14 13 12 11 –T– 6 5 4 3 2 1

Dedication

I dedicate this work first to those who received and carried the message of the Feasts—the Israelites, to whom pertain the adoption as a nation to display who God is, to whom pertain the glory of God, the covenants, the giving of the Law in which we learn of these Feasts, the serving of God in which they celebrated their relationship to God, and the promises God gave concerning His Son who is the fulfillment of these Feasts. I pray for salvation, for the true knowledge of Jesus as the Feast for these of whom are the fathers of the faith and from whom came *"the Christ, according to the flesh, who is Lord over all, the eternally blessed God, Amen"* (Romans 9:4–5; 10:1). May they and multitudes from the nations see that **Jesus Christ is the Feast**—all the Feasts fulfilled in Him. May each hear the call to come to Christ Jesus, to place personal faith in Him. By His Holy Spirit, may any and all who come find Him filling the heart so that each experiences the joy of the Lord, the fullness of **Jesus as The Feast**.

With that, I also dedicate this work to my grandchildren. If the Lord tarries His Return, may they live in the fullness of these Seven Celebrations, experiencing the working of Jesus in their lives in fullest measure. May each experience that **Jesus is the Feast**. *Aidan*, you are first. Lead the way. Become a man of God. Your name means "fire." May your heart *"burn within"* with the Word of God and the personal knowledge of Jesus as your Lord and Savior. *Dakota*, your name means "friend." Become a *"friend of God,"* a woman of God, showing others what it means to know and love Jesus. *Zooey*, your name means "life." May you know the *"eternal life"* of the Lord Jesus by faith. Become a man of God, a man of prayer, a man of faith, experiencing and expressing that life in fullest measure. To my other grandchildren, I do not know your names yet. God does. Let Jesus be your Source of holy fire, of true friendship, of eternal life, experiencing and expressing Him as your Feast, your Living Bread and Spring of Living Water.

Rick Shepherd (*PapaRick*)
Jacksonville, Florida—2011

Acknowledgments

First of all, I thank the Lord Jesus for the work of His Spirit giving continual encouragement, insights, and guidance in this study of The Feasts. Once again, it has been a discovery of my inadequacy and His sufficiency to guide into truth, to bring comments, phrases, or certain verses across my path through others or through what seemed a side path search through a reference tool. Those things that line up with His Word are obviously from Him and I thank Him for His insight. I take responsibility for any inaccurate or misunderstood statements I have made; the downside of writing. As in eating fish, so in the writings of men, one must eat the meat and throw away the bones. Only Scripture is without error, all milk and meat, no bones. I thank the Lord for His guidance. I have much more to learn and apply.

I am extremely grateful to my wife Linda Gail for her continual love, encouragement, prayer support, diligent editing, and helpful comments through this process. I am also grateful for the encouragement I have received from our children along the way. I am certainly indebted to the staff of AMG Publishers, especially Rick Steele, Warren Baker, Trevor Overcash, Dale Anderson, and the late Dan Penwell. Many prayer partners have prayed for and encouraged me these many months. I am grateful for their encouragement and prayers in completing this work. Their contribution will be measured only by eternity I am grateful for the continual encouragement and sense of urgency I hear from so many pastors and lay people across the state of Florida and beyond. I am grateful for the insights gleaned from my pastor Keith Russell, for those Scripture connections I have learned from pastor Mac Brunson, and for the insightful conversations with Al Whittinghill. I thank the Lord for the encouragement to write from those with whom I minister in the Florida Baptist Convention, particularly David Burton, Kathy Walker, and Dr. John Sullivan.

No work is original. There are always many streams flowing into any river. I am grateful for the many tools and reference works consulted in this journey. Two vital tools have been the *Hebrew-Greek Key Study Bible* edited by Spiros Zodhiates and Warren Baker, Revised Edition (Chattanooga: AMG Publishers, 2008) and *The MacArthur Study Bible* edited by John MacArthur (Nashville: Word Publishing, 1997). I am very grateful for the insights of Alfred Edersheim in his works, *The Life and Times of Jesus the Messiah* (Grand Rapids: Wm. B. Eerdmans Publishing Co., [1886] 1971) and *The Temple: Its Ministry and Services As They Were at the Time of Christ* (Grand Rapids: Wm. B. Eerdmans Publishing Co., 1983 Reprint). I appreciate Elwood McQuaid and his excellent work *The Outpouring: Jesus in the Feasts of Israel* (Bellmawr, NJ: The Friends of Israel Gospel Ministry, Inc., 1990). I appreciate the insights of Andrew C. Brunson in *Psalm 118 in the Gospel of John* (Mohr Siebeck, 2003) which confirmed some of my observations in John 7-8. I also acknowledge certain insights gleaned from *The Book of Acts in Its Graeco-Roman Setting*, Vol 2 of *The Book of Acts in Its First Century Setting*, edited by David W. J. Gill and Conrad Gempf (Grand Rapids: Wm. B. Eerdmans Publishing Co., 1994). In addition, I have explored with profit *The New Complete Works of Josephus* (translated by William Whiston), Revised and Expanded Edition (Grand Rapids: Kregel Publications, 1999), Alec Garrard, *The Splendor of the Temple* (Grand Rapids: Kregel Publications, 2000), Kevin Howard and Marvin Rosenthal, *The Feasts of the Lord* (Nashville: Thomas Nelson, 1997), Ceil and Moishe Rosen, *Christ in the Passover: Why Is This Night Different?* (Chicago: Moody Press, 1978), Mitch and Zhava Glaser, *The Fall Feasts of Israel* (Chicago: Moody Press, 1987), Edward Chumney, *The Seven Festivals of Messiah* (Shippensburg, PA: Destiny Image Publishers, Inc., 1994), E. L. C. Austin, *Earth's Greatest Day* (the resurrection) (Grand Rapids: Baker Book House, 1979), Maret H. Dinsmore, *What Really Happened When Christ Died* (Denver: Accent Books, 1979), and Kevin J. Conner, *The Feasts of Israel* (Portland: BT Publishing, 1980). I am grateful for the insightful presentation of Steven Ger in *The Unleavened Messiah: A Portrait of Christ in the Passover* (Garland, TX: Sojourner Ministries, 1996) and his *Exploring the Jewish Heart Series* (Six audio tapes on the Feasts and the Sabbath, 2000). I also appreciate the personal encouragement of John L. Glasser and his notes on *The Seven Feasts of Israel* (Birmingham, AL). May this work, *The Feasts of Israel*, build up believers and bring others to know **Jesus is** the Feast.

RICK SHEPHERD

About the Author

Richard L. Shepherd has been engaged in some form of ministry for over twenty-five years, focusing on areas of teaching, discipleship, and prayer. He has served in churches in Alabama, Florida, Texas, and Tennessee and now serves as Director of Prayer and Spiritual Awakening with the Florida Baptist Convention. For nearly seventeen years (1983–2000), Rick served as an associate pastor at Woodland Park Baptist Church in Chattanooga, Tennessee. The Lord's ministry has taken him to several countries, including Haiti, Romania, Ukraine, Moldova, Italy, Israel, England, and Greece, where he has been involved in training pastors, church leaders, and congregations. Rick has also lectured on college and seminary campuses. He graduated with honors from the University of Mobile and holds a Master of Divinity and a Ph.D. from Southwestern Baptist Theological Seminary in Fort Worth, Texas. He and his wife Linda Gail have four children and make their home in Jacksonville, Florida.

About the Following God Series

Three authors and fellow ministers, Wayne Barber, Eddie Rasnake, and Rick Shepherd, teamed up in 1998 to write a character-based Bible study for AMG Publishers. Their collaboration developed into the title, *Life Principles from the Old Testament*. Since 1998 these same authors and AMG Publishers have produced five more character-based studies—each consisting of twelve lessons geared around a five-day study of a particular Bible personality. More studies of this type are in the works. In 2001, AMG Publishers launched a different Following God category called the Following God™ Discipleship Series. The titles introduced in the Discipleship Series are among the first Following God™ studies to be published in a topically-based format (rather than Bible character-based). However, the interactive study format that readers have come to love remains constant with each new Following God™ release. As new titles and categories are being planned, our focus remains the same: to provide excellent Bible study materials that point people to God's Word in ways that allow them to apply truths to their own lives. More information on this groundbreaking series can be found on the following web pages:

www.amgpublishers.com
www.followinggod.com

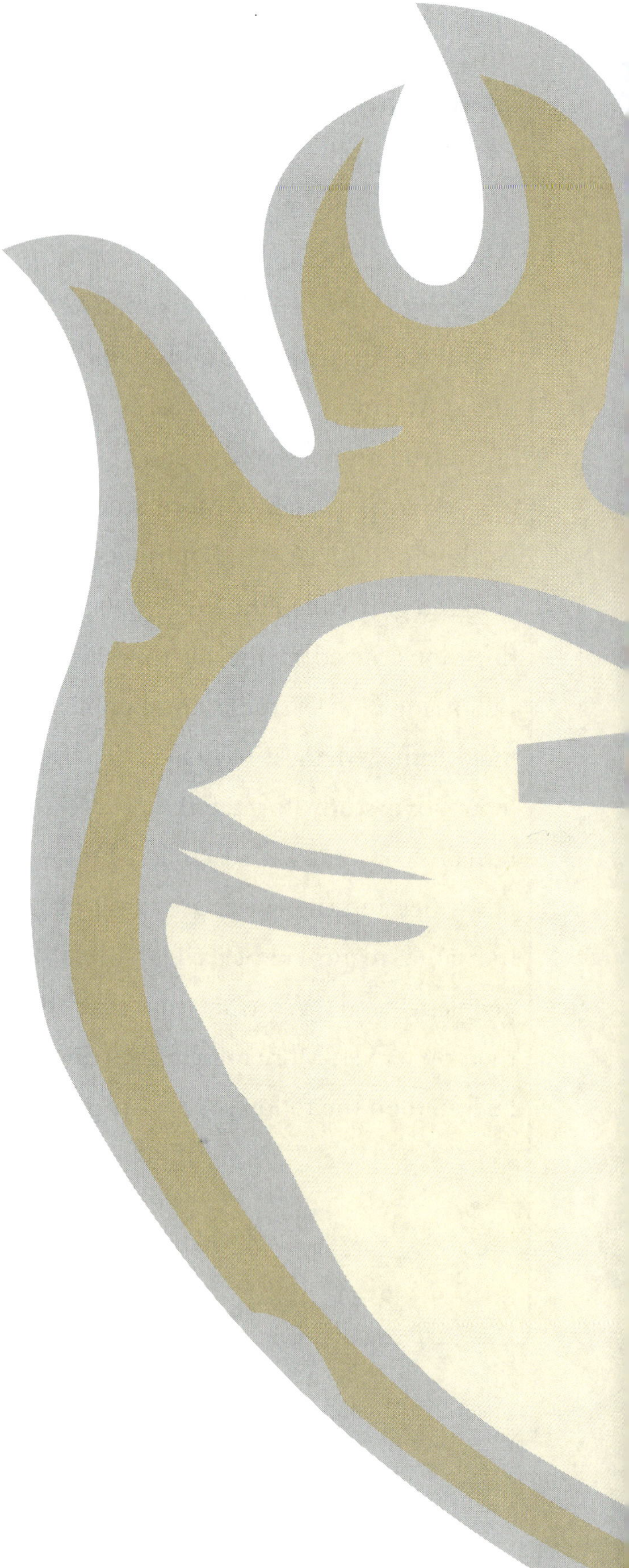

Preface

This journey through **The Feasts of Israel** focuses on the Feasts as practiced in the Old and New Testaments. I have purposefully not dealt with the modern observances of these Feasts, but rather focused on their fulfillment in Jesus and in the believer's walk. While seeking to be thorough, I have not been exhaustive; many additional insights wait to be gleaned.

The Feasts of Israel are actually *"the feasts of the LORD."* He is the focus—Meeting with Him is the point. The historical symbols in each Feast speak a message from His heart to every believer's heart. He calls people to come and worship Him with a heart feasting on Him.

In each Feast is a trail that leads to Jesus—to His Cross, to an Empty Tomb, to His ever-reigning Throne, to His Return and the fulfillment of every promise made in His Word. They lead ultimately to His once and for all established presence with His people in the New Earth with new heavens—all things made new (Revelation 21:5).

As you come to each Feast, think of the questions and paragraphs as a banquet setting with bowls and baskets, plates and platters, cups and saucers, glasses and silverware, all prepared for you. If you only look at the place settings, you will walk away hungry. The feast is found in the Word in these bowls, baskets, platters, and plates. In this Scripture adventure, the true feast is the Lord Himself. **Jesus is the Feast!** The Word of God is Him speaking, leading us to a personal, obedient, experiential relationship with Him day by day. The meat and the milk of the Word are linked to Him who feeds, satisfies, nourishes, and delights the heart (Psalm 119:103; Jeremiah 15:16; 1 Peter 2:1; Hebrews 5:12–14). Your enjoyment of this feast will depend on your participation—**your** personal time with the Lord. Little time with the Lord in the Word, little nourishment; much time with the Lord in the Word, much nourishment.

The call of the Feasts is not a call to accumulate knowledge, but to intensify relationship. Psalm 34:8 calls out, *"Oh, taste and see that the Lord is good; Blessed is the man who trusts in Him!"* Hear the call to greater trust and dependence, not simply knowing *about* Him, but knowing by experience. Psalm 34:10b promises, *"those who seek the Lord shall not lack any good thing."* The Feasts sound the call to seek the Lord, to grow in this relationship, not by simply knowing more Scripture points and principles, but by obeying and walking in that truth. When Jesus and His disciples stopped near the village of Sychar ready for a meal, Jesus mystified His disciples by saying, *"I have food to eat that you do not know about"* and *"My food is to do the will of Him who sent Me, and to finish His work"*—the work of bringing salvation, so multitudes might know Him and bring others to know Him (John 4:32). Jesus feasted doing the Father's will. We can, too. This is not a series of celebrations *"about Him,"* but *"with Him."*

The Feasts are also a call to seek God corporately. Seeking God together in certain Feasts ushered in a period of Spiritual Awakening—a new day and a new people, not a perfect day or a perfect people, but certainly changed. We see that in the Passover in Egypt. God brought true revival through the Passover in Hezekiah's day and at Pentecost in Jesus' day. Every Feast is an invitation to experience the Lord and join in His Kingdom's advance.

Make this your prayer…. *"Lord, open my eyes to see You and Your Word more clearly, so I can **do** Your will."* Remember, **Jesus is the Feast!** Knowing, loving, obeying, and worshiping Him is the goal of every Feast. Celebrate Jesus as Lord—Feast every day, in every place, and bring others to know Him! Feast together!

In Christ,

Richard L. Shepherd

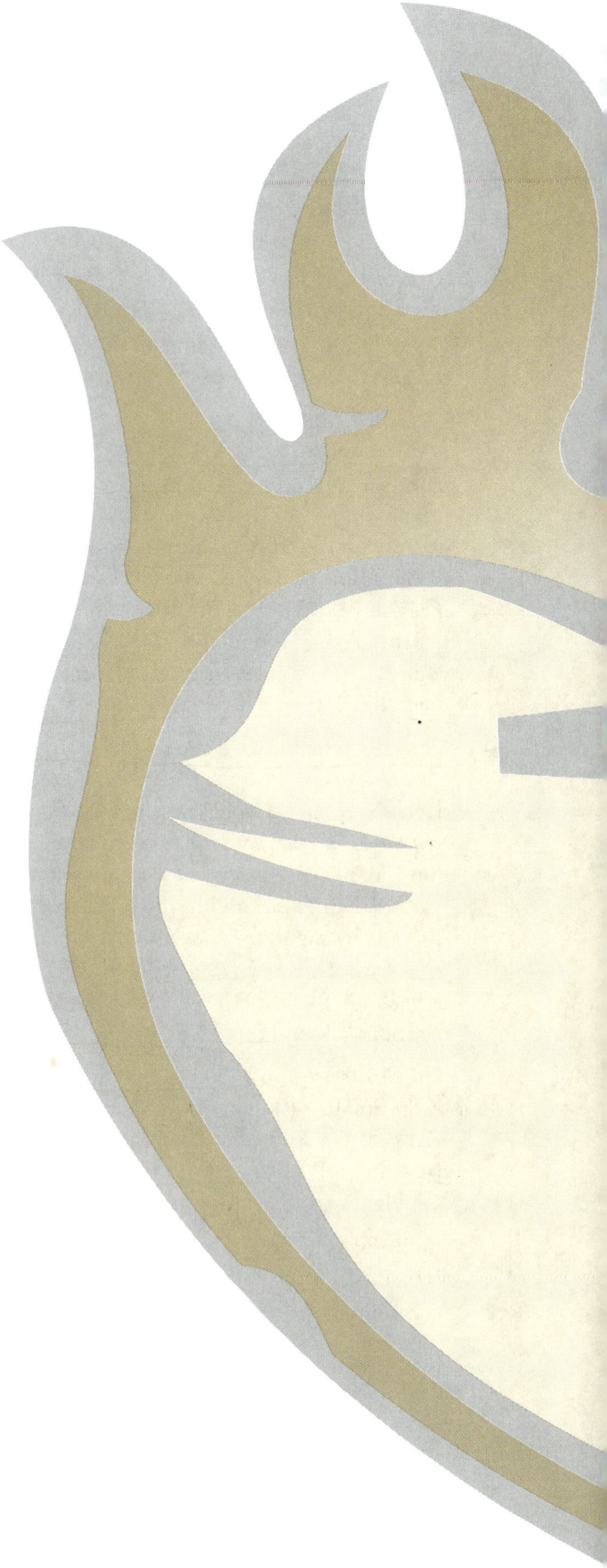

Table of Contents

The Call of the
Feasts of the Lord 1

The Feast of
Passover 25

The Feast of
Unleavened Bread 49

The Feast of
First Fruits 69

The Feast of
Pentecost 95

The Feast of
Trumpets 119

The Day of
Atonement 141

The Feast of
Tabernacles 169

The Call of the Feasts of the Lord

CELEBRATING CHRIST AND HIS SALVATION

In Deuteronomy 12:5, Moses pointed the people to God and to times of celebration before Him. *"But you shall seek the LORD at the place which the LORD your God shall choose from all your tribes, to establish His name there for His dwelling, and there you shall come."* That place would be the location of the Tabernacle for many years and finally the Temple in Jerusalem. In Deuteronomy 16:16, the Lord gave three different seasons for the Feasts, specific times for coming before the Lord in that place. Each was a special time of seeking the Lord and rejoicing together with Him.

The Feasts were an opportunity for undistracted focus on the Lord and one's relationship with Him. It included every aspect of life. Each of the Feasts connected in some way to the agricultural cycle, to the livelihood God gave the people in the land of Israel. They reminded everyone that every workday pointed in some way to the Lord, as did the abundance of fruits and grains harvested and livestock raised each year. They pointed to Him as provider and sustainer, the One who blessed them in the land given by Him. The offerings brought by the people reflected not only His blessings on them, but their grateful response of worship and praise.

Seeking God and celebrating the Feasts go hand in hand. It is the nature of God to celebrate. The Father, the Son, and the Holy Spirit delight in one another. God very much delighted in His creation and rejoices in holiness and love. The Feasts are His gifts to bring people into the celebration of His heart. At the heart of the Feasts is seeking the Lord, answering His call in the **Feasts.**

What we value we seek, and how we seek can make the difference in a life well-spent or a life wasted. The importance of seeking should not surprise us. We were created for seeking. It is part of growing. God made us to grow, to experience more and more of the life He desires to give. We have a seeking mechanism in our souls. We begin life seeking—crying out as a baby for food, attention, touch. We grow up continuing that kind of seeking, but our seeking goes deeper than that. We seek meaning, purpose, significance, plus answers to life's questions and perplexities.

Put Yourself In Their Shoes
GOD'S DESIRE GOD'S CALL

God's call reveals His will, His desire. Deuteronomy 12:5 shows us that **first,** He calls His people to **action**, the action of seeking Him, His person. **Second,** He calls to a place, not merely as a location, but as a **place of interaction**, of meeting with Him. **Third,** God calls them to know a personal **revelation** of Him, that is, *"His name,"* the revelation of His character and His ways. **Fourth,** God calls them to **dwelling** with Him, knowing and practicing His presence in this ongoing, growing relationship. **Fifth,** He calls them to **communication**, to planned time for this ongoing relationship. His heart desire is the same today. We answer His call through Jesus Christ through the **action** of genuine faith, and continue in the **interaction** of a faith walk, through the **revelation** of His Word by His Spirit. This means an ongoing, growing act of **dwelling** with Him along with others in the Body of Christ, and a growing **communication** with Him, practicing His presence, learning from Him and growing in knowing Him. That is His **call**.

When we look at history, we see people seeking greater spiritual reality, often in a variety of ways. God's design in our seeking is a life filled with meaning. He has wired life for seeking that is filled with interactive learning. Scripture reveals that God delights to interact with us and that He longs for us to have that same joy by joining with Him. Therefore, He calls us to seek Him and His ways. If we are to fulfill His design for life, growing in a personal relationship with Him—that for which we were created—we must seek and find and learn in line with His ways. The Scriptures show us those ways through examples, principles, and promises.

However, we have a problem here. Not everyone on earth is seeking God or His ways. Many are self-seeking, selfishly seeking, even using others (many trying to "use" God or a god) for their own desires and ambitions. God is well aware of this. In His mercy, He comes seeking us, as He did with Adam and Eve in the Garden of Eden. In the Scriptures, He has given many examples and principles for seeking and finding Him and His will. One of the ways He has given is **the Feasts of the Lord**. Each Feast is a **call**, an invitation to experience a spiritual reality in a relationship with the Lord. We will see that in the weeks ahead. In this lesson, we will see the big picture presented in the Feasts—what the Scriptures say and what it means to seek Him with a true heart. It is a journey of searching and discovering that can impact every area of your life.

Lesson One — DAY ONE

GOD CALLS HIS PEOPLE TO HIMSELF

Genesis 12—50 chronicles how God called Abram out of Ur of the Chaldeans, how he became Abraham and how God then called Isaac and later his son Jacob to follow Him. He called the family of Jacob into Egypt where they became enslaved for a period of time. Then, He called Moses to deliver the people out of Egyptian slavery and bring them into the promised land of Canaan. Through God's calling His people out of Egypt, we discover many of the inner workings of their relationship with Him. In the call of Abraham, Isaac, Jacob, Moses, and the people of Israel, the call is to God Himself, to a relationship, not just to a land or a religion. Today we will begin to see how important the call of God was in their lives and some of the ways that applies to the follower of Christ today.

📖 The foundation for everything celebrated in the Feasts provides the context of God's calling His people out of Egypt. What does God reveal about Himself in Exodus 6:1? What statement does He make about Himself in verse 2?

God showed His great power!
I Am the Lord.

📖 What did He do as Lord, according to verses 3–4?

Appeared unto Abraham, Isaac and Jacob and established His convenant with them, to give them the land of Canaan.

Did You Know?
"I AM THE LORD"

When the Lord made the statement *"I am the LORD,"* He used a royal formula that most likely would have been familiar to Moses. Kings in the Near East used this formula to begin a royal decree or edict. As an example, John Currid cites the *Legend of Sargon* in Assyria: 'I am Sargon, the mighty king.' In Exodus 6:2, **"The God"** introduces His royal decree revealing His purposes and plans for His covenant people. [For further insights see John D. Currid, *A Study Commentary on Exodus* (Auburn, MA: Evangelical Press, 2000), pp. 136–137]

appeared to them by the name, God Almighty & made agreement with them to give them Canaan, where they lived but didn't own.

📖 What was He doing in Moses' day according to verse 5?

God remembered His covenant
He heard the cry of Israel in Egypt

[margin: listening to the cries of Israel + remembering His agreement]

God promised Moses that He would reveal His power, showing His strong hand, delivering the people out of Egypt. He declared His signature name—*"I am the Lord."* That is the basis of His character and His working. He then recounted His relationship with Abraham, Isaac, and Jacob. With each of them, He made Himself known as *El Shaddai, "God Almighty,"* the all-sufficient God, the God of blessing. Now He is about to make Himself known as Lord/Yahweh. That name had been recognized before, but not like He is about to make Himself known. God repeats His signature, *"I am the Lord,"* four times in this encounter with Moses. In His signature name, He guarantees His presence to accomplish all He promised. This is personal to the Lord, His intense activity in salvation, not merely some religious story. Here is what **He did.** God **appeared** to Abraham, Isaac, and Jacob as *"God Almighty,"* and He **established** His covenant with them, giving them the land of Canaan. Now, God has **heard** the cries of His people in their slavery. God **remembered** His covenant and is now enacting His designs. He gives seven promises

[margin: 4-6-22 How do You want to make Yourself known to me?
to Autumn?
to Hannah?
to Emily?
to Carol?
(+ others)]

📖 Look at Exodus 6:6–8. God declared what He would do because of His covenant with Abraham. He made seven promises, seven *"I will…"* statements. List the first three from verse 6. On what do these first three focus?

I am the Lord, I will bring u out of Egypt
out of bondage, I will redeem u with
stretched out arm and with great jud-
ments

[margin: • save you from the hard work the Egyptians force on you to do.
• I will make you free so you will not be slaves to the Egyptians
• free you by My great power + punish the Egyptians.]

📖 On what do the two promises in verse 7 focus?

(personal) relationship of God with his
people (wants)
relationship w/ Him
+ who He is

📖 On what do the two promises in verse 8 focus?

Bring them into the land and give
it unto them (heritage) Abraham,
Isaac, and Jacob. I am the Lord

[margin: lead them to the land He promised Abraham, Isaac, Jacob + give it to them to own.]

"I am the Lord"—Here is what *I WILL DO* in redeeming you. *"I will bring you out." "I will deliver you from their bondage" "I will redeem you,"* the word "redeem" being the word for a kinsman or near relative who redeems family from some hardship such as slavery (see Leviticus 25:25, 48–49). God is treating them as His family.

"You shall know that I am the Lord"—Here is what you *WILL BE to ME* and what *I WILL BE* to you. *"I will take you for My people, and I will be your God"*—literally, *"I will take you to Me for a people, and I will be to you for*

a God." You to Me, for a people—I to you, for a God. Notice how personal this relationship is. They belong to Him, and He assumes responsibility for them. His signature, "I am the LORD."

His final signature, "I am the LORD," comes after He states what *I WILL GIVE YOU*. "I will bring you" to the Promised Land, and "I will give it to you" for your use. It belongs to Me and I can give it to whom I choose. God promised them a purposeful redemption, a personal relationship, and an exact place to live, the possession He chose for them. God promised what He would DO, what He would BE, and what He would GIVE. That is the nature of His covenant heart and covenant work.

[Handwritten margin notes:]
- *what He did to the people of Egypt*
- *carried them out of Egypt (as if on eagle's wings)*
- *brought you to Me, here.*

📖 God delivered His people out of Egypt and brought them first to Mount Sinai to establish them as a nation. In that meeting at Mount Sinai, God issued His calling for His people. Read Exodus 19:4–6. What three things had Israel "seen" according to verse 4?

what I did to Egyptians, how I bare u on eagles' wings, and brought u unto myself.

God brought Israel to Himself, intending to bring them into a personal relationship and knowledge of God. He emphasized that they had personally experienced the Exodus, "You yourselves have seen. . . ." First, they saw what God did to the Egyptians, judging them as a nation and defeating their gods. Second, they saw that God "bore you on eagles' wings," carefully guiding and protecting them (see Deuteronomy 32:11–12). Third, they saw how God "brought you to [Him]self," to a personal encounter, all intended as part of an ongoing personal relationship.

In Exodus 19:4–6, God uses the language of an ancient covenant agreement with His people. He begins by identifying Himself as the Lord who is entering into this covenant. He has recounted the history of their relationship—what He has done and what they have experienced. Then, He gave the stipulations of the covenant and what it would mean to Israel: "If you will . . . then you shall . . ." What were *they* to do, according to Exodus 19:5?

If u will obey my voice and keep my covenant, then u shall be a peculiar treasure unto me above all people, fr all the earth is mine

God called His people to obey His voice and keep His covenant. That meant listening with a heart to obey, to follow, to trust Him and His ways. He had shown Himself faithful time after time with a people who had shown themselves stubborn time after time. He is mercifully calling them into a covenant relationship with Himself. If they will obey, then they shall know three wonderful facets of being the people of God.

📖 What three things did He promise them in Exodus 19:5–6? What is to mark the people of God? To what are they called?

peculiar property, kingdom of priests, and a Holy Nation

be mine, be My Kingdom of priests, be a holy nation

Did You Know?
ANCIENT COVENANTS

In the encounter at Mount Sinai we see the elements of ancient covenant agreements. At this time in history (around 1445 BC), kings and rulers used a form of treaty or covenant containing five elements all of which are found in Exodus 19:3–8 in the Covenant instituted at Mount Sinai—a **Preamble** introducing the call of the Sovereign or king to enter into an agreement ("*the Lord called to [Moses] from the mountain, saying, "Thus you shall say to the house of Jacob. . . ."*), an historical **Prologue** recounting the nature of the relationship ("*You yourselves have seen what I did to the Egyptians. . . . I bore you on eagles' wings, and brought you to Myself*") **Stipulations** in the relationship ("*obey My voice and keep My covenant*"), **Blessings** promised ("*then you shall be My own possession among all the peoples. . . . and you shall be to Me a kingdom of priests and a holy nation*"), **Agreement and Acceptance** in the assembly of **witnesses** to the covenant ("*Moses called the elders of the people. . . and all the people answered together. . . . "All that the LORD has spoken we will do!" And Moses brought back the words of the people to the LORD.*")

[Handwritten note at bottom:] So He will be w/ us when we worship Him.

God desired in this personal relationship that Israel would know and experience three facets of knowing Him. First, Israel would be *"My own possession,"* the Hebrew word indicating a special treasure, especially one that belonged to a king (for example, 1 Chronicles 29:3). A sense of security and value, of being treasured, and of **belonging**, would mark the people of God. Second, Israel would be *"a kingdom of priests"* to the Lord. They would be uniquely connected by faith to God so they could lead others into a personal relationship with Him. God called them to show other nations what it means to believe in Him and how they, too, could know Him. True **believing** would mark God's people. Third, Israel would be *"a holy nation,"* set apart to the Lord, belonging to Him, unlike any other nations. Holiness and the resultant victorious holy relationships would mark God's people. They were called to belong, to act like God's people. They were called to believe and help others believe. They were called to an obedient, set-apart relationship and lifestyle—set apart to the Lord and His ways. Obedience to the Lord as a nation would mean victorious relationships throughout the nation. As each obeyed, each would experience the joy and victory God desired.

APPLY **Are You Marked as His?**—Being the people of God should carry three marks (Exodus 19:5–6)—1) Being valued by Him in His love, belonging to Him. Each should show His kind of love to others (being His *"own possession"*). Are you marked by that love—confident you are loved and then loving others? 2) Having a voice in prayer before Him and in witness before others (a *"kingdom of priests"* who believe God and serve others by connecting them with God. This means doing things His way, praying His way, and leading others to know Him by faith). Are you marked by praying for and influencing others, believing in His ability? 3) Walking in victorious relationships—a *"holy nation"* should be a nation of people filled with His life, obeying God, walking with a holy lifestyle, having victory over sin, and showing love His way. Are you marked by His victory in daily life? How are you walking?

How did this calling work out in the people of God? How did He bring them out of Egypt and bring them into the Promised Land? And where do the Feasts fit into them fulfilling the calling God had on their lives? We will begin to answer those questions in Days Two and Three.

Put Yourself In Their Shoes
FOLLOWERS OF CHRIST HAVE A CALLING

"But you are A CHOSEN RACE, A *royal* PRIESTHOOD, A HOLY NATION, A PEOPLE FOR *God's* OWN POSSESSION, *that you may proclaim the excellencies of Him who has called you out of darkness into His marvelous light; for you once were* NOT A PEOPLE, *but now you are* THE PEOPLE OF GOD; *you had* NOT RECEIVED MERCY, *but now you have* RECEIVED MERCY*."*

1 Peter 2:9–10

GOD'S PEOPLE IN PLACE ON PURPOSE

Lesson One **DAY TWO**

When we open the pages of the book of Exodus, we see the people of God enslaved in Egypt. God had a design to bring them out of bondage and into His promised land of freedom and joy. Years ago God entered into a covenant with Abraham, promising him a land, a nation of descendants to fill the land, and through that nation a Seed to come who would bless all nations. That Seed would be Jesus Christ.

LESSON ONE – THE CALL OF THE FEASTS OF THE LORD 5

Through the promise of a place, God always pointed to His purpose—for Him to be their God and for them to be His people. He put them in place on purpose. He does the same with each of His children. Before we look at how He implemented that design, we need to see His heart and purpose for these people. What did God want in His relationship with the children of Israel? Where do the Feasts of the Lord fit into the picture? Today we will discover how the Scriptures answer those questions.

> *Did You Know?*
> **SHOWING LOYALTY**
>
> In entering into a covenant with the LORD at Mount Sinai, Israel declared that *"all that the Lord has said we will do, and be obedient."* In essence they proclaimed, "we will worship the Lord, and we will show our loyalty to Him" (Exodus 24:7). During this time in history in the Near East, conquered peoples were required to journey and appear before their ruling king once a year to present tribute and declare their allegiance and loyalty. So Israel journeyed to the place of God's presence (Tabernacle or Temple) to appear before the Lord three times a year and present their offerings, which consisted of offerings in place of their firstborn and offerings of first fruits, the best of their families, fields, and flocks. They also declared their allegiance to their King, offering their lives in worship.

📖 Prior to the children of Israel's entrance into the Promised Land, God spoke through Moses and gave the heart of His purpose for bringing them into the land of Canaan. Those words are recorded in the book of Deuteronomy, Moses' final instructions in what it means to be the people of God. Read Deuteronomy 12:1–7. According to verse 1, by what standard are the Israelites to live?

His laws/commands
worshiping the Lord by his statues and judgments (of God) all the days that ye live upon the earth

📖 What did God say about the worship places and practices of the nations in Canaan? Look at verses 2–3 and summarize what you find.

Don't worship God that way
destroy all places their gods, altars, pillars, groves, graven images and destroy the names of them out of that place from there forever completely DESTROY them & their names

God's Word to the children of Israel gave clear directives, *"statutes"* and *"judgments,"* to guide His people throughout life in the new land. He clearly called them to be different from the nations of the world. Other nations worshipped many gods, many idols, and with that had many corrupt practices—things the Lord called abominable. He wanted every trace of that corruption cleared out of the land of Canaan so that none corrupted His people. Ideas, beliefs, and practices have lasting consequences for evil or good. God wanted His people to know the truth, and with understanding apply that liberating truth.

Again + again + again He repeated to worship at the place He chooses to be worshipped.

Celebrate, Rejoice + Give

📖 Read Deuteronomy 12:4–7. What did God say about Israel's **place** of worship? What specifics did God focus on concerning their **practices** of worship?

the LORD chooses the place, Go there + bring your offerings
God will chose the place of worship
Bring burnt offerings, sacrifaces, tithes and heave offering, vows, freewill, firstlings of herd

📖 Deuteronomy 16:1–17 gives a summary of the Feast Seasons and God's design and purpose. Look at verses 2, 5–6, 11, 15, and 16. What further insights do you find concerning "the place" at which the Feasts were to be celebrated?

The land must be cleansed fr all idolatry bring tithes and offerings, may eat freely what God giveth clean & unclean but do not eat the blood

• offer an animal from your flock or herd
• not in just any town you want, but where He chooses even in the land He gives you.
• Everyone Rejoice before Him
• Celebrate the Feast 7 days
• all men must come to the three Feasts where He chooses + never w/o a gift

6 FOLLOWING GOD – LIFE PRINCIPLES FOR WORSHIP FROM THE FEASTS OF ISRAEL

God had at least three things in mind as He gave instructions about the Feasts. Three elements stand out. First, the **personal** element—God centered His instructions around *"the LORD your God."* Note, *"your God."* It was a personal relationship about which He spoke. He intended everyone to be a joyful participant in that relationship—individually and corporately. Second, He gave a **place** element. He had a chosen a "place" in mind to which they were to come and at which they were to meet together with Him. Third, He gave a **time** element. Specific months, numbers of weeks or days, evenings and mornings, all point to the time element, to specific appointments with the Lord. The three required meetings with the Lord centered around the **Feast of Unleavened Bread** in the Spring (Passover, Unleavened Bread, and First fruits), the **Feast of Weeks** (Pentecost) fifty days later (late spring), and the **Feast of Booths or Tabernacles** which occurred in the Fall. It was connected to the **Feast of Trumpets** and the **Day of Atonement** (these final three occurring in the seventh month of the year).

All three elements—the personal element, the place element, and the time element—concentrate attention on seeking and experiencing God. He is the divine host of each celebration event. Instead of many places of worship, God instructed His people to come to a certain place to *"seek the LORD."* That place would eventually be Jerusalem and the Temple there, His chosen place to *"establish His name"* and His dwelling. God said, *"There you shall come"* with sacrifices, tithes, and various glad offerings. God designed times for the people to come, yearly seasons of feasting at that place. God meant it to be a wonderful meeting with Him and with those from throughout the land.

📖 What is at the heart of God's desire for His people according to Deuteronomy 12:7 and 16:10–12, 14–17?

Eat before the Lord yr God & ye shall rejoice in all that ye put yr hand unto, ye & yr house where the Lord thy God hath blessed thee

In contrast to the corrupt worship and ways of the other nations, God commanded Israel to worship centered around *"the LORD your God."* God desires worship marked by joyful obedience to His Word and remembrance of all His blessings. God set aside a place for Israel to *"rejoice in all your undertakings in which the LORD your God has blessed you"* (12:7). He directed everyone to participate in the Feast seasons—all the family, all the servants, leaders, Levites, orphans and widows, even *"strangers,"* those who were Gentiles but who followed the LORD God. This was a time of celebration, rejoicing, and enjoying the fruits of their labors, the blessings of God. God desired for His people that they *"be altogether joyful"* in coming together seeking Him (16:15).

Part of the joy of these Feasts is found in their giving—giving to the Lord, to His priests, to those in need, and sharing with others during the Feasts. As the Lord had blessed and given to each one, so each one was to give to the Lord and to others. Each time was *"a feast to the LORD your God."* Israel stood as a redeemed community that acted like it belonged to the Lord, showing His kind of love and care for one another. Every year, their calendar reflected their priorities—seeking God, worshiping Him, and celebrating that relationship individually and corporately.

Put Yourself In Their Shoes

TITHES, OFFERINGS, AND FEAST TIMES

God directed the nation of Israel to bring in certain tithes and offerings to meet various needs, including those of the Tabernacle/Temple and priesthood as well as the needs of widows and orphans. Deuteronomy 14:22–26 speaks of the tithe (10 percent) to be brought to the Temple at each of the Feast pilgrimages to be enjoyed by the worshipers in celebration as they ate together with the priests before the Lord. Each of the three required pilgrimages occurred around a harvest time (**Passover** with first fruits, **Pentecost** (another time of first fruits), and **Tabernacles** at the end of the autumn harvest season). God required a second tithe for the priests, Levites, and the work of the Temple (Leviticus 27:30–32; Numbers 18:21–32; Deuteronomy 14:27; Nehemiah 12:44–47; 13:5, 9–13). He also required a third tithe every three years (about 3 percent per year) to be kept in the local community rather than at the Temple. This provided for the Levites, for widows, orphans, and foreigners in each of the towns (Deuteronomy 14:28–29; 26:12–15). Thus the people gave a twenty-three percent tithe to the Lord each year in addition to votive offerings, thank offerings, peace or fellowship offerings, and necessary sin or guilt offerings.

Did You Know?
ISRAEL'S FALSE FEAST AND FALSE WORSHIP

In 931 BC, when Jeroboam I became king of Israel (the Northern Kingdom that split away from Judah), he jealously tried to protect his power. To assure loyalty to himself and to keep people from going to Jerusalem to worship, he created his own priesthood and two new worship sites at Dan (to the north) and Bethel (to the south) with two golden calves to worship. He also invented a new false "feast" on the fifteenth day of the eighth month, one month after the Feast of Tabernacles (1 Kings 12:25–33).

Forgive me God for ever worshipping you my own way (& giving to needy sparingly). 4.7.22

Give me a right heart, God!

Put Yourself In Their Shoes
WHEN JUDGMENT CAME

Lamentations 1:3–5 speaks of the judgment of God on Judah because of their idolatry and sin. As they languished in seventy years of captivity in Babylon, Jeremiah observed, *"the roads to Zion mourn because no one comes to the set feasts"* (NKJV). Their sin and unfaithfulness to the Lord brought judgment for a season. Their Feasts discontinued for seventy years while they endured God's chastening hand.

📖 God's purpose for His people was never a mere external observance of the Feasts. He wanted them to celebrate His working and their relationship with Him. Israel did not always do that. Amos prophesied to the Northern Kingdom of Israel around 760 BC, a time of idolatry and corruption. What did he declare in Amos 5:21–27? What did God say about their feast days? *He hated their religion & feasts*

I hate, I despise your feast days & I will not smell in your solemn assemblies. Warnings of judgement if they do not repent

God gave Amos a message of rebuke, warning, and impending judgment upon Israel if it did not turn from its sin and do what He commanded. He spoke about their Feast days as something He despised and hated. They assembled, but not to truly worship. They offered burnt offerings and peace offerings, but without surrendered hearts. They sang songs and played their musical instruments, but it was only *"noise"* to God. Why? Because their actions did not line up with His Word or His character. They practiced injustice and unrighteousness along with all kinds of idolatry, worshiping the planets and stars and any number of false gods. A Feast celebration or any external worship without a right heart is sickening to God.

📖 Around twenty years later, Isaiah prophesied to the land of Judah and Jerusalem. What do you discover in Isaiah 1:10–15? Note especially verse 14. *Your new moons & your appointed feasts my soul hateth: they are trouble unto me; I am weary to bear them. Even the feasts He Himself appointed He hates if the heart isn't His.*

offerings are like a heavy weight to Him if no heart in it. He turns to curry such false worship

📖 What is God's answer? Read Isaiah 1:16–20 and record your insights. *God call them repentance that may forgiven them and cleanse their hearts, and bring rejoicing back to the people. Repentance is sweet. Stop evil, doing wrong & heartless worship — indeed, do good, help orphans & widows*

The year of these words to Judah and Jerusalem is around 739 BC, a time when many had drifted into an empty formalism in worship. Some were guilty of idolatry. Mere externals characterized their sacrifices and their worship. The people observed the weekly Sabbaths, the monthly New Moons, and even the yearly Feasts, but God hated their observances. Their hearts were not right as evidenced in their treatment of those in real need—the fatherless and the widow. Injustice, evil deeds, and disobedience to His Word filled their lives. Isaiah warned of impending judgment, but offered the merciful forgiveness of God. If they would repent, turn, cleanse their lives, and begin doing what is right, He would forgive, cleanse the heart, and bring rejoicing to the people.

God wanted a heart that worshiped Him and Feasts that truly celebrated the relationship between Him and His people. How should that look? We will discover more of His design in Day Three.

Spending Time with God

Lesson One — **Day Three**

613   Deut 20:4

When the Lord gave Moses the guidelines for their worship and celebration times, He ordered each very specifically. The calendar would not revolve around business or the weather, though those things certainly mattered. The calendar would revolve around their relationship, their walk with the Lord. That meant setting aside set times for worship, for thinking about His Word, for conversations about what it meant to belong to Him, to be His people marked by His character and ways. Today, we will look at some of those guidelines as we discover more of what it means to spend time with God and how the Feasts fit in. *(pg 5)*

📖 In Leviticus 23:2, what is the first truth you discover about the *"the LORD's appointed times"*? *They were considered Holy meetings & His Special Feasts*

The Lord said unto them concerning the feasts of the Lord, which ye shall proclaim to be holy convocations

📖 What is the first appointed time God describes in verse 3?

Six days shall work be done; but the 7th day is the sabbath of rest, a holy convocation; ye shall do no work
7th day a Special day of Rest, for Holy meeting

God called for each appointed time to be a *"holy convocation,"* a gathering to show forth the holy relationship between God and His people. The Lord addressed first the importance of the weekly Sabbath, a time for *"complete rest"* and for a *"holy convocation"* or a *"holy assembly."* It served as a time to cease work, to gather to hear the Word and worship (see Numbers 28:9–10), and for families to seek the Lord more fully. Note that it was more than simply a 'do not work' day. It was a *"holy"* time, a time for the people to live differently and to show forth a different view of the week and of time. The Sabbath served as a time to reflect back on the faithfulness and provision of God in the six days preceding and a time to ready their hearts and their physical strength for the work assignments of the next six days. God never intended it as a legalistic, regimented day, but rather as a weekly day set aside for the holiness and health of His people.

In addition to the **weekly Sabbath**, God called for the **monthly New Moon** celebration at the beginning of each month. That celebration included the blowing of trumpets (Numbers 10:10), a specific burnt offering, and a sin offering (Numbers 28:11–15). We will discover more about this when we look at the Feast of Trumpets in a future lesson.

📖 God also called for "a unique pattern of years." What do you find about the Sabbatical year in Exodus 23:10–11 and Leviticus 25:1–7?

Six years u shall sow your land and gather in its produce. the 7th yr u shall let it rest and lie fallow, that the poor people may eat. the land's year of Rest.

> **Doctrine**
> ## THE SABBATH AS A SIGN
>
> In giving the Ten Commandments, God called for a Sabbath rest, blessing the seventh day as a holy day of rest at creation (Genesis 2:2–3; Exodus 20:11) and noting the rest from slavery He gave in bringing them out of Egypt (Deuteronomy 5:15). Unlike their time in Egypt, working seven days every week, the Israelites now would work only six days and set aside the seventh day as a day of rest and worship. Exodus 31:12–17 speaks of the Sabbath as *"a sign between Me and you throughout your generations, that you may know that I am the LORD who sanctifies you."* The Sabbath served as a way for Israel to testify that they were different, in a class all by themselves. Why? They belonged to the Lord and acknowledged that relationship in a special way by setting apart the seventh day as a Sabbath ("rest") to the Lord, as belonging to Him, set apart (or "holy") to Him. Like Israel, the Sabbath uniquely belonged to the Lord. The Israelites depended on Him for their needs and testified in part through setting aside a day to honor and worship Him. God would take care of them, though they worked one day less, because they would be working with Him, **under His Lordship and blessing.**

LESSON ONE – THE CALL OF THE FEASTS OF THE LORD   9

[Margin note: Be of a giving heart like God's]

📖 What additional insights do you discover in Deuteronomy 15:1–11? Note especially the heart attitude for which God calls in verses 7–11.

Give unto thy brother, the poor and the needy. The Lord will bless thee in all thy work. 14th Day, 1st month Lord's passover

God called for a complete *"sabbath rest"* of the land every seventh year in order for the land to lie fallow. That meant no tilling, sowing, or pruning. God would provide all they needed in the first six years prior to take care of the seventh year. That which grew in the seventh year could be eaten by the poor and by livestock grazing. This would also provide a way for the people to trust Him more fully. In the seventh year, He also commanded a forgiving of debts to all fellow Israelites. The temptation would exist to not loan funds to a poor man as the seventh year approached, since that debt would be forgiven and possibly the person making the loan would not receive all his funds back. God called for a generous heart, not a greedy heart. We are to trust the Lord for provision. Deuteronomy 15:9 uses a Hebrew idiom, the "evil eye," translated a *"hostile"* eye, referring to a stingy, greedy viewpoint that is reluctant or resistant to give to one in need because of losing much or even all of what is given. Not giving would be a sin against God, a show of mistrust toward Him and His provision, and it would also be a sin against the neighbor. God called for a "good" or a generous eye toward one's neighbor in need. To the one who trusted God and displayed a giving heart, the promise states, *"the LORD your God will bless you in all your work and in all your undertakings."*

[Margin note: as represented or illustrated through Joseph in Egypt?]

Put Yourself In Their Shoes
FAILURE TO FOLLOW THE SABBATICAL YEAR

The temptation to worry about provision from the Lord during the sabbatical year, to keep working to make sure all was taken care of, proved a snare to Israel. The nation failed to follow the Lord in taking a sabbatical year. Not only that, their failure to trust the Lord led them to worship and serve false gods like Baal, the supposed god of rain and crops. God's corrective judgment came for their idolatry and for their abuse of the sabbatical year. Jeremiah prophesied that because of their idolatry the people would be taken captive away from the land for seventy years (Jeremiah 29:1–11). In 2 Chronicles 36:21 we read that the land *"enjoyed its Sabbaths . . . until seventy years were complete,"* fulfilling 490 years of history, one year for every seven from 1095 to 605 BC, from King Saul to King Jehoiakim.

📖 Leviticus 23:4 notes the common characteristic of **every** Feast. What is that characteristic? What is significant about that?

These are the feasts of the Lord, even holy convocations which ye shall proclaim in their seasons. (appointed times) "Set times"

The Feasts are called *"the LORD's appointed times."* Like the weekly Sabbath, they are special times for meeting with the Lord, for *"holy convocations"* or *"holy assemblies,"* times set apart **with** Him and **for** Him. While every Feast celebrated a different aspect of the work of God with His people, every Feast had this in common; each celebrated the central aspect of belonging to Him, of being *His holy* people. They assembled for a *"holy"* convocation, a meeting characterized by honoring His holiness and making sure they were walking as He desired. Besides the weekly Sabbath and the monthly New Moon, God gave seven yearly Feasts.

[Margin note: So are self or church is my jealousy or lust or flirting or inappropriate dress or competition honoring His Holiness?!]

📖 Leviticus 23:4–44 gives a quick summary of the Feasts. Read verses 5–44 and list the seven *"appointed times."*

1. Leviticus 23:5 — *In the 14th day of 1st month (passover) beginning at twilight*
2. Leviticus 23:6–8 — *In the 15th day of 1st (unleavened bread) feast*
3. Leviticus 23:9–14 — *(first fruits) of harvest – bring 1st bundle of grain, also offer a male lamb (burnt offering), a grain offering (flour 20?) + drink offering of a quart of wine; do not eat grain (roasted or in) bread until you bring the offering to God — next day*

10 FOLLOWING GOD – LIFE PRINCIPLES FOR WORSHIP FROM THE FEASTS OF ISRAEL

4. Leviticus 23:15–22 _50 day later pentecost_ *[margin: 2 loaves of yeast from 1st harvest of wheat, 2 male sheep, 2 male lambs, grain offering, drink offering, burnt offering, sin offering]*

5. Leviticus 23:23–2 _Feasts of Trumpets 1st day 7 month_ (REST - holy meeting)

6. Leviticus 23:26–32 _Atonement (the day of) cleansing_ - Holy meeting, deny self, don't eat every day

7. Leviticus 23:33–36, 39–44 _feast of booths - celebrate before the Lord, live in shelters_

The first of the Seven Feasts or the *"appointed times"* is Passover or *"the LORD'S Passover."* Closely connected to that is the Feast of Unleavened Bread and the Feast of Firstfruits. Following fifty days later is the Feast of Weeks or Pentecost (Fiftieth Day). Then, in the Fall came the Feast of Trumpets, the Day of Atonement, and the Feast of Booths or Tabernacles (also known as The Feast of Ingathering). Each of these had a prominent place and played a special part in the corporate and personal lives of God's people.

📖 What part do the agricultural seasons play in these Feasts according to Leviticus 23:10, 16, 22, and 39? _early Spring Passover, Fall = harvest season_ *[7 in feast]*
Bring the firstfruits of yr Harvest to Priest, offer a new grain offering to Lord. 50 Days. Keep the feast of the 7 days the 1st & 8th days shall a sabbath - rest. (Lord) *[Lord's Festival]*

The Lord spoke of the new land with new harvests and the offering of first fruits after Passover in the early spring. Then, He spoke of the period fifty days later when another *"new grain offering"* would be offered along with two loaves of bread, lambs, a bull, two rams, a male goat, and libations of wine. One of the indications that this connected to a harvest time around Pentecost is seen in God's call for His people to leave the corners of the fields for the needy and the foreigner to glean food. That occurred during the late spring season. The final Feast occurred in the fall, at the end of harvest season. Recall that the three required meetings with the Lord centered around the Feast of Unleavened Bread (Passover, Unleavened Bread, and First fruits), the Feast of Weeks fifty days later, and the Feast of Booths or Tabernacles which occurred in the Fall and was connected to the Feast of Trumpets and the Day of Atonement (all three occurring in the seventh month in the Fall).

📖 According to Leviticus 23:5, 10, 42–43, what historical events or time periods are mentioned in these Feasts? [We will see much more about the history of Israel in the lessons to come.]
Lord's Passover, Harvest time Firstfruits, feast of booths/shelters. When Lord brought Israel out of Egypt

📖 What historical events are mentioned in Deuteronomy 16:1, 3, 6, 12?
Passover, eat unleaved bread, sacrifice the passover to the Lord, remember u were a slave in Egypt, observe & do these Statues

---

Word Study
"FEAST"

The word *"feast"* referred to in Exodus 23:14–16 and Deuteronomy 16:16 is a translation of the Hebrew word *hagag* or *hag* (or *chag*), a "pilgrim festival," referring to the three yearly feasts God required of all males. The word is rooted in the idea of twirling or moving in a circle of celebration. In Exodus 10:9, Moses spoke of God's call to *"hold a feast to the LORD,"* which they celebrated when they established the covenant at Mount Sinai (Exodus 24:1–11). God called them annually to three feast pilgrimages which recalled the Passover deliverance out of Egypt (Passover and Unleavened Bread), the journey to and settling the Promised Land (First fruits and Pentecost), and their ongoing worship of the Lord as their God (Trumpets, Day of Atonement, Tabernacles). In Leviticus 23:2, *"feasts"* is a translation of *mo'ed* literally meaning an *"appointed time"* or an appointed *"meeting."* Each of these focused on meeting with God in shared worship. All Israel rejoiced before their God through sacrifices, offerings, and gifts. In the New Testament, *"feast"* is a translation of the Greek word *heorte*, used twenty-seven times. The verb *heortazo*, *"to celebrate,"* is used once and emphasizes the daily walk of purity reflective of the believer's relationship to Christ (1 Corinthians 5:8).

Did they "celebrate" at the receiving of the law???

"For Christ our Passover Lamb has been sacrificed. So let us celebrate the feast"

Passover: brought out of Egypt, leaving Egypt (in a hurry) when you left Egypt (sun down) Slavery (of Israel)

LESSON ONE – THE CALL OF THE FEASTS OF THE LORD 11

In giving these seven Feasts, the Lord mentions Passover, the time in which He **passed over** the homes of the Israelites in Egypt ushering them out of slavery. He spoke of the time when they would enter a new land with new harvests. He focused especially on the time when the Lord *"brought them out from the land of Egypt"* (23:43). It must be remembered that in Egypt the Israelites had no holidays and no feast days other than what the Egyptians *may* have had in which they could have allowed these slaves to celebrate. The instructions from the Lord spoke of celebrating a new day for Israel, a new calendar, all new holy days in a new land.

In summary, the Feasts of the Lord present a five-fold focus concerning the relationship of the Lord with Israel. As we walk through these Feasts, these five perspectives will help us understand and apply these Feasts to our walk with God. The Feasts or Festivals are first of all **His** celebrations, "His Feasts," Feasts to the Lord or *"the LORD'S Appointed Times . . . My Appointed Times . . . the Appointed Times of the LORD"* (Leviticus 23:2, 4). Deuteronomy 16:1 speaks of celebrating the first Feast *"to the LORD your God,"* and 16:15 refers to the seventh Feast as *"a feast to the LORD your God,"* focusing attention on Him. Each Feast focused on one's personal relationship to Him as well as the corporate relationship that bonded Israel to the Lord as His people. Within each Feast, we discover something of God's purpose for His people.

Secondly, because of the personal connection to the Lord, these are **holy** celebrations, times when God's people come before Him in *"holy convocations"* or *"assemblies,"* offering *"holy"* offerings *"without defect"* as His set apart or *"holy nation."* The emphases on cleansing, on appropriate sin offerings, and on following His Word point to the holy nature of each Feast. In each Feast, God called His people to purity, personally, as families, and as a nation.

Put Yourself In Their Shoes
CELEBRATING KNOWING THE LORD

The Feasts were a celebration of the Lord, who He is, what He has done, and the salvation He promises and gives. It is a celebration of Him and His work. Therefore, each is a holy celebration. The Feasts were tied to harvest celebrations and to God's acts in history. They were personal and national celebrations, celebrations of the heart. The Feasts picture one's relationship with Jesus Christ and the salvation He bought and brings to each believing heart. These believers make up the harvest of people belonging to Him. Therefore, knowing Jesus as Lord and Savior is meant to be a celebration of Him and of a holy lifestyle. This relationship is grounded in history. It is **History** and becomes a part of each believer's personal history.

Thirdly, these are **harvest** celebrations, a time of remembering, rejoicing, and thanking the Lord for His abundant blessings. Three specific agricultural seasons are early spring (Barley harvest at the time of the first three Feasts), late spring (Wheat harvest, the fourth Feast), and fall (Fruit, olives, and grain harvest, the time of the final three Feasts). Each season celebrated God's provision.

Fourthly, the Feasts are **history** celebrations, a time for remembering historical events and anticipating future events. They give evidence of the workings of God's providence.

Fifthly, these Feasts are **heart** celebrations, connecting each heart to the heart of God in some way, through seven Feast times revealing certain spiritual realities God wants in the heart of each of His children. They show God's personal participation in our lives. We will see each of these as we journey with Israel through the Feasts of the Lord.

APPLY What do you celebrate? What we celebrate tells something about what or who we value. What is valuable to you? What is significant in *your* history? God wants *His* most important things—loving Him with all one's heart, mind, soul, and strength, loving one's neighbor His way, and bringing others to know and love Him—to be the most important things in *your* life. How about you? What do you celebrate? Are you celebrating things that He loves or things He hates? Do you celebrate things that should be a shame to you

12 FOLLOWING GOD – LIFE PRINCIPLES FOR WORSHIP FROM THE FEASTS OF ISRAEL

since they are to Him? Or, are you rejoicing in Him, in His ways, and in your relationship to Him?

The Old Testament Feasts are God's call to Israel to celebrate their relationship with Him. Now let's look at what the New Testament says to the Christian today.

THE CALL OF CHRIST TO HIMSELF

Lesson One — **DAY FOUR**

The call of God to Himself is evident in the Old Testament. We have seen that call especially in the call out of Egypt and into the Promised Land and in the call to seek Him in the seven Feasts. In the New Testament, we hear the call of God to His people, but it goes much deeper than certain locations or outward celebrations. It is not a call to a land but to a life. We will begin looking at how this call is answered today and how it relates to the Feasts. Then, lesson by lesson, we will discover God's call to His people in the Old Testament as well as to us today.

📖 What is Jesus' call to His first disciples as seen in Matthew 4:17–19?

Follow me and I will make u fishers of Men (people). — Repent — the Kingdom of God is at hand

📖 What additional insights do you glean from Jesus' call in Matthew 11:28–30?

Come to me, Take my yoke upon u and learn from me for I am gentle and lowly in heart, u will find rest 4 yr souls

He's calling us to a light load & light burden even to a rest (in Him)

📖 Look at Luke 9:22–26. Jesus' call encompassed time and eternity. What additional aspects of His call do you find in these verses?

If anyone desires to come after me, let him deny himself, and take up his cross daily, and follow Me.

must give up your own wants & life to follow Him. (daily thing)

Jesus began His ministry with the call to repent in preparation for the kingdom of heaven—a new ruler and a new day. John the Baptist had thundered the same message just months before. Jesus called Peter, Andrew, and several others to "follow Me," to become fishers of men, bringing people into a right relationship with God through Jesus. Jesus called people to a change of heart and a change of lifestyle. When He urged people to "come to Me" and "take My yoke," He used the language of a rabbi. The "yoke" was the term used for the lifestyle of the rabbi, the understanding and choices that a rabbi would lead a person to make. Jesus was different than any other rabbi. He would give "rest," and lead with a "gentle" and "humble" heart, not demeaning and arrogant like some. That also meant following His call to a new lifestyle, not seeking one's own will, but willing to die to self, taking up a daily execution of self-will, to walk in His will for His sake. One must trust Him and His words, living expectant of His return and His kingdom.

So perhaps this is why I can't do it bc I am hearing a harsh demeaning command (since trauma). His gentle humble character is what causes us to obey & do & be

Guess I just need to get my sword & renew this traumatized mind.

Margin notes (purple/handwritten):
- Follow Me / come after Me / leaving other gods etc.!
- Believe Christ / Put on the New Self! (Put away the old)
- Begins + Ends w/ Faith
- Faith is how God makes people right w/ Him
- A lifestyle of living by faith!

📖 How does one answer His call according to Ephesians 1:13 and 4:20–24?

through trust and belief in him by word of true we put off the old man and put on the new man.

📖 How does Romans 1:16–17 describe this call and this walk?

The Gospel of Christ is power of God to salvation for everyone who believes, the Jew first and the Greek. The just shall live by faith.

📖 What additional insights do you see in Colossians 2:6–7 and 2:13–15?

As u have received Christ so walk in him, rooted and builded up in him established in faith as u been taught, abounding in it with thanksgiving.

Handwritten annotations: Keeps your focus in Him! / Have your life built on Him / Be strong in faith / Be thankful

Throughout our lives, Jesus calls us to faith *in* Him and a faith walk *with* Him. Paul testified in Romans 1:16 that one who placed faith in Jesus as presented in the gospel message would experience the power of His salvation. God would give the gift of eternal life and a standing of righteousness before God. That standing of righteousness would be matched by a walk of righteousness. The righteous or just man or woman will live by faith, experiencing His power in a faith walk. As we receive Christ into our lives by faith, so we walk with Him by faith. He has rooted us in Himself and now works in us to grow us, to build us up in our relationship with Him. The overflow should be gratitude.

In the context of Colossians 2:6–7, we find Colossians 2:13–15 describing how the Lord Jesus forgives us of all our sins, for every time we have stepped over the line in transgression. He has cleared the slate of our lives. We are no longer in a state of condemnation. He conquered all principalities and powers through His death on the cross, and regardless of their temptations and deceptions, we do not stand condemned, nor can we ever.

What do these truths about our calling and Christ's work have to do with the Feasts? Paul addresses a potential problem in the Colossian church, a problem of misunderstanding what it means to answer Christ's call to follow Him. Some thought it meant being more zealous to follow the Old Testament regulations, but Paul has a word of counsel and correction.

📖 What do you discover in Colossians 2:16?

let no one judge you in food or in drink, or regarding a festival or new moon or sabbaths

Don't let anyone make rules for you about eating + drinking + religious feast or new moon festivals or other sabbaths

📖 Paul is writing under the leadership of the Holy Spirit. What is the focus of the Holy Spirit in Colossians 2:17?

which are a shadow of things to come, but the 'substance is of Christ.' Focus on CHRIST! (rather than rules + regulations of N.T.)

> "Therefore let no one sit in judgment on you in matters of food and drink, or with regard to a feast day or a new moon or a Sabbath. Such [things] are only the shadow of things that are to come, and they have only a symbolic value. But the reality— the substance, the solid fact of what is foreshadowed, the body of it—belongs to Christ."
>
> Colossians 2:16–17 (The Amplified Bible)

What should be the focus of every believer, according to Colossians 2:19? What applications does Paul make in verses 20–23?

As a body of believers our strength come from Christ, who is the head of the body, not the world. CHRIST IS FOCUS!

Evidently, some in the Colossian church were judging one another based on how they were following Jewish dietary laws and the Jewish calendar—Feasts, New Moons, Sabbaths. Certain false teachers were seeking to force their outward regulations on believers, trying to convince them that victory over temptation could be gained by outward rules. They had mistakenly assumed that those external practices must be kept in place, failing to see how Christ had fulfilled all the law. Only in a faith walk with Him could His life be experienced to the fullest. In Old Testament days, each of those practices served as a *"shadow"* of what was to come. They gave a general idea of the shape and size of the greater reality, the Messiah/Christ in His fullness bringing *"the substance."* By knowing Christ, being in union with Him, they had access to His power over fleshly temptations. Like the body linked to the head, so the believer linked to Christ receives His nourishment, His stability, and growth His way. Since every believer died with Christ to the world and the flesh, one should never try to use the world's regulations to achieve the life which God wants us to simply receive by faith. While the world's ways can appear impressive, they usually only mask pride and are powerless against temptation.

How do these truths apply to the Feasts of the Old Testament? Is there any reason to study these Feasts today? We will see in the lessons yet to come how Christ fulfills each Feast and how He wants us to live *in light of His finished work*. As we look at the *"shadow"* of each Feast, we will be better informed to experience *"the substance"* in Christ.

God is faithful, and He remains true to His Word and His promises. The Feasts celebrate what He has done in the past. They also point to the ultimate fellowship and fulfillment of a personal relationship with the Lord Jesus—Feasting with Him now and forever.

ANSWERING THE CALL OF THE FEASTS

The call of the Feasts is a call to come to the Lord. It is a call to journey to His chosen place and there celebrate with others the personal relationship to which He called each one as well as the relationship to which He called the nation as the people of God, That call in the Old Testament Feasts is also God's call in the New Testament, *"in Christ."* The Feasts are the *"shadow"* of all that God desired to show His people, teach His people, and do with His people. Christ is the *"substance,"* the fullness of the will and work of God. He is the way to the Father, to a personal relationship with Him. Through that personal relationship with Him, we walk with God in the realities of all the Feasts. To understand and apply these realities, we must first apply God's call to our lives. Today we will explore that call and discover some of those application points.

Word Study
"FESTAL ASSEMBLY"

Hebrews 12:22–23 states, "but you have come to Mount Zion and to the city of the living God, the heavenly Jerusalem, and to an innumerable company of angels, to the general assembly and church of the first-born who are enrolled in heaven." The phrase "general assembly" is a translation of the Greek word paneguris which some translate as "festal assembly." It refers to a public festal gathering, celebration, or assembly, emphasizing the festive nature of the gathering. Paneguris is used in the Greek Septuagint (LXX) in Ezekiel 46:11 and Hosea 2:11 referring to the "appointed feasts." The Hebrew word that the Septuagint translates as "feasts" is chag, which pictures moving in a circle or marching in a festal procession. It means to celebrate a festival. The glad and festive assembly of heaven in Hebrews 12:23 shows us that our ultimate home is a feast home filled with great joy in which the toil and troubles of earth are past. Our salvation is complete.

Lesson One — DAY FIVE

LESSON ONE – THE CALL OF THE FEASTS OF THE LORD   15

[Handwritten margin notes:]
- *Respect Him + Obey Him*
- *Long life + that all would go well w/ them.*
- *It's a call to love Him w/ all our being.*
- *Always remembering His commands—teaching them to their children—whatever they're doing—instilling in them a lifestyle of His commands.*

📖 What did God desire for His people in bringing them into the land of Canaan, according to Deuteronomy 6:1–3?

God desired that u may fear the Lord, to keep all his Statutes & His commandments, u, your Son, yr Grandson, all the days of yr life

📖 What do you discover about God's call in Deuteronomy 6:4–5?

God is one u shall love the lord with all yr heart, all yr soul, and with all yr might

📖 How did God want His people to walk in this call, according to Deuteronomy 6:6–9? Note the ways God gave to know and fulfill His will.

Words shall be in yr heart, u shall teach them diligently to ur children, talk to them when u sit in ur house, walk by the way lie down and rise up, bind them on thy hand write them on the door posts & gates

God gave His commandments and statutes for living in the land of Canaan. He wanted His people to fear the Lord and obey Him, and thus assure themselves of a well-ordered life in a well-supplied land. The key to this life would be their relationship to the Lord as their God. The foundation stone for every day life and for every relationship would be loving God in every dimension—*"with all [their] heart and with all [their] soul and with all [their] might."* It starts in the heart, the center of one's life, of one's thinking and choosing. We are led by what leads our hearts. What leads our hearts is determined in large measure by what we focus on and listen to. That is why it is so important to pay heed to what enters the heart—and especially to the words God gave.

[handwritten: What leads my heart today? God? Kids? My safety?]

For Israel and for us God's words are to be on our hearts—not just a casual acquaintance or a temporary thought. His words must govern our everyday lives. Notice how involved these words would be with Israel—first *"in your heart,"* believing them, living them, practicing them, then *"teach them diligently"* to your children. How? *"Talk of them"* when sitting in the house, when walking outside, when traveling to and fro, when going to sleep and when waking for each new day. *"Bind them,"* in such a way that you are reminded of them and *"write them"* so that they are seen every time you walk out of or into your house. In other words, make God's Word the foundation for every relationship in life, for every dimension of life, every place in your life, every segment of time—every day, every Sabbath, every New Moon, every Feast time.

📖 What did Jesus say about the heart in Mark 12:29–31?

ur Lord is one, Love ur God with all ur heart, all ur soul, all ur mind, all ur strength, Love ur neighbor as urself.

Love the Lord your God w/ All of it!

In Their Shoes
SEVEN FEASTS—SEVEN REALITIES

The Feasts speak of seven realities in the life of Israel and today picture seven realities for the Christian. 1) **Passover**—Our Redemption by the blood of the Lamb. 2) **Unleavened Bread**—The Purity of an "unleavened" life. 3) **Firstfruits**—Hope in the provision of Christ's resurrection—a new life now and a future resurrection, made forever whole. 4) **Pentecost**—Living by the Spirit's promise and provision as a body of believers. 5) **Trumpets**—Knowing God will call us to assembly and accountability before Him. 6) **Atonement**—Experiencing God's full salvation, sin fully forgiven and forgotten, and His presence fully experienced. 7) **Tabernacles**—God dwelling with us. Celebrating the fullness of God's life and presence on earth and in eternity.

📖 What did Jesus say about heart problems in Mark 7:1–23?

it's not what goes into a man that defiles him but what comes out of his heart that defiles him

📖 What did Jesus say about heart solutions in John 3:3–16?

u most be borned again. from above given a new heart and power to Love like God

must be born again of the Spirit — Believe — hearts must be Saved & reborn by Spirit

As Jesus walked about Israel, teaching, healing, and dealing with people, He continually focused on people's heart condition. In answer to a question about what commandment is the foremost of all, Jesus quoted from Deuteronomy 6:4–5, agreeing that loving God from the heart mattered most. And with that loving one's neighbor as oneself (quoting Leviticus 19:18). Love from the heart in every area of life mattered most.

Jesus did not believe a person could fulfill this on his own. He understood the problems of the heart. Some like the Pharisees tended to focus more on the externals—hand-washing rituals, what one eats or does not eat, and things like that. Jesus went straight to the heart of the matter (which is the heart) in dealing with them. Many were honoring God with their words, their lip service, but their hearts were far from Him. They were marked by the bad fruit Jesus mentions in Mark 7:20–23, things like evil thoughts, thefts, immorality, coveting, pride, and many other similar things. God's goal is a love relationship from the heart, not a "religious" life filled with externals.

Jesus' call is to the heart. That is His focus with Nicodemus in John 3. Every person needs a new birth experience, being born from above, given a new heart and the power to love like God desires. To see that become a reality, Jesus knew He must *"be lifted up"* like the serpent Moses lifted up in the wilderness. All who looked were made whole (see Numbers 21:5–9). Jesus would eventually be lifted up on a cross, die for our sins, and rise again to give us new life. As those in the Old Testament found God's healing by looking upon the serpent, those that look to Jesus find new life in Him. The Old Testament prophets spoke of *"a new heart"* in Ezekiel 36:25–28 and *"a new covenant"* in Jeremiah 31:31–34. Jesus brought both in His call to the heart.

APPLY **How's Your Heart?**—Do you have a personal relationship with Jesus Christ as your Lord and Savior? Have you looked to Him, asked Him to forgive and cleanse you? Has He given you a new heart? Are you born from above or *"born again"*? Are you walking in fellowship with Him from the heart, or is there some issue that is interfering with your fellowship? Stop and pray. Talk to Him and deal with anything He brings up in prayer or in your time in His Word. Remember, 1 John 1:7–9 promises His forgiveness and fellowship with Him.

📖 God's call is always to become His, to belong to Him. Appearing almost fifty times in the Old Testament is the phrase "You will be My people and I will be your God" (or similar). [Examples include Genesis 17:7–8; Exodus 6:7; 29:45–46; Leviticus 26:12; Jeremiah 7:23; 11:4; 24:7; 30:22; 31:33; Ezekiel

LESSON ONE – THE CALL OF THE FEASTS OF THE LORD 17

36:28; 37:27.] How do we apply that today? What does God say to the New Testament believer, to each follower of Christ? Paul the Apostle wrote concerning this in several passages. Look at these and write a summary statement of each one.

Acts 20:28 with Ephesians 1:7, 13–14

We have redemption through His blood / we are his

> [margin note:] The Blood He shed was to purchase us. We have forgiveness & redemption through that blood, by Grace. When we believed He SEALED us w/ His Holy Spirit.

1 Corinthians 6:19–20 *we aren't our own – we are His temple where His Spirit lives! Our body is the Temple of the Holy Spirit, bought with a price. our body is to Glorify God!*

1 Corinthians 10:31–33

whatever you do, do all to the glory of GoD & do not for our benefit but for Others' benefit – that they may be Saved.

2 Corinthians 6:14–18; 7:1

Do not be unequally yoked together with unbelievers, be Holy

> "Celebrate the Feast."
>
> "Rejoice in the Lord always."
>
> 1 Corinthians 5:8; Philippians 4:4

Paul told the elders in Ephesus that Jesus purchased the church with His own blood. He redeemed or bought each one at an inestimable price. All those who trust in Him through the word of truth, the message of salvation through Jesus, are His *"purchased possession."* Each believer in Christ belongs to Him. He or she has been bought with a price, the price of His life on the cross. Therefore, everything we do is to glorify or show forth who He is and what it means to belong to Him—everything—eating, drinking, every relationship, every action, every word spoken. We are not to be yoked or partnered with unbelievers in their thinking or their choices. We should be marked as those who know the presence of the Lord and walk accordingly. That does not mean perfection, but it does mean dealing with temptation and sin, seeking to walk rightly, growing in knowing Him and His Word.

📖 God's consistent call in the Old and New Testaments is to be holy. Leviticus 11:45 states, *"For I am the LORD, who brought you up from the land of Egypt, to be your God; thus you shall be holy for I am holy."* In the context, God was speaking of what they ate, guarding them against anything unclean. How does that apply to us today? One application is apparent—everything, including something as simple as food, matters to God. God wants us to walk holy or set apart to Him. Does the New Testament have anything to say to this? Read 1 Peter 1:14–25 and summarize your insights.

Our GoD wants us to be like him, for He created us in image and his likeness, for he is a Holy GoD and His wants his children to be Holy also. He wants close personal relationship with us.

> [margin note:] V15 Be holy in your conduct – in reverence & love one another constantly... no longer think & act & live as you formerly did.

Peter encapsulates all three truths concerning our walk with God—God's call is to the **Heart**, to be **His**, and to be **Holy**. First, consider the **Heart**—In hearing, **believing**, and obeying the truth, the message of the gospel, each soul stands purified by the blood of Jesus, "born again." From that new heart God commands each to "love one another from the heart." **Consider being His**—Each is a child of God, with His spiritual DNA in the heart. Each one answers to the Father and has been purchased by the "precious blood" of Christ. We **belong** to Him and should act accordingly. **Consider being Holy**—He is holy and because we are now born into the family, we should reflect that family likeness—"You shall be holy, for I am holy." That should be true in all our choices, all our **behavior**.

These three truths—God's call to the heart, the call to be His, and the call to be holy—are interwoven in every part of the relationship between God and His people. Everything in the Christian life ultimately links to knowing Jesus Christ and walking with Him in a personal, heart-to-heart relationship. God wants us to celebrate that relationship, to "rejoice in the Lord always" (Philippians 4:4). That brings us back to the Feasts. The Feasts are times of celebrating the relationship of God's people with Himself, because of what He has done for them to make them **His** in **heart** for a **holy** walk. We will see this several times as we journey through the Feasts. We will look at what it means to celebrate the Feasts "in Christ" and rejoice in all God has done, is doing, and promises to do yet future.

APPLY — **The Heart that is His**—What do these truths mean to you? In the space below, write your reflections on each of the truths we have looked at in Day Five.

Because of His call to my **Heart**, I respond with this prayer:
Thank u Lord for saving me. You called to my heart & I responded, so I have a new holy heart now & purity by Jesus' Blood, Thank you! (Help me believe it so deep that it affects how I live). Glory!

Because I am called to be **His**, I respond with this prayer:
Thank u Lord, I give myself to u. I still belong to you, God, (trauma doesn't change that - shattered emotions don't change that), help me truly believe it in my core belief system so I will act out of this truth. Thank you! Glory!

Because I am called to be **Holy**, I respond with this prayer:
Thank u Lord, help me to be Holy, 4 thy are Holy. God you called me to be holy & gave me your Spirit to help me be that. Help me believe by Your Spirit, I can be holy & let my life show I believe it to my core. (Bc I think I don't live more holy because I don't believe it enough).

Matt. 8:13

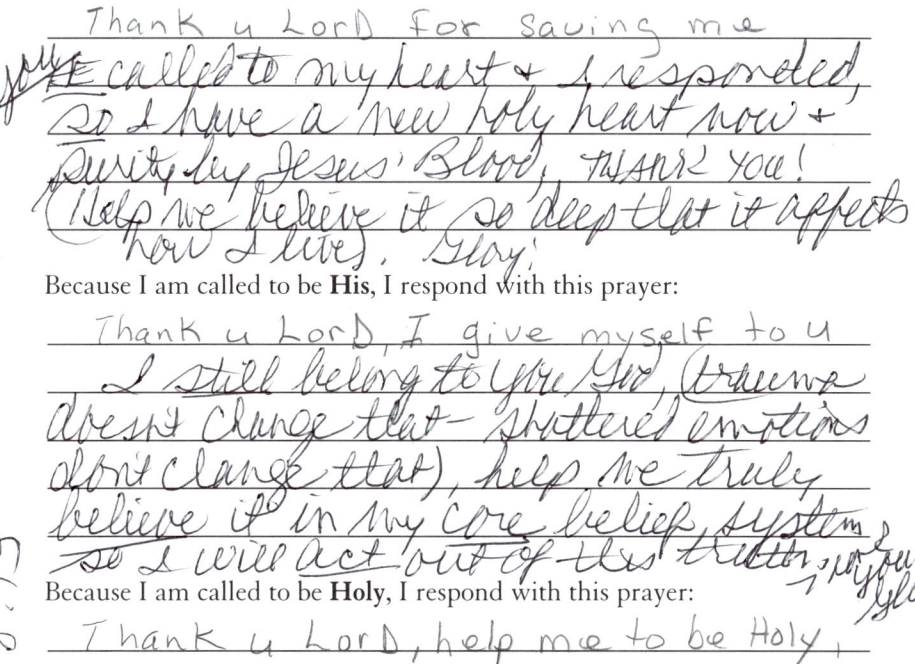

> **Did You Know?**
> ## "I AM THE LORD"
>
> Jesus spoke in parabolic form of the future, using the imagery of a great Feast. Matthew 8:11; Luke 14:15–24; and Matthew 24:1–14 speak of the future kingdom comparing it to a great marriage celebration feast. Isaiah 25:6–8 speaks of a great feast on Mount Zion in which the Lord provides the best for His people, a time yet future when there will be no death nor tears nor disgrace. Revelation 19:6–9 speaks of the awe-inspiring Marriage Supper of the Lamb in which the Bride of Jesus Christ (the Christian church) rejoices with Him in great celebration. Revelation 21—22 describes the conditions of a perpetual feast in the presence of the Lord in the New Jerusalem with a new heaven and new earth. Each of the Feasts is ultimately fulfilled in this forever reality of a secure relationship and joyful fellowship between the Lord and His people.

Carol

That's them (in eternity) but we celebrate by faith now.

LESSON ONE – THE CALL OF THE FEASTS OF THE LORD

> *Wow! Israel's whole calendar was centered around God & remembrance*

Lord, I want to answer Your call in the Feasts. I want to walk in a heart-to-heart fellowship with You, experiencing what it means to belong to You. Show me more clearly what it means to walk holy in all I do or say or think. As I walk through each of the Feasts, help me understand the way You work with Your people, the way You bring salvation, and <u>the continual call to celebrate You in the Feasts on a daily basis</u>—*in Christ*. <u>Open my eyes to see</u>, my ears to hear, <u>my mind to understand</u>, and <u>my heart to wholeheartedly obey and worship</u>. May I truly answer Your call in the Feasts, and personally celebrate Christ. In Jesus' name, amen.

Change me + my whole life of this, Lord! 4-21-22

ISRAEL'S CALENDAR

Religious Calendar	Civil Calendar	Gregorian Calendar	Main Events and Agricultural Events	Feasts or Special Days
1. Abib / Nisan First Month of the Religious Year	7. Seventh month of the Civil Year	March—April	*Pilgrimage* to the Tabernacle / Temple for the Feast of Unleavened Bread Celebrated the *Exodus* out of Egypt. **First Month/ Beginning of the Religious Year** Latter Rains Conclude Barley and Flax Harvests	**1. Passover** (Nisan 14)—Exodus 12:1–11; Leviticus 23:5 **2. Feast of Unleavened Bread** (Nisan 15–21)—Leviticus 23:6–8 **3. Feast of First Fruits** Leviticus 23:9–14
2. Ziv / Iyyar	8. Eighth month/Civil	April—May	Dry Period Grain Harvest Continues	
3. Sivan	9. Ninth month/Civil	May—June	*Pilgrimage* to the Tabernacle / Temple for the Feast of Weeks (sometimes called Firstfruits) Firstfruits of Wheat Harvest Figs begin ripening	**4. Feast of Weeks or Pentecost** (Sivan 6) (50 Days after Firstfruits) Leviticus 23:9–14
4. Tammuz	10. Tenth month/Civil	June—July	Full Wheat Harvest Begin Grape Harvest	
5. Ab	11. Eleventh month/Civil	July—August	Full Grape Harvest Olive Harvest	
6. Elul	12. Twelfth month/Civil	August—September	Dates Harvest Summer Figs Harvest	
7. Ethanim / Tishri Sabbatical Month of the Religious Year	1. First Month of the Civil Year	September—October	*Pilgrimage* to the Tabernacle / Temple for the Feast of Booths / Tabernacles **Sabbatical Month** **Tishri 1**—Jewish **New Year,** *Rosh Hashanah* (*Hebrew* for "Head of the Year") Former or Early Rains Begin Plowing Fields	**5. Feast of Trumpets** (Tishri 1) Leviticus 23:15–22 **6. Day of Atonement** (Tishri 10) Leviticus 16; 23:26–32 **7. Feast of Booths / Tabernacles / Ingathering** (Tishri 15–22) Leviticus 33–36
8. Bul / Marchesvan	2. Second month/Civil	October—November	Plowing Fields, Rains Sowing Barley and Wheat	
9. Chislev (or Kislev)	3. Third month/Civil	November—December	Winter Season	**Dedication / Hanukkah** (Chislev 25) John 10:22
10. Tebeth	4. Fourth month/Civil	December—January	Winter Rains	
11. Shebat	5. Fifth month / Civil	January—February	Almond Trees Blossom	
12. Adar	6. Sixth month/ Civil	February—March	Beginning of Latter Rains Citrus Fruit Harvest	**Purim** (Adar 13–14) Esther 9:26–28

THE FEASTS AND FESTIVALS OF ISRAEL
ALONG WITH THE FEASTS OF PURIM, DEDICATION, AND THE SABBATH

FEAST	WHEN	WHAT	WHY	SCRIPTURE
Passover	Nisan 14 (First month of religious calendar—end of March)—(Lamb selection, Nisan 10)	Lamb slain for the deliverance of the household from death and from Egyptian slavery	Remember and celebrate the Lord's deliverance of Israel through the exodus from Egypt	Exodus 12 Leviticus 23:5 Deuteronomy 16:1–7
Unleavened Bread	Nisan 15–21 (around April 1–7)	No leaven eaten. Remembrance of their hasty departure from Egypt and symbol of cleansing from corruption	Part of the celebration of the Passover when they had no time for bread to rise. Part of deliverance from Egypt	Leviticus 23:6–8 Deuteronomy 16:8
Firstfruits	Sunday morning after Sabbath after Passover during the Week of Unleavened Bread	First barley sheaves offered as a Wave offering before the Lord, plus a Burnt Offering of a male lamb, grain, oil, and wine	Celebrate the beginning, the "firstfruits," of the harvest and worship God as the giver of all	Leviticus 23:9–14
Feast of Weeks or Pentecost	50 Days after First Fruits (Seven Weeks/Sabbaths after the Day of Firstfruits). This places Day 50 on a Sunday.	Offer a Wave Offering of two leavened loaves of wheat before the Lord, a Burnt Offering of 7 lambs, one bull, 2 rams, grain, oil, wine, a Sin Offering of a male goat, a Peace Offering of 2 male lambs	Celebrate the ingathering of the Spring Harvest. Moses and the people also received the Law (Ten Commandments, etc.) at Mount Sinai on this day.	Leviticus 23:15–21, 22 Deuteronomy 16:9–12
Trumpets	Tishri 1 (Seventh month, around mid-September)	Trumpets Call Israel to Assembly and to Accountability. An ingathering of the people	To gather to the Lord, to prepare to meet with Him.	Leviticus 23:23–25
Day of Atonement *Yom Kippur* A Day of Fasting	Tishri 10, (Seventh month, around late September)	The Day the High Priest went into the Holy of Holies to present the offering of blood of bull and goat on the Mercy Seat to cover sins.	God called for the yearly Day of Atonement for the covering of the people's sins for the past year.	Leviticus 23:26–32 and 16:1–34
Feast of Tabernacles or Booths or Ingathering	Tishri 15–21, plus Tishri 22 (the 8th day as a holy assembly) (early October)	For one week, the people lived in makeshift Booths of leafy branches symbolizing their journey through the Wilderness to the Promised Land.	Celebration of God's provision and protection in the Wilderness and His provision of harvests in the Promised Land.	Leviticus 23:33–44 Deuteronomy 16:13–17
Purim	Adar 14–15 (around March 1)	Celebration of the Deliverance God provided through Esther and Mordecai (ca 473 BC)	To celebrate the victory God gave over the enemies of the Jews (Esther 9:22)	Esther 1–10, note chapter 3 and 9:17–32
Dedication, Hanukkah, or Feast of Lights	Chislev/Kislev 25 (around December 10)	Commemoration of the Jews' Deliverance and cleansing of the Temple in 164 BC.	To celebrate the victory of the Hasmoneans against Antiocus Epiphanes and the Syrians during the Maccabean Revolt	John 10:22–39 Many expected the Messiah to reveal Himself at this time (10:24)
Sabbath	The Seventh Day of every Week (Saturday) and every called Sabbath during a Feast time	A Day of Rest (No work) to focus on the Lord, His Word, the relationship of the people with Him, and worship of Him.	God rested. He wanted His people to rest in order to seek Him, know Him, and worship Him.	Genesis 2:2–3 Exodus 20:8–11; 23:12; 31:13–16 Leviticus 23:3 Deuteronomy 5:12

THE OFFERINGS OF THE FEASTS
Including Daily, Weekly Sabbath, and Monthly New Moon Offerings

DAYS/CALENDAR	OFFERINGS	SCRIPTURE
Daily Offerings, one at 9:00 AM and one at 3:00 PM	Burnt Offering—One year male lamb, grain and olive oil, plus wine every morning and every evening	Exodus 29:38–42 Numbers 28:3–8
Weekly **Sabbath** Offering	Burnt Offering—Two male lambs plus the grain, oil, and wine offerings for each animal. Plus the Daily Burnt Offering	Leviticus 23:3 Numbers 28:9–10
Monthly **New Moon** Offering	Burnt Offerings—Two young bulls, one ram, seven male lambs plus the grain, oil, and wine offerings for each animal. Sin Offering—one male goat. Plus the Daily Burnt Offerings	Numbers 28:11–15
Passover—Nisan 14	A Passover lamb	Exodus 12:14–28,42–51
Unleavened Bread—Nisan 15–21 (joined to Passover beginning on the night of Abib/Nisan 14) **Holy Convocation** on the **first** day (Nisan 15) and the **seventh** day (Nisan 21)	Burnt Offerings for each day for seven days— Two young bulls each day plus grain, oil, and wine, One ram plus grain, oil, wine Seven male lambs plus grain, oil, wine Sin Offering—One male goat each day. Plus the Daily Burnt Offerings	Exodus 12:15–20 Leviticus 23:4–8 Numbers 28:16–25
Feast of Firstfruits—The day after the Sabbath after Passover (Leviticus 23:15). During the week of Nisan 15–21	Wave Offering—One sheaf (omer) of barley Burnt Offering—One-year-old male lamb plus grain, oil, and wine. Plus Daily Burnt Offerings.	Leviticus 23:9–15
Feast of Weeks / Harvest/ Pentecost—Fifty days (seven Sabbaths plus one day) after the Feast of Firstfruits—The month Sivan (late May, early June) **Holy Convocation** on Pentecost	Wave Offering—Two loaves of leavened bread (wheat) Burnt Offerings—Two young bulls plus grain, oil, and wine One Ram plus grain, oil, wine Seven male lambs plus grain, oil, wine Sin Offering—One male goat. Plus Daily Burnt Offerings	Leviticus 23:15–21 Numbers 28:26–31
Feast of Trumpets—Tishri 1 (seventh month) **Holy Convocation** on Tishri 1	Burnt Offerings— One young bull plus grain, oil, and wine. One ram plus grain, oil, and wine Seven male lambs plus grain, oil, wine for each Sin Offering—One male goat. Plus Monthly New Moon Offering. Plus Daily Burnt Offering	Leviticus 23:22–25 Numbers 29:1–6
Day of Atonement—Tishri 10 **Holy Convocation** on Tishri 10	Burnt Offerings of one ram for the High Priest and one ram for the Nation. Plus, Burnt Offerings of One young bull plus grain, oil, wine, One ram plus grain, oil, wine and Seven male lambs plus grain, oil, wine for each Sin Offerings—One bull for the High Priest, one male goat for the nation and one male goat as the Scapegoat for the nation, plus one kid of the goats as a sin offering. Plus Daily burnt offerings	Leviticus 16:1–28; 23:26–32 Numbers 29:7–11
Feast of Tabernacles/ Booths / Ingathering—Tishri 15–22 **Holy Convocation** on **Day 1** (Tishri 15) and **Day 8** (Tishri 22) **7 Days** of **Holy Convocations** each year Offerings for the 7 Days of the Feast totaled 70 bulls, 14 rams, 98 lambs, 7 goats (189 animals—7x7x3), in addition to those of Day 8 and the Daily Burnt Offerings. Total: 215 animals in 8 days.	Burnt Offerings— Day 1—13 bulls, 2 rams, 14 lambs plus grain offering Day 2—12 bulls, 2 rams, 14 lambs plus grain offering. Day 3—11 bulls, 2 rams, 14 lambs plus grain offering Day 4—10 bulls, 2 rams, 14 lambs plus grain offering Day 5—9 bulls, 2 rams, 14 lambs plus grain offering Day 6—8 bulls, 2 rams, 14 lambs plus grain offering Day 7—7 bulls, 2 rams, 14 lambs plus grain ofeing Day 8—1 bull, 1 ram, 7 male lambs plus grain offering. Sin Offering of one male goat daily—Daily Burnt Offering	Leviticus 23:33–36, 39–43 Numbers 29:12–38
Sin Offerings and Trespass Offerings Any day by individuals or groups	Sin Offerings and Trespass Offerings—According to the guidelines for priests, congregation, rulers, and individuals	Leviticus 4:1–35; 5:1–18; 6:1–7
Various Offerings Any day by Anyone	Various Worship Offerings—Vow or Votive Offerings, Freewill Offerings, Thank Offerings, Peace/Fellowship Offerings	Leviticus 3:1–17; 7:15–18; 22:18–33; 23:38; Numbers 29:39

THE SABBATH
The Call of the Every-Week "Feast"

"… The LORD'S appointed times which you shall proclaim as holy convocations—My appointed times are these: For six days work may be done; but on the seventh day there is a sabbath of complete rest, a holy convocation. You shall not do any work; it is a sabbath to the LORD in all your dwellings" (Leviticus 23:2–3). God intended the Sabbath as a weekly "Feast" time in the spirit of the Seven "Feasts" or *"appointed times"* given in Leviticus 23. The seventh day served as a weekly call to seek God, to proclaim His Word, and to remember the covenant relationship in which they lived. The day gave the people opportunity to find refreshment physically in the day of rest as well as refreshment spiritually in time set aside hearing and **reflecting** on His Word, **remembering** His faithfulness, **rejoicing** in His provision in the week past, and **recalling** His promises for the week ahead.

SABBATH GUIDELINES	SCRIPTURE
God rested on the seventh day of **Creation** and set it aside as a day of **rest and remembering.**	Genesis 2:2–3; Exodus 20:8–11; 31:17
God put the Sabbath observance in place as the Israelites journeyed from Egypt to Mount Sinai. It served as a **test** of their trust and obedience.	Exodus 16:4–5
God provided **manna** each morning. On the sixth day, He provided enough for two days so that the Sabbath required no work. Through the Sabbath observance, God called the Israelites to **rest**, refreshment, and **remembrance** of their deliverance from Egypt and its slavery.	Exodus 16:13–36; Deuteronomy 5:15
God gave the **Ten Commandments** at Mount Sinai. In the fourth commandment, He set aside the Sabbath as a holy, blessed day for rest, for **remembering** and seeking Him, for hearing His Word, for worship, and for growing in the relationship His people had with Him. God repeated this command in several different contexts, explaining varying details.	Exodus 20:8–11; 23:12; 34:21; 35:3; Leviticus 23:3; Numbers 28:9–10; Deuteronomy 5:12–15; Nehemiah 9:13–14; 13:15–19
The Sabbath is a **sign** of the **covenant** relationship of His people with Himself. It pointed to the Lord sanctifying (setting apart) His people Israel. The Sabbath served as one way in which they were different from other nations.	Exodus 31:12–17; 35:1–3; Leviticus 26:2
God warned against any **violation** of the Sabbath as a serious offense punishable by being cut off from the people of God, even by **death.**	Exodus 31:14–15; 35:2
During the **Wilderness wanderings**, a man defiantly **violated** the Sabbath by his working. God judged him with the death penalty.	Numbers 15:32–36 (see Exodus 31:15; 35:2)
God spoke through Isaiah and Jeremiah to Israel about the way they **dishonored** the Sabbath and the Lord. They were focusing on personal pleasure and personal opinions rather than the Word and will of the Lord.	Isaiah 56:2, 4, 6; 58:13–14; Jeremiah 17:21–27
Nehemiah and the people agreed to **honor** the Sabbath in a renewal of the covenant (10:31, ca 445 BC). During his second term of leadership in Jerusalem, Nehemiah also dealt with Sabbath **violations** (ca 424 BC).	Nehemiah 10:31; 13:15–22

IN THE NEW TESTAMENT

Jesus is LORD OF THE SABBATH. He made it clear that this is a day for remembering the Lord and one's relationship to Him, for worshiping and obeying Him, and for loving and benefiting others.	Matthew 12:1–21 (v.8); Mark 2:23–28 (v.28); Luke 6:1–5 (v.5); Colossians 2:16–17
Jesus healed many on the Sabbath. In this way, He showed one way the Sabbath could fulfill its intent—*"the Sabbath was made for man, and not man for the Sabbath"* (Mark 2:27); *"a day to do good… to save life"* (Luke 6:9).	Matthew 12:9–14, 15–21; Mark 3:1–6, 7–12; Luke 6:6–11; 13:10–17; 14:1–6; John 5:1–19; 7:14–24; 9:1–41
There is a **Sabbath Rest, a rest of soul,** God desires for His people through a personal relationship with Jesus Christ, the Lord of the Sabbath.	Psalm 132:8–18; Matthew 11:28–30; Hebrews 4:1–11
Many see in the Scriptures a future and further fulfillment of the promise of a Sabbath rest in a **Sabbath Era**, the promised **Millennium**, in which the **Sabbath rest** and the **Feast of Tabernacles** are fulfilled.	Isaiah 11:10; Zechariah 14:4–11, 16, 20–21; Luke 1:68–75

THE CALL OF THE FEASTS OF THE LORD
Viewed from the Fullness of the Work of Christ in the New Testament

SEASON/DATE	FEAST	CALL OF THE FEAST	SCRIPTURE
\multicolumn{4}{l}{The ongoing call of the first three **Feasts** is **the CALL to CELEBRATE the FATHER'S love and purpose through our JUSTIFICATION in His SON, Jesus Christ.** We experience the fullness of *"the love of God"* who *"gave His only begotten Son"* (2 Corinthians 13:14; John 3:16). Romans 3—5 speak of the work of Christ in bringing forgiveness of sin and justification by faith. Faith is reckoned to the believer *"as righteousness"* (Romans 4:22). The call is to any *"who believe in Him who raised Jesus our Lord from the dead, He who was delivered up because of our transgressions, and was raised because of our justification"* (Romans 4:25). The feasts are *"a shadow"*; Christ is the *"substance"* (Colossians 2:16–17).}
Spring Nisan 14	1. Passover	**The Call to Redemption.** Jesus Christ, the Lamb of God is *"our Passover"* who *"takes away the sin of the world."* We are redeemed *"with precious blood, as of a lamb unblemished and spotless, the blood of Christ."*	John 1:29, 36 1 Corinthians 5:7 1 Peter 1:18–19
Spring Nisan 15–21	2. Unleavened Bread	**The Call to Purity**, to an "Unleavened" life. Jesus knew no sin, nor was any deceit found in Him. He was unblemished and spotless. He was made sin for us that we could be made the righteousness of God in Him. This "Christ life" is to be lived in and through us, in our words, deeds, thoughts and attitudes.	1 Corinthians 5:8 1 Peter 1:13–18; 3:22–24 2 Corinthians 5:21 Philippians 1:21; 2:3–5; 3:8; 4:13
Spring Nisan 17	3. First Fruits	**The Call to Resurrection Hope**, a *"living hope."* Christ is *"the first fruits"* of the resurrection, *"after that those who are Christ's at His coming."*	1 Corinthians 15:23 1 Peter 1:1–11
\multicolumn{4}{l}{The ongoing call of the Feast of Pentecost is **the CALL to CELEBRATE our SANCTIFICATION, the ongoing work of the HOLY SPIRIT.** We are born of the Spirit, nurtured by the Spirit, so that we grow **"in Christ,"** experiencing *"the fellowship of the Spirit"* (2 Corinthians 13:14).}
Late Spring Sivan 6	4. Pentecost / Weeks	**The Call to the Spirit-filled Life.** We are sealed in Him for the day of redemption. This is also the call to Spirit-filled living as part of the Body of Christ—loving one another and all people by the fruit of the Spirit.	Ephesians 1:13–14; 4:30; 5:18–21; 1 Corinthians 12:12–13; Galatians 5:22–23
\multicolumn{4}{l}{The ongoing call of the last three **Feasts** is the **CALL to CELEBRATE our GLORIFICATION—the finished work of the SON** (Romans 8:28–30), **the fullness of** *"the grace of the Lord Jesus Christ"* (2 Corinthians 13:14) **now**, and *"in the ages to come… the surpassing riches of His grace"* (Ephesians 2:7).}
Fall Tishri 1	5. Trumpets	**The Call to Assembly and Accountability** in the Presence (*parousia*) of the Lord and at the Judgment Seat of Christ. This is seen in the Trumpet call of the Resurrection and of our Bridegroom, Jesus Christ for His Bride. We will meet Him *"in the air"* and gather *"to the marriage supper of the lamb."*	2 Corinthians 5:10; 1 Corinthians 3:10–15; 4:4–5; 15:52; 1 Thessalonians 4:13–18; Revelation 19:6–9
Fall Tishri 10	6. Day of Atonement	**The Call to Eternally Secure Salvation.** We can be confident and hopeful in His Atonement for our sins *"once for all."* Christ is our High Priest and our sacrifice for sin.	Hebrews 2:17–18; 3:1; 7–8, 9–10
Fall Tishri 15–22	7. Tabernacles / Booths / Ingathering	**The Call to Practice His Presence and look forward to His Kingdom and Rewards from Him.** What each does is not without His gaze and the opportunity for His *"well done, good and faithful servant. Enter into the joy of your Lord."* This occurs in the Millennial Kingdom and the New Heaven and New Earth to come.	2 Corinthians 6:14–18 Matthew 25:21 2 Timothy 4:1, 8 2 Peter 3:3–13 Revelation 20:4–6

The Feast of Passover

The Call to Remember and Celebrate Your Redemption in Christ

The call of the Feasts of the Lord is a call to seek God, to come before Him, listen to Him, learn from Him, and rejoice in Him and with Him. Many today do not seek the Lord; even many Christians do not daily spend time with the Lord or seek to grow in knowing Him. Each of the Feasts is a call to come, a call to know Him better, a call to walk with Him more consistently. Each one presents a reality of God's work with His people Israel, and it also speaks of the work of Jesus Christ and the relationship He desires with each believer today.

The Feast of Passover is the first of the Feasts and the foundation for all the Feasts. Without Passover there could be no Feasts, no celebrations, no rejoicing in the freedom God brings. It is Passover that is the doorway into freedom and the relationship God desires with His people. It is the starting point, God even declaring that the month of events surrounding Passover would be the first month in Israel's religious calendar. With Passover we begin a journey into history and a journey into the heart of God for His people. On that journey we will also discover His heart for each of His children. The spiritual realities seen in the Feasts connect to the New Testament as well. The Christian life is a life of answering the call of each Feast and celebrating the relationship pictured there.

This Journey through the Feasts is presented with the desire that in seeking God in each of these Scripture points, we will find Him in such a way that the walk of each seeker is more intimate with Him, more obviously filled with His likeness and power, and more instructive to others about what it means to know Him in His fullness. The Path of the Feasts is a path upon which to seek and find the Lord, to fellowship, walk and work with Him with greater intensity, and to worship Him more wholeheartedly. Each Feast presents something of the reality of knowing and worshiping God. God began instructing His people with the Passover. It is the first Feast. In it we, too, can begin our journey and in this Feast begin to discover the heart of God for His people—for you and for me.

> **Passover is the first of the Feasts and the foundation of all the Feasts...**

Lesson Two — DAY ONE

THE PEOPLE OF GOD IN GREAT NEED

When we turn to the book of Exodus, we find the people of God in great need. They were enslaved in Egypt, but God had a plan to deal with that slavery. He chose a man named Moses through whom He would work. What did God want for His people? In one word, "relationship." But that relationship needed work, a God-work if it was to be the reality He desired. The people of Israel enslaved in Egypt were not zealous for a relationship with God. Surely some prayed, but most simply endured another day of Egyptian slavery. God had a plan to carry out. Let's look at some of the details of His working.

📖 Exodus 1—4 gives us the history of Israel in Egypt and the mission of Moses to bring them out of Egypt into the Promised Land of Canaan. What do you discover about the purpose and plan of God in Exodus 3:13–22? Summarize what you find.

The people will know me as I am. God is about bring his people out of the slavery of the Egyptians, and bring them to a land flowing with milk and honey. He wants them to know him & know he cares what happened to them & will lead them out to a fertile land.

God chose Moses to go in His power, in the authority of His name as the "I AM WHO I AM," the God who created and sustains all that is. God is also the covenant-keeping God, fulfilling His promises to Abraham, Isaac, and Jacob. He showed His evident concern for His covenant people and promised to bring them "out of the affliction of Egypt" to the Promised Land of Canaan, "a land flowing with milk and honey."

📖 After some reluctance, Moses went to Egypt and along with Aaron his brother (Exodus 4:27–31), confronted Pharaoh as God directed. Conditions became ever harsher for the Israelites. Then God began sending plagues upon the land of Egypt, one after another, each an assault on one or more of the gods of Egypt. [You can read the account in Exodus 4—10.] After nine plagues, Pharaoh had grown more and more hard-hearted and stubborn in his resistance to letting the people of Israel go. God had one more plague to deliver. What is God's point in this matter according to Exodus 4:21–23?

God give Pharoah one last chance, to let his son go, his first born. If u refuse, I will kill your son, your first born. (life and death)

📖 How did God see His people, His "first-born," according to Exodus 6:1–8?

God saw the people as his sons. As the people of his promise to Abraham.

📖 What was God's plan for the tenth plague according to Exodus 11:1?

God plan to judgement upon Pharoah and the egyptians. "Power of release" the "Passover" To make Pharoah push God's people out of Egypt.

26 FOLLOWING GOD – LIFE PRINCIPLES FOR WORSHIP FROM THE FEASTS OF ISRAEL

God took a personal interest in His people, Israel. Israel mattered to God. God considered His people to be *"My son, My firstborn,"* greatly valued and loved. God would do whatever it took to secure Israel's release from Egyptian bondage. He sent words of warning through Moses, *"If you refuse to let him go, indeed I will kill your son, your firstborn."* This was a matter of fighting for the life of one God loved, a matter of war, of life, and death. It was also a matter of God's covenant and His promises to Abraham, Isaac, and Jacob. As *"the LORD,"* the I AM, *Yahweh* [the "I will be Who I have been"], He would faithfully keep His Word and bring His people into the Promised Land of Canaan. He is able and He would do it. His name ever stands behind everything He says. The tenth plague, *"one more plague,"* the *"LORD's Passover,"* would bring the power of release.

📖 Describe the night of the Passover, according to Exodus 12:3–13, 21–22.

They kill the Passover lamb, put the blood on the door posts, and they eat the flesh that night

On the tenth day of Nisan, each household selected a one year old male lamb without blemish and kept it for four days, guarding it lest some injury occur. It must be without blemish. That lamb became the Passover lamb and more personally, *"your lamb."* God consistently calls people to a personal relationship with Himself, a personal interaction in life. On the fourteenth day, each family sacrificed their lamb at twilight. Literally, the wording is "between the evenings," referring to between Noon and 6:00 PM, which puts the sacrifice at around 3:00 PM. They caught the blood of the lamb in a basin and took *"a bunch of hyssop,"* dipped it into the basin and then sprinkled the blood on the side doorposts and the top lentil of each home. Interestingly, that makes the motions of a Cross.

Moses instructed the people to stay in the house. *"None of you shall go outside the door of his house until morning."* That night they roasted the lamb and ate it, careful not to break any bone. Along with the lamb they ate bitter herbs and unleavened bread (since there was no time for leaven to rise before they ate the bread). Israel must eat it **ready to go** (Exodus 12:11). The Lord promised to **pass over** homes where the blood of the lamb had been applied. Death to a lamb had already occurred there. The lambs were the substitutes for the people, saving them from death and judgment by the Lord. Each house marked by the blood of the lamb would be a haven of salvation, a place safe from judgment. Where there was no application of the blood, no obedience to the Lord's direction, no faith in the Lord's way, judgment would strike at Midnight.

📖 It is important to note the connections to the promises of God. He is faithful. Read Genesis 15:13–16. What did the Lord promise Abram?

He said to Abram your descendants will be strangers in a land that is not theirs, & serve them, they will afflict them 400 years

The Lord promised Abram many things, specifically eight promises related to his descendants and where and how they would live. First, his descendants would be *"strangers in a land that is not theirs."* Second, they would

Word Study
THE SACRIFICE OF A LAMB

On the fourteenth day of Nisan, the Israelites killed the Passover lamb (Exodus 12:6, 21, 28). The Hebrew word for *"kill,"* *shachat*, means to slaughter in sacrifice. The Septuagint (LXX) translation uses the Greek word *sphazo* which means to slay or slaughter (Exodus 12:6). The same word is used in Revelation 5:6, 12, and 13:8 of Jesus as the Lamb (*arnion*) slain (*sphazo*).

LESSON TWO – THE FEAST OF PASSOVER 27

Put Yourself In Their Shoes
PASSOVER ESSENTIALS

In New Testament days, the Jews considered certain teachings essential in the Passover observance. Rabbi Gamaliel, the teacher of the Apostle Paul noted three essentials. "Whoever does not explain three things in the Passover has not fulfilled the duty incumbent on him. These three things are: the Passover lamb, the unleavened bread, and the bitter herbs. *The Passover lamb* means that God passed over the blood-sprinkled place on the houses of our fathers in Egypt; *the unleavened bread* means that our fathers were delivered out of Egypt (in haste); and *the bitter herbs* mean that the Egyptians made bitter the lives of our fathers in Egypt." (*Mishnah, Pes.* x. 15 as found in Alfred Edersheim, *The Temple*, p. 237)

Put Yourself In Their Shoes
GOD AND HIS PEOPLE

God's watchful care for **His** people is seen from many directions. He delivered, redeemed, purchased, covered, and protected by the blood **over them**. He remained **with them**, leading them and they obediently followed Him (Exodus 13:18–22). He blessed and enriched them, showing that He was **for them** (Exodus 12:35–36; Genesis 15:14). They journeyed out of Egypt in the strength of the lamb; the lamb was **in them**, a prophetic picture of the indwelling strength of the Lamb to come.

---

serve that land. Third, they would be afflicted by the people of that land. Fourth, the duration would be four hundred years. Fifth, that nation would be judged. Sixth, the children of Abram would come out of that land. Seventh, they would come out with great possessions. Eighth, they would return to the land of Abram, the land of Canaan.

📖 How did the Lord fulfill His promises according to Exodus 11:2–3; 12:35–36, 40–41?

They asked for silver and gold, and clothes and the Lord gave they favor in the sight of Egyptians and they gave them what they asked. They lived in Egypt 430 yrs.

The children of Israel went into Egypt in the days of Jacob and Joseph, settling in the land of Goshen. Later, the Egyptians enslaved them, afflicting them with harsh labor. God raised up Moses to deliver His people and Moses obeyed. In preparation for the day in which they would leave, by faith Moses instructed the people to ask for *"articles of silver, articles of gold, and clothing."* They obeyed during the days before the tenth plague. When the Passover occurred, that night the people of Egypt began urging Israelites to leave—**now!!!**—and with them went so much treasure that the Israelites in effect *"plundered the Egyptians"* like a victorious army. Their sojourn in Egypt lasted 430 years *"to the very day,"* fulfilling the summary statement given to Abram that his descendants would be there 400 years. Egypt certainly faced judgment through the ten plagues, and Israel journeyed ready to enter the Promised Land, the land of Canaan.

📖 How significant was this night? What does God say in Exodus 12:1–2? What additional truths do you find in Exodus 12:24–27? What added note is found in Exodus 13:8?

He made it a feast + a Passover to remember + to tell their children! This shall be the 1st month of the year. That's how significant it was! you and yours sons shall observe this ordinance forever. tell what the did for me when I came out of Egypt

So significant was this Passover and the Exodus from Egypt, that God changed the calendar. The month Abib (later called Nisan, our mid-March to mid-April) occurred as the seventh month in Israel's civil calendar. God gave Israel a new calendar, a religious calendar with Abib/Nisan as the first month of the year. God focused attention on this month and commanded Israel to do the same, to make it a priority month. Each year Israel would *"observe this event,"* making it a family priority, a time for parents and children to focus attention on the redemption God provided—God brought them out of the slavery of Egypt into the freedom of the Promised Land. God called them to testify yearly that He had *"passed over"* their homes, struck the Egyptian homes, but *"spared* [literally, *"delivered"*] *our homes."* The **personal** note is also emphasized, *"what the LORD did for me when I came out of Egypt"* (13:8). By way of application, God still calls us to testify of how He has delivered and redeemed us through the death and resurrection of Jesus Christ. We will see that in Day's Three and Four.

28 FOLLOWING GOD – LIFE PRINCIPLES FOR WORSHIP FROM THE FEASTS OF ISRAEL

📖 What happened on Passover night, according to Exodus 12:29–41?

THe first born of Egypt dead (died) that night & Pharaoh told Moses & Aaron go from among my people. They left with silver, gold, and clothing. Mixed multitude the people of Egypt also told them hurry & go!

At midnight, God *"struck all the first-born"* of Egypt, touching every strata of society from Pharaoh in the palace to the prisoner in the dungeon, as well as livestock. Egypt experienced a grievous social and economic calamity. Immediately, he and the Egyptians urged Israel to leave—**now!!** The Israelites hastily took their bowls of unleavened dough as God had instructed. Six hundred thousand men plus women and children (an estimated total of one to two million) marched out of Egypt carrying the many treasured articles they had requested in the days prior. A *"mixed multitude"* of Israelites, some Egyptians and other nationalities, and *"a very large number of livestock"* journeyed toward the Promised Land.

It was official. Israel was now a nation set apart, no longer simply descendants of twelve sons of Jacob, but a unified nation of twelve tribes known as "Israel," the new name God had given Jacob on the night He had wrestled with him (Genesis 32:22–31). This nation would encounter many challenges over the next years and centuries, but there would always be a unifying thread of the work of God, especially this work of being redeemed out of Egypt. The phrase *"out of Egypt"* or similar occurs more than 150 times in the Old Testament. It stands as the defining moment for Israel as a nation under the leadership of the Lord. A look at some of the observances of the Passover in the history of Israel will help us further see the significance of this event in Israel, in the life and ministry of Jesus, and in our lives. We turn now to Day Two.

> "It is a night to be observed for the LORD for having brought them out from the land of Egypt; this night is for the LORD, to be observed by all the sons of Israel throughout their generations."
>
> **Exodus 12:42**

Sianterfication

redeemsions.

ISRAEL REMEMBERS GOD'S WORKINGS

Lesson Two — **DAY TWO**

In the Old Testament, we find only a few references to Israel celebrating the Passover, not a record of every time, but a record of significant times. In those times, we see a marker in the nation's life, a reminder of God's faithfulness and His workings. Today, we will review some of those instances and look at the personal applications to our daily walks.

📖 The very first year after leaving Egypt, Israel celebrated the Passover in the wilderness of Sinai. Read Numbers 9:1–8. What issue surfaced in the celebration of the Passover? Numbers 5:1–4 may give you some further insight.

Some could not celebrate of Israel bc touched a dead body & thus were unclean.

There men that were defiled by a dead body. GOD command they out of the Camp Put every leper, every one who has a discharge, who ever becomes defiled by a dead body. unclean

LESSON TWO – THE FEAST OF PASSOVER 29

📖 According to Numbers 9:9–12, what solution did the Lord give?

If anyone y are unclean because of a dead body, or on a far journey, he may still keep the Lord's Passover but at twilight on the 14th day of second Month

📖 What further restrictions did the Lord give in Numbers 9:13–14?

There shall be one statue, both for the stranger and the native of the land.

[Margin note: anyone who is clean + not away on a trip but doesn't celebrate Passover will be CUT OFF from the people.]

📖 Exodus 12:43–49 gives the *"ordinance"* related to the Passover and participation by any *"foreigner."* What do these restrictions tell you about the Lord, His view toward His people, and how He wanted them to view the Passover?

God want them to worship and Love him with a pure heart in holiness.

[Margin note: View the Passover as a serious celebration to God + only for Israel not foreigners freely in the land. He viewed His people as a set apart people holy unto Him.]

The Israelites observed the Passover *"according to all its statutes and . . . ordinances,"* following God's guidelines. However, some of the men could not participate because they were ceremonially unclean, having touched a dead person. The requirements for outward cleanliness, for avoidance of defilement, pointed to God's call to inward cleanliness, to a pure heart that loved and worshiped Him in holiness. God gave external boundary lines to Israel so they could better understand the internal boundary lines as God's holy people. Throughout Scripture God calls attention to the issues of the heart. That included how they celebrated the Passover in the land God gave, the land set apart by God for His people.

God wanted His people to celebrate before Him, but not in an unclean state nor in a foreign land. In His gracious care, He provided a second opportunity for those who faced this dilemma during Passover. Instead of participating in the first month, they could celebrate one month later, on the fourteenth of the second month following the same order. However, those who refused to participate in the Passover, even though clean and there in the land of Israel, would be *"cut off from his people,"* ostracized because of *"his sin."* They were refusing to join with the people of God as they recalled the redemption He had given. If someone from another nation desired to celebrate, God gladly welcomed that one if he would simply follow the Lord's regulations which included circumcision, the mark of putting away the old life and joining the people of God and His way (Exodus 12:48).

Two truths weave themselves throughout God's workings relative to Passover. **First,** God acted in a **personal** way because of His **personal relationship** to the children of Israel. He wanted a personal response from them in all they did. **Second,** God delivered and redeemed the people out of Egypt to be a **holy, loving** people, set apart to God, to know Him, and to live out that **holy, loving relationship** as a demonstration of knowing the true God. God meant them to be a witness nation to the other nations of the world—this is what it means to know and follow the Lord God. Anyone who submits to Him and His Word can enter into that kind of

> **Did You Know?**
> **NO PASSOVER IN THE WILDERNESS**
>
> After Israel celebrated the Passover on the one-year anniversary of their exodus from Egypt, there is no record of them celebrating until Joshua led them into the land of Canaan almost forty years later. Why? One reason is their ceremonial uncleanness. They circumcised no one during the wilderness wanderings. Joshua 5:2–10 records the circumcision event followed by the celebration of Passover in the land of Canaan.

30 FOLLOWING GOD – LIFE PRINCIPLES FOR WORSHIP FROM THE FEASTS OF ISRAEL

personal, holy, loving relationship and experience His working. The celebration of the Passover focused on being His people, redeemed to know and follow Him.

📖 After the Wilderness wanderings, Moses reviewed what God required of the nation in their new land. Deuteronomy 16:1–16 speaks of the three Feasts required of all the men. Each was to be celebrated in the chosen place where the Tabernacle rested (and later the Temple). Read verses 1–7. What is the focus of this observance in verse 1?

To Observe the passover at it appointed time. that he brought you out of Egypt by night

📖 What does the Lord emphasize in verse 3? Why does He require this Feast along with Unleavened Bread? *Don't eat yeast 7 days that u remember the day which u came out of Egypt all the days of your life*

📖 Where must the Passover sacrifice occur and be eaten according to verses 5–7? How is this different from what occurred in Egypt?

At the places the Lord God Chooses! Each in own homes in Egypt. Now together where He says to.

The focus of the Passover observance is remembering the Lord's deliverance of Israel out of Egypt. They must not forget from where they had come, nor fail to remember how God had redeemed them. This Feast along with Unleavened Bread is designed to call to mind their affliction and their deliverance. *"Remember"*—that is the key word for this celebration. Remember who you were and where you were. Remember who God is and what He did. Remember how He brought you to Canaan and all He has given and done for you. Remember your redemption for *"all the days of your life."*

This Feast is one of the three Feast seasons to be celebrated at the chosen central place of worship where the Tabernacle (later the Temple) rested. God did not want them celebrating the Feast in their separate towns and villages, but rather together in His chosen place. Rather than slaying a lamb in each household in various villages, the Passover lambs would be sacrificed, roasted, and eaten at this chosen location. Together they would worship and remember all God had done. This would continually unify them as God's chosen people, uniquely redeemed out of Egypt.

The next detailed written account of the Passover occurred hundreds of years later around 715 BC, early in Hezekiah's reign (715–686 BC). Second Chronicles 29 gives the account of the cleansing of the Temple in the first month (Nisan), which the priests completed on the sixteenth (29:17). The next day, the seventeenth was a new day. Sin offerings and burnt offerings followed, and the people rejoiced greatly (29:20–36). Chapter 30 then records the events surrounding Hezekiah's call to celebrate the Passover.

Put Yourself In Their Shoes
REMEMBER YOUR REDEMPTION

"Remember" is the key word for the Passover celebration (Exodus 13:3). Remember who you were and where you were. Remember who God is and what He did. Remember how He brought you to Canaan and all He has given and done for you. Remember your redemption for *"all the days of your life"* (Deuteronomy 16:3). Jesus said the same about the New Covenant in His body given and blood poured out; eat this bread and drink this cup *"in remembrance of Me."* proclaiming *"the Lord's death until He comes"* and your full redemption is seen (1 Corinthians 11:24–26; Ephesians 1:7, 13–14; 4:30; Romans 8:23–25).

📖 After cleansing the Temple and consecrating the priesthood because of past sins and the failure to follow the Lord, Hezekiah called for the celebration of the Passover. Read the account in 2 Chronicles 30:1–27. What is the date given in verse 2? Why is this date given, according to verse 3?

In the second month, because sufficient number of Priests had not santified themselves nor the people gathered at Jerusalem

📖 What do these verses reveal about the heart of God for His people?

The great Love God has for his people give more time for them get in line with His will. He's merciful, full of grace + patient towards them. (forgiving)

Hezekiah called for the celebration of the Passover in the second month because *"the priests had not consecrated themselves in sufficient numbers,"* nor had people gathered to Jerusalem from throughout the country. In Numbers 9:6–12, God graciously gave the second month as an opportunity for those who could not come in the first month. This incident reveals the heart of God for His people, giving them time to cleanse the Temple and the priesthood, time to order their lives in line with God's heart and His holy standards.

> "Yield yourselves to the LORD.... for the LORD your God is gracious and merciful, and will not turn His face from you if you return to Him."
>
> 2 Chronicles 30:8, 9 NKJV

To understand all that is going on, it is important to grasp the historical events surrounding this time. Israel and Judah were facing a measure of the judgment of God. Judah had encounters with Aram (Syria), Edom, the Philistines, and northern Israel in which several died in battle and several were taken captive (2 Chronicles 28:5–8, 17, 18). Why? Second Chronicles 28:9 reports the anger of the Lord against Judah because of their sins, their unfaithfulness to the Lord. King Ahaz, Hezekiah's father, *"had brought about a lack of restraint in Judah"* and proved himself unfaithful to the Lord. Second Chronicles 28:11–13 reports the Lord's anger against Samaria and northern Israel, so much so that in 722 BC, God allowed the Assyrian army to sweep into Israel, conquering and captivating the ten northern tribes in the region of Samaria. Many, but not all, were taken captive into other countries (2 Kings 17:6). Some remained. A measure of hope remained that God could restore His people.

📖 What did Hezekiah focus on according to 2 Chronicles 30:5–9?

The Lord is gracious and merciful, and will not turn His face from u if you return to Him

📖 What different responses to the invitation to the Passover do you note in 2 Chronicles 30:10–12?

Some laughed them to scorn and mocked them. Gods hand was Judah to do his commandments at the word of the Lord. Some were sorry for what they'd done + they went to Jerushlem.

32 FOLLOWING GOD – LIFE PRINCIPLES FOR WORSHIP FROM THE FEASTS OF ISRAEL

Hezekiah issued a decree calling all of Israel (those remaining in the north and Judah in the south) to come to Jerusalem to celebrate the Passover. He dispatched swift couriers "from Beersheba to Dan" (farthest south to farthest north), reminding the people of the ways of some in Israel who had encountered judgment because of their idolatry and unholiness. They had become "a horror" to those around them. He called them to "return to the LORD God of Abraham, Isaac, and Israel, that He may return to . . . you." Hezekiah entreated them to "yield to the Lord and enter His sanctuary . . . and serve the LORD your God." Stop stubbornly resisting Him in self will and selfishness. God would be "gracious and compassionate" and not turn His face against those who "return to Him." Some in the northern tribes laughed with scorn and mocked the messengers; their hearts unrepentant, hardened by sin. Others listened, responded in humility, and set out for Jerusalem. God was working there and in Judah; "the hand of God was also on Judah to give them one heart to do what the king and the princes commanded by the word of the LORD."

[margin note: userpon not where we should be. Faithful with what He all ready give u]

What kind of actions occurred according to 2 Chronicles 30:13–20?

The multitude of people came had not cleansed themselves Removed alters + incense to other gods, came together to celebrate Passover leaders took their regular places in the temple.

What do you discover about the people and about the Lord in 2 Chronicles 30:18–20?

The people did not do as the word of God said but Hezekiah prayed and God listened to Hezekiah and healed the people

Describe the celebration given in 2 Chronicles 30:21–27. Note the many different words that picture the scene and how the people interacted.

there great joy & celebration so much so they extended the celetion for another seven days. Praised the Lord w/ loud music, feasted 7 days, offered fellowship offerings all very happy, Priests/Levites stood & blessed the people. God heard their prayers reached Heaven, His Holy Home.

The people journeyed to Jerusalem, a "very large assembly" gathered. Several began removing altars to false gods left from the reign of Ahaz. As the Passover began, many priests and Levites consecrated themselves afresh. Many came ceremonially unclean, yet ate the Passover anyway. Apparently, God chastened some with sickness. Hezekiah asked God to forgive them and look at the heart seeking God. The Lord mercifully heard and healed the people. This was yet another mark of the redemption God purchased for His people, not only the remembrance of a deliverance centuries before, but a present-day, ongoing redemption. Their personal relationship to the Lord included diligently seeking Him and receiving from Him forgiveness, grace, and mercy. They also received the opportunity for a fresh start, a new day in that relationship. These believers celebrated with great joy, so much so that they extended the celebration for another seven days. "Great joy," praise, thanksgiving, and rejoicing marked those days, "because there was nothing like this in Jerusalem since the days of Solomon."

LESSON TWO – THE FEAST OF PASSOVER   33

EXTRA MILE
JOSIAH'S PASSOVER AND EZRA'S PASSOVER

Another significant Passover celebration occurred in the days of King Josiah (640–609 BC), around 614 BC. Spiritual awakening came in some measure. Second Chronicles 35:18 states, *"there had not been celebrated a Passover like it in Israel since the days of Samuel,"* referring to the fervor and devotion of Josiah and the priests of his day. Look at the details in 2 Chronicles 34 and 35:1–19. Explore another significant Passover in Ezra 6:19–22. This occurred around 515 BC, after the completion of the second Temple (516 BC).

📖 Second Chronicles 31 describes the ongoing purge of idolatry along with other marks of this return to the Lord. Read verses 20–21 that summarize Hezekiah's attitude and actions. What distinguishing marks do you find there?

whatever he did for the Lord God, he did it with all his heart.

Hezekiah provided many animals and goods for the offerings and called the people to give. They did so in abundance, following the lead of Hezekiah, an excellent example of one who sought the LORD *"with all his heart."* Part of that seeking occurred in his call to celebrate Passover at the Temple in Jerusalem. That is the call of each of the Feasts, seeking God with a whole heart, to follow, love, and obey Him.

🛑 **APPLY**

What Do You Seek?—How you spend your time, how you spend or save or give your money, how you interact with people and whom you choose to interact with, are all indicators of what you seek, of what is important or a priority in your life. Ask the Lord to give you insight into how well you are seeking **Him**. What call are you answering in your daily life? To what siren sound do you respond? Remember, the Feasts are about seeking God as a year-long lifestyle, year after year and day by day, whatever the season of the year and whatever the season of your life.

Lesson Two — DAY THREE

JESUS AND THE PASSOVER CELEBRATIONS

When we turn to the pages of the New Testament we find the Passover at the center of much that took place in the days of Jesus. The historical events teach us plenty about the days of Jesus, but even more about Jesus Himself, the redemption He gives, and the relationship He desires with each of us. Today, we will explore the Passover in Jesus' day and see applications to our day.

📖 When would Jesus have first encountered the Passover celebration? Read Luke 2:41–51. On what was the twelve-year-old Jesus focused?

When He 12 they went up to Jerusalem according to the custom of the feast. He was about His Father's business.

📖 What possible connections do you see between *"My Father's business"* or *"the things of My Father"* and all the events surrounding the celebration of the Passover?

Redemption and Relationship with us

📖 The historical point of Passover focused on bringing a people **out of** slavery in Egypt and **into** the Promised Land. In this first Passover experience, what animated Jesus? What did people need to be brought *out of* and what did the Father desire to bring them *into*?

Out of the World, into the Kingdom of God; from death - to everlasting life

Luke 2 gives us some of the details of Jesus' celebration of the Passover at the age of twelve. It is likely He had been to Jerusalem with His family several times before this since we read they *"went to Jerusalem every year."* We see Christ's clear focus at age twelve on being *"about My Father's business"* (NKJV) or *"in My Father's house"* (NASB), literally *"in the things of My Father."* He questioned why Mary and Joseph were not aware of or did not *"know"* this. The Old Testament record would obviously lead one to see the Father's business as redeeming a people for His name and His purposes. Passover stood at the heart of His work of doing that. It was the first Feast occurring in the first month. The priority should be clearly seen. The historical events of bringing people out of slavery, redeemed to be brought into the Promised Land, pointed to a holy purpose—a holy people walking by faith, worshiping the true God with true hearts. Jesus echoed these truths throughout His life on earth, especially in His ministry, and certainly in His death and resurrection.

> **Did You Know?**
>
> **THE LAMB FOR ALL**
>
> When Abel offered an animal (perhaps a lamb), and when Abraham and Isaac spoke of a lamb on Mount Moriah, they pointed to a lamb **for one person**. When the Israelites sacrificed a lamb at the Passover, it was a lamb **for a family, a household**. When the Day of Atonement came, the animals sacrificed were **for the nation**. When John the Baptist pointed to Jesus, he spoke of Him as *"the Lamb of God who takes away the sin of the world,"* the lamb **for the world**.

📖 Jesus' ministry lasted approximately three and a half years. He experienced four Passovers during that time (John 2:13–25; John 5:1; 6:4; 11:55). The first and last of His ministry proved most significant. What do you see about God's heart for redemption in the first Passover of Jesus' ministry as recorded in John 2:13–25? What did Jesus observe in the Temple, according to verses 14–15?

He found those who sold oxen, and sheep, and doves, and moneychangers doing business.

📖 According to John 2:16, what verdict did Jesus give concerning the actions of those in the Temple?

Do not make My Father's House a house of merchandise

📖 How did the disciples of Jesus see His actions (later as they reflected on all He had done), according to John 2:17?

They remembered that it was written "Zeal for your house has eaten Me up"

📖 Jesus' focus never changed—from age 12 to age 30 to age 33. What is His focus in John 2:16–17?

His focus redemption and and relationship. (Father's Will)

> *"Jesus therefore said, 'When you lift up the Son of Man, then you will know that I am He, and I do nothing on My own initiative, but I speak these things as the Father taught Me. And He who sent Me is with Me; He has not left Me alone, for I always do the things that are pleasing to Him.'"*
>
> John 8:28–29

Along with many others who had come to Jerusalem during the Passover week, Jesus went to the Temple area. Those who traveled from outside Jerusalem or from great distances outside Israel would need to procure a sacrifice in Jerusalem. Those who wished to give money in the Temple or pay the obligatory Temple tax (Exodus 30:13–14) would need to exchange their currency for the Jewish currency. This necessitated people being available to sell approved sacrificial animals and doves as well as those who would exchange currency. However, those who did so in Jesus' day took advantage of others, raising prices or charging excess fees and thus making exorbitant profits. In the words of Christ, they had made *"My Father's house a house of merchandise!"* Their focus was wrong. They were not merely providing a service or help for worshipers. They were making excess money off of the worshipers. The disciples later called to mind the words of David in Psalm 69:9, pointing to a heart of *"zeal"* for the Lord and His worship. Jesus consistently showed His love and zeal for His Father and His Father's will. Pure worship and uncorrupted devotion occupied Jesus' thoughts and ministry.

📖 How did Jesus answer the questions of the Jewish authorities over His actions in the Temple? What did He declare in John 2:19? What did the Jews think He meant according to verse 20?

Destroy this temple and in three days I will raise it up; 40 years to build will u raise it up in 3 days the old day.

📖 What truth did the disciples recognize as they thought back on these events, looking at them from the view point of the crucifixion and resurrection, according to John 2:21–22?

He spoke of the temple of His body the disciples remembered that had said this to them

📖 One other incident in Jesus' life helps connect this event with the events of Passover. Look at Luke 9:28–31, especially verse 31. The word translated *"decease"* or *"departure"* is a translation of the Greek word *exodos*, referring to going "out by a way," of being separated from one place to another.

The Jewish authorities, possibly members of the Sanhedrin who exercised a measure of control over the Temple, questioned Jesus' actions. They wanted a tangible *"sign"* or miraculous display. They failed to discern the purity and power of Jesus in Himself, the authority He bore as the Son of God. Jesus spoke of destroying the Temple and raising it in three days. Here the Greek word translated *"temple"* is *naos* referring to the inner sanctuary, the Holy of Holies, the place of God's Presence. Jesus Himself was the Tabernacle or Temple, the Holy of Holies of God (John 1:14). They could only see externals and focused on the ongoing Temple building/remodeling, forty-six years at that point [approximately 20/19 BC to 27 AD]. Jesus referred to the tearing down of His body in crucifixion and His resurrection from the dead. Jesus knew that His crucifixion would lead to an exodus from the Cross and the tomb in Jerusalem to heaven and eventually the eternal kingdom. With Him would go all who believe in Him for eternal life.

Passover brought the nation of Israel out of Egyptian bondage and death into the Promised Land and the life God desired for His people. Just so, Jesus as the Passover would bring millions out of bondage to sin and death and into eternal life and all the promises of God. He would fulfill all the Scriptures in bringing many to pure, uncorrupt worship and would even make each believer a God-glorifying Temple (*naos*) of the Holy Spirit (1 Corinthians 6:19–20). In Days Four and Five, we will see how He accomplished this and what He is doing today as *"our Passover."*

JESUS AND THE DISCIPLES CELEBRATE PASSOVER–JESUS OUR PASSOVER

Lesson Two — **DAY FOUR**

The last Passover of Jesus brings us to the main point of His ministry. On His way to Jerusalem and the Passover celebration, just days before His crucifixion, Jesus spoke about His mission. He knew very well that the Passover was His destiny. It was why He came, but it was not the end of His destiny. It would be the beginning of a new day with a new destiny for millions whom He would redeem. We will see that in today's lesson.

📖 Jesus understood His mission. He knew the Father's will and how He would fulfill all the Father desired. We find a clear record of that mission and how clearly Jesus understood it. Read the following verses and record what you find about the heart and mission of Jesus.

📖 Matthew 20:17–28 (note verse 28)

He said I came not to be ministered unto but to minister and to give His life a ransom for many

📖 Luke 19:1–10 (note verse 10)

For the Son of man is come to seek and save that which was lost

📖 Matthew 26:1–2

Ye know that after 2 days is the feast of passover & the Son of man is betrayed to be crucified.

Just before Jesus and His disciples traveled to Jerusalem for the Passover celebration, He spoke to the disciples about His coming crucifixion and resurrection. Jesus also spoke to them about His coming *"to serve, and to give His life a ransom for many."* As they journeyed, most likely with several others making the annual pilgrimage, His route took Him through Jericho where He met Zaccheus. In that encounter, Jesus declared He had come *"to seek*

> **Did You Know?**
>
> **WHEN THEY SANG THE *HALLEL***
>
> The Jews sang the *Hallel*, Psalms 113–118, during eighteen days and one night each year. They sang it over the Passover sacrifice, at the Feast of Pentecost, all eight days of the Feast of Tabernacles in the Autumn and the eight-day feast of the Dedication (Restoration) of the Temple after the victory of Judas Maccabeus over the Syrians in 164 BC (celebrated in *Hanukkah*). The only night on which the Jews sang the *Hallel* was the night of the Passover Supper. Jesus and His disciples included *"a hymn,"* the *Hallel* in their observance of the Passover (Matthew 26:30; Mark 14:26). (See Alfred Edersheim, *The Temple*, p. 225.)

LESSON TWO – THE FEAST OF PASSOVER 37

and to save that which was lost." Two days before the Passover, Jesus pointed to the Passover as the time of His crucifixion. What would Jesus say as He and the disciples celebrated the Passover together?

The Son of man is betrayed to be crucified. Jesus? You didn't celebrate its coming... did you?!
5-25-22 *LK 22:15*

📖 Read the account of Jesus' Passover with His disciples in Matthew 26:17–30. (The other accounts are given in Mark 14:12–25; Luke 22:7–34; John 13–14). What occurred? Briefly outline what happened.

He sends the disciples to prepare the passover. As sat He said one u shall betray me. Disciples said is it I. Jesus said thu who dip with me in the dish. Take, eat, this is my body. He took the cup, This is my blood of the new testament, which is shed for many

📖 What is the main point upon which Jesus focused, according to Matthew 26:26–28?

redemption from sin through faith, His Blood The Covenant

📖 Matthew 26:30 states that "after singing a hymn, they went out to the Mount of Olives." That hymn would have been part of the Hallel, Psalm 113—118. Note the final words of Psalm 118, verses 19–29. What connections do you see to what occurred in Jesus' crucifixion?

O Give thanks unto the Lord; for he is good; for his mercy endureth for ever. WOW! Open the Gates- He's willing to v. 27 be bound as Sacrifice. It's all prophecy about why He had to come!

This Passover event can be summarized in four movements, like a symphony. First is the **preparation** for the Passover in which some of the disciples prepared for the actual meal in Jerusalem. Before the meal, Jesus prepared them for what He knew would occur—a betrayal by one of them. He also purposefully served each of them, washing their feet. Second, we see the **celebration** of the Passover, the meal and all that occurred with it. Third, we see the initiation of the Lord's Supper in which Jesus changed the order of the traditional Passover emphasizing His words about His body being broken like the bread and His blood being poured out like the fruit of the vine. It was the **initiation** of the New Covenant in His blood which included the life-saving fact of forgiveness of sins—the fulfillment of His mission. Finally, we see Jesus preparing them for the **manifestation** of Himself as *The Passover Lamb*. The hymn they sang from Psalms 113—118 pointed to the saving work of God and even to the rejoicing His salvation would bring.

PSALM 118:21–25a, 26–29

"I will praise You, for You have answered me, and have become my salvation. The stone which the builders rejected has become the chief cornerstone. This was the Lord's doing; it is marvelous in our eyes. This is the day the Lord has made; we will rejoice and be glad in it. Save now, I pray, O Lord; O Lord, I pray, send now prosperity. Blessed is he who comes in the name of the Lord! We have blessed You from the house of the Lord. God is the Lord, and He has given us light; Bind the sacrifice with cords to the horns of the altar. You are my God, and I will praise You; You are my God, I will exalt You. Oh, give thanks to the Lord, for He is good! For His mercy endures forever."

He demonstrated servant leader + just servant-mentality we should have of one another

WOW!

38 FOLLOWING GOD – LIFE PRINCIPLES FOR WORSHIP FROM THE FEASTS OF ISRAEL

📖 The chart, THE EVENTS OF THE PASSOVER WITH JESUS AND HIS DISCIPLES, given at the end of this lesson, shows the events of a Passover celebration from the first century AD with the changes made by Jesus in the initiation of the Lord's Supper. For a fuller understanding of what Jesus did and how that applies to us today, carefully review these events. Consider how they more fully reveal the ministry and mission of Jesus *"who gave Himself for us, that He might redeem us . . . and purify for Himself a people for His own possession"* (Titus 2:14). Record any new insights and applications the Spirit of God shows you.

_____
_____
_____
_____
_____

📖 What did Jesus point to that would occur **after** this Passover? Note His words in each of the following passages:

Matthew 26:29
I will drink not until day I drink it new with u in my Father's Kingdom

Luke 22:15–16, 18
I say unto u, I will not drink of the fruit of the vine, until the kingdom of God shall come

Luke 22:28–30
And I appoint unto you a kingdom as my Father hath appointed unto me

Luke 22:37
He was numbered with the transgressors, he the sin of many, made intercession for the transgressors

John 13:36 with 14:1–3.
He (Jesus) would prepare a eternal Home them, (us).

✓ Jesus spoke of His kingdom in which His disciples would reign with him on earth and in which He would drink of the fruit of the vine once again. He would soon leave them, but only for a time. In that time, He would prepare a place for them and then return to receive them to Himself so that they would forever be with Him. He would eventually bring them out of this present evil age, out of their sin, and into the life of His Spirit with Him forever. The place He would prepare would be an eternal home, that which other Scriptures point to as new heavens and a new earth.

Did You Know?
GOD'S "I WILL'S" IN THE PASSOVER CELEBRATION

Based on four *"I will"* promises of Exodus 6:6–7, the Jews in Jesus' day drank four specific cups of the fruit of the vine during the Passover celebration. The LORD said, "**I will** *bring you out. . . .* **I will** *deliver you. . . .* **I will** *also redeem you. . . .* **I will** *take you for My people, and* **I will** *be your God."* The participants drank one cup connected to each of the "I wills" of God— 1) the Cup of Sanctification, acknowledging Israel being brought out and set apart, 2) the Cup of Wrath, recalling God's wrath poured out on Egypt as He delivered Israel, 3) the Cup of Redemption (also known as "the Cup of Blessing"), remembering their being redeemed out of slavery, and 4) the Cup of Consummation or Covenant Relationship, celebrating belonging to the Lord.

It is important to note at this point that Jesus spoke about preparing a place immediately **after** the third cup in the Passover celebration. He spoke of going to **His Father's house** to prepare a place, promising to come again to receive His own to Himself (John 14:1–3). That was a familiar promise and the common language of a bridegroom proposing to his bride after they had drunk from the common cup that accompanied a proposal of marriage. John 14 records what Jesus then spoke about the soon coming indwelling of the Holy Spirit (the guarantee and seal of the covenant relationship similar to an "engagement ring," Ephesians 1:13–14). He said this before they left the Upper Room (see John 14:31).

As we have noted earlier, part of the makeup of the Passover Feast is its historical roots, celebrating the deliverance of Israel out of Egypt. Those roots ultimately point to the fruit of the life, death, and resurrection of Jesus the Messiah in the first century AD. The historical celebration of the Passover by Jesus with His disciples had in view the fuller purpose of God. Jesus realized in greater ways than the disciples could comprehend the full redemption God had in mind. The historical event of redemption out of idolatrous, enslaving Egypt pictured the future full redemption out of this enslaving evil age and the idolatrous world system independent of God.

> On Passover night, God redeemed Israel from slavery in Egypt. The New Testament speaks of being *"redeemed"* from slavery using the Greek word *lutrosis*, "to ransom." It is from the word *lutron* which refers to "something to loosen with, that is, a redemption price" (*Key Word Study Bible* New Testament Dictionary, #3083, p. 2216). What does 1 Peter 1:18–19 reveal about our redemption price?

Not redeemed with corruptible things, but with the precious blood of Christ, as a lamb without blemish and without spot

> Ephesians 1:7 and 1:13–14 speak of our redemption using the Greek word *apolutrosis*, an intensified form of the word *lutron*. The prefix *apo* speaks of separation, of being redeemed from something, to be set free for a ransom, to be ransomed in full. What do you find about our redemption in Ephesians 1:7, 13–14; 4:30? What are we redeemed from? What are we redeemed to?

In whom we have redemption through his blood, the forgiveness of sins, according to the riches of his grace.

> What additional insights do you glean from Acts 20:28?

Feed the church of God, which he hath purchased with his own blood.

Peter speaks of the great redemption price Jesus paid, revealing both His great, eternal love and the value He placed on those He redeemed. No amount of silver and gold could redeem one person, nor could all the silver and gold in the world equal one drop of the *"precious blood . . . of Christ."* The Lord redeemed Israel out of Egypt on Passover night through a slain

---

Did You Know?
PETER'S PASSOVER "EXODUS"

Jesus spoke in parabolic form of the In the first **Passover**, God rescued the enslaved Jews on the **night** of the *"Passover,"* leaving in haste the next morning, with their *"loins girded, your sandals on your feet"* (Exodus 12:11–12), following the Angel of the Lord by the light of a Pillar of Fire. The Red Sea opened and they escaped from Pharaoh's soldiers who soon after died. The Greek translation (LXX) of Moses' testimony states, *"God . . . rescued me out of the hand of Pharaoh"* (Exodus 18:4, 10). Consider the parallels in Acts 12:1–24, the rescue of Peter from prison during Passover Week. Like the Hebrew children, Peter was imprisoned, rescued at night by an angel of the Lord with a light shining in the prison. He told Peter to *"get up* **quickly***,"* *"gird yourself and put on sandals,"* and *"follow me."* Peter followed escaping from the soldiers as the prison doors opened. He then reported to the praying people. Acts 12:11 records Peter's words, like those Moses used, *"the Lord . . . rescued me out of the hand of Herod."* The soldiers were executed (12:19), Herod soon after met his death at the hands of God (12:23), and the church continued their mission declaring to the nations *"the word of the Lord,"* that Jesus is Lord (Acts 12:24). God rescues us **out of** our "chains," "prisons," and certain death and **unto** Himself, His life, and His eternal, holy purposes.

lamb, promising them a full inheritance in the Promised Land of Canaan. Jesus paid the redemption price for us on the Cross as *"the Lamb of God,"* becoming *"our Passover,"* releasing us from our slavery to sin, self, and the devil. He fully released us from our sins, forgiving us all *"our trespasses."* Not only that, He gave us His Spirit as the seal of our redemption, the *"pledge"* or guarantee that His inheritance belongs to us and we belong to Him.

Using the Greek verb *peripoieomai,* which literally means "to make around oneself," to make one's own, Acts 20:28 states that God *"purchased"* or *"acquired"* the church *"with His own blood,"* making every believer His own possession, greatly loved and treasured and called to a holy and loving lifestyle empowered by His Spirit. We are redeemed, purchased, changed, and freed to walk a new walk as God's own possession. Ultimately, the people of God are redeemed to reveal daily the treasure of who Jesus is and glorify Him forever.

How significantly did (does) Jesus' death and resurrection impact you? How do we apply this to our daily lives? How do we celebrate the Passover today? What is God's call of the Feasts to us today, especially the Feast of Passover? We will see these application points in Day Five.

FOR ME TO CELEBRATE THE FEAST— OBEYING THE CALL OF PASSOVER

Lesson Two **DAY FIVE**

REMEMBER THE REALITY OF REDEMPTION

Every detail of the first Passover and every subsequent Passover celebration is a celebration of the reality of redemption. God redeemed Israel from the slavery of Egypt. The innocent blood of a lamb sprinkled on the doorposts provided a covering of protection and the doorway to redemption—a picture of Israel being bought out of slavery into freedom as children of God. God delivered His *"son Israel, My first-born"* just as He had promised Moses He would.

How do we **remember** this Feast in our daily lives? How do you and I answer the Call of the Feast of Passover? What do the Scriptures show us about this Feast and its applications to those who believe in and follow Jesus Christ as Lord and Savior? Carefully read 1 Corinthians 5:7–8. What should we remember?

Let us keep the feast, not with old leaven, neither with the leaven of malice and wickedness; but with the unleaven bread of sincerity and truth.

First Corinthians 5:1–8 records the failure of the Corinthian church to deal with a professed believer living in immorality. The Spirit of God led Paul to rebuke them sharply and call them to holy thinking and holy and loving actions. The foundation for his counsel to them is the reality pictured in the

> *"Clean out the old leaven, that you may be a new lump, just as you are in fact unleavened. For Christ our Passover also has been sacrificed. Let us therefore celebrate the feast, not with old leaven, nor with the leaven of malice and wickedness, but with the unleavened bread of sincerity and truth."*
>
> **1 Corinthians 5:7–8**

> *"Grace to you and peace ... from Jesus Christ, the faithful witness, the first-born from the dead, and the ruler of the kings of the earth. To Him who loves us, and released us from our sins by His blood, and He has made us to be a kingdom, priests to His God and Father; to Him be the glory and the dominion forever and ever. Amen."*
>
> **Revelation 1:4a, 5–6**

Passover, the reality of genuine redemption. God has done something through Jesus Christ that should change the way a believer in Christ lives every day. What Christ did in being *"our Passover,"* giving Himself to be *"sacrificed"* on the Cross, did something that should change the way each believer lives. What should we do? How does every believer answer the Call of the Feast of the Passover?

First Corinthians 5:8 calls us to *"celebrate the Feast"* or *"keep the Feast,"* referring to the Feast of Unleavened Bread as it is tied to Passover. We will discover the fuller meaning of that Feast in our next lesson. The key point in this lesson is the Feast of Passover. **The Passover is the Foundation of all the Feasts**, for without Passover occurring, there can be no other Feasts, there can be no celebrating, there can be no freedom, only slavery and death. With the Passover we can celebrate all the Feasts. Here is the main point. Passover pictures the **power of release**.

Jesus is *"our Passover."* Remember the first Passover. That Passover proved to be the Power of Release for the children of Israel. The first nine plagues in Egypt simply made Pharaoh's heart harder and harder. The tenth plague dealt the death blow to Pharaoh's and his son's claim to be "gods." This event proved to be the force of Israel's release out of Egypt **that night**, propelling God's people into the wilderness toward the Promised Land. They exited Egypt immediately.

REMEMBER THE POWER OF RELEASE

Jesus is *"our Passover,"* our **power of release**. What power of release has Christ provided? Look at each of the following verses and passages and record your insights about the power of release given by Jesus to every believer. Note in each passage what **Jesus** releases us **from** or **out of** AND/OR what He releases us *into*.

Luke 4:18–19
He release us from sin, guilt, condemnation, judgment

Luke 24:46–47
It behooved Christ to suffer, and rise from the dead the 3rd day. Repentance, remission of sins be preached in all nation in his name

Revelation 1:5
He washed our sins by his blood

Acts 13:37–39
By him all that believe are justified from all thing

Galatians 5:1, 13–14

All the law is fulfilled in one word; Thou shall Love Thy neighbor as Thyself

Colossians 2:13–14

He made us alive through his forgiveness

Hebrews 2:14–18 with 1 John 3:8

For the son of God was manifested, that He might destroy the works of the devil

Jesus came to **release** the captives **out of** captivity to sin, guilt, condemnation, and judgment, out of captivity to a broken heart, to death and the bondage that accompanies the fear of death. He came to release us **from** our sins by His blood. He came to forgive us. He freed us **from** those things from which rules, regulations, and laws could not free us. External rules cannot produce an internal change. Jesus can. He released us **from** a legalistic system of trying to earn our way to heaven or outweigh good deeds over bad deeds. By His payment for our sins on the cross, He released us **from** our debt of sin, wiping clean the massive *"certificate of debt,"* taking it out of the way, no longer to be held over us, condemning us.

He released us bringing us **into** a living, personal relationship with Jesus as our Lord, our Savior and Redeemer. He released us **into** freedom, not the freedom to do what we want, but the freedom to do what we ought. We are **free** to love others, to serve others, rather than manipulate or use others. He released us **into** being priests, those connected to God who believe Him and help others believe and become His. He released us **into** His kingdom, to reign with Him,

APPLY Write a prayer of thanks to the Lord for what He has released you **from** and what He has released you **into**.

_____
_____
_____
_____
_____
_____
_____
_____
_____

REMEMBER TO REMEMBER WHAT JESUS DID AND WHAT JESUS SAID

Jesus gave us a clear application of the Passover in one of the two ordinances He gave to His church. In Matthew 28:18–20, He instructed His disciples to **baptize** everyone who comes to faith in Christ and to teach every disciple to obey what He taught. He instructed the church to observe/participate in **the**

Word Study
"FORGIVENESS"

The Greek word most often used for "forgiveness" is *aphiemi*, made up of two Greek words, *apo*, "off or away from" denoting a separation and *hiemi*, "to send" or "to let go." It refers to a release of sins, a sending away from one, or a removing off of one. When Jesus forgives sin, He removes it from us *"as far as the east is from the west"* (Psalm 103:12). He casts our sins *"into the depths of the sea"* (Micah 7:19), the idea being that He makes them inaccessible to all. Hebrews 10:17 quoting Jeremiah 31:34 declares, *"AND THEIR SINS AND THEIR LAWLESS DEEDS I WILL REMEMBER NO MORE."* Hebrews 10:18 therefore states, *"Now where there is forgiveness of these things, there is no longer any offering for sin."* Our sins are released from us and from hindering our eternity with the Lord.

[Jesus said] *"Do this in remembrance of Me. . . . For as often as you eat this bread and drink the cup, you proclaim the Lord's death until He comes."*

I Corinthians 24b, 26

Lord's Supper *"until He comes."* Read over His instructions as given to Paul in **1 Corinthians 11:23–32.** What did Jesus want His disciples to **remember**, according to verses 24–25? Note what He says in Matthew 26:28 also. (You may want to review the summary given in the chart, "THE EVENTS OF THE PASSOVER WITH JESUS AND HIS DISCIPLES.")

📖 What would believers be doing each time they participated in this *"supper,"* according to verse 26?

proclaim the Lord's death till He come

📖 To what would believers look forward according to verse 26?

The coming of Lord Jesus return

📖 What attitude is crucial according to verse 27?

Thanksgiving; for what He has done and will do

📖 What instruction does the Spirit of God give through Paul in verse 28?

Let a man examine himself

📖 What warning did Paul give the Corinthian church in verses 29–32?

He who eateth and drinketh unworthily does does damnation to him.

Jesus wanted His disciples to remember Him and His sacrifice when they came together and broke the bread and drank of the fruit of the vine. Specifically, this symbolic meal pointed to Jesus' body given and broken *"for you"* and His blood poured out *"for the forgiveness of sins"* (Matthew 26:28). In partaking of this together, believers would be proclaiming the Lord's death, pointing any who would believe to the salvation He alone can give. They would also be looking forward to His *"return."* As noted earlier, this would be the return of a Bridegroom for His bride, the church. This also speaks of a continual love and loyalty to the Lord, being faithful awaiting His return.

An essential in honoring the Lord is the attitude of reverence in celebrating this meal. That means treating the Lord and His sacrifice in a worthy manner, not merely going through a religious formula or ritual, or even worse, treating Him with dishonor or disrespect. This necessitates examining oneself in the light of Scripture, under the guidance of His Spirit, and partaking of this meal, trusting Him for His forgiveness of any and all sin. Paul warned the Corinthians of God's judgment on some of them for their obvious irreverence. Some had become sick, and some had died under the chastening hand of God. How crucial to examine one's heart and life, continually repenting of any sin. We must remember that when God chastens, it is to correct and bring us to maturity. Hebrews 12:5–11 speaks of the ongoing chastening and child-training work of the Lord with His children.

Each time one partakes of the Lord's Supper, he or she should **look together** as part of the body of Christ, **look up,** remembering the Lord Himself and one's relationship with Him, **look back** on the Lord's death for sin, **look**

seder [handwritten annotation]

within to one's heart (attitudes and actions), **look out** on others who need to hear, see, receive, and believe the message proclaimed, **look forward** to the resurrected Lord's return, ready to **look forever** on Him and the vast family of which we will be part.

REMEMBER *YOUR* REDEMPTION… DAILY

📖 **A DAILY REMEMBRANCE—A DAILY REALITY**—The Seven Feasts present seven realities God desires in each of His children. Passover presents **the reality of redemption**, an unimaginable price paid by Jesus, the Lamb slain, for the unfathomable sin in each person. Each day one should **remember** and live in the **reality of redemption**. Read this **confession of redemption** below. Then, add to it your own words of testimony, praise, and thanksgiving.

I am redeemed, *"purchased"* with the *"precious blood"* of Jesus *"as of a lamb unblemished and spotless"* (Acts 20:28; 1 Peter 1:18–19). I am loved and valued by God. I am undeserving of this redemption. I cannot earn this redemption, nor pay it back. I am thankful for this redemption. I exalt my Lord and Savior Jesus Christ for the price He paid. May I be holy, conducting myself in reverence and fear before the Father with fervent and sincere love toward Him and one another (1 Peter 1:15–17, 22) . . . .

_____
_____
_____
_____
_____
_____
_____
_____
_____

🙏 **Lord,** thank You for taking the initiative to come and die, to redeem me from my sin, my selfishness, from the power of sin's enslavement, and one day the very presence of sin. I praise You for the price You paid in Your holiness and love—Your holiness required this price if I would be redeemed, freed, delivered out of bondage to the devil, the flesh, and the world system. Your love gave what You required. Thank You. I was and am powerless apart from You. Thank you for the power of release You gave and continue to give for my daily struggles, for the temptations I face, for the waywardness of my flesh, and the battles in the world arena. Thank You that by the cross I am crucified with You; my flesh has a place of death, the only place that fits it, the only place that truly deals with it, so that I can be free of its wickedness. May I walk *"by faith in the Son of God who loved me and gave Himself for me"* and never *"set aside the grace of God,"* trying in my own power to deal with old "Egyptian" thinking and living (Galatians 2:20–21). You displayed the riches of grace in Your sacrifice. In my life, may You clearly see and empower my choices to live in that grace day by day. In Jesus' name, amen.

📜 *Word Study*

"CELEBRATE THE FEAST"

The phrase *"celebrate the Feast"* or *"keep the Feast"* in 1 Corinthians 5:8 is a translation of the Greek word *heortazo*, used only here in the New Testament. It is a present tense verb meaning to continually celebrate, not just once a year, not just when one partakes of the Lord's Supper, but all day, every day. It is also in the subjunctive mood which means that each person has a choice—I should and I could celebrate, but I may or may not. The choice is open, every day, every moment of every day as to **if** or **how well** each of us celebrates.

THE EVENTS OF THE PASSOVER WITH JESUS AND HIS DISCIPLES

The accounts of the Passover events are given in Matthew 26:17–30; Mark 14:12–25; Luke 22:7–34; John 13–14. The Passover events of Jesus with His disciples can be summarized in four movements, like a symphony. First there was the **preparation** for the Passover. Jesus spoke of His betrayal and crucifixion at least six months prior to prepare them for what He knew would occur. His triumphal entry on Sunday (Nisan 10) prior to the Passover set everything in motion. Second, there was the **celebration** of the Passover itself, the meal and all that occurred with it. Third, we see the **initiation** of the Lord's Supper in which Jesus changed the order of the traditional Passover, adding another breaking of bread and His words about His body being broken like the bread and His blood being poured out like the fruit of the vine. It was the initiation of the New Covenant in His blood for forgiveness of sins. Finally, Jesus spoke to them about the **manifestation** of Himself as **The Passover**, something they did not fully comprehend until after His resurrection.

PREPARATION

Sunday, Nisan 10—Passover Lamb Selection day followed by three days of examining the lamb to assure an unblemished Passover lamb. That day Jesus rode into Jerusalem in His triumphal entry with the people crying out, *"Hosanna* (meaning "save now"), *. . . Blessed is He who comes in the name of the Lord"* (Matthew 21:9). Then, many examined Him, questioned, tested, and plotted against Him over the next three days. The Passover lambs were slain on Nisan 14.

In preparation for the Passover, Peter and John brought the slain lamb from the Temple to the previously arranged Upper Room. The setting included a low-lying table around which the disciples reclined with feet facing outward from the table. The reclining arrangement most likely followed the oldest to the youngest. Judas reclined to Jesus' left and was likely the oldest. John reclined to Jesus right (likely the youngest) (John 13:23–26).

In the evening, as they began the Passover celebration, Jesus spoke of His desire to eat the Passover with His disciples (Luke 22:15–16). He Himself was to be **their** Passover Lamb, their substitution for sin and covering from the judgment of God.

CELEBRATION

In New Testament times, the participants drank **Four Cups** of the fruit of the vine in a certain order during the Passover celebration—1) the Cup of Sanctification, recalling Israel being brought out and set apart, 2) the Cup of Wrath, remembering God's wrath poured out on Egypt, 3) the Cup of Redemption (also known as *"the Cup of Blessing"*), redeeming out of slavery, and 4) the Cup of Consummation or Covenant Relationship, celebrating belonging to the Lord. The Jews based this four-fold designation on four promises of Exodus 6:6–7—The LORD said, *"I will bring you out. . . . I will deliver you. . . . I will also redeem you. . . . I will take you for My people, and I will be your God."* (The following general order is based on the four Gospels and the accounts proposed in various historical documents, most notably *The Temple: Its Ministry and Services as They Were in the Time of Christ* [pages 208–248] by Alfred Edersheim [Grand Rapids: Wm. B. Eerdmans Publishing Co., 1983 Reprint]. Scriptures are listed where the events are recorded.)

1. The First Cup is filled with *"the fruit of the vine"* (Matthew 26:29; Mark 14:25; Luke 22:18). The father or the Host/Head of the Feast said a prayer of thanks for the **Cup of Sanctification**, setting apart the day and the meal of celebration to the Lord. Luke 22:17 records this first cup. All **drank the First Cup.**

2. Washing of hands. Jesus would be considered the Host of the meal and would wash first. This may be the time at which Jesus washed the disciples' feet (knowing the contentious attitude with which they viewed their own position and importance) (Luke 22:24–27; John 13:3–17).

3. The Head of the Feast dipped **bitter herbs** in salt water or vinegar (reminders of bitter slavery and tears), spoke a prayer of blessing, and gave to all.

4. The Second Cup (the Cup of Wrath) poured and set aside. Based on Exodus 13:1–10, one (often a child in a family) would ask Questions about the Passover—"Why is this night different from all other nights?" The father or the Head of the Feast then told of the Passover and the Exodus, including the significance of the lamb, the bitter herbs, and the unleavened bread. The answers emphasized the reality of personal redemption, speaking of *"what the Lord did for me when I came out of Egypt"* (13:8).

5. The participants recited the first part of the *Hallel* (*"the praise,"* Psalms 113—114).

6. The participants **drank the Second Cup** followed by the second **washing** of hands.

THE EVENTS OF THE PASSOVER WITH JESUS AND HIS DISCIPLES

7. Unleavened Bread and Bitter Herbs. The Head of the Feast took one of two pieces of unleavened bread, broke it, then spoke a prayer of thanks and blessing, and gave each a piece of the bread with bitter herbs to dip in *Charoseth* (a sauce of crushed berries or raisins mixed with vinegar). This was known as *"the sop"* or *"the morsel"* and would be given to all, including Judas. Jesus *"became troubled in spirit"* stating that one of them would betray Him (John 13:18, 21–30; Matthew 26:21–25). Jesus dipped *"the morsel"* and gave it to Judas first (John 13:26) because he was at the seat to Jesus' left (the chief and first place at the table, often reserved for the oldest). It is likely that Judas exited after this point without finishing the Passover meal (John 13:27–30).

8. The participants ate **the Passover Meal** of bitter herbs, unleavened bread, the *Chagigah* (a festival offering *"from the flock and the herd"*—Deuteronomy 16:2), and roasted lamb. The **third hand washing** occurred after the meal.

9. Then, Jesus poured the Third Cup (the Cup of Redemption, also known as the Cup of Blessing).

INITIATION OF THE LORD'S SUPPER

10. Departing from the traditional order and instituting **a new order**, Jesus took <u>Bread</u> *"after supper"* (1 Corinthians 11:25), gave thanks, blessed it, broke the bread, and gave it to the disciples. *"Take, eat; this is My body"* (Matthew 26:26; 1 Corinthians 11:23–24).

Passover Traditions Today—What about the *aphikomen*? The modern Passover includes the placing together of three pieces of unleavened bread with a linen napkin between each piece. After the second cup, the host takes the middle piece, breaks it, wraps it in a linen napkin, and puts it aside (hidden) for after supper [the Greek word *aphikomen* means "after-dish"]. After the meal, children look for the *aphikomen*, find it, take it out of the linen wrapping and share it among all. Some scholars believe this aspect of Passover began in the first century as a result of Jewish Christians including it in their observance since Jesus had added the blessing and breaking of a piece of unleavened bread *"after supper."* After the Temple was destroyed in AD 70, there were no more Passover lambs, so they used unleavened bread to represent the lamb. It is thought that some of the Jews picked up the custom of the three pieces, with the middle piece being broken and wrapped, not recognizing the significance of that piece picturing Jesus the Messiah broken in death, wrapped in linen, hidden away in burial, and brought out for all to partake of. Today, the *aphikomen* is a regular part of the Passover Seder.

11. Jesus took The Third Cup (the Cup of Redemption also known as **the Cup of Blessing**—1 Corinthians 10:16), gave thanks, blessed it, and gave the cup to the disciples, speaking of **the New Covenant in His blood**. *"Drink from it, all of you; for this is My blood of the covenant, which is poured out for many for forgiveness of sins"* (Matthew 26:27–28). *"This cup is the new covenant in My blood; do this, as often as you drink it, in remembrance of Me"* (1 Corinthians 11:25).

12. Immediately **after** these statements, Jesus spoke of going to **His Father's house** to prepare a place, promising to come again to receive His own to Himself (John 14:1–3). That was a familiar promise and the common language of a bridegroom proposing to his bride. John 14:16–18 records what Jesus then spoke about the soon coming and indwelling of the Holy Spirit (*"the guarantee"* of the covenant relationship, similar to an "engagement ring"—Ephesians 1:13–14).

Note **three** truths—**1)** The new significance of **Jesus as the Passover Lamb** and **Jesus as the unleavened bread broken**. **2)** Jesus offering Himself **as that Passover Lamb** was also **the bride price** to be paid for His new bride (the Christian church). **3)** Jesus commanded them to partake of the Lord's Supper *"in remembrance of Me,"* doing so *"until He returns"* (1 Corinthians 11:24–26). He has just proposed to His disciples the wedding vows of that day. He promised to return when all things are ready.

13. Jesus poured **The Fourth Cup (the Cup of Consummation)** and the disciples drank **the Fourth Cup**. Some think that Jesus did not drink the fourth cup.

In Matthew 26:20, Jesus stated after He had given them **the Third Cup**, *"the cup of blessing,"* and most likely after pouring **the Fourth Cup**, that He would *"not drink of this fruit of the vine from now on until that day when I drink it new with you in My Father's kingdom"* (Matthew 26:29). Luke 22:18 adds, *"until the kingdom of God comes."* That would coincide with the consummation of the Marriage Feast (Revelation 19:7–9) and the fullness of the kingdom on earth.

14. At the conclusion of the Supper, they sang a **hymn** (the remainder of the *Hallel*—Psalm 115—118 or Psalm 136) and *"went out to the Mount of Olives"* (Matthew 26:30). John records that while still in the Upper Room, after Jesus spoke to them about leaving, preparing a place, coming back to receive them, and the promise and work of the Holy Spirit, He then said *"arise, let us go from here"* (John 14:31).

LESSON TWO – THE FEAST OF PASSOVER   47

The Events of the Passover with Jesus and His Disciples (cont.)

MANIFESTATION of the Passover Lamb

15. Jesus prepared them for the **manifestation** of Himself as **The Passover**. After the Supper, Jesus spoke of fulfilling the prophecy from Isaiah 53:12, *"He was numbered with Transgressors"* (Luke 22:37). The hymn they sang, either the remaining portion of the *Hallel* (Psalms 115—118) or possibly Psalms 136, pointed to the saving work of God and even to the rejoicing His salvation would bring.

They walked from the Upper Room to the Garden of Gethsemane (John 15—18:1). The route would have taken them past the glorious Temple of white marble and gold trim, shining in the light of a full moon. Hanging over the entry at the Porch of the Temple leading into the Holy Place was a massive, beautiful golden vine. As they passed the Temple, perhaps Jesus looked up and pointed to that vine and spoke of Himself as the **True Vine**, the true source of life, the **true temple** of God who was about to be torn down and raised again the third day (John 15:1–8; 2:18–22).

As Jesus and the disciples walked toward the Garden of Gethsemane, He offered what is commonly called His high priestly prayer in John 17. **After this,** they crossed the Kidron ravine over the Brook Kidron, red with the blood of thousands of lambs slain, the blood draining from the altar area to the Kidron Brook just a few yards away. The evident fragrance of blood and the aroma of lambs roasted over the fire filled the night air as Jesus walked into the garden. There in great agony, He prayed three times, then faced the betrayal by Judas. He was arrested, abandoned by His disciples, and forced to endure three Jewish trials followed by three Roman trials, none of which could find any sin, guilt, or fault in Him. Jesus stood as the unblemished **Passover Lamb** who gave Himself to be crucified (John 10:17–18). Paul later wrote,

"…indeed Christ, our Passover, was sacrificed for us. Therefore let us celebrate the feast"
(1 Corinthians 5:7–8).

The Feast of Unleavened Bread

The Call to Experience the Unleavened Life of Christ

As we explore the Feasts of the Lord, it is vital to remember, each Feast is a **"Him"** celebration, a Feast focused on the Lord Himself and one's relationship to Him. The **Feast of Unleavened Bread** is the **second** of seven Feasts given by the Lord, each one **celebrating** one's covenant relationship and walk with Him. Each Feast is also a **call** to focus on the Lord, to rejoice in Him and learn from Him. In addition, each Feast is connected to the **calendar** of God's work in Israel and in the world related to historical events in which He reveals more of His redemptive work. The Feasts also reveal His care and control over the matters of humankind as He works among the nations. Most importantly, each Feast foreshadows and pictures something about the person and work of **Christ**. God's redemptive work through Christ brings us into the fullness of a personal relationship with Him and the freedom He longs for us to experience.

We see in these Feasts God's design for us to walk in a God-blessed relationship with Him (going back to His Covenant with Abraham and even further to His original intent in the creation in which God blessed all He had done—Genesis 1:28; 12:2–3). God wants us to walk in a believing relationship with Him, as seen in Abraham, in Moses, and in the Passover and Exodus. God wants His best in our lives, growing out of this blessed relationship of faith.

The Feast of Unleavened Bread gives us another picture of the relationship God offers to any who will place faith in Him. This Feast is part of the harvest celebration associated with the Feast of First fruits (beginning of the barley harvest). Unleavened Bread is also part of the history celebration of the nation of Israel. We will see the historical dimension in Israel's exodus from Egypt as well as in the events surrounding Jesus' life and ministry. We will also see how God desires us to walk in an "unleavened life" experiencing the purity of His life and His will.

> **The Feast of Unleavened Bread points us to "unleavened living," a walk experiencing the Unleavened Life of Christ, walking in the purity and joy of His Spirit.**

Lesson Three — DAY ONE

HURRY UP AND LEAVE EGYPT

Interestingly interwoven in the Exodus event is the eating of unleavened bread. However, God never meant unleavened bread only as a circumstantial or dietary matter. It was much, much more than a dietary incidental. It spoke to the work of God in the people, individually, and corporately. That experience in the Old Testament took on even more significance in the New Testament, as we will see in exploring this Feast. Where did unleavened bread fit in the Exodus events? How did it relate to the ways and works of God? We will begin to see in today's lesson.

📖 Review God's directions for the people of Israel in Exodus 23:14–17. What do you discover about the Feast of Unleavened Bread?

Three times a year thou shall feast unto me. Thou shall keep the feast of unleavened bread, eat it 7 days

📖 What additional insights do you discover in Exodus 34:23–24? You may also want to refer to Deuteronomy 16:16.

I will cast out the nations before thee and enlarge thy borders: neither shall any man desire thy land, when they go before the Lord 3 times a yr

God required all the males to appear before Him three times a year. The Feast of Unleavened Bread occurred during the first of those times, in the early spring. The other two times were in late spring at the Feast of Harvest or Weeks (Pentecost), and in the autumn at the Feast of Ingathering or Booths/Tabernacles. This meant in most cases that whole families journeyed to the place of the Feasts to worship and celebrate their relationship with the Lord, to give offerings to Him, and to share with family and friends.

📖 Read about the preparation for the Exodus in Exodus 12:14–20. What importance did God place on this event according to verse 14?

This day shall to u far a memorial: ye shall keep it a feast to the Lord through out yr generations ye shall keep it for ever

📖 As you consider this verse, think about how significant national holidays are in any nation. According to verse 14, what do you see about the Lord's relationship to Israel and their relationship to Him in this event?

God wanted his to celebrate what He had done and who they were to Him, and who He was to them as a nation and as individuals for ever

God ordered the events of the Exodus to be memorialized in a yearly feast, a time to celebrate what He had done, who they were to Him, and who He was to them as a nation and as individuals. He ordered it not only as a yearly feast, but as *"a permanent ordinance,"* literally *"an eternal ordinance."* God called for a celebration for all time, and even more, since God intended a relationship with Him and the salvation He gave to last forever,

📖 How did unleavened bread fit into the actual events of the exodus from Egypt? Read the account in Exodus 12:33–39 and record your insights.

And the Egyptians were urgent upon the people, that they might send them out of the land in haste. So the people took their dough before it was leavened, kneading bowls

After the Lord passed through the land, judging every home where they did not apply the blood of a lamb, the Egyptians quickly urged the Israelites to leave. That necessitated hurriedly picking up everything and moving. They gathered their kneading bowls filled with unleavened dough and marched out of Egypt without delay. When they set up camp, they quickly baked the unleavened bread. God acted quickly. That meant His people had to follow quickly, promptly obeying the instructions He had given through Moses.

📖 How crucial was this dietary detail in the relationship between God and Israel? What rested on one's obedience or failure to obey this ordinance, according to Exodus 12:15, 19?

remove the leaven ur house
7 days u shall eat unleavened bread from the 1st day until the 7st day that person shall be cut off from Isreal. No work shall be done on the 1st day or the 7st day

Technically, leaven or yeast caused bread to rise from the reaction of the ingredients. In the exodus event, the hasty departure necessitated unleavened bread—no time for leaven to rise. The unleavened bread of the yearly feast focused on recalling the quick exodus from Egypt. It also pointed to removal of any corrupting influence in the nation. God did not want any of the "leaven" of Egypt traveling with His people, nor did He want any kind of corrupting influence in His people once they moved into the Promised Land. God clearly warned that anyone who ate leavened bread or anything with leaven in it would be *"cut off from Israel."* That meant being excommunicated from the people of God, left on one's own. It could also mean being executed as a rebellious member of the community. This was no mild suggestion. It was crucial and essential that the people follow the Lord's instructions, that they symbolically show the uncorrupt nature of the redemption God had given them.

📖 God desired that His people celebrate together as His people. Read Exodus 12:16. What does the requirement for a holy assembly say about the responsibility of the people as a whole, as a nation set apart to a relationship with the Lord God?

Holy convocation on the 1st and 7st days. No manner of work shall be done on them. but that everyone must eat - that only be prepared by you.

Put Yourself In Their Shoes
GOD CAN BRING SALVATION QUICKLY

In the exodus from Egypt, God acted quickly, bringing deliverance out of the slavery of Egypt and into a new day of freedom. When God brings salvation, He often moves quickly. The testimony of Scripture is clear that anytime a person calls on the Lord for salvation, He responds quickly, without delay. Call on Him. At that moment, He will save anyone from the slavery and judgment of sin and give His salvation and freedom. Romans 10:13, quoting the Old Testament prophet Joel (2:32), assures us, *"WHOEVER WILL CALL UPON THE NAME OF THE LORD WILL BE SAVED."* God can also work quickly to restore Christians who have wandered into the wilderness of unbelief or pride or foolish choices, not because they have lost their salvation—that cannot happen—but because foolish choices are possible. U-turns are also possible and God can quickly respond. God is ready to quickly restore the repentant heart.

LESSON THREE – THE FEAST OF UNLEAVENED BREAD

Put Yourself In Their Shoes
WORTH FORSAKING— WORTH REMEMBERING

God worked to deliver His people form the enslavement of Egypt and the corruption of Egyptian thinking. Leaven symbolized corruption, the evil of their enslavement, as well as the influences of thinking about Egyptian gods and ways. This was **worth forsaking**. God had better for His people. He desired an uncorrupt relationship in an uncorrupt land. Part of the celebration of leaving Egypt was the anticipation of a new land, a new life, of leaving the old—symbolized in leaven—and preparing for the new. All that God did in bringing them out was certainly **worth remembering** every year (Exodus 12:15–20). What is worth forsaking in your life? Forsake what God says to forsake. What is worth remembering? Call to mind what God has done. Thank Him and celebrate your relationship with Him.

📖 What additional insights do you find in Exodus 12:19–20 that relate to the responsibilities and relationships of each family in the nation?

No leavened shall be found in ur house whoever eat leavened shall be cut off from the congregation of Isreal. You shall unleavened bread only.

📖 What would family members think of this time? As a family, how would they view this no-leaven week?

Everybody must follow GoD's instutions No leavened in the house of no kind.

God called His people to assemble together in worship twice during the week of Unleavened Bread, the first day and the last day. It was important to make sure all leaven was gone and to worship from the start and then to conclude the week in worship and reflection for what God had done and for the relationship with Him they were privileged to know. God required the entire nation, every family, to participate in the Feast, a requirement meant to build the relationship with Himself and with one another. That relationship building had to be part of *every* household. Each family and every family member must be diligent in removing leaven and in eating only unleavened bread. God also stipulated there could be nothing else with leaven in the house. God required that no person—Israelite, foreigner, or native of the land—partake of leaven. To do so would be to symbolically allow corruption in the relationship with God and with the people of Israel, a sin in God's sight. The yearly feast reminded the people of an unleavened, uncorrupted relationship with God and with one another—as a nation, as a household, and as an individual.

How did Israel celebrate this Feast through the years? What truths highlighted their celebrations? We will see in Day Two.

Lesson Three — DAY TWO
ISRAEL REMEMBERED WHAT GOD HAD DONE

Built into the accounts in Exodus are the remembrances of these events. This was important for the people and for their relationship with the Lord. The book of Deuteronomy further emphasized this. It records the second giving of the law plus instructions needed for entering the Promised Land. It had been forty years since the exodus of the people of Israel from the slavery of Egypt. A new generation faced the future. What did God want them to remember? How were they to celebrate His working? Today, we will look at Israel as they prepared to enter the land and at certain examples of how they celebrated through the years.

📖 Exodus 13:3–10 gives further guidelines for the Feast of Unleavened Bread. What did Moses emphasize in verse 3?

Remember this day which you went out of Egypt. by strength of hand the Lord brought u out

📖 What did God want the people to remember, according to verse 8?

This is done because of what the Lord did for me when I came out from Egypt. (Tell yours Sons)

God wanted His people to remember the slavery of Egypt and what He had done on their behalf to deliver them. He desired that they remember and celebrate His powerful hand in their historical deliverance. To emphasize their departure and separation from Egypt and all its bondage and corruption, God called them to absolute separation from leaven in any form. His working merited a week of celebration. To highlight what God had done, He called the fathers to testify to their children about the work God had done. The emphasis year after year would be *"what the Lord did for me when I came out of Egypt."* Note the **personal** pronouns. God meant for this testimony of salvation to remain personal. Even hundreds of years past the exodus event, God wanted the people of Israel to recognize their connection to those who had gone before. In delivering the fathers of long ago, God was delivering future generations. Every generation must remember what God has done. It applied to all who had a faith relationship to the Lord.

📖 According to Exodus 13:9, what additional truths did the Lord want His people to remember? Note the word pictures He used as memory aids.

A sign; for with a strong hand the Lord brought u out of Egypt. Sign on the hand and between your eyes.

God put this Feast in place to be *"a sign"* so significant that it would be like a memorable mark on the hand or the forehead, pointing to His word and being able to call to mind all He had spoken. The people were to remember and speak about the Lord and what He had done, the deliverance He provided. At any point, God desired that they could remember and testify that *"with a strong hand the LORD has brought you out of Egypt."* This annual observance helped Israel remember and testify to others about what the Lord did for them.

📖 Look at the guidelines in Deuteronomy 16:1–4, 8. What description of this bread do you find in verse 3?

_____
_____
_____

📖 What additional afflictions took place during the **first seven days** out of Egypt (Nisan 15–21), the days in which they would be eating unleavened bread? What details of this week do you find in an overview of Exodus 13:17–22; 14:1–30; 15:22–25. Note that the Israelites left Egypt on Nisan

LESSON THREE – THE FEAST OF UNLEAVENED BREAD 53

15, crossed through the Red Sea in the early morning of the seventeenth, then marched for three days to the waters of Marah (around Nisan 18–20).

📖 What did God want His people to remember?

Did You Know?

JOSHUA AND ISRAEL CELEBRATED THE FEAST OF UNLEAVENED BREAD

On Nisan 10, the people crossed the Jordan River into the Promised Land, the land of Canaan. Joshua 5:10–12 records the celebration of the Passover on Nisan 14 and Unleavened Bread beginning on Nisan 15.

The Feast of Unleavened Bread, which lasted seven days, provided an opportunity to call to mind deliverance from the days of affliction in Egypt by the kmemory of *"the bread of affliction."* One of the marks of that bread was the fact that it had to be eaten on the run out of Egypt. That included the first two days in which Pharaoh's army pursued and hemmed in the Israelites at the Red Sea (Nisan 15–16) before the Lord miraculously delivered them (Nisan 17). That also included the three days' journey in the Wilderness of Sin and the experience of the bitter waters of Marah (Nisan 18–20) before finally coming to the Wells of Elim, presumably at the end of the week. Those seven days recalled the days of affliction in Egypt and the week of afflictions they faced in leaving Egypt. God wanted His people to remember the days and the way He brought them out. The annual holy assembly at the end of the seven day feast would help them focus on the Lord, on their relationship to Him and their responsibilities before Him as His people.

APPLY **Recalling and Telling What God Has Done**—What has God done in your life? First of all, has He saved you? Do you know Jesus Christ as your personal Lord and Savior? Do you remember what your life was like before He changed your heart and life? What changes is He working on now? What expectations do you have for the days ahead? For eternity with Him? Each of us should be able to say, "Because of Jesus, I am grateful I am not where I once was, I am prayerful about where I am now, and I am expectant about what He is doing and where He is taking me." Each of God's children is a grace-work of art in progress—Ephesians 2:10.

📖 One of the more remarkable observances of the Feast of Unleavened Bread occurred in the reign of Hezekiah around 715 BC. The account begins in 2 Chronicles 30:13 and is linked with the celebration of Passover on the fourteenth of the month. What did the people do in preparation, according to verses 13–14?

they assembled at Jerusalem, took away all the altars and casted them Brook Kidron

📖 How do these events in Hezekiah's day relate to the practice of clearing out any leaven in one's house?

the same; take away a present of sin, and focus on God

[Handwritten at top: People was willing to change]

📖 Read 2 Chronicles 30:21–22 and summarize this particular celebration. What stands out to you?

The people Celebrated with a pure Heart; they rejoiced in their relationship with God

The people celebrated the Feast of Unleavened Bread with the heart attitude God intended. They removed not only leaven from their houses, but more significantly the corrupting influences of idol altars. King Ahaz had allowed these, even encouraging people to do as they pleased against what God said. Now King Hezekiah focused all attention on the Lord and worship at His Temple. In Jerusalem, the people from near and far helped remove the altars dedicated to idols and false gods. Then they celebrated the Passover and the Feast of Unleavened Bread with great joy and gladness. Jerusalem became a city cleansed of corrupt worship, filled with joyous songs and celebration of pure worship as the people rejoiced in their relationship to God. They followed the orders God had given, they listened as the Levites *"taught the good knowledge of the LORD,"* and they enjoyed the days of feasting.

📖 Look at 2 Chronicles 30:23–27. What was unique about this celebration of the Feast of Unleavened Bread? What characteristics are given in this account?

The people worshiped God with their whole heart

📖 What happened as a result of the whole-hearted focus on the Lord and His word according to 2 Chronicles 31:1?

The people went home and destroyed their false altars and idols

The great joy of this Feast caused the people to extend the Feast for another seven days. King Hezekiah and the leaders gladly joined in, providing food in abundance for the people. Great gladness filled the city as people from the northern regions of Israel and from the surrounding region of Judah joined with those who lived in Jerusalem. *"Since the time of Solomon . . . there had been nothing like this in Jerusalem."* As the priests and Levites prayed and blessed the people, God heard their prayers. As a result of this renewal, after the extended Feast, the people returned to their cities and homes and began destroying false altars and idols. This revival spread to regions of Judah and Benjamin in the south and Ephraim and Manasseh in the north. The symbol of an unleavened feast became for a time the reality of joyous unleavened living in the land of Israel and Judah.

What can we learn about the Feast of Unleavened Bread from the New Testament? In Day Three, we will begin looking at the life of Jesus and how He fulfilled this Feast. We will also begin to see how this Feast should be connected to our daily living so that we are answering the **call of the Feast** of Unleavened Bread.

Did You Know?
THE FESTIVAL OFFERINGS

With each Feast, God required certain unique offerings during the week. Each Feast was different in the required offerings. For the Feast of Unleavened Bread, Numbers 28:17–25 delineates the offering of two bulls, one ram, and seven lambs as burnt offerings, one goat as a sin offering, grain offerings with the burnt offerings, plus the regular daily burnt offerings. The Feast of Unleavened Bread was a time of remembrance that focused on Israel's relationship with the Lord, a holy relationship marked by yielded, obedient lives.

[Handwritten: God want our heart / Love / Motovated]

EXTRA MILE
CELEBRATIONS OF THE FEAST

For further insight about the times of Unleavened Bread in the Old Testament, look at 2 Chronicles 8:13; 35:17 and Ezra 6:22.

Lesson Three — DAY THREE

JESUS LIVED AN "UNLEAVENED" LIFE

When we turn to the pages of the New Testament, we find the celebration of the Feast of Unleavened Bread a significant part of the yearly schedule of the Israelites. It was inseparably tied to Passover, the names being interchangeable for the two celebrations. We saw in Lesson 2 how Jesus celebrated the Passover, becoming the Passover Lamb procuring our deliverance from sin and judgment. The Feast of Unleavened Bread coincides with Passover and, in the life of Jesus, with His crucifixion, burial, and resurrection. He fulfills the heart of each Feast. In the case of unleavened bread, Scripture reveals Jesus as the "unleavened" Savior in His sinless life and ministry. While the Jews celebrated the Feast of Unleavened Bread, the sinless Son of God lay buried in a borrowed tomb. What connections can we see between His crucifixion and burial and the Feast of Unleavened Bread? What fuller picture do the Scriptures reveal about Jesus and this Feast?

📖 The Jewish leaders arrested Jesus and brought Him before Annas for the first of three Jewish trials. What did they discover about Jesus in that midnight trial? Review John 18:12–13, 19–24 and notate your insights.

They could not find no fault in him, Jesus told them to bear witness of the wrong that did.

📖 The second trial occurred before Caiaphas. Review Matthew 26:57–68. What conclusions did they reach in verses 59–60?

The chief priests and elders and all the council, sought false witness against Jesus at the last two false witnesses.

📖 What do you discover about Jesus in the early dawn trial before the Sanhedrin, according to Luke 22:66–71?

Jesus was in total control, saying to them bear witness of the wrong

Did You Know?
TWO OR THREE WITNESSES

Old Testament law required that there be two or three witnesses to confirm the guilt or innocence of a person. One witness alone was never enough to convict a person of a crime. Deuteronomy 19:15–21 gave very clear regulations on trials and the necessity of two or three witnesses. A false witness, if found out, would suffer the penalty he wrongly sought to place on the accused. God wanted them to *"put away the evil from among you"* (19:19-NKJV). In the events surrounding the crucifixion, more than three witnesses agreed that Jesus was without guilt, innocent, and righteous.

The first trial could not produce any credible accusations against Jesus. He told them to question those who heard Him. If any wrong was spoken by Him, He commanded that they *"bear witness"* of the wrong. They could not. In the second trial they *"sought false testimony,"* but produced only confused *"witnesses"* until *"two false witnesses"* twisted His words in an attempt to produce a guilty verdict. They finally accused Him of wrong for being who He is, *"the Christ, the Son of God"* and *"the Son of Man."* The early dawn trial before the Sanhedrin produced no true accusations of wrong doing or wrong speaking, only evidences of their own unbelief.

📖 What did Judas say about Jesus in Matthew 27:4?

I have sinned in that I have betrayed the innocent blood.

📖 What about the trials before Pilate? Record what you find in Luke 23:1–25, especially verses 4, 14, 15, and 22.

Pilate said to chief Priests and to the people, I find no fault in this man

📖 What additional action did Pilate take according to Matthew 27:24? For additional insight look at Deuteronomy 21:6–9.

He took water and washed his hands before them saying I am innocent of the blood of this just person: see ye to it.

📖 What did Pilate's wife say in Matthew 27:19?

Have nothing to do with that just man: I have suffered many things in a dream because of him

📖 Those at the cross saw how Jesus responded to His crucifixion. What did the thief on the cross say about Jesus in Luke 23:39–42?

Remember me when u come into thy Kingdom: today shalt thou be with me in paradise.

📖 What did the Roman Centurion at the cross declare, according to Luke 23:47? What about his fellow soldiers? What did they declare according to Matthew 27:54?

when saw the earthquake and the things that were done, feared greatly, saying Truly this was the Son of God.

In three Jewish trials, then three Roman trials (two before Pilate and one before Herod), no one found anything wrong in Jesus. Three times Pilate said he found no guilt in Jesus. He even used a Jewish ceremonial washing ritual attempting to clear himself of the guilt of condemning Jesus. Pilate's wife spoke of Jesus as *"that righteous Man,"* and the Roman Centurion declared Him to be *"innocent"* or *"righteous."* His fellow soldiers recognized Jesus as no ordinary man. One of the thieves being crucified next to Jesus, a Jewish criminal, began mocking Jesus (Matthew 27:44), but then changed, proclaiming *"this man has done nothing wrong."* Judas declared that he had betrayed *"innocent blood."* Romans, Jews, leaders, and criminals all pointed to Jesus as a righteous man. Jesus had lived an "unleavened" life.

📖 Peter knew Jesus as well as anyone. He walked with Him for over three years and was eyewitness to the resurrected Jesus. What did Peter say about Jesus in his Pentecost sermon, especially Acts 2:22–24? Read Acts 2:31 as well and note his additional statements about Jesus.

Jesus of Nazareth, a man approved of God among u by miracles and wonders and signs, which God did by him, in the midst of u

---

Margin notes:

God is showing us how to walk with him
Pilate
Authority to judge but not to wash his hands

90.73

LESSON THREE – THE FEAST OF UNLEAVENED BREAD   57

> **Did You Know?**
> **"WITHOUT DEFECT"**
>
> Throughout the Old Testament, the term *"without defect"* or *"without blemish"* is used of the offerings to be brought to the Lord, first mentioned in Exodus 12:5 of the Passover lamb. The pattern is clear from the earliest days when Noah offered up *"clean"* animals rather than *"unclean"* (Genesis 8:20–21). Any gift, offering, or sacrifice must be pure, whole, clean, and unblemished. We read this of the sacrifices that consecrated the priests (Exodus 29:1), all the offerings of Leviticus (for example, 1:3,10; 3:1, 6; 4:3, 23, 28, 32), the red heifer (Numbers 19:2), the daily burnt offerings of two lambs (Numbers 28:3), and all the Sabbath and Feast offerings (Numbers 28–29). Israel greatly grieved the Lord in Malachi's day, bringing *"defiled food,"* and *"blind . . . lame and sick"* animals (Malachi 1:7–8, 13) Jesus was free of defect in every way, fulfilling all the offerings of the Old Testament, pleasing the Father in all of life and becoming *"an offering and a sacrifice to God as a fragrant aroma"* (Isaiah 53:10; John 1:29, 8:29; 2 Corinthians 5:21; Ephesians 5:2).

📖 What additional truths do you discover in Peter's sermon in Acts 3, especially verses 14?

But ye denied the Holy One and Just and desired a murderer to be granted unto u

📖 Read the Spirit-inspired testimony Peter penned in 1 Peter 1:18–20. What do you find about Jesus?

Jesus was like a lamb without blemish and without spot: ordained before the was but manifest in these last times for you

📖 What record about Jesus do you find in 1 Peter 2:22–23?

who did no sin, Neither was guile found in his mouth: but committed himself to him that judgeth righteously

Jesus was *"attested to you by God"* or clearly exhibited as God's Messiah. God's seal of approval was on Jesus in every way. After speaking of the miraculous life and ministry of Jesus, Peter pointed to His resurrection, noting that even in His burial His flesh did not *"suffer decay"* or as one translation states, *"see corruption."* There was nothing in Jesus that had any measure of decay or corruption. He was and is *"the Holy and Righteous One"* who willingly went to the cross to pay the just price for our sins and opened the way for us to have His righteousness and His kind of life given to us by faith.

Peter wrote that Jesus was like *"a lamb unblemished"* (Greek-*amomos*) *"and spotless"* (Greek-*aspilos*) and His pure blood redeemed us from death and judgment. The Greek word *amomos* refers to no internal blemish, whereas *aspilos* refers to no external spot or stain. In His trials and on the cross, He never spoke deceitfully, never reviled anyone, and made no bitter threats. Jesus *"committed no sin"* in words or in deeds. Within and without, Jesus was without "leaven," as testified by Jews and Romans, by those who placed no faith in Him and those who followed Him faithfully.

✓ 📖 What connections do you find between Jesus' life and your life in John 1:12?

Many as recieved him to them he gave power to become the sons of God; believed his name

📖 In Galatians 2:20?

I am crucified with Christ: yet I live; yet not I, but Christ liveth in me; and the life which I live in the flesh I live by faith of the Son God

📖 In Colossians 3:4?

when Christ, who is our life, shall appear, then shall ye also appear with him in glory

📖 In 2 Peter 1:3–4?

According as his divine power hath given unto us all things that pertain unto life an godliness

Jesus Christ places His life in those who by faith receive Him as Lord and Savior. They become children of God with His nature in them. Therefore, the daily answer for our old life is crucifixion moment by moment, a *"by faith"* application of His death and burial and a dependence on His resurrection life. The cross is the only remedy for the "flesh" or the old nature—to be put to death daily. Christ is our life for each day, for every circumstance. He has made us *"partakers of the divine nature, having escaped the corruption that is in the world by lust."* The world constantly experiences and expresses the corruption of selfish desires, lusts that deceive and defeat and bring more of the stench of death. Jesus' life is marked by His purity, godliness, and power. His will for each of His followers is to experience and express that 'unleavened' "life."

📖 Jesus warned of *"leaven"* and its influence. Look at Matthew 16:1–12. What did Jesus say about leaven in these verses?

Take heed and beware of the leaven of the Pharisees and of the Sadducees

What were the disciples confused about? What did Jesus say to clarify their understanding?

I speak it not to you concerning bread, that ye should beware of the leaven of the Pharisees and of the Sadducees

About what type of *"leaven"* is Jesus warning them (and us)?

He wanted the disciples to recognize the evil influence and teaching of the Pharisees and Sadducees

The Pharisees continually tested Jesus, not to discover truth or to learn from Him, but to trap Him, seeking to defeat and destroy Him. They hated Him. Jesus clearly stated that they were acting like an *"evil and adulterous generation."* Jesus' statement was enough for anyone sensitive to the working of God to recognize and come to personal repentance over one's evil heart. The Pharisees refused to believe or heed His words. Jesus wanted His disciples to recognize the evil influence of the teaching of the Pharisees and Sadducees. They were slow to understand. Jesus called them *"men of little faith"* and then sought to build up their faith. In what He said, Jesus was warning and redirecting. He showed them their need for a genuine faith walk.

What He said that day reveals the fact that genuine faith deals with the past, the present, and the future. He spoke of how to walk rightly related to the Lord in the present and He reminded them of the past workings of God. Genuine faith remembers the **past**, especially what God has done, like the feeding of the five thousand or of the four thousand. Jesus warned them

---

Acts 20:16

Relationship – God

Religion

Put Yourself In Their Shoes
THE INFLUENCE OF WORDS

The statement "One idea can change a person's life" is of great weight. One idea can influence a person to turn to God or away from God, to His Word or away from His Word, to what is right or to what is wrong. Jesus made it clear that **words** have powerful influence. They can be like honey sweet to the soul, like a refreshing spring rain, like cool water to a parched heart, or like bitter poison that cripples or kills. One idea can change a life, a ministry, a church, a community, a nation—for good or for evil. We must watch what we say and carefully evaluate what we hear, for what we hear we can easily heed.

LESSON THREE – THE FEAST OF UNLEAVENED BREAD 59

about the present, what they might hear. Genuine faith evaluates the **present**, cautious about what one listens to. Jesus stated clearly, *"beware,"* watch out for the teaching of the Pharisees and Sadducees. It matters what you feed on **now**, because it can affect your **future**, your beliefs and actions. That on which you feed, leads to what you heed. They did not have the trained ear they needed to discern the nature of the *leaven-like words* of the Pharisees. Therefore, Jesus continued to train them. What you listen to influences you. What you receive and believe affects your present and future choices.

What further Scriptural insights do we find about leaven? Of what do we need to be aware? We will discover in Day Four.

Lesson Three — Day Four

LEAVENED OR UNLEAVENED LIVING? WHICH WILL IT BE?

As we have seen, in Jesus' ministry, He often spoke of leaven. The apostle Paul did the same years later. Throughout Scripture, leaven always speaks of influence; sometimes good, most of the time evil. Most of the time leaven is used of that which corrupts and a few times of that which brings a holy influence. Ultimately, God designed that followers of Jesus experience the spiritual truths of this Feast on a daily basis. In today's lesson, we will look further at these truths to more fully understand and apply the reality of the Feast of Unleavened Bread. We need to answer the question, "Leavened or unleavened living, which will it be?"

📖 What warning did Jesus give about leaven in Luke 12:1?

Beware ye of the leaven of the Pharisees which is hypocrisy

📖 Jesus spoke of the hypocrisy of the Pharisees in great detail in Matthew 23:1–37, pronouncing seven woes of judgment on their hypocrisy. Read through His statements and summarize the key points.

They are full of hypocrisy and lawlessness on inside while appearing to be righteous to men. Speaking one way and acting differently.

Jesus pointed to yet another aspect of the leaven of the Pharisees that must be guarded against—their hypocrisy. They said one thing and did another. They set forth many rules and regulations for others to follow, but did not follow those regulations themselves. If they spoke the word of God, they often followed only an outward form, an external rule, but failed to understand and apply the heart of that law. At other times, they added to what God had said, making His law burdensome with man-made additions, regulations, things He never intended. Jesus said they were *"full of hypocrisy and lawlessness"* on the inside while appearing to be righteous to men (23:28).

Did You Know?
PHARISEES

The name "Pharisee" means "separated one," a name of honor when this group first started. They wanted to do the right thing. However, over the years, those "separated ones" became severely and proudly separated to a strict interpretation of the Law, so much so that they added stringent rules, regulations, and rituals, like special handwashings and rigid Sabbath rules. This sect within Judaism boasted about six thousand adherents. They continually challenged Jesus and His teachings and ways. He did not fit their religious mold, and because He did not fit, they wanted to destroy Him. He, on the other hand continually rebuked them for straining at fine points of their law while failing to genuinely care for people. Jesus often condemned their hypocrisy, even pronouncing seven *"woes"* over them in Matthew 23:1–36.

Lawlessness is the opposite extreme of following faithfully. Speaking one way and acting differently is lawlessness, not godliness. That two-faced lifestyle is the heart of the word "hypocrisy" from the Greek word *hupokrisis*. It was a word used of stage actors, of those who wore masks, who played a part. That kind of unreal living is bad leaven, an unwanted influence.

📖 In Mark 8:15, Jesus warned His followers about *"the leaven of Herod."* What did He mean? What do you find about Herod in Matthew 14:1–11?

It referred to the worldliness, compromise and the corruption of Herod

📖 What additional insights do you glean from Mark 3:6 and Matthew 22:15–16?

It corrupted all that it touched, Jesus told his disciples to guard their hearts and minds of this influence

> **Word Study**
> **"HYPOCRISY"**
>
> is rooted in the Greek word *hupokrino* which is a combination of the words *hupo*, "under," and *krino*, "to judge, to divide or separate based on evaluation, to decide." In its original sense, it meant to divide under, to divide secretly, that is, to get under the true meaning. The Greeks first used it of one who sought to interpret dreams. Then, it came to mean one who represented, acted, or simulated anything, like a stage actor. In Attic Greek it was used of actors in a play and from that became synonymous with one who acts a part or pretends to be what he is not.

The *"leaven of Herod"* referred to the worldliness, compromise, and corruption of Herod Antipas, son of Herod the Great. His immoral ways, as well as those of his family, were well known. For example, Herod took Herodius, his niece and the wife of his brother Philip as his own wife, committing incest and violating the clear command of Leviticus 18:16. When John the Baptist preached against his sin, he arrested John and then, at a dinner party when pressured by his illegitimate wife, his sensuous step-daughter, and his craving for the approval of his dinner guests, he had John beheaded—showing his unprincipled, corrupt heart. The Herodians, a Jewish political party that supported Rome and Herod Antipas, actually joined with the Pharisees seeking to destroy Jesus. This *"leaven"* corrupted all that it touched and Jesus wanted His disciples warned of its destructive influence. The world system does the same today and one must guard the mind and heart of this influence.

📖 The Sadducees had their influence as well. What did Jesus say about their *"leaven"* in Matthew 16:6, 11–12?

beware of doctrine of the Pharisees and Sadducees

📖 What doctrines or teachings do you find the Sadducees advocating in Matthew 22:23–33, especially verses 23 and 29? What additional teaching do you find in Acts 23:8?

They were concerned about appearance of outside but not theirs hearts on inside

📖 How did John the Baptist describe the Sadducees in Matthew 3:7? To what did he call their attention in verses 8–9?

poisonous snakes, bring evidence of repentence

LESSON THREE – THE FEAST OF UNLEAVENED BREAD

📖 What did the Sadducees think of Jesus (the high priest and many other priests were Sadducees)? Read John 11:45–53 and note your insights.

They were against and plotted to kill him (Jesus).

Jesus warned His disciples about the deadly leaven of the Sadducees. John the Baptist even described them as venomous snakes, spreading the venom of their teachings. They rested on their physical lineage to Abraham as sufficient for salvation, not ready to repent from the heart and change their actions or ways. They opposed Jesus at every turn, even plotting to destroy Him. They did not believe in the resurrection of the dead nor in angels or spirits, adhering only to rationalistic and anti-supernatural beliefs. They desired power and control in Jerusalem, not a holy and loving faith relationship with God.

📖 The apostle Paul also spoke of *"leaven"* in Galatians 5:9. He described it as a *"persuasion"* in Galatians 5:8. What kind of *"persuasion"* was he dealing with? Read Galatians 5:1, 5–9 and record what you discover? For a fuller picture read Galatians 5:10–25.

They persuaded into returning to be justified by the works of the law or rituals or work of the flesh. A little leaven leavens the whole lump

📖 How was this *"leaven"* or *"persuasion"* affecting the Galatian believers according to Galatians 3:1–14 and 5:7, 13–16?

The people were doing whatever they wanted. Slave to the work of law

Paul painted a very clear picture; *"a little leaven leavens the whole lump of dough."* Throughout the letter to the Galatians, Paul dealt with those being persuaded either to begin or return to living by law, by legalistic works, or by rituals such as circumcision rather than simple faith in Christ and His finished work on the cross. It was a faith in Christ PLUS a "law," but that "law" or formula or ritual contradicted the Scriptures and genuine faith. God wants a trust relationship lived under the Lordship of Jesus, or to put it another way, He wants us to *"walk by the Spirit,"* or be *"led by the Spirit"* (5:16, 18).

He wants believers to experience the freedom found in a faith relationship to Christ, not the freedom to do whatever one wants, whatever the flesh desires. God desires for each believer the freedom to do the will of God in the fullness of His Spirit with the fruit of His Spirit being experienced and expressed in all relationships (5:16–25). That kind of daily walk means freedom in relationship to Jesus and freedom in relationships with others. Enslavement to man-made regulations and opinions never builds relationships. God meant circumcision to be a symbol and sign of a new relationship between Abraham and Himself, a relationship of cutting away the corrupt

---

Did You Know?
SADDUCEES

In New Testament days, the Sadducees, a sect of wealthy members of the priesthood, controlled the Temple. Many were Herodians who treated Rome as a friend to promote their own power and position. Rationalism and anti-supernaturalism marked their doctrine (no resurrection, no angels or spirits). They adhered only to the Pentateuch and shunned legalism, being nothing like the separatist Pharisees. Sadducees readily compromised the Scriptures and moral principles for personal or political advancement. Along with the Pharisees, they sought to destroy Jesus and His followers (Matthew 22:15–34; John 11:47–53; 12:9–11; Acts 4:1–3; 5:17–18).

flesh. God was not giving a legalistic ritual. Jesus came to fulfill the law, pay the penalty for our sin, our law breaking, and then indwell believers by His Spirit, so that we could experience a relationship of freedom and continue growing in that relationship. Such a walk following the leadership of the Spirit means showing love to others, serving others, not using others.

The leaven of strict rituals and legalism always leads to an enslaving concern over keeping the rules, not concern over the needs of others and how one might serve them—it is personal **"faith** (confident trust in Jesus and His life and abilities) **working** (words and actions) **through** (Spirit-empowered) **love."** The *"leaven,"* the *"persuasion"* of the legalists, focused on adherence to their "law," not the Law of God, but a man-made, man-regulated "law" of "you must do things this way (my way) and no other way." They considered external regulations as of prime importance, an absolute, rather than living in the freedom of *"faith working through love."*

Genuine faith means a relationship marked by the freedom, purity, and creativity of the Holy Spirit. That legalistic *"persuasion"* was indeed a corrupting *"leaven,"* leading them away from dependence on the Holy Spirit and into following the desires of the flesh. It sometimes seems easier to have the forms of a "religion" rather than the reality of a genuine relationship. That influence was spreading throughout the *"churches of Galatia"* (1:2) and the relationships within those churches. Paul, led by the Holy Spirit, sought to stop the spread of this influence and bring the people in these churches back to daily dependence on the Spirit of God.

📖 The Corinthian church had some problems with leaven, the leaven of immorality. Paul wrote concerning this. Read 1 Corinthians 5:1–8. What do you see about leaven in 1 Corinthians 5:6? What kind of leaven is Paul speaking of?

One of members of the church had taken his stepmother to wife... (incest)

📖 How should one deal with this *"old leaven"* according to 1 Corinthians 5:7?

purge out the old leaven

Someone in the Corinthian church had an immoral relationship with *"his father's wife,"* most likely his stepmother. Paul grieved when he heard this. He expected the church to mourn over such a grievous sin. Instead, they were acting with an arrogant attitude, ignoring the sin rather than humbly, honestly, lovingly going to the supposed believer and dealing with his actions as sin, calling him to repentance and restoration. Not even the unbelieving Gentile world accepted such immorality. Left unchecked, this kind of attitude would affect (and infect) the whole body of believers like leaven affects the *"whole lump of dough."* Paul called this sin *"old leaven"* and expected the church to remove it, to call this man to repentance or face removal from the fellowship of the church. The *"old leaven"* of Egypt symbolized the leaven of the world, that is, traces of Egypt remaining in one's thinking or in one's life. It must be removed. Because it so easily leads to corrupt living, we must remove any old ways of thinking and decision-making not in line with the Word of God or the Spirit of God.

Leviticus 23:

> *"... a little leaven leavens the whole lump of dough."*
>
> **Galatians 5:9 and 1 Corinthians 5:6**

LESSON THREE – THE FEAST OF UNLEAVENED BREAD

Put Yourself In Their Shoes

THE LEAVEN OF PRIDE

Boasting and arrogance marked the Corinthian church in failing to deal with the sin in their midst. Some refer to this as the leaven of boasting or pride. To be arrogant is to be puffed up, appearing to be more than one is. It is a picture of being filled with yeast and its influence. In the Old Testament, the Hebrew word for leaven is *chometz* meaning bitter or sour. Sin, especially the sin of pride, brings a measure of bitterness into our lives. Pride makes us bitter, sour, and harsh, and as leaven causes bread to puff up, so pride puffs up people with an arrogant attitude.

Put Yourself In Their Shoes

AN UNLEAVENED LIFE LOOKS LIKE THIS

In 2 Timothy 2:19–22, Paul spoke to Timothy about how he should live every day. What he told him looks like an unleavened life. "Nevertheless, the firm foundation of God stands, having this seal, 'The Lord knows those who are His,' and, 'Let everyone who names the name of the Lord abstain from wickedness.' Now in a large house there are not only gold and silver vessels, but also vessels of wood and of earthenware, and some to honor and some to dishonor. Therefore, if a man cleanses himself from these things, he will be a vessel for honor, sanctified, useful to the Master, prepared for every good work. Now flee from youthful lusts, and pursue righteousness, faith, love and peace, with those who call on the Lord from a pure heart."

📖 What other deadly leaven surfaces in 1 Corinthians 5:8?

malice & wickerness

📖 What is the answer to dealing with this or any other *"leaven"* in a Christian's life or in the fellowship of a local church? How should followers of Christ celebrate *"the Feast"* according to 1 Corinthians 5:8?

with sincerity and truth, by removing the leaven

Paul spoke of the *"leaven of malice and wickedness,"* two deadly sins in any context. *"Malice"* (Greek, *kakias*) refers to an evil disposition, a vicious attitude, or a readiness to do wrong and *"wickedness"* (Greek, *ponerios*), refers to the accompanying evil action, the active exercise of that disposition. God is not without a remedy for these kinds of leaven. Paul spoke of the sacrifice of Christ as our Passover, the Feast inseparably connected to the Feast of Unleavened Bread. Jesus fulfills all the Feasts, beginning with Passover and Unleavened Bread. He died as our Passover Lamb, delivering us from all that enslaves us in "Egypt" and from the leaven, the wickedness and ways of "Egypt" or the world system. That is not just for consideration one day or one week a year. God calls us to *"celebrate the feast"* (present tense) every day by the continual removal of any leaven. In Christ, we have His power, His Spirit to search out and shine the light on any leaven, repent of it, remove it, and then live out the reality of His unleavened life.

📖 By what should our lives be characterized? What kind of *"unleavened bread"* should be our daily experience according to 1 Corinthians 5:8?

Sincerity and truth

Having dealt with the *"leaven"* that is to have no part in a believer's life, Paul goes on to characterize our celebrating *"with the unleavened bread of sincerity and truth."* *"Sincerity"* (Greek, *eilekrines*) literally means to be judged by the sunlight, that is, a life that has nothing hidden in darkness. That life can be displayed in the open as revealing Christ because it is His *"unleavened"* life showing. Our English word "sincerity" comes to us via the Latin *sincere*, "without wax," referring to the practice of certain pottery makers filling cracks in the pottery with wax and then painting over the surface to hide the defect. By exposing the defective pottery to the sunlight the wax would soften and the vessel would be seen in its true light. God wants us to be "without wax," not covered with cosmetic Christianity, but walking in sincerity, integrity, and honesty.

According to 1 Corinthians 5:8, this life is also marked by *"truth"* (from the Greek word *aletheia*). *Aletheia* literally means "not hidden" or "not concealed." In other words, a life of truth is a life open to inspection. It is clear to others that there is no deception. This refers to a life of integrity. One believes the truth, speaks the truth, and deals truthfully with others. This believer is honest, not a cheat or a liar, and one whose heart and conscience does not condemn him or her. The daily experience of a believer should be Christ's unleavened life produced by His Spirit, who is in fact the Spirit of Truth (John 16:13).

How are we to apply these principles? How are we to walk in an "unleavened life"? We will explore these application points in *Day Five*.

For Me to "Celebrate the Feast"

Lesson Three — **DAY FIVE**

Leaven thrives in the dark. An unleavened life walks in the light, the light of sincerity and truth. How are we to walk this way? How are we to walk without leaven? It is not enough just to **watch out** for leaven. We must also actively **walk** without leaven. The Christians life was never meant to be only a matter of what is **not in** our lives, but more about what **is in** our lives because of our connection to and relationship with Jesus Christ. The fruit of His Life, of His Spirit should be clearly experienced and seen in us, through the words we speak and the deeds we live out.

How do we "Celebrate the Feast"?

First, we must make sure about the Connection to Passover, Old and New Testament—<u>Jesus</u> is the Passover Lamb who takes away our sin, delivers us from judgment, condemnation, and death, and leads us out of a failing, faltering, condemned world system marked by **death**. Think of what He delivered us **from** and what He brings us to? Throughout Scripture, God first leads His people away from measuring life the way the world measures. Read Hebrews 11:24–26 and consider these three "Velcro" points to which you can attach your life.

1. In Moses' day, God delivered them out of the empty measure of Egypt, Egypt's ways, Pharaoh's standards or, to coin a word, "Pharaoh-ism." Arrogant pride is the measure of Egypt or of Pharaoh-ism. Hebrews 11:24 alludes to this, to the proud standards of Pharaoh as the measure of life.
2. God delivered them out of the passing pleasures of Egypt. Hebrews 11:25 speaks of this. The pleasures of Egypt refer to the empty lusts and desires characteristic of Egypt.
3. God delivered them out of the temporary treasures of Egypt. Hebrews 11:26 speaks of this. This points to the temporary and decaying things and possessions of Egypt's empire (the treasures of Egypt).

We have been delivered **out of** the thinking, believing, and living of *"Egypt"* and **into** the thinking, believing, and living of God. What does that mean?

1. He gives us a **New Measure—the Measure of Christ**—He leads us into Life through humility not pride (by surrendering our agendas and opinions and taking the measure of Christ as our measure for all things). We find that measure in the Word of God, in viewing the life of Jesus Christ as applied in a Spirit-filled life.
2. He gives us **New Pleasures—the Pleasures of Christ**—He calls to a Life marked by pleasing Christ, making Him preeminent. This means daily surrender to the Spirit of God.
3. He gives us **New Treasures—the Treasures of Christ**—He wants us to experience lasting riches by investing in lives, eternal lives, helping others know Jesus as Lord and Savior and grow in a relationship to Him, to please and glorify Him.

> *"By faith Moses, when he had grown up, refused to be called the son of Pharaoh's daughter; choosing rather to endure ill treatment with the people of God than to enjoy the passing pleasures of sin; considering the reproach of Christ greater riches than the treasures of Egypt; for he was looking to the reward."*
>
> Hebrews 11:24–26

Put Yourself In Their Shoes

THE LORD'S SUPPER AND UNLEAVENED LIVING

As we partake of the Lord's Supper (1 Corinthians 11:23–31), we **remember** Jesus—all He is, all He has done, all He has promised. That means we also seek to walk in purity by His Spirit, examining ourselves under the guidance of His Spirit and honoring His blood poured out and His body broken. Then, we partake of the bread and the fruit of the vine, knowing they represent Jesus Christ in His death for us and His forgiveness of us. In this, we proclaim the Lord's death (the price paid) until He returns. We also prepare for His return day by day, like a bride awaiting the Bridegroom—We live an unleavened life.

The measure, pleasure, and treasure of the Feast of Unleavened Bread is holiness of life—a life that is marked by forgiveness and cleansing from sin, by the removal of any *"leaven"* in our lives, and by the abiding presence and experience of the unleavened life of Christ's Spirit. Jesus leads us in a life away from leaven, always removing leaven (anything that corrupts, that grows in the darkness, that puffs up like pride, that causes decay, that churns up the flesh). By His Spirit and through His Word, He shows us what is "leaven-like" in our lives. He leads us in cleaning that leaven out, and He leads us to replace it with the Bread of His Life, His Word, His Truth. Replacing leaven in our lives is a step toward walking in freedom away from bondage—just as the Israelites walked away from Egyptian bondage into greater and greater freedom.

The Lord led His people to Sinai to give them the Law, His clear boundaries, and blessed ways for life. This could give them a walk of freedom because it was a walk in the truth. However, they had no power over sin. That was the problem. Jesus solved that problem by His death and resurrection. He died for us to deal with the sin problem. He lives in us to empower obedience. His Father-pleasing life is in us by His Spirit. Now, by faith in Him, we can walk moment by moment in the "unleavened life" He gives. Remember, every Feast is a **heart celebration**. How do we celebrate the Feast of Unleavened Bread? Day by day, **we honor and obey and trust** Christ as our Passover Lamb, sacrificed for us—to cleanse us, deliver us, and lead us in that Unleavened Life.

APPLY As 1 Corinthians 5:7–8 notes, we must be *watching out* for any kind of *"old leaven,"* ever cautious, ever aware that the world, the flesh, and the devil are still around, still tempting, still deceiving, still bringing battles. There are seven areas—**Seven Leavens** to watch out for. Look at each of these, think about the questions, and answer them honestly. What leavens do you need to get rid of? What steps can you take today to put away one or more of these influences, these leavens?

1. Leaven of the **Pharisees—Hypocrisy**—Are you being influenced in any ways that cause you to be two-faced, to speak one way, but live another. Are you being influenced to lie about who you really are, to put on a mask to hide the real you?
2. Leaven of **Legalism**—Are you being influenced by any brand of legalism or some man-made rule or ritual to find fulfillment? Are you trying to live by a legalistic code rather than by the working of the Spirit of God using the Word of God?
3. Leaven of the **Sadducees—False teaching** filled with **Rationalism, Anti-supernaturalism,** and **Compromise**—Are you being influenced by rationalistic, anti-supernatural thinking that leaves out the power and ways of God in your life? Are you accepting elements of false teaching that allow you to "fit in" more comfortably with the world? Do you believe in teaching that allows you to rationalize wrong behavior? Are you compromising biblical standards or moral truths to gain some personal advantage—political (in an organization, in government, in church circles), professional, positional, or prestige-related?
4. Leaven of **Herod**—Compromise and worldliness leading to **corruption**—Are you being influenced by compromising with the world system's way of thinking, by compromising with anything immoral, unethical, or improper (words, deeds, thoughts)?

5. Leaven of **Immorality**—Are you being influenced by any kind of immoral thinking or immoral actions of others? Is the leaven of lust corrupting your thinking or your choices?
6. Leaven of **Pride/Arrogance**—Are you being influenced to make yourself look better than you are? Are you concerned about selfishly promoting your "image" and making sure you have the "approval" of others, of the "right people"? Are you arrogant in heart or words, in attitudes or deeds?
7. Leaven of **Wickedness and Malice**—Are you being influenced by thoughts of wickedness, of indulging in some sin? Are you being corrupted by thoughts of wrong toward others, of being malicious and hurtful, so you can get your way or so you can "get even" with someone who has hurt you? Are you only concerned about what you want, regardless of who it affects or how it affects others?

Instead of feeding on any of these kinds of leaven, the Word of God commands us to *"celebrate the* **Feast***"* with *"the* **unleavened** *bread of sincerity and truth."* Consider these application questions related to this. Write a response to what the Spirit of God is showing you. Are there any steps He is leading you to take to either 1) remove a certain kind of leaven or 2) put in place that which is unleavened? Can you say you are celebrating the Feast God's way?

1. <u>Sincerity</u>—(Greek—*eilikrineia*—literally, "judged of in sunshine," therefore one seen as genuine, pure, clear as light)—This refers to your **vertical life, in line with God**. Are you rightly aligned with God? Are you genuine? Are you walking in mental and moral purity? Is your thinking clear or clouded—clear with the mind of Christ and the perspective of the Word of God or clouded with *"earthly"* wisdom (James 3:13–16) of *"this present evil age"* (Galatians 1:4; Romans 12:2)?

By the Power of the Spirit, I need to REMOVE the Leaven(s) of…

_____
_____
_____
_____
_____

By the Power of Christ, I need to PUT IN PLACE His "Unleavened Life" in the Area of…

_____
_____
_____
_____
_____

2. <u>Truth</u>—This refers to your **horizontal life**, a life of integrity, **in line with others**. Are you rightly aligned with others? Do you believe the Truth, speak the Truth, deal truthfully with others? Are you honest, not a cheat, not a liar? Does your heart/conscience not condemn you? Are you walking in the truth? Are you honest with yourself about your personal weaknesses and strengths? Are you careful about ways in which you could trip or fall in

> *"Who may ascend into the hill of the LORD? And who may stand in His holy place? He who has clean hands and a pure heart, who has not lifted up his soul to falsehood and has not sworn deceitfully. He shall receive a blessing from the LORD and righteousness from the God of his salvation. Such is the generation of those who seek Him, who seek Your face."*
>
> **Psalm 24:3–6**

your thinking or your choices? Are you living with a steady diet of truth—from the Word of God, from Spirit-filled believers, from a God-centered body of believers? What most influences you—the Scriptures—the Internet—Movies/TV shows—Blogs—Your email inbox—Text messages—The latest best seller—Books and articles in your field of work—Magazines or Newspapers—Biblically based men and women—World system thinkers without the Wisdom of God?

By the Power of the Spirit, I need to Remove the Leaven(s) of…

_____
_____
_____
_____
_____

By the Power of Christ, I need to Put in Place His "Unleavened Life" in the Area of…

_____
_____
_____
_____
_____

> "O Lord, who may abide in Your tent? Who may dwell on Your holy hill? He walks with integrity, and works righteousness, and speaks truth in his heart" and "Behold You desire truth in the innermost being"
>
> **Psalm 15:1–2 and Psalm 51:6a**

Passover 4-6 Evening (Fri.) 8 days
unleaven 4-7th Evening (sat) E
First Fruit 4-7th (Sat-E)
Thur 4-12 Sabbath E

Lord, I come to You concerning this matter of leaven in my life. Thank You for showing me these areas of grave concern, areas I must deal with Your way. I confess where I have sinned. I turn from my wrong ways, wrong choices, wrong words, and wrong deeds. I turn to You and Your way, Your Word. I ask You to forgive me, cleanse me, and clear out these strongholds in my life. I receive Your Word in each of these areas. Lord, I admit I cannot produce this kind of life. I can't do it, but **You** can. I ask You to fill me with Your Spirit, with Your "Unleavened Life" and live in me and through me to reveal Your character and conduct. May people see the fruit of Your life being worked out and lived out in the everyday things I face. May this "Unleavened Life" mark my relationship with others. I know that You will receive the credit, the honor for what You do and I will be eternally grateful. May I *"celebrate the Feast"* with You and with others. May I live rightly aligned vertically *and* horizontally. May I be empowered to lead others to know You and Your "Unleavened Life." May they experience the joy of celebrating *"the Feast"* in their lives. I thank You and praise You, Lord Jesus, for all You have done to make this celebration a reality. Amen.

lesson 4 — Jeremiah 7:20

The Feast of First Fruits

THE CALL TO LIVE IN THE REALITY OF RESURRECTION LIFE

The idea of first fruits goes back to the very beginning of time and the family of Adam. Genesis 4 speaks of Adam's son, Abel, bringing the first of his flock as an offering to the Lord. The Lord was pleased with Abel's offering and his heart of faith, his show of dependence and gratitude to the Lord. Inherent in any offering of first fruits is the matter of thanksgiving to God for His full provision. Expressing thanks goes with the attitude of dependence on God for His blessing on the entire harvest, whether of grain or livestock.

God gave various regulations to Israel concerning the matter of first fruits. Each showed some aspect of acknowledging God as God and the giver of all (Exodus 22:29; 23:19; Deuteronomy 26:1–11). This included the firstborn of children and of livestock. The first fruits of the ground, the grains, the fruits of the trees and of the vine, all belonged to the Lord. In giving offerings to Him, the people recognized Him as their provider and their God. It served as a demonstration of gratitude and continued faith in Him. These offerings were the appropriate response of worship, of a heart of surrender, love, and continued devotion to the Lord.

The yearly Feast of First Fruits served as a focal point for this attitude of thanksgiving and worship as well as a yearly offering revealing their dependence on and trust in the Lord. First Fruits, the third of the seven Feasts, occurred during the week of Unleavened Bread on the Sunday after Passover. It linked the Passover and Unleavened Bread celebrations to the celebration of Pentecost, since that Feast celebrated the full wheat harvest exactly fifty days after First Fruits (Exodus 34:22, 26; Leviticus 23:9–22).

We have much to discover about the Feast of First Fruits. This celebration consisted in harvesting a few sheaves to offer to the Lord, acknowledging Him as the giver of the harvest, thanking Him, and dedicating the entire harvest to Him. This was also a time to ask His blessings on the full harvest. Offering the first fruits of the harvest was a way of sanctifying the entire

> *The Feast of First Fruits connected the people as the glad, grateful recipients with the Lord God as the generous Giver of all.*

LESSON FOUR – THE FEAST OF FIRST FRUITS   69

harvest to the Lord, seeking the blessing of God on the harvest so that it could be used and enjoyed by Israel as its people lived out their lives as the people of God.

When we turn to the New Testament, we see even more meaning in the celebration of First Fruits. Each Feast pictures for us the **shadow** of Christ and in the New Testament we see the **substance**. We will discover how Christ fulfills this Feast and how we fit into His designs of the full harvest. The journey into the Feast of First Fruits covers many paths with many application points. The call of the Feast of First Fruits is indeed a call to celebration in what Christ has done and promises yet to do.

Lesson Four · DAY ONE

THE MYSTERIES OF HISTORY

God orders times and seasons to fulfill His will and His purposes. When we look at the order of the Feasts in Israel's calendar and compare that with His workings in the history of His people, we discover some amazing connections. We see a history tapestry with God weaving people and nations to fulfill His purposes. In this lesson, we will look at some of God's workings in the history of His people and begin to see how He used this in fulfilling His will. We will also see some of His ways and how He uses both the passage of *time* and His unique *timing* to work out the details of His will and to show us His ways with each of us. Today we will review certain events occurring on or around the seventeenth of the month Abib or Nisan, the general timing of the Feast of First Fruits (Sunday after the Sabbath after Passover) Let's explore these mysteries of history.

📖 One of the first significant events of history occurring on the seventeenth of Abib/Nisan is found in Genesis 7–8, the Flood in Noah's day. The rains and flood waters began on the seventeenth day of the second month (Genesis 7:11) and increased for forty days (Genesis 7:12, 17). They prevailed over the earth for 150 days (Genesis 7:24). What do you find in Genesis 8:1–3?

God remembered Noah and every living thing God made the wind to pass over the earth and the waters subsided.

📖 What occurred in Genesis 8:4?

The Ark rested in the 7th month, 17th day of the month, on the mountains of Ararat.

The floodwaters of judgment began on the seventeenth day of the second month and prevailed for 150 days. After 150 days when the waters were at their peak, *"God caused a wind to pass over the earth, and the water subsided."* Specifically, it began to decrease after the 150 days, on Day 151. The record in Genesis 8:4 gives the seventeenth day of the seventh month as that day, also the day the Ark rested on the mountains of Ararat. This speaks of the seventh month of the civil calendar. When God instituted the Passover celebration, that month became the first month (Abib/Nisan) in the religious calendar. On the seventeenth of Nisan, the Ark rested, and the waters of

70 FOLLOWING GOD – LIFE PRINCIPLES FOR WORSHIP FROM THE FEASTS OF ISRAEL

judgment were finished. Judgment had passed. A new day dawned for Noah and his family, a new beginning.

Genesis 8:5–19 records that after this, Noah and his family waited until the floodwaters had completely receded and the ground dried sufficiently for them to exit the Ark. They first had some assurance with the evidence of new growth from the olive branch brought by the dove. Then, on the twenty–seventh day of the second month, when the earth was dry, God spoke, commanding Noah and his family along with the animals to leave the Ark and begin their new lives.

📖 Dates given in Scripture are never random or accidental. Each is significant in some measure. Think of the dates of the Exodus. We saw in Lesson 3 that the children of Israel came out of Egypt 430 years after going in, *"to the very day"* (Exodus 12:41). Look at the following Scriptures and make the connections. What day did they partake of the Passover lamb according to Exodus 12:6? What time of day did the meal take place according to Exodus 12:8?

14th day of same month, it took place at night

📖 According to Exodus 12:22, when were they to leave their houses?

not go out till morning

📖 When did the Lord *"pass over"* Egypt, according to Exodus 12:29?

at midnight

📖 If the selection of the Passover lamb occurred on Nisan 10, followed by four days to Passover on Nisan 14, on what date would their exodus occur? What do you discover in Numbers 33:3?

15th day of the 1st month, day after passover

📖 How did God lead the people according to Exodus 13:17–20? What does Numbers 33:5–8 record? From their camp at Etham, where did they go? See Exodus 14:1–2?

the Red sea, wilderness — habiroth, at Red sea

📖 What occurred when they reached the Red Sea, according to Exodus 14:10?

The Egyptians followed them

📖 What did the Lord instruct them to do in Exodus 14:13–18?

Stand still and see the salvation of the Lord. THE Lord will fight for u and u shall hold your peace

---

Put Yourself In Their Shoes
JACOB'S NEW DAY

Exodus 12:41 states that Israel departed Egypt after 430 years *"to the very day,"* placing their entrance into Egypt on Nisan 15. Jacob's official welcome by Pharaoh and placement in Goshen likely occurred within one or two days after his arrival, making Jacob's new day on or around Nisan 17 (a day of new beginnings). What kind of new day was it? During Joseph's first years in Egypt, Genesis 37 reveals that Judah and those around him were being corrupted by Canaanite influences—Judah married a Canaanite woman and saw the birth of three sons, two of whom were slain by the Lord for their wickedness. Because Egyptians despised shepherds, Israel's placement in Goshen also kept them away from many Egyptian influences. God has a way of bringing His people into a new day, guiding them away from corruption into the fulfillment of His purposes as He did with Israel during these 430 years. This new beginning fit into the purposes of God in making them a cohesive nation. They came to Egypt numbering seventy and left almost two million (Exodus 1:1–7; Numbers 1:46).

LESSON FOUR – THE FEAST OF FIRST FRUITS

📖 Read the account in Exodus 14:24–31. What happened on that night and the next morning, possibly the morning of Nisan 17 or 18?

Lord removed wheels from chariots that they moved difficulty, God drowed them in the Red Sea

📖 Read 1 Corinthians 10:1–2. Record any insights and connections you see.

all ours Fathers were under the cloud and all passed through the sea

God instructed the Israelites to select the Passover lambs on the tenth of Nisan, keep them protected for four days, and then sacrifice them on the fourteenth. They ate the Passover meal that night with sandals on, robes girded, and staff in hand, ready to depart. The Passover occurred at Midnight, and Egyptians became astir with grief—urging the Israelites to leave. They departed immediately on the fifteenth of Nisan traveling east, stopping at Succoth. From there they journeyed to Etham. The next day, the Lord led them to turn toward the Red Sea, where Pharaoh's armies caught up with them. There the Angel of the Lord shielded His people from the Egyptian army and the Lord began parting the waters of the Red Sea.

That night the people began marching through on dry land, apparently in the light of the Pillar of Fire. Pharaoh's armies finally began pursuing. In *"the morning watch"* (2:00 AM—6:00 AM), the Angel of the Lord looked down and confused the Egyptian army, striking their chariot wheels so that they *"drove them with difficulty."* Finally, God brought the waters of the Red Sea upon the fleeing army and drowned them. When morning dawned, likely the morning of Nisan 17, the Israelites saw their enemies defeated, dead on the seashore. The people of God crossed through the Red Sea into a new life in a new land, no longer in Egypt. It occurred within the time frame when they would later celebrate First Fruits in Canaan.

That morning the Israelites were free. It was a new day. Judgment had fallen on Egypt, Pharaoh, and his army. Israel experienced a new day of freedom. First Corinthians 10:1–2 says, *"our fathers were all under the cloud, and all passed through the sea; and all were baptized into Moses in the cloud and in the sea."* What does that mean? First Corinthians 10:6 goes on to say that these events serve as examples to us today. Israel was symbolically immersed into Moses and the sea, that is, baptized or identified in him as their leader, the sea as the symbolic path of death, burial, and rising again.

They passed through the waters of the Red Sea as one passes through the waters of baptism—a picture of judgment, death, burial, and rising again. Rising out of those waters, they walked onto a new shore, into a new land, a new life, and new freedom following the Lord—free of Egypt, Pharaoh, and his taskmasters. Their newly found freedom symbolized freedom from the power of the world, the flesh, the Devil, and the enslavement of sin. God's people experienced a new day with a new lifestyle, no longer enduring days as slaves, but now free to follow and obey their Lord, the one who desires His best for each one. We will see in Day Four how these symbolic pictures are fulfilled in Christ.

Word Study
"BAPTIZED"

When 1 Corinthians 10:2 speaks of the nation of Israel being *"baptized into Moses in the cloud and in the sea,"* it is speaking of being identified with Moses and the Lord *"in the cloud,"* following His leadership via the Shekinah Glory *"cloud"* and Pillar of Fire through the Red Sea. The verb *"baptized"* is a translation of the Greek word *baptizo*, which means to immerse, to be totally engulfed. It was used of a ship sinking, becoming identified with the sea. It was used of dying cloth, the cloth totally immersed and identified with a new color. The Israelites identified with the waters of the Red Sea. In Scripture, the sea is often used to imply separation. In the journey through the Red Sea, Israel experienced its final separation from Egypt, dying to an old way and rising to a new way and a new day.

📖 We find another instance of a new day occurring on Nisan 17. Read the account of Ahaz and Hezekiah in 2 Chronicles 28:22–25 and 29:1–36. What was the condition of Jerusalem under Ahaz?

The city of Jerusalem was in ruin because King Ahaz unfaithfulness and idolatry

📖 What changes did Hezekiah make?

He purified the Temple and restored Temple worship

📖 What day did they begin cleansing and consecrating the Temple, and when did they finish, according to verse 17?

The 1st day of the 1st month and the 16th day of the first month they finished

📖 What did Hezekiah do the next day, the seventeenth of Nisan ("*the first month*"), according to verses 20–36?

He gathered the leader and made preperation to worship the Lord

Second Chronicles 28:22–25 records the unfaithfulness and idolatry of King Ahaz. When he died, his son Hezekiah came to the throne with a different heart. In the first year and the first month (Nisan) of Hezekiah's reign, this twenty-five year old king called for the priests and Levites to begin cleansing the Temple (715 BC). They began on the first day, taking eight days to cleanse and consecrate the outer court, followed by eight days of cleansing the inner Temple. They finished on the sixteenth of the month. Hezekiah "*arose early*" the next day, the seventeenth of Nisan, and assembled the princes of the city. They joined with the priests at the Temple and offered many burnt offerings and a sin offering to cleanse the altar, the king, the leaders, and the people. As they offered these in worship, the various Levites and priests sang "*the song to the Lord . . . accompanied by the instruments*" while the assembly of the people worshiped with great joy. More thank offerings, burnt offerings, and peace offerings followed as the people "*rejoiced over what God had prepared for the people.*" It was a new day for Judah and Jerusalem, a day of a revived priesthood and a truly worship-filled Temple, a day of cleansing and rejoicing.

Each of these historical examples of the timeframe on or around the seventeenth of Nisan point to a new day, a new beginning in some way. They chronicle a change. How do these events relate to the Feast of First Fruits? We will begin to make more connections in Day Two.

Did You Know?
ESTHER'S NEW DAY

In 474 BC, in the courts of Ahasuerus (Xerxes) and Esther, Esther 3:12 records that on the thirteenth of Nisan, Ahasuerus and Haman the Agagite (descendant of Amalek, one of the sons of Esau, Genesis 36:12) issued a decree to destroy the Jews in the Persian Kingdom. Haman is a type of Satan and the antichrist seeking to destroy God's people. Interestingly, the thirteenth of Nisan is the same night Judas agreed to betray and hand over Jesus for thirty pieces of silver. The king told Haman, "*the silver is yours*" (3:11). Mordecai mourned, called Esther to approach the king, and seek deliverance. Esther called for three days of fasting (possibly Nisan 14, 15, 16), with a banquet for the King and Haman on the sixteenth, followed by a second banquet on the seventeenth. On that day Haman was accused, found guilty, judged, condemned, and hanged on the gallows he had prepared for Mordecai. Mordecai was exalted to reign in the empire and brought about a counter-decree that saved the Jews from extermination. It was a day of new life, the people spared from destruction, delivered from the hands of a betrayer and wicked men. They had a new freedom.

Lesson Four — DAY TWO

GOD'S CALL TO OFFER FIRST FRUITS

The giving of first fruits acknowledges God as the giver of provision and the one upon whom we depend for all our needs. Without His working, without His gifts to us, we would be without any help or hope. He provides for us our necessary food and more. Acknowledging God's sustaining power with a spirit of thanksgiving is our proper response. Today we will begin looking at the importance of giving to God the first—the firstborn and the first fruits. We will also look at the Feast of First Fruits and how Israel celebrated this third Feast.

📖 In the midst of the events surrounding the Exodus, God gave Moses very clear instruction concerning the firstborn. Read Exodus 13:1–2, 11–16. What does God require according to verse 2?

Sanctify all the first born among the children of Israel, both of man and animal (mine)

📖 In Exodus 13:11–16, what additional instructions did He give Israel for when they began living in the land of Canaan? Additional insights are found in Numbers 18:15–18.

_____
_____
_____

📖 In the context, God was speaking just before the day when Israeli families left Egypt in the Exodus. What happened to the firstborn of Egypt the night before the Exodus, according to Exodus 12:29–30?

_____
_____

📖 In contrast, what happened to the firstborn of the children of Israel the night before the Exodus—to each of those who were in a house marked by the blood of a lamb, according to Exodus 12:13, 22–23, 27?

_____
_____

God redeemed the firstborn in every Israeli home, both of children and of livestock where the blood of the lamb covered the doorposts—the tenth plague touched none of them. In contrast, every Egyptian home faced the death of the firstborn child and of livestock, since none had applied the blood of the Passover lamb. Everyone deserved death because of sin, but God provided a merciful way for a substitute to die—an unblemished lamb. Many were given a sense of new life that day. Since God delivered the firstborn of Israel, they rightly belonged to Him and to His service. God required this of His people.

They needed a continual reminder of His gift of life. He made it an ordinance for the people of Israel when they settled in the Promised Land that every firstborn male and animal belonged to Him. Since He had spared the firstborn sons of Israel, they belonged to Him. Every future firstborn son also would belong to Him. This would serve as a sign of the relationship between God and Israel, a mark of ownership, of being valuable to God, of bringing honor to Him and of receiving mercy from Him.

The redemption of the firstborn continually pointed to His merciful redemptive work in bringing Israel out of Egypt. It also gave clear evidence that Israel belonged to Him. In Exodus 13:13, God called the people to redeem the firstborn by an offering to the Lord—a lamb as a substitute for a donkey and five shekels as the redemption price for a male (later instruction given in Numbers 18:16). Like one's hands or one's face ever in sight, so the reality of redemption was ever to be before the eyes of Israel. Every time a father saw the face of his firstborn, it would be a reminder of God's deliverance of him and of all of them. The regulations of the firstborn, like those for first fruits were another reminder that all belonged to God. He designed for Israel to walk in a personal, faith relationship of worship and obedient following.

> First fruits were also important to the Lord. The Lord gave clear regulations about bringing first fruits to Him during the year. What do you discover in Exodus 23:16–17, 19; 34:22 and Numbers 15:18–21?

_____
_____
_____

> How did the Lord provide for the priests according to Numbers 18:12 and Deuteronomy 18:4–5?

_____
_____

> What additional guidelines do you find in Deuteronomy 26:1–11?

_____
_____
_____

The Lord called for the people to offer the first fruits of their crops at the three required annual Feast times. He also required an offering of the first of their ground grain (meal) during the year. In Deuteronomy 26:1–11, God called for a special first fruits offering after they settled in the Promised Land. That offering would be part of their worship of the Lord and rejoicing in Him and His promised provision. The Lord designed that the peoples' regular first fruits offerings of grain, fruit, and livestock would provide for the needs of the priests and their families. Each offering of first fruits acknowledged the Lord as provider, the One who blessed each family in abundantly fulfilling their needs.

> What guidelines did God give concerning the special Feast of First Fruits during the week of Unleavened Bread? Read Leviticus 23:9–14. What were the people to do once they settled in the land of Canaan, according to verses 10–11?

_____
_____

Did You Know?
THE TRIBE OF LEVI IN PLACE OF THE FIRSTBORN

In the Passover and Exodus events, the Lord redeemed and set apart to Himself the firstborn of Israel, claiming special ownership of the firstborn. In place of every firstborn male of Israel, the Lord chose the tribe of Levi to be His to minister alongside the priests from the line of Aaron (Numbers 3:12–13; 4:1–49; and 8:13–19). They ministered in the Tabernacle on behalf of the nation. God moved the priestly duties from the firstborn of each family to the tribe of Levi on behalf of all the families of Israel. God instructed Israel to provide for them through the various offerings and sacrifices of the people (Leviticus 27:30–33; Numbers 18:8–20, 21–32; Deuteronomy 14:27).

📖 What additional sacrifice did God require, according to Leviticus 23:12–13?

_____

_____

📖 What guidelines did God give concerning the new spring harvest and its use in verse 14?

_____

_____

When the people settled in the land of Canaan, God prescribed a yearly Feast of First Fruits to be carried out during the week of Unleavened Bread. On the day after the Sabbath, each family was to bring in the first sheaf of their harvest to the priest who would wave that before the Lord, acknowledging Him as the Giver of the harvest. This offering dedicated the entire harvest to Him and showed their gratitude for His provision.

In addition, the people offered a burnt offering, normally consisting of three main items—a one-year-old male lamb along with a grain offering of fine flour mixed with olive oil, plus a drink offering of wine. The burnt offering was totally consumed in the fires of the altar, picturing a heart of surrender totally consumed with the Lord as God. The heartbeat of the nation and of each Israelite should be to follow Him in every detail of life, including the grateful receiving of every morsel of food and drink.

Giving thanks to the Lord and acknowledging their dependence upon Him allowed the worshiper to enjoy the remainder of the harvest in the days, weeks, and months to come. No one was to eat any of the harvest until after the offering of first fruits. It was a matter of reverence, of respect, of acknowledging one's total dependence on the Lord.

The guidelines for the Feasts were given to Israel at Mount Sinai for their implementation in the land of Canaan. How did this work out in the history of Israel? Consider the workings of God in this matter.

📖 Israel came to the Promised Land in the spring of 1405 BC, after forty years of wandering in the wilderness. Joshua led them to the Jordan River. When did they cross that river, according to Joshua 4:19?

_____

📖 What occurred at Gilgal, according to Joshua 5:10?

_____

📖 According to Joshua 5:11, what happened the next day, the fifteenth of Nisan?

_____

📖 What did they experience over the next three days, the fifteenth, sixteenth, and seventeenth of Nisan? Review the events in Joshua 5:11–12. What differences do you see in each of the days, especially in the food provided?

Did You Know?
"MILK AND HONEY"

God promised Israel a land *"flowing with milk and honey"* (Exodus 3:8, 17; 13:5; 33:3), a phrase used 20 times in the Old Testament (e.g., Leviticus 20:24; Numbers 13:27; 14:8; 16:13–14, Deuteronomy 6:3; 11:9; 26:9, 15; 27:3; 31:20; Joshua 5:6; Jeremiah 11:5; 32:22; Ezekiel 20:6, 15). Ezekiel 20:6 uses the phrase speaking of the land of Israel and adds *"which is the glory of all lands,"* a land carefully chosen and especially favored and blessed by the Lord for His people. It refers to the natural blessing of *"honey"* in a land marked by abundance of bees, flowers, streams, fountains, springs, and rainfall (Deuteronomy 8:7–10; 11:9–12), as well as the cultivated blessing of *"milk"* from sheep, goats, and cows. In this land blessed by the Lord, there would be no harsh enslavement, no need to irrigate as in Egypt, but rather abundant opportunity to reap and enjoy God's provision.

_____

_____

_____

The people of Israel entered the Promised Land exactly in synch with the season of the Feasts, crossing the Jordan River on the tenth of Nisan and setting up camp at Gilgal. There, on the fourteenth, they celebrated the Passover. The next day, the fifteenth, they ate unleavened bread along with manna and some of the fruit of Canaan. On the sixteenth, they ate unleavened bread, and their last day of manna. The manna ceased after the sixteenth, so that on the seventeenth of Nisan, they ate only unleavened bread and the promised fruit of Canaan. It was the **first fruits** of the Promised Land. All kinds of fruit would be theirs now, including grapes, olives, dates, figs, pomegranates, barley, wheat, and honey. It was a day of new provision, a new day with a new diet in the new land, promised and provided by the Lord.

In Day Three, we will turn to the days of the New Testament where we see the celebration of first fruits with a few more detailed customs. In Jesus' life, words, and ministry, we will also find the fulfillment of the Feast of First Fruits. We will see Him fulfilling this Feast in ways beyond what any would have ever thought.

First Fruits in New Testament Days

Lesson Four — **DAY THREE**

We have noted that in every Feast there is some connection to a harvest or to a harvest season. The Feast of First fruits is obviously directly connected to the Spring harvest season, specifically to the first of the barley harvest in late March. Generally speaking, Israel celebrated this Feast by the priests offering a sheaf of barley or later a handful of barley flour from the barley harvest. He waved it before the Lord on the day after the Sabbath after Passover. When we turn to the first century AD, we find that the Jews had developed a more elaborate ritual for this celebration. A review of that celebration will help us see how Jesus fulfilled this Feast and how we can make applications to our daily walk.

Preparation for the Feast of First Fruits. In Jerusalem, during the autumn, the priests plowed a special field in the Ashes Valley (the place where the sin offerings and ashes of the Red Heifer were burned) across the Kidron Valley from the Temple at the Mount of Olives. Then seventy days before the Feast of First Fruits (mid to late January), they planted the special field with barley to be harvested and presented on the Feast of First Fruits, the day after the Sabbath in the Week of the Feast of Unleavened Bread. The field could not be artificially watered or fertilized, but must be allowed to grow naturally. In the days leading up to Passover, certain members of the Sanhedrin marked the place where the first sheaf would be harvested. They did this by tying the still-standing barley in bundles and marking them to be cut and harvested for the offering.

Procedures of the Feast of First Fruits. The night before the day of First fruits (Saturday after sunset) three priests made their way in a procession from the Temple to that barley field. They carried sickles and baskets with which to

> ### Did You Know?
> ### WAVE OFFERING WORSHIP
>
> For certain offerings, God instructed the priests to *"wave"* the offering before the Lord, lifting it up to Him as a symbol of first giving it to Him after which it could be used as directed and blessed by Him (see Exodus 29:24–27; 35:22; Leviticus 7:30–34). God instructed the giving of a sheaf of grain as a wave offering in the Feast of First Fruits (Leviticus 23:11–12). This principle of offering is also seen when God told Moses to throw down his staff. After seeing the *"serpent"* in his staff, God told him to pick it up (a step of surrender and faith for Moses). From that point forward, it was known as *"the rod of God,"* having been given up to Him, now useful by Him to bless His people. God worked in many ways through that staff, for example, in parting the waters of the Red Sea, in bringing water from the rock in the wilderness, and in giving victory over the Amalekites (Exodus 14:16, 26–27; 17:5–6, 9–13). What we give to God is His to use as He pleases to fulfill His purposes.

gather the first fruits offering of barley. They asked five questions of those who had come with them, 'Has the sun set?' 'With this sickle?' 'Into this basket?' 'On this Sabbath?' 'Shall I reap?' Then they cut the marked sheaves and gathered one ephah of barley (about twenty quarts).

That was taken to the Temple courts, threshed with rods or stalks, then parched over a flame, winnowed in the wind to remove the chaff, milled, and sifted into extremely fine flour. The priests set aside one omer of flour or about five pints to offer, mixed with three-fourths pint of olive oil and some frankincense. On Sunday morning the priest walked to the altar to present to the Lord this one omer (five pints) of barley flour as a wave offering. The priest raised and waved this before the Lord, then took only a handful and burned it on the altar. He gave the remainder to the Levites and priests to eat. This was the form in which the First Sheaf was presented on the Feast of First Fruits Day in New Testament days.

Individuals with their families would bring a sheaf of the first fruits of their harvest to the priest and offer a burnt offering as well (lamb or two doves, etc.) on this day. This was a way of thanking God for the first fruits of the harvest, of giving to Him those first fruits, acknowledging the grain as a gift from Him, and of setting aside or sanctifying the remainder of the harvest to Him. This offering served as a way of connecting to God, seeking the blessing of God and His fruitfulness over the entire harvest as it grew to maturity. It all belonged to Him and was a gift from Him. This was a harvest celebration, but it was more. As we will see, it pointed to Christ and His redemptive work.

📖 There are parallels between Jesus and the barley first fruits. Barley was considered the common man's grain. Jesus certainly spoke to and loved the common people (Mark 12:37). First, read Luke 9:18–22. According to verse 22, what did Jesus say would soon occur in Jerusalem? [Jesus spoke this about nine months before His crucifixion.]

_____
_____

📖 Think of how Jesus was treated as He went into Jerusalem that final Passover season (see Matthew 21:7–11; Luke 19:35–40). What did Caiaphas, the high priest, say about Jesus in John 11:47–53 and 18:14?

_____
_____
_____

📖 What did His enemies do to Jesus when they arrested Him, according to John 18:12, 24?

_____
_____

📖 What happened a short while later, according to Matthew 27:26–30?

_____
_____
_____
_____

📖 What does Isaiah 53:4–5, 10 say about this *"Man of sorrows"*?

_____

_____

Jesus predicted in Luke 9:22 that the leaders of His day, the *"elders and chief priests and scribes,"* would reject Him as Messiah and kill Him. He also said He would rise on the third day. Several days before Passover, Caiaphas selected Jesus to die—*"one man should die for the people."* Like the barley sheaf, Jesus was selected and bound the night of His betrayal. Later, He was beaten with a reed, with fists, and with a Roman scourge. He endured the fiery pain of that, the first flames of God's wrath. He was crushed (milled and sifted) for our iniquities. On the cross, He was lifted from the earth, in a sense waved before the Father as our sin offering, our burnt offering, our peace offering, all preparing to fulfill God's plan as the first fruits offering.

📖 What occurred at the cross? Look at the following Scriptures from Matthew 27 and give a brief summary of the events. These are preparation for Jesus fulfilling all the prophecies and purposes of the Father.

verse 45

_____

_____

verse 46

_____

_____

verse 50

_____

_____

verse 51

_____

_____

verse 52a

_____

_____

verse 54

_____

_____

verses 57–60

_____

_____

_____

> *Did You Know?*
>
> ### GOD SPEAKING THROUGH EARTHQUAKES IN SCRIPTURE
>
> God has used earthquakes in many ways—He works through them to get people's attention, to prepare people to hear from Him, to emphasize His revelation or an event, to deal in judgment, or to awaken one to His mercy. An earthquake occurred when Jesus died on the cross (Matthew 27:51). A *"great earthquake"* occurred on resurrection morning as the angel descended and rolled away the stone from the tomb (Matthew 28:2). Earthquakes often signaled a message from God—"God is speaking! Listen!" We see earthquakes at Mount Sinai with the giving of the Ten Commandments (Exodus 19:18), at the Red Sea when Israel crossed on dry land (Psalms 77:16–20), in dealing with the rebellion of Korah (Numbers 16:31–34), and in the New Testament in the Philippian jail where Paul and Silas were praising God (Acts 16:25–30). We discover several in Revelation (6:12; 8:5; 11:13–19). Other examples in the Old Testament include 1 Kings 19:11; Job 9:6; Psalms 18:7; 68:8; Isaiah 3:13; 5:25; 13:13; 24:18; 29:6; Jeremiah 10:10; 49:21; Joel 2:10; Nahum 1:5; Haggai 2:6.

After Jesus had spoken of those around Him, asking the Father to forgive them, after taking care of His mother Mary, and giving assurance to the repentant thief beside Him, He became silent for several hours. Darkness enveloped the land from Noon to 3:00 PM. Then, at 3:00, Jesus cried out *"My God, My God, why have You forsaken Me."* John 19:28 and 30 record His next two statements, *"I thirst"* and *"It is finished."* Luke 23:46 records His final prayer, *"Father, into Your hands I commit My spirit,"* before He breathed His last. With Christ's death several things occurred. The **darkness** ended (3:00 PM). The massive veil of the Temple was torn in two from top to bottom, opening the way to the Holy of Holies. An **earthquake** occurred. **Rocks** split and **tombs** opened. The rugged, experienced Roman **centurion** and those with him were struck with great fear and declared about Jesus, *"Truly this was the Son of God!"* When Jesus was confirmed dead, Joseph of Arimathea came with Nicodemus, took the body, wrapped it in strips of clean linen cloth with 100 pounds of myrrh resin, aloes, and spices (John 19:38–42). He laid Jesus in his new tomb and rolled a stone against the door of the tomb. Jesus lay **buried**. All heaven and earth awaited His prophesied resurrection. Not far away from that tomb stood that special field of barley.

📖 The field of barley was carefully guarded and protected by the priests. What about Jesus in the tomb? What occurred after Joseph buried Him there, according to Matthew 27:62–66?

_____

_____

_____

Word Study
SEISMOS

The Greek word *seismos* refers to quaking, a shaking, an earthquake. It is used of the earthquakes that occurred in Jerusalem when Jesus died on the cross and on resurrection morning when a *"great earthquake"* (*seismos* with *megas*) occurred (Matthew 27:51, 54; 28:2). The word is also used of the quaking of the fierce Roman soldiers guarding the tomb of Jesus. When the earth quaked, an angel descended, rolled away the stone, and the guards *"shook for fear of him, and became like dead men"* (Matthew 28:4). An earthquake followed by a 'guard-quake.' Interestingly, when the women saw the angel they were frightened, but did not quake or faint. What a difference!

The Jewish authorities went to Pilate to seek a guard for the tomb of Jesus, saying they feared His disciples might attempt to steal His body and deceive others into thinking He had risen from the dead. Pilate granted their request. The day after He died, Jesus' tomb was sealed under the Roman governor's authority and could not be broken without Roman authority. Perhaps as many as twelve Roman soldiers closely guarded the tomb. This number would match the twelve disciples whom the Jews considered a threat. At the same time, the barley field stood nearby awaiting the harvest of first fruits. On Saturday after sunset, the priests cut the first sheaves and went to the Temple and prepared to present them the next morning as the offering for the Feast of First Fruits.

Jesus lay buried in the tomb, waiting the morning of the resurrection. What was going on during the time His body lay in the grave? It is important to understand this to fully grasp all that Jesus' death and resurrection meant then, today, and forever. Consider what the Scriptures say concerning the time between Jesus' death and His resurrection.

📖 What did Jesus say to the repentant thief on the cross, according to Luke 23:43? Where would they be later that day?

_____

_____

_____

📖 What do you discover in Colossians 2:13–14?

_____

_____

Think of the events leading up to and following Jesus' death. The thief on the cross turned in repentance from reviling Jesus to recognizing Him as the true King of the Jews. He asked in faith that Jesus would remember him when He comes in His Kingdom. Jesus assured him that *"today"* he would experience *"Paradise"* with Him, a home in heaven, the home of the righteous after death.

What Jesus did for the thief, He can do for anyone. On the cross, Jesus paid for sin and provided all that was needed for full forgiveness. Through His work on the cross, He wiped away (or erased) the "certificate of debt," the record of all our sins, every violation of God's law. In the first century, a "certificate of debt" referred to the charges against a person for which he could be executed. Jesus took the penalty for all our charges, all our transgressions. The one who places faith in Jesus experiences His forgiveness and is made righteous, given a new heart, a new nature, and thus made fit for heaven. Why? Paul states that each "certificate" was nailed to the cross in Christ, thus fully erasing the penalty for our sins. The Roman placard nailed over Jesus' head said He was guilty of being *"King of the Jews"* and therefore must die, but that was no crime. Jesus died instead for your sins and my sins—the real placard placed there by the Father was the "certificates" of all our sins. We owed a sin debt we could never pay. Jesus fully paid the price for that debt He did not owe.

📖 Because of what Jesus did in paying for our sins, He also dealt a death blow to all evil as God had promised in Genesis 3:15. What do you find in Colossians 2:15?

_____
_____
_____

📖 What additional thoughts do you find about what Jesus did according to Hebrews 2:14–18? As an additional reference, look at 1 John 3:8 and note what Jesus came to do.

_____
_____
_____

By paying for our sin, Jesus nullified or removed any condemnation against those who receive His salvation by faith. He thus defeated the devil, taking away his power of death. When Jesus died, He *"disarmed principalities and powers,"* defeating Satan and all demonic forces along with their power to accuse and condemn. In Colossians 2:15, Paul painted the picture of Jesus being like a conquering Roman general making a public display of the enemy's defeat and His triumph. Jesus came to destroy the works of the devil, deliver us from the fear of death, and one day from death itself.

📖 What insights are added by 1 Peter 3:18–19, 22?

_____
_____
_____

📖 What occurred in the process of Christ's descending to earth and then ascending *"far above all the heavens"* according to Ephesians 4:7–10? You may find additional insights in Ephesians 2:4–10, especially verse 6.

Word Study
"PARADISE"

The term *"paradise"* is a translation of the Greek word is *paradeisos*, which, in turn, is a Persian loan word picturing a park or enclosed garden. It is used in the Septuagint (Greek Old Testament) in several places. It is used of the Garden of Eden (Genesis 2:8, 10, 15, 16; 3:3, 4, 9, 24, 25), of a well-watered garden in Jerusalem where Solomon meets with his bride, a place of closest companionship (Song of Solomon 4:13). In 2 Corinthians 12:2, 4, Paul speaks of being *"caught up to the third heaven.… caught up into Paradise and heard inexpressible words, which it is not lawful for a man to utter."* Jesus promised the thief on the cross, *"Truly, I say to you, today, you shall be with Me in Paradise"* (Luke 23:43). Jesus promised the one who overcomes He *"will give to eat from the Tree of Life, which is in the midst of the Paradise of God"* (Revelation 2:7-NKJV). Revelation 22:2, 14 places the Tree of Life in the New Jerusalem, thus linking it to paradise (Revelation 22:2, 14). Paradise is a place of beauty, of closest relationship, of revelation and insight, of healing and well-being, and the place where those redeemed by Christ walk with Him in the fullness of His presence.

Word Study
"RESURRECTION"

The Greek word *anastasis* translated "resurrection" is from the word *anistemi* meaning to "stand up again, arise, raise up, rise again." This word picture matches the picture of sleep. The body lies down in sleep and rises when awake. The physical body lies down in the physical "sleep" of death, and Jesus calls each body from the grave to "stand up" or "rise" in resurrection (John 5:28–29; 6:39). Just as Jesus began revealing His power, telling the physically helpless paralytic to *"rise and walk,"* so He will do in the day of resurrection (see Mark 2:1–12; Luke 5:17–26).

> **Doctrine**
> **THE SECOND ADAM WON**
>
> The first Adam faced temptation and failed. As a result death entered earth, eventually bringing Adam's death and death to all his offspring. Jesus came as the Second Adam. He was *"tempted in all things as we are, yet without sin"* (Hebrews 4:15). He won over temptation at every turn, over Satan in the Wilderness and on the cross (Matthew 4:1–10; Colossians 1:15; 1 Peter 3:18–19, 22; Genesis 3:15; John 12:31; 16:11), and over Death and Hades in His death and resurrection (Revelation 1:18). He gives life, victory, and resurrection to everyone who turns to Him in repentance and faith (John 1:12; 1 Corinthians 15:45–57).

Jesus died and arose to *"bring us to God."* Peter explains that after Jesus died and was made alive in the Spirit, He made a proclamation of His victory over sin, death, Satan, and all the forces of evil. That proclamation reached the farthest bounds of the spirit world and of the *"spirits now in prison,"* those disobedient before the Flood. He made known His triumph to the fullest. Those suffering in Peter's day (as today) could know they were included in His ultimate victory over death. On the third day, Jesus resurrected and opened the way to lead *"captivity captive."* In other words, those captive to sin, death, and the devil, could now be released and brought to God because of Jesus' triumph on the cross and in the resurrection. Ephesians 2:6 speaks of believers now raised up and seated *"in the heavenly places in Christ Jesus,"* to minister as His saints on earth (4:12–16) and glorify Christ **now** *and* to experience the *"riches of His grace"* in *"the ages to come"* (2:7).

When Jesus died on the cross, no one thought He would rise from the dead. No one expected such a miracle, but Jesus had predicted His resurrection. We will see how that occurred on Day Four.

Lesson Four — DAY FOUR

JESUS CHRIST, THE FIRST FRUITS OF THE RESURRECTION

The Sabbath drew to a close, and the priests made their way to the special barley field on the Mount of Olives. They cut the selected sheaves and took them to the Temple, where they were winnowed, crushed, and sifted into fine flour. The next morning the first fruits offering would be waved before the Lord and a special burnt offering would ascend to the Lord as part of the worship of the day. What occurred at the Garden tomb?

📖 What occurred at the Garden tomb on Sunday morning? Read each of the verses from Matthew 28 listed here and record each event. [Note: The verses are listed as the events occurred chronologically.]

verse 6a

verse 2

verses 3–4

verse 1

_____

_____

verse 5

_____

_____

verse 7

_____

_____

Very early in the morning while it was still dark, Jesus arose from the dead. Soon after, a great earthquake occurred, and a shining angel descended in the presence of the guards. The seemingly fearless Roman guards became so greatly frightened they shook with fear and fainted. The angel rolled away the stone from the tomb to reveal that Jesus was not there; He was risen, the First Fruits of the Resurrection. Then, Mary Magdalene and Mary (the mother of James the Less, and wife of Clopas, Matthew 27:56; Mark 15:40; John 19:25) came to the tomb. They saw the angel who told them Jesus *"is risen"* and commanded them to go and tell the disciples. They quickly ran and told them all that happened.

📖 How does Jesus' resurrection on Sunday connect with the Feast of First Fruits? What do you discover about first fruits in 1 Corinthians 15:20–23? What is Christ called in these verses?

_____

_____

_____

First of all, Jesus' resurrection occurred on the very day of the celebration of the Feast of First Fruits. He is the sheaf of barley waved before the Heavenly Father as the first fruits. Paul wrote to the Corinthian believers to clarify the certainty of the believer's resurrection. When he did so, one of the first things he noted was the certainty that Jesus Christ had resurrected. Christ is called *"the first fruits"* of the resurrection, the first to rise from the dead. *"Christ is risen from the dead, and has become the first fruits of those who have fallen asleep."* Jesus died. He arose first. All those who belong to Him will also be raised as the after fruits.

📖 What about the **appearances of Christ**? He rose from the dead on the morning of the Feast of First Fruits. As the priest was waving the barley sheaf before the Lord in the Temple, Christ was beginning to show Himself to His followers. He **first** appeared to Mary Magdalene. Read the account in John 20:1–18. What occurred first, according to verses 1–10? (Note: This first visit to the tomb was most likely with *"the other Mary"* mentioned in Matthew 28:1.)

_____

_____

Did You Know?
JESUS' GRAVE CLOTHS

Joseph of Arimathea secured the body of Jesus after He died and wrapped it in linen cloths along with the aromatic spices provided by Nicodemus. Together they transported the body of Jesus to the new tomb Joseph provided. The linen strips wrapped around Jesus' body were saturated with *"myrrh and aloes,"* over 100 Roman pounds (*litas*) (about 65 lbs or 30 kg) equivalent to that for a king. The spices consisted of a sticky myrrh resin (from the Balsamodendron tree) mixed with sandalwood powder from the Agallocha tree, and perhaps other spices. They would have formed a loose covering, adhering to the body with separate cloths (*soudarion*, a jaw band, face cloth, handkerchief, or sweat cloth) wrapped around the head. When Jesus resurrected, He did not unwrap the cloths. He simply left that encasing intact with the face cloth folded or *"rolled up . . . by itself."* The message of the grave cloths—Jesus really died. He was loved and honored in His burial. Yet He had no struggle rising from the dead or exiting the wrappings or the tomb. He is the living Lord and Savior, the First Fruits of the Resurrection.

LESSON FOUR – THE FEAST OF FIRST FRUITS   83

Doctrine
RESURRECTION ORDER

In 1 Corinthians 15:23, Paul speaks of a resurrection order: *"Christ the first fruits, after that those who are Christ's at His coming."* The Scriptures reveal the following *"order"* (Greek—*tagma* from *tasso*, to arrange in an orderly manner or in sequence) of the resurrection: **1)** Christ as *"the first fruits,"* **2)** deceased saints exiting their graves after Christ resurrected (Matthew 27:52–53), **3)** the church—the *"dead in Christ . . . first,"* followed immediately by those *"who are alive and remain"* (1 Thessalonians 4:16–17), **4)** the *"Two Witnesses"* of Revelation 11:11–12, **5)** Tribulation saints (Revelation 20:4–6), **6)** Old Testament Saints (Daniel 12:2; Luke 14:14; Revelation 20:6), **7)** the *"unjust"* or unbelievers (Acts 24:15; Revelation 20:5, 12–15; John 5:28, 29b).

Doctrine
"MY BRETHREN"

After His resurrection, after Jesus had fully paid the price for their salvation, He called His disciples *"My brethren,"* something He had not done before (Matthew 28:10; John 20:17). In Hebrews 2:9–13, we find the details of Christ first tasting death for everyone. Why? It was necessary for Jesus to suffer and die to bring *"many sons to glory,"* sons (and daughters) who are from one Father. Therefore, *"He is not ashamed to call them brethren."* Jesus fully identified with humankind to make us family. We belong. All who place faith in Jesus and His finished work become family. The marks of family are belonging and obedience to the Father (Matthew 12:50; Luke 8:21).

📖 Mary stayed at the tomb after Peter and John had left. She wept there, stooped to look in the tomb. What did she encounter, according to verses 11–13?

_____
_____
_____

📖 What happened next? Read John 20:14–16 and record your insights.

_____
_____
_____

Jesus appeared to different people five times on resurrection Sunday. Mary Magdalene came to the tomb first while it was still dark with *"the other Mary"* (sometime before 6:00 AM), saw the stone already taken away from the tomb, and ran to tell the others. Matthew 28:5–7 adds that the angel appeared to these two and told them to tell the disciples. Simon Peter and John heard Mary Magdalene's story and ran to the tomb. There they saw the tomb empty except for the linen cloths lying there cocoon-like without Jesus inside them. No one had come and unwrapped those cloths. Jesus in His glorified body had simply exited the cloths and the tomb. They went back home. Mary stayed there and wept. She looked inside the empty tomb and saw two angels who questioned her weeping. *"Why are you weeping?"* She still thought someone had taken Jesus' body away. She turned around and saw a man standing there, whom she supposed to be the gardener. It was Jesus who asked her, *"Woman, why are you weeping? Whom are you seeking?"* She repeated her puzzlement. Then Jesus simply said, *"Mary!"* and she recognized His voice and cried out *"Rabboni!"* which means "my teacher." She reached for Him with great astonishment.

📖 According to John 20:17, what did Jesus say to Mary after she recognized Him? What significance does this statement hold?

_____
_____
_____

Jesus told Mary, *"Stop clinging to Me."* Some translate this as *"do not cling to Me"* or *"do not touch Me,"* indicating that perhaps she tried to cling but then Jesus had a word of instruction first, before she could touch Him. He then said, *"for I have not yet ascended to the Father; but go to My brethren, and say to them, 'I ascend to My Father and your Father, and My God and your God.'"* What did this mean? There are two lines of thinking here. One that Jesus is simply reminding Mary to tell His disciples that He is alive and has not yet ascended to the Father. They will see Him too. The night before His crucifixion, Jesus had told His disciples that He would be going away and they could not go with Him there yet (John 13:33, 36; 14:2; 16:5).

The second line of thinking is that Jesus was speaking of immediately ascending to the Father on Resurrection Sunday to sprinkle His blood on the true Mercy Seat in the true Tabernacle in Heaven and to be waved before the Father as the sheaf of First Fruits of the Resurrection. If this day was not the day His heavenly ministry occurred, then certainly this occurred at His ascension, forty days later (Acts 1:9–11). Whichever time this occurred, His work in this regard is presented in Hebrews 8:1–2; 9:11–14, 22–26. The most vital fact is that it did occur. He fulfilled all the Scriptures in this regard.

📖 What other appearances occurred on Resurrection Sunday? What do you find in the following verses?

Matthew 28:9–10

___

Luke 24:34

___

Luke 24:13–35

___

Later in the morning, soon after appearing to Mary Magdalene, Jesus met the group of **women** on the road, those who had been at the tomb, and told them to tell of His Resurrection. Later that day, Jesus appeared to **Simon Peter**. Then, that afternoon, near evening, Jesus walked with the two on the **road to Emmaus** and manifested Himself to them at their house as He blessed and broke bread.

📖 What occurred that Sunday night, according to John 20:19–23 and Luke 24:36–48? These accounts contain a unique encounter. Describe what occurred.

___

On Sunday night, the ten disciples (without Thomas but with the two Emmaus disciples present) were meeting locked away, hiding in fear, when Jesus suddenly appeared. He calmed their fears with His words, *"peace to you."* At His appearance, they became frightened, joyful, and wondering all at the same time. He showed them the covenant marks, His hands and His feet, then ate some fish and honeycomb revealing He was real, not a disembodied spirit. Then Jesus explained everything that had happened in the light of the Old Testament Scriptures. As the Father sent Him, so He sent them, giving them His commission to tell the message of Jesus and of repentance and forgiveness of sins through Him.

In giving them this commission, Jesus did something very unique. He breathed on them and said, *"Receive the Holy Spirit."* Did they receive the Spirit at that moment? No, because we find Him later commanding them to tarry in Jerusalem until they are endued with power by the promised

> *Did You Know?*
>
> ## THE APPEARANCES OF THE RESURRECTED CHRIST
>
> There are ten appearances of Christ in the forty days after His Resurrection, five on Resurrection Sunday, five in the following days, then several in the account of the Early Church. **1)** He appeared first at the tomb to Mary Magdalene (John 20:11–18), **2)** to the women as they walked on the road (Matthew 28:9–10), **3)** to Peter (Luke 24:34), **4)** to the two journeying to Emmaus (Luke 24:24:13–32), **5)** to the Ten disciples without Thomas (Luke 24:36–43; John 20:19–25), **6)** eight days later to the eleven disciples with Thomas (John 20:26–31), **7)** to more than 500 believers (likely in Galilee) (1 Corinthians 15:6), **8)** to James the half-brother of Jesus (1 Corinthians 15:7), **9)** to the seven disciples on the shore of Galilee (John 21:1–25), **10)** to the disciples at His ascension (Acts 1:3–11). He later appeared to Stephen at his martyrdom (Acts 7:55–56), to Saul/Paul on the road to Damascus (Acts 9:3–9; 1 Corinthians 15:8) and to John on Patmos (Revelation 1:9–18).

> **Since Christ had no problem in creating the first time or in rising from the dead, He is more than adequate to bring about the resurrection of every believer and all the New Creation. Consider this: He made everything out of nothing, so He is certainly able to make something new out of something old.**

Holy Spirit. Another account in Acts 1:2–9 gives more detail about His instructions and their waiting on the coming of the Spirit. What did this encounter on Resurrection Sunday mean? Does this have something to do with the Feast of First Fruits?

Consider this parallel. Christ is the Creator (John 1:1–3, 10; Colossians 1:16–17). In the Garden of Eden, He breathed into the face of Adam, and he became a living soul, in the first Creation. On Resurrection Sunday night, Jesus breathed into the faces of His disciples, commanding them to receive the Holy Spirit. They did not receive His Spirit that night. That occurred fifty days later during the Feast of Pentecost. This encounter is a preview of the start of the New Creation; Christ is risen from the dead, the First Fruits of the Resurrection, the beginning of a new day. Jesus says in essence, 'when the Holy Spirit comes, receive Him as though He were My very breath, because He is. We are one. You are part of the New Creation in Christ.' The disciples did not grasp all this meant until after Pentecost. Under the teaching of the Spirit, they began to piece together all the things Jesus had done and said. They saw how His death and resurrection fulfilled Old Testament prophecies and promises.

📖 There is one more connection to the Feast of First Fruits on this Resurrection Sunday. Read Matthew 27:51–53. From these verses, piece together what occurred on the day Jesus died.

_____
_____
_____

📖 What occurred *"after His resurrection,"* according to verses 52 and 53? What connection do you see to First fruits?

_____
_____
_____

The moment Jesus died, an earthquake struck Jerusalem, powerful enough to split the rocks, particularly the stones that sealed many graves. Those tombs opened that day, but remained silent, undisturbed, until Sunday. *"After"* Jesus' resurrection, *"many"* Old Testament saints *"were raised"* and came into Jerusalem and *"appeared to many."* When the priest offered the sheaves of barley in the first fruits offering on Sunday morning, he offered the grain of many sheaves, a picture of the first of the harvest of people. When Jesus resurrected, He was not the only sheaf that arose. God raised several saints, many sheaves.

The priests cut and presented a full bundle of barley sheaves on the morning of the Feast of First Fruits. The Old Testament saints raised that day were part of the first sheaves of the harvest, a testimony of their faith in the coming Messiah and of Jesus' resurrection power. Jesus arose as the first fruits on Resurrection Sunday, and with Him He raised the first sheaves of the greater harvest to come. Some see these as simply resuscitated like Lazarus and so would die again. Others see these as literally resurrected like Jesus. Where did they go? Scripture does not say. If they were resurrected saints, it is likely that they ascended to heaven soon after or with Jesus in His ascension. The main point in the historical events of that Feast of First

Fruits that became known as Resurrection Sunday **is** that *Jesus as the First fruits of the resurrection brought about the greater fulfillment of the Feast*. In the historical events of Resurrection Sunday, He also pointed to the time in which He will resurrect all who belong to Him, a preview of what He will do. That is our confident expectation.

How are we to apply the truths of the Feast of First fruits to our daily lives as followers of Christ? We will look at several application points in Day Five.

THE CALL OF THE FEAST OF FIRST FRUITS—RESURRECTION CERTAINTY

Lesson Four — DAY FIVE

What does the Feast of First Fruits say to followers of Christ today? We have seen that Christ is the First Fruits of the Resurrection, the guarantee that more will follow. In His first fruits offering are the blessing and the setting apart or sanctifying of the entire harvest to the Father and a preview of what the resurrection will be like for every believer. What application points can we see concerning the Feast of First Fruits in our lives today? Today, we will explore some of those application points centered on the resurrection of Christ, how that impacts our daily living, and our future forever.

📖 **What** promises or guarantees does Peter give the believer in 1 Peter 1:3–9? What do we have *"through the resurrection,"* according to verse 3? What additional promise is described in verses 4–5?

_____
_____
_____
_____

📖 **How** does the reality of Christ's resurrection help the believer face various trials according to 1 Peter 1:6–9?

_____
_____
_____

Through the resurrection of Jesus Christ, believers have *"a living hope."* Because He overcame death and lives today, every born-again follower of Christ is connected to Him and His power. Each also has the assurance of an eternal inheritance, *"imperishable and undefiled . . . [one that] will not fade away, reserved in heaven for you."* We are also *"protected by the power of God."* That's security, especially in the uncertain times and the insecurities of life on earth—health issues, financial and employment issues, wars, conflicts, robberies, and spiritual battles. Peter speaks of being *"distressed by various trials,"* the word *"various,"* being a translation of *poikilos*, meaning multi-colored. We face all kinds of trials, all shapes and sizes and colors that can cause pain, but God is still at work, and we are secure.

Word Study
A TREASURY OF SECURITY

First Peter 1:4–5 records five words that stand as a treasury of security for the believer. **"Imperishable"** (Gr. *Aphthartos*) refers to never rotting or being spoiled. **"Undefiled"** (*amiantos*) means unstained by any evil. **"Unfading"** (*amarantos*) "was used of flowers and suggests a supernatural beauty that time does not impair. [The three words here] indicate that the inheritance is untouched by death, unstained by evil, unimpaired by time. It is composed of immortality, purity, and beauty (Beare)." [Cleon L. Rogers, Jr and Cleon L. Rogers III, *The New Linguistic and Exegetical Key to the Greek New Testament* (Grand Rapids: Zondervan Publishing House, 1998), p. 567] Our **inheritance** is secure as well. *Tereo*, translated **"reserved,"** means to be guarded, kept, or taken care of. The Greek word translated **"protected"** comes from the Greek word *phroupeo*, to watch over, used of a military guard continually watching.

Each believer's faith is tested through all kinds of trials like metal tested in a fire. Even gold, the best of metals, is not as valuable as a believer's faith that has been tested and shown to be genuine. Faith that is focused on and resting in Jesus will bring recognition, glory, and honor to Him when we are resurrected. He, too, will be fully revealed at His return when He resurrects His own. Because Jesus resurrected, we can face trials with a sense of purpose, even in pain. His full salvation awaits us.

📖 **When** will those *"in Christ"* or *"those who are Christ's"* (they belong to Him) be resurrected according to 1 Corinthians 15:23?

_____

_____

📖 What do you find about this future work in 1 Thessalonians 4:13–18?

_____

_____

📖 What further revelation does Paul give about **when** those in Christ will be resurrected? Look at 1 Corinthians 15:51–54 and record your insights.

_____

_____

_____

📖 Revelation 20:4–6 summarizes the *"first resurrection."* What happens with those who are part of *"the first resurrection"*? When do the remainder of humankind resurrect, according to verse 5?

_____

_____

_____

The *"first resurrection"* will occur at the Lord's return, His *parousia* or the coming of His kingly presence. The first manifestation of that will be at what is often called the "rapture" of the church, the Greek word *harpazo* painting the picture of being suddenly snatched up. The *"dead in Christ shall rise first"* and then those believers who remain alive will be *"caught up together with them in the clouds to meet the Lord in the air, and thus we shall always be with the Lord."* Paul speaks of *"the trumpet of God"* in 1 Thessalonians and *"the last trumpet"* in 1 Corinthians, both referring to God's call to assemble, to meet with Him. (We will see more about this in the Feast of Trumpets in a later lesson.)

📖 What do you discover in 1 Corinthians 15:35–49 about the resurrection of those in Christ?

_____

_____

_____

📖 What related promise do you find in Philippians 3:20–21?

_____

Doctrine
THE *"SLEEP"* OF DEATH

Paul speaks of those who have *"fallen asleep,"* referring to those who have died (1 Corinthians 15:20; 1 Thessalonians 4:13, 14, 15). Specifically, the physical body lies down in the sleep of death and will be raised in the power of the resurrection, awakened to all the promises of the salvation Jesus Christ purchased in His death and resurrection. This is no doctrine of "soul sleep," since 2 Corinthians 5:1–8 gives great detail about our being in the Lord's presence immediately after we die, clothed with our heavenly dwelling, full of life, alert to the Lord and all He has in heaven. Verse 8 declares that one who is *"absent from the body"* is *"present with the Lord."* Paul testified in Philippians 1:23 of *"having a desire to depart and be with Christ, which is far better,"* the idea being that of immediately rejoicing in His conscious presence.

📖 What do you discover about our future in 1 John 3:1–3?

_____

_____

The resurrection of believers in Christ means a magnificent change from a corruptible and weak body to one incorruptible and glorious, touched and changed by the power of God. Philippians 3:20–21 ascends to the heights of wonder in describing our resurrection—*"For our citizenship is in heaven, from which also we eagerly wait for a Savior, the Lord Jesus Christ, who will transform the body of our humble state into conformity with the body of His glory, by the exertion of the power that He has even to subject all things to Himself."* John confidently exclaims, *"We know that when He is revealed, we shall be like Him."* We are not destined to stay as we are. We are destined to a glorious resurrection body and wondrous resurrection realities with Christ forever. The resurrection of Christ as the fulfillment of the Feast of First fruits gives hope and confidence that He will resurrect every believer when He returns.

There are two aspects to the resurrection of Jesus, one for now and one forever. **Forever**, we will know His resurrection perfection—a perfect body in a perfect world, in perfect fellowship with a perfect Lord and Savior and with a perfect family. For **now**, we can know His resurrection power in daily life, the power to walk in *"newness of life,"* putting away the deeds of the flesh, yielding our members as instruments of righteousness in everyday interactions. **Each** of us has the need for power **now**. **Power** and **Perfection**—power for now and perfection forever. What security!

Colossians 3:1–4 relates to now and forever. It speaks of being raised with Christ as a *present* reality. Because that is true, because we have His power now, God calls us to seek the things which are above, to set our minds on things above. We have died, and our lives are currently *"hidden with Christ in God."* But one day we will live forever *"with Him in glory."* Romans 6:4–14 assures that we have been given resurrection life, that we have been raised to walk in newness of life, His kind of life *now*. This is a life of dying to "self," to the "I, me, my, mine" lifestyle, saying "no" to self agendas and "yes" to Jesus agendas. This is a life of *His* life at work in us and through us. Paul testified of his life, *"for me to live is Christ"* (Philippians 1:21). This means Jesus died **for us** to give His life **to us**, to live His life **in us**, to express His life **through us**.

APPLY **Power Now**—Are you experiencing the power of Jesus in your life now? Is your daily life marked by His character being expressed in you and through you? Can people see in you, in the way you handle some of the issues listed below. Can people see Jesus' impact on you and His power through you? They should be able to look and say, "So, that's how Jesus would handle _____." Consider these situations. If you see an area that needs God's attention, *circle* it and *tell* Him. Ask Him for His power now. If you see a relationship that needs mending, talk to the Lord about it. Take the first step in His power now.

Doctrine
OUR GUARANTEE

"Christ's resurrection is the pledge of His people's resurrection, just as the first-fruits were the pledge of the harvest to come. Christ is the first to be raised from the dead, and so stands in the front rank alone, as the first-fruits were plucked before the rest of the produce was ripe; but, just as certainly as the harvest in due time followed the first-fruits, so shall those who sleep in Christ be raised up in due time, and stand in the second rank after Him." [J. Soutar, *"First Fruits"* in **Dictionary of Christ and the Gospels**, vol. 1, James Hastings, ed. (Grand Rapids: Baker Book House, reprint 1973 from New York: Charles Scribner's Sons, 1906), p. 597]

Jesus died for us— To give His life to us—To live His life in us—To express His life through us.

Doctrine
NEW CREATION

Jesus arose as the **First Fruits** of the Resurrection and thus of a New Creation. We can become part of that new creation by faith in Jesus Christ and His finished work on the cross and in the resurrection (Galatians 2:20; 3:22; 6:14–15). *"Therefore if any man is in Christ, he is a new creature; the old things passed away; behold, new things have come"* (2 Corinthians 5:17). That means a new lifestyle and new works that have His nature about them. Ephesians 2:10 speaks about being *"His workmanship, created in Christ Jesus for good works which God prepared beforehand, that we should walk in them."* Colossians 3:10–11 speaks about putting on *"the new man"* and experiencing His renewing work of making us into the *"image of the One who created him."* This new creation means new thinking, new actions, and living a new way by the power of the resurrected Christ (Ephesians 4:22–32). One day it means a new resurrection body and living in a resurrected New Earth with a New Heaven (Isaiah 65:17–19; 66:22; Romans 8:16–30; 2 Peter 3:`13; Revelations 21:1).

- Traffic
- Dealing with Income Taxes
- Your eating
- What you laugh at
- When someone does you wrong
- How you treat someone you do not need
- Politics (office, local, state, national)
- Home life
- When you have been wronged
- How hard you work
- How you spend spare time
- How someone has treated you
- Waiting in line
- Family disagreements
- Your words/Conversations
- Extra money (or *any* money)
- A flat tire
- Attitude toward a superior (boss, owner, officer)
- Honesty in school
- How well you do a job
- Praise from others
- Complaints from others
- Faithfulness in ministry

APPLY **New Start Now**—Consider these truths. First, read and think through the paragraphs below, Reflect back over what we have seen in this lesson. **Remember** how God has given new beginnings to many. Then, consider and **Rejoice** in how Jesus could work in anyone's life… including yours. Make a **Request** of Him for your life or for someone you know.

Reflect—The Timing of First Fruits, A New Beginning. In every historical example of the timeframe surrounding the Feast of First fruits (around Nisan 17), there are **eight** realities at work. First, there is a judgment on a wicked world. Second, we see the salvation of God's people. Third, for God's people there is a dying to an old order and fourth, a moving into a new order, a new life and lifestyle. Fifth, in this new lifestyle, the righteous must live by the power of God. Sixth, they must live by faith in God. Seventh, every example is followed by the challenge of faith obedience in carrying out the eighth factor, the new assignments God gives that will take His wisdom, power, and grace.

Remember—Think of how this is seen in the biblical examples. It is true of Noah coming out of the corruption of the world and the judgment of the flood, and reestablishing life on earth, of Moses and the people moving out of Egypt and slavery into a new day and new freedom, of Joshua leading the people out of the wilderness and into conquering Canaan and establishing the nation there, of Hezekiah leading the people out of the corruption of idolatry into a new day of true worship, of Mordecai and Esther leading the people of God out of the threat of genocide and into the ongoing challenges of living in a Persian culture, of every believer dying to self and the world and living out a resurrection empowered life in the daily stuff of life, by faith, by grace, by His Spirit within.

Rejoice—As part of applying these truths to your life, think of how Jesus fulfills all these Biblical examples in bringing a new day, a new beginning, giving a new life. Jesus is the **Greater Noah** who brings 'rest,' no longer under judgment, but living in the dawning of a new day, a new beginning, a new creation. Jesus is the **Greater Moses**, the prophet like Moses who brings us through the "Red Sea" deliverance onto a new shore, a new day with a new lifestyle, no longer oppressed and enslaved. Jesus is the **Greater Joshua** [*"Jehovah Is Salvation"*] bringing us through the Jordan River, no longer in the wilderness of unbelief, into a day of new provision. Jesus is the **Greater Hezekiah**, cleansing our lives of the rebellion and corruption of idolatry. He leads us into true worship in spirit and truth. Jesus is the **Greater Mordecai**, directing us to walk in faith, in the calling of God, no longer under the sentence of death, but living in the day of a new life, spared from destruction and judgment. At the Garden Tomb, Jesus is the **Greater Adam**, the Last Adam in the garden. He has won over temptation, sin, death, the devil, and hell. The new creation and the resurrection harvest have begun. In His Word, God reveals that He is bringing about a new order, making us new creatures *"in Christ"* and bringing us one day to our new home in the New Jerusalem with a new heaven and a new earth. He declares triumphantly, *"Behold, I am making all things new"* (Revelations 21:5).

<u>My Request</u> for a New Start—Where do you need a new start? Or, do you know of someone who is in great need of a new beginning? Pause and pray for your own life or for someone you know who needs the Lord's work in his or her life—giving a new day, a fresh start, a new beginning. You may want to write your prayer or perhaps a Letter to God in the space below. Include a prayer of praise and thanks that Jesus grants new beginnings. Perhaps there are some things for which You can thank Him today. Write any requests you have of Him regarding a new start.

_____
_____
_____
_____
_____
_____
_____
_____
_____
_____
_____
_____
_____
_____

Lord, thank You that You are the God of a new day, of new beginnings. Thank you for the testimony of Your work in Noah, Moses, Joshua, Hezekiah, but most of all in Your Son, our Lord Jesus Christ. Thank You that You give new life and with that a new start each day as I follow You. I pray for clearer understanding about Your resurrection life and how that should impact my daily decisions and all my relationships. May I be a faithful witness to others of the change You can make, of the new start You can give to anyone who repents of sin and places faith in You. Thank you for the hope, the certainty of the resurrection, of **my** resurrection because of the work **You** have done. Remind me of this *"living hope"* as I

Doctrine
WHAT YOU <u>DO</u> IN THE BODY MATTERS

In 2 Timothy 2, we find a way of winning and reward and a way of losing and lies. To experience all Christ desires now and in eternity, **believe** and **teach** *"the word of truth"* and **behave** empowered by *"the grace"* of Christ, staying away from anything wicked and staying close to all that is pure and Jesus-centered. The soldier, athlete, and farmer receive rewards by doing right. The pure vessel is useful, honored to convey the Master's blessings to others. Paul spoke of two who spoke lies saying our resurrection already occurred, emphasizing the "spiritual" and deemphasizing the body, thus leading some away from God and into corrupt living (since the body does not matter, either do as you please or deny yourself to extremes). Spirit *and* body matter. Godliness faithfully honors both with balance and receives eternal rewards in the resurrection. Belief in the resurrection keeps accountability on one's future agenda and makes a difference in behavior. What we do in the body matters—we will answer to God and He will reward accordingly.

> *Did You Know?*
> **RESURRECTION REALITY NOW**
>
> The lifestyle pictured in being raised to *"walk in newness of life"* is sometimes called "resurrection living." In reality, it goes by many names: **Abiding in the Vine** (John 15:1–8), **Walking in the Light** (1 John 1:5–9), **The Spirit-filled Walk** (Ephesians 5:18–21), **The Word-filled Walk**, letting the Word richly indwell (Colossians 3:16–17), **The New Man,** putting off the old man and putting on the new (Ephesians 4:20–24), **The Walk of Worship/Surrender** (Romans 12:1–2), **The Crucified Life** (Galatians 2:20), **The Cross-filled life,** taking up my cross (Luke 9:23), **The Imitation of Christ** (1 Corinthians 11:1), **Following Jesus** (Matthew 4:19).

face the various trials of life. I pray for Your grace and mercy, Your wisdom and insight to live out the *"newness of life"* You have provided in Your resurrection. May I continually yield my members as instruments of righteousness, empowered by You. May I bring You glory and honor in how I live surrendered to You, allowing You to live Your life in me and through me. In Jesus' name, Amen.

Notes

Notes

The Feast of Pentecost

The Call of God to Spirit-Filled Relationships

The Feasts of the Lord give us the yearly calendar of the nation of Israel and the eternal calendar of the people of God. In **Passover** we see our Redemption from slavery and release into the land of God's promises (and for the Christian a release into the "eternal Life" He promises). In **Unleavened Bread** we see an unleavened life—walking in purity and holiness—a walk of sincerity and truth. In **First Fruits** we see Jesus as the First Fruits of the Resurrection with the promise of many sons and daughters being raised up in resurrection life and power. His present-day followers know the reality of His gift of that resurrection life. The fourth Feast known as the **Feast of Pentecost** gives yet another picture of the life God desires for His people.

The fullness of the Feast of First Fruits reveals God's display of the resurrected Lord Jesus, the First Fruits of the Resurrection. As such, He revealed the kind of life He promised to all who would follow Him in repentance and faith. He would give each of His children resurrection life, a life with His power designed to display His character. The Feast of First Fruits points to our confident hope in the resurrection to come. So, the initial coming of the Spirit at Pentecost is the first manifestation of the earnest or guarantee of our full redemption, which culminates in the resurrection.

The Feast of First Fruits is linked to the Feast of Pentecost, as the first of the harvest is linked to the end of the harvest. Pentecost is the fulfillment of the spring harvest, the offering of two loaves of wheat being the first fruits of that harvest. As the Feast of First fruits symbolized the resurrection of Christ, Jesus being the first fruits of the resurrection, so the Feast of Pentecost symbolizes the first fruits of the Spirit, the birth of the church and the ingathering of an additional 3000 believers, revealing the first work of the Spirit in bringing in the harvest.

The period of Pentecost celebrates the harvest of the wheat, the end of the spring harvest season before the coming of the summer planting in preparation for the final harvest of the fall. Just so, in Pentecost we celebrate the first

> *Did you know?*
> **THE NAME "PENTECOST"**
>
> For the fourth Feast, the New Testament uses the name **"Pentecost"** (the Greek word, *pentekoste*, meaning "fiftieth") since it came on the fiftieth day after First Fruits. The name *"Feast of Weeks"* (Deuteronomy 16:10) refers to the fact that this Feast occurred on the Sunday after completion of *"the seventh Sabbath"* (seven weeks) after First Fruits (Leviticus 23:16–17). This Feast was also called *"the Feast of Harvest"* (Exodus 23:16) and *"the day of the first fruits,"* since it celebrated the first fruits of the wheat harvest (Numbers 28:26; Leviticus 23:17).

Lesson Five — DAY ONE

THE HISTORY OF PENTECOST

The Fourth Feast is known as the Feast of Weeks or the Feast of Harvest. It occurred **seven weeks** and one day (or fifty days) after First Fruits and was to be observed as a celebration of the full wheat harvest. In the New Testament it came to be known as Pentecost based on the Greek word *pentekoste,* associated with the number fifty. Does this Feast have any meaning for us? What is the historical background of this Feast and how does that connect to today? We must clearly see the historical matters to understand God's application for our daily lives. This Feast is wrapped up in what God did with His people in bringing them out of Egypt and into the Promised Land. It gives us the foundation for understanding and applying the call of the Feast of Pentecost to our daily walk. First, let's explore the history of Pentecost.

📖 What is the name given to the fourth Feast in Numbers 28:26 and Deuteronomy 16:9–10?

Feast of Weeks

📖 Read Leviticus 23:15–16. What specific instructions did God give concerning **when** to celebrate this fourth Feast?

Count 50 days to the day after the 7th sabbath; then u offer a new grain offering to the Lord

The Feast of First Fruits occurred on the day after the Sabbath during the week of Unleavened Bread. That placed it on a Sunday. From that day, the Israelites were to count seven complete Sabbaths or seven full weeks, equaling 49 days. The fourth Feast known as **"the Feast of Weeks"** would then occur on the fiftieth day, also a Sunday, since it was after the seventh Sabbath (Saturday).

📖 Consider the historical foundation. What occurred on the fiftieth day after the children of Israel left Egypt? Since the name "Pentecost" focuses on the number "fifty," encompassing the "seven weeks" and a day, we must look for the significance in the Scripture for delineating that number of days. Usually the number "seven" denotes completion, seven complete weeks, bringing them to the completion of the spring harvest. Read the following verses and note the specific day to which each refers. Follow the trail of days they experienced from Egypt to Mount Sinai. Note the fiftieth day in Exodus 19:16. Where were they when this occurred according to Exodus 19:1–3? *Mount Sinai*

Put Yourself In Their Shoes

THE SEVENS CYCLE

The people of Israel followed a pattern of sevens in their calendars and their celebrations, a part of experiencing the order and care of God. Consider the **lifestyle calendar**. They observed a **weekly** Sabbath every Saturday, a Sabbath **month** in the fall, a Sabbatical **year** every seventh year, and a **generational** Sabbath year, the year of Jubilee (seven times seven years plus one to bring about the fiftieth year). Consider the **yearly celebration calendar**. Within each year there were **seven special Sabbath rests** as part of the **Feasts**. (For more information, see the chart on page 199.)

Exodus 12:3 _Take them a lamb 10th day_

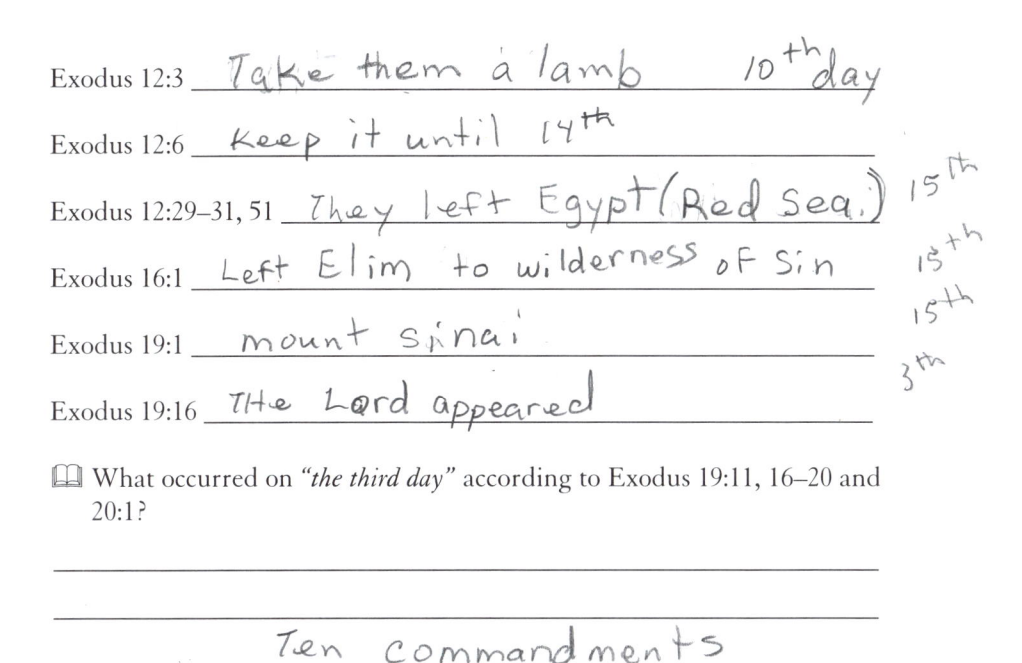

Exodus 12:6 _Keep it until 14th_

Exodus 12:29–31, 51 _They left Egypt (Red Sea)_ 15th

Exodus 16:1 _Left Elim to wilderness of Sin_ 15th

Exodus 19:1 _mount Sinai_ 15th

Exodus 19:16 _The Lord appeared_ 3th

📖 What occurred on *"the third day"* according to Exodus 19:11, 16–20 and 20:1?

Ten commandments

Each family of Israelites selected a Passover lamb on the tenth of the month and then slew it on the fourteenth. That night they ate it with sandals on, ready to depart Egypt. When the Lord passed over the land of Egypt and the firstborn died, the Egyptians urged them to leave. They departed, traveling on the fifteenth of the month. Exodus 16:1 points to the fifteenth day of the second month when they came to the Wilderness of Sin, thirty days after their departure. They arrived in the Wilderness of Sinai on the first day of the third month. From the fifteenth of the first month to the first of the third month we calculate them traveling 16 days the first month plus 30 days the second month. That is 46 days. The first of the third month is Day 47. Moses apparently went up to the mount to meet the Lord the next day, Day 48. God gave instructions for Moses to *"consecrate"* the people *"today"* (Day 48), *"and tomorrow"* (Day 49), and *"be ready for the third day"* (Day 50). On that day, the Lord appeared to them in Mount Sinai in fire, smoke, the quaking of the mountain, the sound of His trumpet (*shofar*), lightning, thunder, and finally His Voice giving them the Ten Commandments.

📖 We saw the call of God to His people in Lesson One. Review what God showed them about their purpose in Exodus 19:4–6? What three characteristics were to mark the people of God?

Holy Nation, a Kingdom of priests
my own possession

God called the children of Israel *"My own possession,"* **belonging** to Him as **His** special treasure, highly valued, greatly invested in by the Lord. They were also to be *"a kingdom of priests,"* a people truly **believing** God so that they connect with Him and help others connect with Him in true belief, worship, and obedience. That was their job, their mission to the nations of the world. The third purpose for which God called them was to be *"a holy nation,"* a nation set apart to God in a personal relationship **behaving** set apart as a testimony of what it means to belong to and obey God and His Word. They were to walk holy with God, to show themselves as His people with Him as their God.

> *"I . . . brought you to Myself. Now then, if you will indeed obey My voice and keep My covenant, then you shall be My own possession (a special treasure to Me) among all the peoples; for all the earth is Mine; and you shall be to Me a kingdom of priests and a holy nation."*
>
> **Exodus 19:4b, 5–6**

LESSON FIVE – THE FEAST OF PENTECOST 97

📖 After God gave the people His call as His people, what did they promise God, according to Exodus 19:8? From your knowledge of the people of Israel, what do you think of their follow through? How well did they do?

they broke the law

The people stated simply, *"all that the Lord has spoken we will do!"* However, the record of the people actually obeying what He said proved them to be a dismal failure. They did not have the power and often failed to have the will to obey God. It was a continual issue with them, year after year for hundreds of years. They needed more than simply *saying* they would obey. They needed the power to fulfill those words. We will look at that in Day Three, but first, what did they actually do to celebrate this Feast in the Old Testament? We will explore that in Day Two.

Lesson Five — Day Two

Celebrating the Feast of Weeks

The name *"Feast of Weeks"* refers to the fact that Israel's fourth feast occurred on the day after completion of seven weeks. The precise count of weeks began on the Sunday of the Feast of First fruits leading up to the Sunday of the Feast of Weeks, fifty days exactly (Leviticus 23:16–17). The New Testament uses the name "Pentecost" (Greek, *pentekoste*, "fiftieth") since it came on the fiftieth day after First Fruits. This Feast was also called the Feast of Harvest because it celebrated the wheat harvest, a time of rejoicing over God's provision. How did they celebrate this Feast? We will explore that now.

📖 God wanted His people to *"appear before the Lord"* in His chosen place three times a year, the second of which was the Feast of Weeks in the late Spring. What did God require them to do at this Feast according to Deuteronomy 16:10, 16–17?

📖 Who participated according to Deuteronomy 16:11?

📖 What did God require of them as found in Leviticus 23:21 and Numbers 28:26?

📖 What additional direction do you discover in Leviticus 23:16–17?

_____

_____

_____

God called all His people to join together, each family member, every servant, the Levites from the various communities spread throughout Israel, the fatherless and widow, many of whom would face greater need, as well as the stranger or foreigner in the land. The Feast provided an opportunity for them to remember what God had done and rejoice before the Lord, centering attention on Him and their relationship with Him. Worship to Him and thanksgiving for His abundant provision would fill this Feast. Part of their time together included a *"holy convocation"* or assembly to worship the Lord at the Tabernacle (and later the Temple). The people practiced a special day of rest, *"no laborious work"* being done on this day, so that all could participate wholeheartedly. He wanted their attention on Him and what He had done and given to them. Part of this time according to historians included the public reading of Ezekiel 1. The Lord directed His people not to come to the Feast *"empty-handed"* but with a generous offering out of what God had given, each *"as he is able, according to the blessing of the LORD your God which He has given you."* With the wheat harvest completed, the people rejoiced over the abundance God had given.

This voluntary or *"freewill offering"* would be combined with the required and unique new grain offering. God gave the priests specific instructions for this unique offering. He required that they offer *a wave offering of two loaves* of wheat bread mixed *with leaven*, a departure from the regular offerings that never allowed for leaven (see Leviticus 2:11; 6:17), though this offering was not placed on the fires of the altar. The daily bread that they ate normally contained leaven, and these two loaves reflected that as an offering of thanks for God's abundant provision. Each loaf weighed about five pounds.

📖 What additional offering did the Lord require as stipulated in Leviticus 23:18–19?

_____

_____

_____

Along with waving the bread offering, the Lord required the priests to bring a burnt offering composed of two young bulls, one ram, seven one year old male lambs plus a grain offering of fine flour mixed with olive oil along with drink offerings of wine. In addition, they offered a goat as a sin offering, *"to make atonement for you."*

The offerings raised and waved pictured the heart lifted up in thanks for the abundant harvest as well as the heart offered up in surrender like the burnt offerings, showing one totally consumed with the Lord. They must ever deal with sin God's way, making the sin offering for atonement. The priests also offered the daily required burnt offerings in the morning and in the afternoon, a reminder and picture of the continual dependence and surrender in following the Lord as their God.

> *Did You Know?*
> ## EZEKIEL AND PENTECOST
>
> On the day of Pentecost, the Jews read Ezekiel 1 as part of their worship assemblies. Ezekiel describes the vision of the creatures near God's throne, noting the flashes of lightning, a dark cloud, and sounds like roaring waters or the movement of a mighty army. He also describes seeing the majestic, brilliant throne of God surrounded by the appearance of a rainbow and the figure of a fiery-looking man with the radiance of the glory of God all around. That prepared Ezekiel for the message God commanded Him to proclaim. This vision resembled the vision at **Mount Sinai** (Exodus 19—24). The Jews connected the giving of the Law there with the timing of Pentecost. They heard and saw the Lord, which prepared them for the message of the covenant. In **Acts 2**, the disciples praying in the Temple (*"house"*) suddenly heard the noise of a *"violent, rushing wind"* or breath which filled the *"house."* They saw tongues or pillars *"as of fire,"* bright, burning, spreading out and resting on the head of each of the 120, all preparing them for proclaiming the message. They immediately experienced being *"filled with the Holy Spirit"* and began speaking many dialects telling *"the mighty deeds of God."*

Did You Know?
WHY LEAVENED LOAVES?

Questions sometimes arise over why the loaves offered at Pentecost contained leaven. The offerings on the altar never contained leaven (Leviticus 2:11; 6:17). One of the reasons for that concerned the corrupting nature of leaven. The offerings must ever be pure, uncorrupted, even as each animal must be without blemish or defect (Numbers 28:31). Why leaven in the Pentecost offerings? These loaves represented the daily bread of the people provided in abundance with the latest harvest. The Feast of Weeks gave opportunity to thank the Lord for His abundant provision in the full harvest. It may be noted that the offering of the loaves at Pentecost was waved before the Lord, not burned on the altar.

Did You Know?
THE FIRST FRUITS AND PENTECOST

The Lord connected the Feasts of First Fruits and Pentecost as the start and the close of the spring harvests, calling for an exact counting of days between them. During the Feast of First Fruits, the priests waved the first sheaf of the barley harvest before the Lord, thanking the Lord for and consecrating the entire harvest to Him. In the Feast of Weeks or Pentecost, the priest waved two loaves before the Lord as representative of the first fruits of the wheat harvest and the culmination of the entire fifty days of full growth and harvest. Both acknowledged and thanked the Lord as the provider, anticipating the harvest at First Fruits and reflecting back on the harvest at Pentecost.

📖 God also required a *"peace"* or *"fellowship offering."* What did God command the priests to do with the two lambs of the *"peace offering"* or *"fellowship offering"* according to Leviticus 23:20?

_____

_____

The people gave two lambs as a <u>peace offering</u> or <u>fellowship offering</u> to the priests who waved them before the Lord, a picture of their surrender to and dependence upon the Lord. Those lambs then served as food for the priests for their service in the Tabernacle or Temple. The priests belonged to the Lord in a unique way. As the people gave their offerings to the Lord, these holy (or set apart) offerings provided for the priests and their families. They could join in the peaceful fellowship of a people united in worshiping the one true God. The joy would be intensified by the purity and generosity of hearts following God together.

📖 According to Deuteronomy 16:12, what did God want them to remember as they celebrated this Feast? Why do you think this was important?

_____

_____

_____

_____

📖 What additional guideline did God give to the people in Leviticus 23:22? How does this relate to what God said in Deuteronomy 16:12?

_____

_____

_____

God called His people to remember from where the Lord had brought them, the years of slavery in Egypt from which the Lord had delivered them. That thought would help keep things in perspective. They would certainly tend to be more grateful knowing how far they had come as a nation and how much God had blessed them year by year. One regulation God gave them that had significant impact concerned reserving the corners of the harvest field and the gleanings *"for the needy and the alien,"* the foreigner who would have no roots and potentially have great need. God called His people to generosity in their offerings to Him, in their celebration together, and in their concern for the needs of others. As their Lord, He promised to provide and wanted their lives to reflect His care through their gratitude and generosity.

How did the celebration of the Feast of Weeks occur in New Testament days? We will begin to see that in Days Three and Four.

THE PROMISE OF PENTECOST

Lesson Five — **DAY THREE**

When we turn to the New Testament, we find the Feast of Weeks or Pentecost full of activity, especially as recorded in Acts 2. How did Jesus view this day? What did His disciples think of this Feast? As Jesus taught them the details of His work and what future days held, He spoke of a day when the work of the Holy Spirit would become more evident. He spoke to them of how they would be affected. Today, we will look at some of these teachings and promises from Jesus and how they connect to Pentecost.

📖 The first mention of the Holy Spirit in the ministry of Jesus is inseparably linked to the *"kingdom"* at hand and the call to *"repent,"* getting the heart ready for the Lord's presence. This mention of the Holy Spirit is found in the prophetic words of John the Baptist. What do you discover in Matthew 3:11?

_____

_____

_____

📖 How did Jesus see this prophecy? Read Jesus' words in Acts 1:5. With what did Jesus connect this, according to Acts 1:4?

_____

_____

_____

John prophesied that *"the kingdom of heaven is at hand"* and therefore people must be prepared. Repentance of sin must come first, setting the heart to receive the Lord, the Messiah to come. John then connected his ministry with the soon to be unveiled ministry of the Messiah. As John "the baptizer" baptized people *"with water"* so the Messiah would *"baptize you with the Holy Spirit and fire."* In speaking to His disciples forty days after His resurrection, just before He ascended back to heaven, Jesus connected this prophecy of John with what He had told them when He spoke of what *"the Father had promised."* That would occur *"not many days from now."* What other promises did Jesus make? Let's explore a few of those.

📖 The night before Jesus was crucified He spoke of the coming of the Holy Spirit. What did Jesus say to His disciples about the Holy Spirit? Look at John 14:16–20. What did Jesus promise?

_____

_____

_____

📖 What ministry would the Spirit fulfill in the disciples according to John 14:25–27?

_____

_____

Doctrine
"BAPTIZE... WITH THE HOLY SPIRIT AND FIRE"

To "baptize" means to identify or mark when understood in its primary meaning. *Baptizo*, "to baptize," meant to immerse as when one immersed cloth in a dye. The cloth is identified with or marked by a new color, a new identity. John the Baptist prophesied, and Jesus promised that He would baptize His followers with the Holy Spirit (see Matthew 3:11; Acts 1:5). Jesus said His followers would be marked by the Holy Spirit indwelling each—filling, controlling, influencing, and identifying each of them as belonging to Him for His witness. This "baptism" occurred on Pentecost Sunday (Acts 2:1–4). Since then believers, any who place faith in Jesus, are *"baptized"*—identified, immersed—into the Body of Christ by the Holy Spirit (Romans 8:9–17; 1 Corinthians 12:13; Ephesians 1:13–14; 4:4–6; 1 John 3:24; 4:13).

📖 What would be one of the main ministries of the Spirit according to John 15:26–27?

_____
_____
_____

> *Doctrine*
> ### THE UNITY OF THE SPIRIT
>
> In John 17, Jesus **prayed** for the unity of His disciples, that they would be one as He and the Father are one. He also prayed for their protection from the evil one, the one who divides. He prayed for all His disciples to be *"sanctified in truth,"* in His word (John 17:9–26). That prayer included all who believe today (John 17:20). God also calls us to *"preserve the unity of the Spirit"* (Ephesians 4:3). *"Preserve"* is a translation of the Greek word *tereo*, which focuses on guarding or watching over. That begins with **personal** dependence on the Spirit, since this unity is given and maintained by the Spirit's **power**. When one resists or quenches the Spirit by disobedience, power is disconnected and disunity with others soon follows. When one sins against another, unity is broken and that grieves the Holy Spirit. We must carefully guard against these enemy traps. Do nothing to disrupt or corrupt the unity between believers, for in this unity the testimony of Jesus is seen. Others know we belong to Jesus by our love for one another, the love that is the fruit of His Spirit (John 13:35; Galatians 5:22–23). This unity of the Spirit **points** others to Jesus Christ and brings glory to Him.

Jesus said He would not leave His disciples *"as orphans,"* but through His Spirit would continue this closest of relationships. He promised to ask the Father who would in turn give the disciples *"another Helper"* who would be *"with you forever."* This Helper is *"the Spirit of truth,"* never deceitful, always speaking and acting in line with the truth, with the truthfulness of God. Not only would this Holy Spirit be **with** the disciples, He would also *"be in you"*—residing **in** each disciple giving each eternal life. He is now with and in everyone who believes on His name, just as He was with Christ's disciples (*"I will come to you . . . I in you."*). The Holy Spirit would teach the things of Jesus, bearing witness of Him so that the disciples could effectively bear witness of Jesus to others. By the Spirit's working, each believer would also experience the peace Jesus promised.

📖 On Resurrection Sunday, Jesus appeared to ten of His disciples plus the two from Emmaus. In that meeting, He spoke of the Holy Spirit. What did He say, according to John 20:19–22?

_____
_____

📖 What instructions did Jesus give about the days ahead in Luke 24:49?

_____
_____

📖 We have seen some of what Jesus said on the day He ascended. On that occasion, what further promises did Jesus give concerning the Holy Spirit? Read Acts 1:3–9, noting verses 6–8 in particular. Note how He connected this with the upcoming days (Pentecost was ten days away).

_____
_____

We reviewed this Resurrection Sunday event in the previous lesson by looking at the Feast of First Fruits.. Consider the connections of First Fruits to the Feast of Pentecost. On Resurrection Sunday, after Jesus made it obvious He was real and resurrected; He explained everything that had happened in the light of the Old Testament Scriptures. As the Father sent Him, so Jesus that night was sending His disciples, giving them His commission to tell the message of Jesus and of repentance and forgiveness of sins through Him.

In giving them this commission, Jesus did something very unique. He breathed on them and said, *"Receive the Holy Spirit."* Did they receive the Spirit at that moment? No, because we find Him forty days later commanding them to tarry in Jerusalem until He sent *"the Promise of My Father"* when they would be *"endued with power from on high"* by the Holy Spirit (Luke 24:49; Acts 1:5, 8).

First Fruits spoke of the beginning of the harvest and the preparation for the fullness of that harvest. Pentecost pointed to the bringing in of the harvest, the promise of First Fruits beginning to be fulfilled in the joy of the full Pentecost harvest.

Jesus spoke of His disciples being *"baptized with the Holy Spirit not many days from now."* That work of the Spirit would identify them with Jesus and empower them as witnesses of Jesus. Jesus commissioned them to communicate the message of His life, death, resurrection, forgiveness of sins, and eternal life through faith in Him. From Jerusalem that witness would extend to the ends of the earth.

What connection did the Resurrection Sunday encounter have with Pentecost? Where did the Holy Spirit fit into these events? Consider this parallel. Christ is the Creator (John 1:1–3, 10; Colossians 1:16–17). In the Garden of Eden in the first Creation, He breathed into the face of Adam who became a living soul. On Resurrection Sunday night, Jesus breathed into the faces of His disciples, commanding them to receive the Holy Spirit. They did not receive His Spirit that night. That occurred fifty days later during the Feast of Pentecost. The Resurrection Day encounter is a preview of the start of the New Creation; Christ is risen from the dead, the first fruits of the resurrection, the beginning of a new day. Jesus is saying in essence, "when the Holy Spirit comes, receive Him as though He were My very breath, because He is. We are one. You are part of the New Creation in Christ." The disciples did not grasp this until after Pentecost. Under the teaching of the Spirit, they began to piece together all the things Jesus had done and said. They saw how His death and resurrection fulfilled Old Testament prophecies and promises.

- There were fifty days from the Feast of First Fruits to the Feast of Pentecost. What occurred during the first forty days after Jesus resurrection, according to Acts 1:1–3?

  _____
  _____

- What did Jesus do on Day 40, according to Luke 24:49–51 and Acts 1:4–9?

  _____
  _____
  _____

- What did the disciples do from Day 40 to the Feast of Pentecost, according to Luke 24:52–53 and Acts 1:10–26?

  _____
  _____
  _____

After Jesus appeared to the disciples on Resurrection Sunday, He appeared five other times in the forty day period before His Ascension. On Day 40, Jesus led them to Bethany, a village on the Mount of Olives, where He focused their attention on their calling—to be witnesses of Him starting in Jerusalem, and going into Judea, Samaria, and to the ends of the earth. To do that they must follow His instruction, not focusing yet on the kingdom to be restored to Israel, but intent on proclaiming the message

Did You Know?

THE FORTY DAYS AFTER JESUS' RESURRECTION

Jesus resurrected on Sunday, the day of the Feast of First fruits. He appeared five times that day to different disciples. Over the next 39 days, He appeared five other times—

1) eight days after His resurrection to the eleven disciples with Thomas (John 20:26–31),

2) to more than 500 believers at one time (1 Corinthians 15:6—possibly the occasion in Galilee in which He gave the Great Commission as recorded in Matthew 28:16–20),

3) to James the half-brother of Jesus (1 Corinthians 15:7),

4) to the seven disciples on the shore of Galilee (John 21:1–25), and

5) to the disciples at His ascension (Luke 24:49–52; Acts 1:3–11).

of Jesus and faith in Him. He assured them of the coming and empowering of His Spirit, *"the Promise of My Father."* Jesus lifted His hands and blessed His disciples and then ascended, likely into the Shekinah Cloud of Glory, and then He exited earth. The disciples hearing and seeing this wholeheartedly *"worshiped Him"* as He departed into heaven.

After hearing the *"two men in white clothing"* promise that this Jesus would return in the same way He had gone into heaven, the eleven disciples returned to the upper room where they were staying. There with several men and women, including Jesus' mother Mary and *"His brothers,"* they spent extended time in prayer. That time in prayer continued day after day with about 120 involved. Part of that time also included *"praising and blessing God"* in the temple, most likely referring to the daily hours of prayer centered around the offering of incense at 9:00 AM and 3:00 PM (see for example, Luke 1:9–10). As they prayed, they sought the Lord about Judas' replacement and chose Matthias. The time of the Feast of Pentecost approached. What would this Feast bring? We will see in Day Four.

Lesson Five — DAY FOUR

THE POWER OF PENTECOST

Did You Know?
THE TEMPLE AREA

The Temple located on Mount Moriah in Jerusalem was surrounded by a platform built by Herod, measuring over 900 feet by 1000 feet, almost 35 acres. Surrounding the platform was a succession of porticoes. On the east side stood Solomon's Porch, about 50 feet wide with 3 rows of white marble columns about 40 feet high covered with a wooden roof. Included in these were markets for sacrificial items. There visitors came; rabbis often gathered their students, and several synagogue congregations met on the Sabbath. At the age of 12, Jesus had His first discussions with the Jewish leaders in this Temple area (Luke 2:43–50). On the south side stood the two-storied Royal Porch, 600 feet long by 100 feet wide. The Sanhedrin met there. Estimates of how many the entire platform could hold are from 100,000 to 250,000 people. Many would have crowded in during Feast times. This is the setting for Pentecost in Acts 2 and for continued ministry there by the early church. It could have easily been the place of the 3000 being baptized on Pentecost Sunday (Acts 2:41, 46; 3:1–26; 4:1–3; 5:20–32, 42; 21:26—22:29).

What occurred at the Feast of Weeks/Pentecost in Acts 2? How did these events connect with the celebrations of the Feast of Weeks/Pentecost from years past? In the account in Acts, what new insights can we glean from the celebration of Pentecost by the disciples, the followers of Jesus the Messiah? How can we apply those insights to our walk with Him today? We will begin to explore these matters now.

📖 The fiftieth day arrived. The Feast of Pentecost in Jerusalem saw multitudes from many nations. What occurred this day? Read Acts 2:1–16 and answer the following question? What time were the disciples gathered together according to Acts 2:15? Compare Exodus 30:7 and Luke 1:8–10 for what occurred in the morning at the Temple. Remember that this Sunday is a Feast day and a Sabbath rest day for a holy convocation.

_____
_____
_____
_____

📖 Where were they gathered according to Acts 2:1 and 2:2? Notice the word *"house"* and compare 1 Kings 8:10–11.

_____
_____
_____

📖 What did they hear as recorded in Acts 2:2? Compare the sound the disciples would have heard in John 20:22 when Jesus *"breathed (Greek—emphusao) on them."*

_____

104   FOLLOWING GOD – LIFE PRINCIPLES FOR WORSHIP FROM THE FEASTS OF ISRAEL

📖 What did they see according to Acts 2:3? Compare Exodus 40:38 and 2 Chronicles 7:1–3 and record any connections you see.

📖 What did they experience according to Acts 2:4a? Compare 1 Corinthians 6:19–20 and record your insights.

The 120 were gathered around 9:00 AM in the *"house,"* a term that referred to the Temple, the *"house of the LORD."* The morning burnt offering and incense offering occurred at this hour in which the people gathered for *"prayer."* Since this is a Feast day, a day for a *"holy convocation"* in which no one did any work, it is likely that all in Jerusalem were gathered at the Temple for this time of prayer. As the 120 prayed they heard *"a noise like a violent rushing wind"* filling *"the whole house."* The word translated *"wind"* (*pnoe*) could be translated *"breath"* as it is in Acts 17:25. This can be seen as the fulfillment of what Jesus did when He breathed on the disciples telling them to receive the Holy Spirit, for in that moment *"tongues as of fire"* rested on each of the 120 and *"they were all filled with the Holy Spirit."*

As in the Tabernacle and Temple of old, the Spirit of God seen as a pillar of fire took up residence upon and in these 120, each person becoming a *"temple of the Holy Spirit."* At this moment Jesus fulfilled the promise He made to His disciples as recorded in Luke 24:49: *And behold, I am sending forth the promise of My Father upon you; but you are to stay in the city until you are clothed with power from on high.* As part of fulfilling this promise, Christ baptized them with the Holy Spirit and fire. To baptize is to immerse, the picture of identifying one with that in which he is baptized. The disciples entered into an internal and eternal identity with the Spirit of God as He took up residence within each of them. John baptized with water, identifying those preparing for the coming kingdom of the Messiah. Jesus baptized with the Spirit, identifying those who were now one with Him, believers indwelt by His very Spirit. What would these people then do?

📖 What did the 120 begin to do, according to Acts 2:4b?

📖 Who heard these languages (dialects), and from where did these people come according to Acts 2:5, 9–11?

Did You Know?
OUTPOURING AND HARVESTING

How does the harvest celebration of Pentecost in the Old Testament connect with the coming of the Holy Spirit in the New Testament? When the apostle Peter sought to explain the coming of the Holy Spirit on Pentecost, he quoted the passage from Joel 2:28–29 referring to the outpouring of the Spirit. Immediately before that passage on the outpouring of the Holy Spirit, Joel spoke about the outpouring of abundant rains leading to *"threshing floors full of wheat,"* abundant food, and exuberant worship by God's people (2:23–24, 26). Pentecost in the New Testament continued to celebrate the wheat harvest, then in Acts 2 we see the outpouring of the Spirit, exuberant worship, and the abundant harvest of the 3,000 believers—beginning the fulfillment of Joel's promise that *"whoever calls on the name of the Lord shall be saved"* (2:28, 29, 32). Pentecost was a celebration of the wheat harvest and was called *"the day of the first fruits"* in reference to the wheat (Numbers 28:26). In the New Testament, God poured out His Spirit, and with this pouring came an abundant harvest of people into the church, the first fruits of the newly born church (Acts 2:39–41; cf. John 4:34–42; Matthew 9:35–38).

📖 What did the people from various nations hear according to Acts 2:6–8, 11?

_____
_____
_____

📖 What was their response to what they heard according to Acts 2:6, 12–13?

_____
_____
_____

📖 According to Acts 2:14–36, what did Peter say concerning all that occurred the morning of the Feast of Pentecost?

_____
_____
_____
_____

📖 What did Peter say about the Holy Spirit? Look at Acts 2:33, 38–39 and record your insights.

_____
_____
_____
_____

📖 How did the people respond to Peter's message according to Acts 2:37–41?

_____
_____

Put Yourself In Their Shoes
"THREE THOUSAND WORSHIPERS"

At Mount Sinai, on the Day of Pentecost around 1445 BC, Moses and the people met the Lord and heard His word. Soon after, many revealed their unbelief in what they had seen and heard and instead reveled in the worship of a golden calf. When Moses confronted the people, many continued their very public idolatrous and immoral worship of that golden calf. That day 3000 died under the judgment of God (Exodus 32:1–28). Acts 2:41 speaks of 3000 who heard Peter, *"received his word,"* and were then *"baptized"* in public declaration of their faith and worship of Jesus as Lord and Savior. When the people of Acts 2 began reflecting over the events of the Day of Pentecost, surely they saw the wonder of grace on those who just over 50 days earlier, had been part of the crowds standing before Jesus crying *"crucify Him."* Now, with their hearts and lives, they were crying *"worship Him."*

Those filled with the Holy Spirit began to speak in various languages, even individual dialects (Acts 2:6—Greek, *dialektos*), including the languages of the Parthians, Medes, Elamites, Mesopotamians, Judeans, as well as those of Cappadocia, Pontus, Asia, Phrygia, Pamphylia, Egypt, Libya, Cyrene, Rome, Crete, and Arabia. They heard the 120 *"speaking of the mighty deeds of God."* The people stood amazed, wondering and discussing what this could mean. Some mocked them, saying they were affected by wine. Peter confidently declared this had no connection to wine, but rather to a fulfillment of what Joel prophesied; it was the pouring out of the Holy Spirit because of the work of the crucified, resurrected, exalted Messiah Jesus. The promise of the Father, the Holy Spirit, was seen in His working that very morning. Anyone who would repent and turn to this Jesus as Messiah, Lord, and Savior would receive forgiveness of sins and the indwelling of this same Holy Spirit. Many who heard were *"pierced to the heart,"* or *"smitten in conscience"* and cried out *"what shall we do?"* About three thousand *"received his word and were baptized,"* identifying themselves with Jesus and His followers.

📖 What occurred after this? What evidence do you find of the work of the Spirit and of a harvest of people coming into the family of God? Record your insights from the following verses:

Acts 2:47 _____

_____

4:4 _____

_____

4:33 _____

_____

5:14, 42 _____

_____

6:7 _____

_____

9:31 _____

_____

11:19–26 _____

_____

13:52 _____

_____

14:26–27 _____

_____

Immediately after the Feast of Pentecost, the church continued to grow. Three thousand were added from the original 120 followed by five thousand men, meaning probably more than ten thousand others came, as wives and children placed faith in Christ along with the men. The apostles and disciples in the church continued to give witness of the resurrection of Christ. The grace of God worked in them and through them to see multitudes come to Christ. The church increased *"greatly in Jerusalem,"* then began to spread *"throughout all Judea and Galilee and Samaria."* Other passages tell the story of Peter in Caesarea with the Gentiles. In Antioch *"considerable numbers were brought to the Lord"* and taught the Scriptures by Paul and Barnabas. Then, Paul and Barnabas saw many come to faith in Christ as they traveled the various cities in Asia Minor (modern Turkey). What Jesus said about the work of the Holy Spirit began to be fulfilled as obedient disciples spoke the message of salvation in Christ to Jews and Gentiles from Jerusalem, to Judea, Samaria, and into the ends of the earth.

📖 What connection do you see between Leviticus 23:22, Acts 2:44–47 and 4:32–37?

_____

_____

_____

_____

> *Did You Know?*
> ### PENTECOST AS BABEL REVERSED
>
> Some see the events of Pentecost Sunday as a movement of Babel reversed. In Genesis 11:1–9, God came down where all were gathered in one place. There at Babel, He confused the one language into many and the people scattered. In Acts 2, God came down where all were gathered in one place at Pentecost, and the 120 spoke many different languages and dialects that united all to understand about Jesus. They spoke one unified message about the mighty deeds of God. At Babel, they spoke one unified message about the mighty deeds of man. God had to confuse the languages to restrain them from carrying out their wayward plans to make a name for themselves. At Pentecost, God brought clarity to everyone as He released His disciples to carry out the wondrous Christ-centered plans of the Father and glorify the name of Jesus. From Babel they went to the ends of the earth, most holding on to their misguided thoughts and glorifying man. From Jerusalem, the disciples went to the ends of the earth with the message of life in Christ, what the angel called *"the whole message of this Life"* (Acts 5:20). They continually glorified Jesus Christ. The Lord Jesus still reverses lives, ends confusion, and unites hearts today.

📖 What aspects of the Feast of Pentecost do you see being fulfilled in these events?

_____
_____
_____

Included in the guidelines for the Feast of Weeks or Pentecost is the regulation about reserving the corners of the fields and the *"gleanings"* for the poor, the stranger or foreigner, as well as the widows and orphans. God showed His concern for these and wanted His people to show care for those in need. When we turn to the New Testament, we see the new believers sharing with one another and looking out for one another as needs arose. This was not a general fund for the entire community, but for those in the church, *"the congregation of those who believed"* who had needs. This is not a surrender of all personal property, but the voluntary giving to needs as they arose. This is clear in the account in Acts 5 in which Peter told Ananias that his property remained his while unsold and continued *"under your control"* after it sold. These believers, filled with the Spirit showed the generous heart of God and took care of one another, a fulfillment of the Lord's desire in the Feast of Weeks or Pentecost.

📖 The offering of two leavened loaves occurred on the morning of the Feast of Pentecost. Is there a fuller meaning to this than simply offering the bread of the harvest? What occurred in Acts 2, Acts 10, and Acts 19:1–7 that relates to "Pentecost" and a "harvest"? Note your thoughts.

_____
_____
_____
_____

📖 What did Paul later tell the Christians in Ephesus about God's work among Gentiles? Read Ephesians 2:11–22 and 3:3–7 and summarize your insights in light of what God did in the Pentecost events.

_____
_____
_____
_____

📖 What further insights do you discover from Revelation 5:8–10, especially verse 9, concerning those who will worship before the Lamb, the Lord Jesus?

_____
_____
_____

In Acts 2, 10, and 19, a great multitude came to faith in Christ and received the Holy Spirit to indwell forever. The 3,000 in Acts 2 were Jews and those in Cornelius' house were Gentiles, while those in Ephesus could have been either, but all received the same Holy Spirit like those in Acts 2. Here we see

Did You Know?
THE HARVEST OF THE NATIONS BEGINNING AT PENTECOST

Jesus often spoke of the turning of people to follow Him as Lord and Savior in terms of *"the harvest"* (Matthew 9:35–38; John 4:34–42). Acts 2:5 speaks of men *"from every nation"* gathered at Pentecost and gives a representative list (2:9–11) related to the Table of Nations in Genesis 10 (children of Shem, Ham, and Japheth). The book of Acts follows a general geographic pattern of witnessing of Jesus from Jerusalem to Judea (Acts 2—7) to Samaria (and Ethiopia) (8) to the ends of the earth (9—28), corresponding to the sons of Shem (Jerusalem, Judea, and Samaria), the sons of Ham (Ethiopia), and the sons of Japheth (from Caesarea to Europe and *"the ends of the earth"*—Acts 1:8; 13:47). In Stephen's witness, he speaks of seeing *"the Son of Man"* (Acts 7:56) whom Daniel prophesied would be *"given dominion and glory and a kingdom, that all peoples, nations, and languages should serve Him"* (Daniel 7:14). *"The harvest"* of the nations continues as we walk in "Acts 29."

108 FOLLOWING GOD – LIFE PRINCIPLES FOR WORSHIP FROM THE FEASTS OF ISRAEL

that of which Paul spoke in Ephesians 2. The Gentiles, formerly *"excluded from the commonwealth of Israel, and strangers to the covenants of promise"* have been *"brought near by the blood of Christ."* He made both groups into one, creating *"one new man,"* who has *"access in one Spirit to the Father."* Jews and Gentiles are now *"fellow citizens,"* both part of *"God's household,"* part of *"a holy temple in the Lord."*

When the priests on Pentecost morning offered two loaves, they offered leavened loaves, unlike any other offering. Many see this as a picture of the newly born church composed of *"two loaves"* now made one in Christ. Jews and Gentiles are still marked by "leaven," a picture of the influence of sin, but they are brought near to God and cleansed by the blood of Jesus. Two loaves offered, but from one harvest, the harvest that was pictured in Jesus' first fruits resurrection. He died on the cross to save Jews and Gentiles, terms that include people from *"every tribe and tongue and people and nation."*

What can we learn from viewing the celebration of the Feast of Weeks/Pentecost? How are we to apply the truths found in this Feast? What spiritual and relational realities does God want in the life of each of His children? We will see certain applications in Day Five.

ANSWERING THE CALL OF THE FEAST OF PENTECOST

Lesson Five — **DAY FIVE**

In Their Shoes
THE EARLY CHURCH AND UNITY OF THE SPIRIT

Jesus fulfilled the Feast of First Fruits in His resurrection. For us today, the fulfillment of the Feast of First Fruits occurs now and in the future—now as we walk *"in newness of life,"* in His resurrection power. In the future, it will be fully manifested in the resurrection of believers. In Israel's calendar and in the harvest season, First Fruits is linked to Pentecost. In the life of the Church, the two Feasts link in spiritual fulfillment. We **walk** daily in resurrection power and promise, and we **witness** of that in the power of the Spirit. The fulfillment of Pentecost occurs today as believers walk in the power of the Spirit and in Spirit-filled, Spirit-directed, Spirit-empowered witness to who Jesus is and what Jesus promises He can do. How should we answer the call of the Feast of Pentecost today? What application points can we make to our daily walk?

📖 What did Jesus promise His disciples about the work of the Spirit and their witness? Read Luke 12:11–12?

_____

_____

📖 How did the disciples see this promise and this Feast being fulfilled in their daily lives? What do you discover in Acts 4:8–12?

_____

_____

_____

The book of Acts often speaks of the unity of the Spirit among believers. They were united on Pentecost Sunday as the Spirit indwelt and filled them. They spoke one message—*"the mighty deeds of God"* (2:4, 11) and received one salvation (*"forgiveness of sins"* and the indwelling of *"the Holy Spirit"*—2:38). They fellowshipped and ministered and prayed in *"one accord"* (2:42–47; 4:24; 5:12). They *"were of one heart and one soul"* and shared freely with one another as needs arose (4:32–35). As they testified about the resurrection of Jesus, *"abundant grace was upon them all"* (4:33). Later, even in the midst of questions about the gospel and ministry, they carefully clarified the meaning of the gospel, *"having become of one mind"* being led by the Holy Spirit (Acts 15:25–29).

📖 What occurred with all the disciples in Acts 4:31?

_____
_____

📖 How did this reality occur in the lives of those in Acts 6:1–7? Note especially verses 3, 5, and 7.

_____
_____
_____

Jesus told His disciples that they would have many opportunities to speak the message of who He is as the Messiah, the Lord and Savior. Some would oppose them and the message. He promised that in those situations, the Spirit of God would give each what to say, according to the need of the moment. They certainly experienced that on the Day of Pentecost as Peter explained the meaning of all that occurred. Many came to personal faith in Jesus as the Messiah and Savior. Later, when the Jewish authorities arrested Peter and John, Peter, *"filled with the Holy Spirit,"* gave an explanation of who Jesus is and how His crucifixion and resurrection applied to the lame man who had been healed. He declared with boldness concerning Jesus, *"there is salvation in no one else; for there is no other name under heaven that has been given among men, by which we must be saved"* (Acts 4:12).

After being released and reporting the threats from the officials about speaking of this Jesus, Peter and John, along with those gathered, prayed, asking the Lord for boldness in declaring the message of the crucified, resurrected Jesus. God answered, *"and they were all filled with the Holy Spirit, and they spoke the word of God with boldness."* Pentecost continued to be fulfilled with a harvest of people coming into the church—believing in Jesus as Lord and Savior, made children of God, indwelt by His Holy Spirit, and showing His character in their actions and words. This reality continued to be revealed as the church grew in numbers. When a disagreement arose over the care of the widows, the apostles looked for Spirit-filled men to serve in that needed ministry. As a result, these men took care of the ministry as well as being faithful witnesses of Christ. The church continued to grow in even greater ways as they followed the leadership of the Spirit.

📖 What applications do you see for today in Ephesians 5:18–21?

_____
_____
_____
_____

📖 What additional insights do you see in Ephesians 6:17–20?

_____
_____
_____
_____

> *"Do not become anxious about how or what you should speak . . . for the Holy Spirit will teach you in that very hour what you ought to say"*
>
> Luke 12:11–12

📖 What do you discover in Colossians 4:2–6?

_____

_____

_____

_____

Paul instructed the Ephesian believers in God's will for each Christian—to be *"filled with the Spirit"*—literally, "be being filled," continuously submitting to the leadership and empowering of the Holy Spirit. The result would be self-control, a joyous heart filled with a song, continually giving thanks to the Father, and living with a servant's heart toward one another. Paul asked these same believers to live in the strength of the Lord and with *"the armor of God."* That included the *"helmet of salvation"* and *"the sword of the Spirit, which is the word of God."* That sword of the word should be the basis of all praying, as the Spirit directs and empowers prayer for *"all the saints"* (all believers), especially for the confident witness of those like Paul as they spoke the message of the gospel or good news of Jesus. Paul asked the Colossian believers to pray for open doors *"for the word"* and the ability to speak it clearly as he ought. He also urged those believers to speak *"with grace"* and wisdom, knowing how to answer each situation, each encounter, each conversation with others.

📖 The apostle Peter, who experienced the work of the Holy Spirit on Pentecost and beyond and who saw the Lord empower his witness wrote to believers concerning these things. Read 1 Peter 3:8–17. What do you see about *being* a witness?

_____

_____

_____

_____

📖 What do you see about *speaking* in witness of who Jesus is?

_____

_____

_____

_____

Peter experienced the working of the Spirit of God, the effective communication of what he had seen and heard from the Lord Jesus. He urged his readers to live out love for one another within the church in words and deeds. That lifestyle should be carried into all relationships of daily life. Some will oppose the Christian and the message of salvation through Jesus. Some will threaten Christians. The answer: *"sanctify"* or set apart *"Christ as Lord in your hearts"*—let your heart be the place of worship, of heart-to-heart interaction with Christ. Live in loving obedience to His Lordship in every detail of life. Then you will be ready to give a clear answer for why you follow Jesus and why you believe what He says, why you have a confident hope in Him. On Pentecost Sunday, Peter had given a clear reason for what they were doing and why they were speaking of the *"the mighty deeds*

📖 *Doctrine*
THE REALITY OF "ONENESS"

T. W. Hunt has said that God's favorite number is "one." Jesus said, *"I and the Father are one,"* expressing the essential oneness they share. That same oneness exists between the Son and the Spirit and between the Father and the Spirit. We see that expressed in their working, and we see that in the church born of God. Jesus prayed to His Father for His followers *"that they may be one, even as We are"* (John 17:11, 21–22). The early church was marked by *"one mind,"* *"one heart and soul,"* often praying with *"one accord"* (Acts 2:46; 4:24, 32). There were times in which it took time to discuss and search the Scriptures to become of *"one mind"* (Acts 15:25). We are *"one body"* in Christ (1 Corinthians 10:17; 12:13, 27; Ephesians 3:6; 5:30). Ephesians 4:4–6 celebrates this truth expressed by the Father, Son, and Spirit, *"there is one body and one Spirit, . . . you were called in one hope . . . one Lord, one faith, one baptism, one God and Father of all who is over all and through all and in all."* God calls us to express that through oneness in sharing the gospel and in relationships with one another (Philippians 1:27; 2:2–5; 4:2; 1 Peter 3:8).

> *Ask the Lord to make you an effective witness, experiencing the fullness of His Spirit in your lifestyle and the power of the Spirit in effectively speaking the message of who Jesus is, of His claims as Lord, and of His call to place faith in Him and follow obediently!*

of God" (Acts 2:11, see 2:14–40). Maintain a good conscience so that no one can unjustly accuse you. Do what is right whatever the cost, even if suffering is involved. *Be* a real witness of what you believe and *speak* a clear witness of what you believe.

APPLY **What about You?**—Are you a follower and disciple of Jesus Christ? Have you been born again? Are you walking under the control or filling of the Spirit of God? How is your testimony to others? Do people see in you the life of a Christ follower? How is your witness to others—family, neighbors, coworkers, fellow students, members of the community? **Pause** and reflect. **Pray.** Ask the Lord to make you an effective witness (even this day), experiencing the reality of Pentecost—the fullness of His Spirit in your lifestyle and the power of the Spirit in effectively speaking the message of who Jesus is, of His claims as Lord, and of His call to place faith in Him and follow obediently. Call people to trust and receive what Jesus can do in any life.

📖 What does God want from His family today? What did Jesus say would mark His disciples according to John 13:35? Record your insights and then walk through the **Stop and Apply** exercise.

_____
_____

APPLY **"How to Treat One Another"**—Jesus said His disciples would be marked by love for one another. This is *agape* love, a love that chooses to benefit others regardless of how one feels. It is God's kind of love, the fruit of the Spirit empowered by the Spirit. How are you doing in showing love to fellow believers and to those who are not yet believers?

1. As a check-up, walk through the chart at the end of this lesson, "How to Treat One Another" Where there is need for repentance, repent. Where there is need for clearing up relationships, go to that person and make things right. To help you, there is a second chart entitled "How to Deal with Sin" that gives some basic guidelines.

2. As a step-forward, *pray* in line with 1 Thessalonians 3:12, *"And may the Lord cause you to increase and abound in love for one another, and for all men"* **Learn** in line with 1 Thessalonians 4:9, *"for you yourselves are taught by God to love one another."* Ask the Spirit of God to do this in your life—increase and abound in love and learn how to love God's way, not only for believers, but for *"all men."*

After walking through these steps, record any thoughts, insights or a prayer concerning what God has shown you. Then, reflect on the prayer given here and offer your prayer to the Lord.

_____
_____
_____
_____

"**Lord**, thank You for making provision for me to come to You as part of a leavened loaf, influenced by evil, but forgiven and cleansed through Your blood on the cross. Thank You that I can be a part of the Body of Christ, part of that *"one new man"* to show and tell others who You are, what You can do, and Your offer of salvation from sin and the gift of eternal life. May I walk in the fullness of Your Spirit so that I faithfully and clearly declare Your message—in the way I live my life and in the words that I speak. May I be part of increasing the harvest of believers as I help 'cultivate' the soil, 'plant' the seed of Your Word, 'water' the seeds already planted, or even have a part in 'harvesting' the sheaves of new believers. May You be pleased, glorified, and magnified by my life under Your Spirit's control. In Jesus' name, Amen."

HOW TO TREAT "ONE ANOTHER"
God's Commands About Blessing, Protecting, and Building Up Others

COMMAND	SCRIPTURE
Do not steal, deal falsely, nor lie to one another	Leviticus 19:11
"You shall not hate your fellow countryman [brother] in your heart."	Leviticus 19:17
"You shall not take vengeance, nor bear any grudge against the sons of your people."	Leviticus 19:18a
"… You shall love your neighbor as yourself; I am the LORD."	Leviticus 19:18b
Do not wrong one another in business matters	Leviticus 25:14–17
"Two are better than one" Their work together is profitable. Each can lift up the other if one falls.	Ecclesiastes 4:9–12
"Be at peace with one another"	Mark 9:50
Do not seek glory or honor from one another	John 5:44
"…you also ought to wash one another's feet. For I gave you an example…"	John 13:14–15
"Love one another"	John 13:34–35; 2 John 1:5
"This is My commandment, that you love one another, just as I have loved you."	John 15:12; 1 John 3:10–11
"Be devoted to one another in brotherly love"	Romans 12:10
"Give preference to one another in honor"	Romans 12:10
"Be of the same mind toward one another"	Romans 12:16;15:5
"Respect what is right in the sight of all men"	Romans 12:17
"If possible, so far as it depends on you be at peace with all men"	Romans 12:18
"Owe nothing … except to love one another"	Romans 13:8
"Let us not judge one another anymore"	Romans 14:13
"Let us pursue the things which make for peace and the building up of one another"	Romans 14:19
"We… ought to bear the weaknesses of those without strength and not just please ourselves. Let each of us please his neighbor for his good, to his edification."	Romans 15:1–2 Proverbs 17:17
May God "grant you to be of the same mind with one another according to Christ Jesus; that with one accord you may with one voice glorify" Him.	Romans 15:5–6; Psalm 133:1
"Wherefore, accept one another, just as Christ also accepted us to the glory of God."	Romans 15:7
"[You are] able also to admonish one another."	Romans 15:14
"Greet one another with a holy kiss."	Romans 16:16
Do not "become arrogant/puffed up in behalf of one against the other" (taking sides).	1 Corinthians 4:6
Do not pursue lawsuits against one another. Do not wrong and defraud one another.	1 Corinthians 6:5–8

COMMAND	SCRIPTURE
"Stop depriving one another [in marriage], except by agreement for a time that you may devote yourselves to prayer…"	1 Corinthians 7:5
Do not wound another's conscience or cause another to stumble by what you do or say, but seek the good of your brother or your neighbor.	1 Corinthians 8:7–13; 10:23–33
"Have the same care for one another."	1 Corinthians 12:25–27
"Through love serve one another."	Galatians 5:13
"Do not bite and devour one another."	Galatians 5:15
"Do not challenge one another."	Galatians 5:26
"Do not envy one another."	Galatians 5:26
"Bear one another's burdens."	Galatians 6:2
"Do good to all men, and especially to those who are of the household of the faith."	Galatians 6:10
"With all humility and gentleness, with patience, showing forbearance to one another in love."	Ephesians 4:2
"Laying aside falsehood, speak truth, each one of you, with his neighbor."	Ephesians 4:25; Zechariah 8:16
Labor "in order that [you] may have something to share with him who has need."	Ephesians 4:28
Speak words of grace that build up, not "unwholesome" words that tear down.	Ephesians 4:29
"Be kind to one another."	Ephesians 4:32
"[Be] tenderhearted [to one another]."	Ephesians 4:32
"Forgiving each other, just as God in Christ also has forgiven you"	Ephesians 4:32
"…Be filled with the Spirit, speaking to one another in psalms and hymns and spiritual songs."	Ephesians 5:18–19
"Be subject to one another in the fear of Christ."	Ephesians 5:21
"[Be] of the same mind, maintaining the same love, united in spirit, intent on one purpose."	Philippians 2:2
"With humility of mind let each of you regard one another as more important than himself."	Philippians 2:3
"Do not lie to one another."	Colossians 3:9
"Bearing with one another"	Colossians 3:13
"Forgiving each other, whoever has a complaint against anyone"	Colossians 3:13
"Let the word of Christ richly dwell within you, with all wisdom teaching and admonishing one another…"	Colossians 3:16
"We give thanks to God…making mention of you in our prayers." "Brethren, pray for us."	1 Thessalonians 1:2; 5:25
"May the Lord cause you to increase and abound in love for one another …"	1 Thessalonians 3:12
"May the Lord cause you to increase and abound in love … for all men"	1 Thessalonians 3:12
"Excel still more" in love for one another.	1 Thessalonians 4:10
"Comfort one another with these words."	1 Thessalonians 4:18

HOW TO TREAT "ONE ANOTHER" (CONT.)
God's Commands About Blessing, Protecting, and Building Up Others

COMMAND	SCRIPTURE
"Encourage one another…just as you are doing."	1 Thessalonians 5:11
"Build up one another, just as you are doing."	1 Thessalonians 5:11
"Live in peace with one another."	1 Thessalonians 5:13
"Admonish the unruly, encourage the fainthearted, help the weak, be patient with all men."	1 Thessalonians 5:14; Proverbs 27:5–6
"See that no one repays another with evil for evil, but always seek after that which is good for one another and for all men."	1 Thessalonians 5:15
"Remind them… to be ready for every good deed, to malign no one, to be uncontentious, gentle, showing every consideration for all men."	Titus 3:1–2
"Encourage one another day after day…lest any one of you be hardened by the deceitfulness of sin."	Hebrews 3:13; 10:25
"Stimulate one another to love and good deeds."	Hebrews 10:24
"Let love of the brethren continue."	Hebrews 13:1
"Do not neglect to show hospitality to strangers, for by this some have entertained angels."	Hebrews 13:2
"Remember the prisoners [in prison for their faith], as though in prison with them, and those who are ill-treated, since you … also are in the body."	Hebrews 13:3
Care for widows, orphans and others "in their distress" [times of pressure, affliction, and need].	James 1:27
Do not show favoritism or partiality to one another.	James 2:1–9
"Do not speak against one another, brethren."	James 4:11
"Do not complain, brethren, against one another."	James 5:9
"Confess your sins to one another."	James 5:16
"Pray for one another."	James 5:16
"Fervently love one another from the heart."	1 Peter 1:22; 4:8
"Not returning evil for evil, or insult for insult, but giving a blessing instead"	1 Peter 3:9; Zechariah 7:10
"Be hospitable to one another without complaint."	1 Peter 4:9
"Serving one another" with your spiritual gift through words and/or deeds.	1 Peter 4:10
"… And all of you, clothe yourselves with humility toward one another."	1 Peter 5:5
"If we walk in the light, as He Himself is in the light, we have fellowship with one another."	1 John 1:7
"We ought to lay down our lives for the brethren."	1 John 3:16
Love not "with word…, but in deed and truth."	1 John 3:17–18
"This is His commandment, that we believe in … Jesus Christ, and love one another…"	1 John 3:23
"Beloved, if God so loved us, we also ought to love one another."	1 John 4:11 (7–21)

HOW TO DEAL WITH SIN
DEALING WITH YOUR PERSONAL SIN

- **God Is Faithful to Convict.** As you read the Word of God, study with a small group, or listen to a message being preached or taught, God will often convict of some sin. He wants us to come to Him, agree with Him about the sin, agree to turn from that sin, agree to turn to what is right in that area or in that relationship, and by faith receive His forgiveness and cleansing for that sin (1 John 1:5–9).

- **Ask God.** If you think there is a fellowship break between you and the Lord, go to Him in prayer asking Him to show you what is displeasing to Him. Ask Him to reveal anywhere you have stepped over the line of His Word, anywhere you have grieved or quenched His Spirit. He promises to show us where there is sin (John 16:8–11).

- **Watch Out for False Guilt and Lies.** The enemy, the evil one is also called the adversary—he is against God, against God's people, and against God's purposes. He is also the accuser against God and *"the brethren"*—all believers (Revelation 12:10). He is the father of lies and spreads untruth anywhere he can—lies about God, about God's Word, about God's people, about anything—to create division, discord, and distrust. When it comes to the lives of individual believers, he shoots "thought darts" to accuse—either of sin we have committed or even of sin which we have faced in temptation but have not committed—anything to confuse, frustrate, condemn, and make us feel guilty. Remember, to be tempted is not a sin, to have a tempting thought is not sin. It is not a sin until we act on that temptation, or continue to cradle a thought such as lust or anger. When we do, we need to confess it and make it right.

- **The Spirit is Specific.** When the Holy Spirit convicts of sin, He is specific so we can confess specifically—"Lord, here is what I did, when I did it. I was wrong. I turn from it. I want to do the right thing. Thank You for forgiving me." Satan is often general, condemning and confusing—"you are bad, weak, foolish, etc." Trust God to guide in truth. *"The wisdom from above is first pure, then peaceable, gentle, reasonable, full of mercy and good fruits, unwavering, without hypocrisy"* (James 3:17)

- **God Does Not Remember Sins so as to Use Them Against Us.** The Holy Spirit does not bring up old sins. Those are removed, forgiven and forgotten. Satan uses instant replay to remind us, hassle us, depress us, defeat us. He nags at us—"Remember how many times you've done that. You will never change. You cannot do anything right. Remember." Simply remember the promises of the Word of God and hold to them. (Hebrews 10:17–18)

- **Receive Forgiveness by Faith Not Feeling.** Trust the Word of God to be true, as true as the God of the Word. Deal with bedrock facts, not shifting-sands feelings. Jesus died to forgive, not condemn.

DEALING WITH YOUR PERSONAL SINS AGAINST OTHERS

- **When Someone Has Something Against You.** First, if someone has something against you, you need to go to that person (or persons)—face to face if possible, by a phone call if not face to face (Matthew 5:23–24). If you cannot reach them either way, seek the next best way, the fastest way possible. Ephesians 4:26 says, *"Do not let the sun go down on your anger."* In other words, deal with any sin, especially anger, on the day you face it. It is like household garbage; the longer you wait to get rid of it, the worse it stinks. What if he or she does not receive you or your attempt to get things right or does not forgive you? You are responsible for you. Let God deal with that person.
- **The Circle of Confession** is as big as the circle of offense. If your sin is against God, confess it to Him. If you have sinned against an individual, go to that indi-

vidual, confess, and make it right. If you have sinned against a group, make it right with the group.

- **Restitution.** If there is need for **restitution**—financial, material, property lost or stolen, whatever—make it right as much as is possible. The burden may seem heavy now, but making it right makes the burden on your heart turn into wings for your soul.

Dealing with Others Who Have Sinned Against You

- **When Someone Sins Against You**, first have a forgiving, kind attitude toward that one, *"forgiving each other, just as God in Christ also has forgiven you."* (Eph. 4:32) What if he or she does not ask for forgiveness? You are responsible for you. Obey God. Show love. Let God deal with that person.

- **Two Options.** To get things right, you have **one of two choices**. **Forget it** and do not mention it. The person may be unaware he has offended you in some way. *"Love covers a multitude of sins."* (1 Peter 4:8) OR…**Go to** him or her and point out the offense in order to restore the relationship (not in order to make the person feel bad or feel guilty) (Matthew 18:15–20; Galatians 6:1; 2 Thessalonians 3:15). God's goal is oneness with Him and with one another—walk in harmony, peace—real love toward one another (1 Peter 3:8–18) *"As much as depends on you, live peaceably with all men."* (Romans 12:18)

✓ The Feast of Trumpets

THE CALL TO ASSEMBLY AND ACCOUNTABILITY BEFORE THE LORD

With the Feast of Trumpets we come to the Fall Feasts in the seventh month of Israel's calendar, the month Tishri (our September–October). There are three Feasts in this month—The Feast of Trumpets on the first of the month, the Day of Atonement on the tenth, and the Feast of Tabernacles the fifteenth through the twenty-second. These three events complete the religious calendar of Israel regarding the Feasts. They also speak of our future and of the end of days.

Between the Feast of Pentecost in the third month and the Feast of Trumpets in the seventh month, cultivating, sowing, and preparing for the fall harvests occupied the people of Israel. They stayed active in the fields, in the vineyards, and in the olive groves and fruit orchards looking forward to a great harvest. In a similar way, we are spiritually now in the post-Pentecost era when we are cultivating the ground, sowing the seed of the Word, gathering some of the harvest, and preparing for the final harvest. The Feast of Trumpets comes at the point of the season of final harvest.

God directed His priests to call all His people to attention, to walk in the reality of the Feast of Trumpets. We will see that God had something He wanted them to remember (a mind issue), something He wanted them to schedule (a time issue), something He wanted them to offer (a heart issue), and something to which He wanted them to be alert (an action issue [trumpets always alerted, calling to attention and action]).

In the Feast of Trumpets, God called His people to assemble with Him and to accountability before Him. The Day of Atonement was ten days away, a day of humbling oneself before Him, the entire nation anticipating the sin-atoning work of the High Priest in his annual entering of the Holy of Holies with the blood of the slain animals. The Feast of Trumpets therefore was a call to sober, serious reflection, to repentance where needed, to seeking the Lord with more intensity. Over the years, the ten days from Tishri 1 to Tishri 10 became known as the "Days of Awe," because of the seriousness of

> **Did You Know?**
> ### THE CELEBRATION OF ROSH HASHANNAH
>
> The modern Jewish celebration connected to the Feast of Trumpets is Rosh Hashannah, Israel's civil New Year. Rosh Hashannah means "head of the year," pointing to Tishri as the first month in the civil calendar. In the religious calendar, Nisan is the first month (March–April) with Tishri being the seventh or Sabbatical month.

> **Did You Know?**
> **CREATION, CHRIST, AND THE MONTH TISHRI**
>
> Many of the Jews of biblical days dated the Creation from the month Tishri as the first month, with Adam and Eve being created on Tishri 1. Some calculate the birth of Christ on Tishri 15, the beginning of the Feast of Tabernacles. Tishri is also the month in which many date His baptism by John the Baptist before He went into the Wilderness Temptation for forty days.

this season. The Trumpets of that first day were indeed a call to attention as a nation and as individuals. Added to this, many set aside the previous thirty days of the month Elul as a time of heart searching along with the ten days of awe, a forty-day period of reflection, repentance, and restoration of relationships with the Lord and with others.

The trumpet blasts of this day called all to look back over the year now past, to reflect and adjust. The first of Tishri is the start of a new civil year, a time to look forward to the year ahead, to the Day of Atonement ten days away followed by the greatest of celebrations, the Feast of Tabernacles when the harvests are complete, the work is done, and a time of gratitude and celebration is in order. Tishri is also the seventh month in the religious year, the Sabbatical month and thus the most sacred to many—a time of greatest reflection, of deepest repentance, and of most exuberant rejoicing.

Several questions come to mind as we explore this Feast. How did Israel view the Feast of Trumpets? What significance did God intend for His people Israel? What is the call of the Feast of Trumpets to each of His children today? Our Scripture adventure with the Feast of Trumpets will help us discover answers to these and other questions and lead us to answer the call of the Feast of Trumpets.

Lesson Six — **DAY ONE**

TRUMPETS SPEAK

> **Did You Know?**
> **THE SOUND OF SILVER**
>
> God instructed that two trumpets be made of silver to signal Israel and the leaders for various purposes. Silver is one of the purest metals and produces one of the clearest sounds. It pictures a pure message—*"The words of the LORD are pure words; as silver tried in a furnace on the earth, refined seven times"* (Psalm 12:6) and *"the tongue of the righteous is as choice silver"* (Proverbs 10:20). **The Silver Trumpets sounded** 1) over the offerings, 2) to summon leaders, 3) to summon the people, 4) to warn of war or danger, 5) to call on the Lord in the midst of an attack by an enemy, 6) to begin each Feast, and 7) to begin each New Moon observance (Numbers 10:1–10).

Trumpets speak a particular message in Scripture. God had a message to convey in His guidelines for the uses of various trumpets. In the nation of Israel, Scripture shows trumpets being used in many ways in daily life, both in their religious life and in their civil life. What images and ideas came to mind when the Israelites heard the sound of the trumpet? What did the trumpets say? What message do their announcements convey? We will see in today's Scripture adventure.

📖 There were two kinds of trumpets used by Israel, the silver trumpet (Hebrew—*chatsotsrah*) used in the Tabernacle and later in the Temple, and the ram's horn trumpet (Hebrew—*shofar*). First, consider the silver trumpets the Lord instructed Moses to construct for signaling the people of God. Numbers 10:1–10 gives the various times when trumpets were to be used. List the various ways they used the silver trumpets.

Used for calling of assembly and for directing the movement of the camp

📖 In 2 Chronicles 29:27–28, we find the trumpets sounding. What occasion did they celebrate?

Trumpets were blowed when the burned offering began.

120 FOLLOWING GOD – LIFE PRINCIPLES FOR WORSHIP FROM THE FEASTS OF ISRAEL

Prayer Warriors

📖 Look at 2 Chronicles 5:11–13, the celebration and dedication of the Temple in Solomon's day. What do you find in verse 12 about the silver trumpets in the days of Solomon?

They celebrated with cymbals, stringed instruments and harps, and 120 priests sounding with trumpets

The Lord instructed the priests to signal the people through the use of the trumpets—1) for their **assemblies**, 2) for their **journeys**, 3) for their **battles**, and 4) for their **festivities**.

<u>Assemblies</u>—He commanded that <u>both</u> silver trumpets be used to summon or gather the congregation together while the leaders of Israel gathered when only <u>one</u> trumpet signaled.

<u>Journeys</u>—Both trumpets signaled the people to set out marching to the next campsite. Various signals announced the movement of different parts of the camp (east side, south side, etc.).

<u>Battles</u>—When an enemy attacked, the priests sounded the alarm to warn the people and to call the Lord to deliver them.

<u>Festivities</u>—They used the trumpet to signal the beginning of each of the *"appointed feasts"* as well as the New Moon/first of each month. They used the silver trumpets to sound *"in the day of your gladness,"* referring to special occasions of victory and rejoicing as well as to the weekly Sabbath. The priests also blew the trumpets over each of the sacrifices such as the burnt offerings and peace offerings *"as a reminder of you before your God,"* humbly calling on the Lord and directing attention to their relationship to Him as their God.

Examples from history include those of Solomon's day, when he, the priests, and the people celebrated the dedication of the Temple in Jerusalem. There we see 120 priests with 120 trumpets, expanding the number of trumpets along with numerous other instruments previously introduced by David in his reign. Later, in Hezekiah's day, other instruments and Levitical singers joined in the celebrations over the offerings.

📖 The second kind of trumpet used by Israel is the *shofar* or ram's horn trumpet. The *shofar* trumpet is first mentioned in Exodus 19 when Israel met with the Lord at Mount Sinai. Read Exodus 19:10–25 and note the use of the *shofar* or ram's horn (verses 13, 16, 19). Record your insights.

This was very long and loud horn or Trumpet. The Lord call his people to mt. Sinai to gave the law and make a covenant with them

At Mount Sinai, God instructed Moses to prepare the people for the awestruck moment of meeting Him, coming into His presence, and hearing from Him. There the people heard the sound of the trumpet of the Lord, a ram's horn trumpet (Hebrew, *shofar*), it's long blast signaling the people to come before the Lord. It sounded *"very loud,"* growing louder and louder.

Did You Know?
THE SIGNAL SOUNDS OF THE TRUMPETS

The Silver Trumpets (around 12 to 20 inches in length) and the *Shofar* (ram's horn) had distinct sounds, and the use of the trumpets varied dependent on the message conveyed and the occasion for which it was used. Consider the different blasts on the trumpets or the *shofar*. One long blast using both silver trumpets sounded to gather people together for worship. One trumpet alone sounded to call together the leaders. Three repeated blasts or a "broken sound" (Hebrew, *trugnah*) sounded the "alarm" as the signal for all to go forward. There are three types of *shofar* blasts according to the Mishna—1) a **sustained** blast equal to three quavering notes, 2) a **quavering** note equal to three wailing notes, and 3) the short **wailing** note. (9 of these equaled one sustained note.) (See Numbers 10:2–7, 9.)

Put Yourself In Their Shoes
SIGNALS OF THE HEART

Under King Abijah, Judah with an army of 400,000 faced the idolatrous northern kingdom of Israel with 800,000 led by Jeroboam. When confronted with an ambush, *"the priests blew the trumpets,"* and the army *"cried to the LORD."* God routed the armies of Jeroboam and gave Judah a great victory. The summary of that event declares *"the sons of Judah conquered because they trusted in the LORD, the God of their fathers."* The silver trumpets signaled the cry of their heart of trust in the Lord (2 Chronicles 13:1–18). They obeyed Numbers 10:9, and God answered.

This was the most momentous event the people had ever seen or heard, God calling His people to gather before Him for the giving of the Law and the establishment of the covenant. It was seen as a marriage covenant with the Lord, calling Israel to be His bride (Jeremiah 2:2). They and their relationship with the Lord would never be the same.

📖 Israel used the ram's horn (*shofar*) in many different instances. Record your insights into the following accounts that speak of the use of the ram's horn as it relates to **Israel's battles**.

Joshua 6:4–20

Rams horn was blown when marched around the wall of Jericho

Judges 3:27

blew the trumpets in the mountains of Ephraim and killed the moabites

Judges 6:34

when the spirit of the lord came upon Gideon he blew the trumpet

Judges 7:1–8, 16–22

The men blew the trumpets broke pitcher Lord had every man's sword against companion

Nehemiah 4:20

Trumpets used on wall to rally them our God will fight for us

Did You Know?
THE SHOFAR

The *shofar* trumpet (ram's horn) was used

1) to call warriors to battle (Judges 3:27; 7:20),

2) at the attack of Jericho (Joshua 6:4–5),

3) by the watchmen of a city to call the city to arms or to warning (1 Samuel 13:3–4; Ezekiel 33:2–9),

4) at the coronation of a king (1 Kings 1:34; 2 Kings 9:13),

5) by David when he brought the Ark of the Covenant to Jerusalem (2 Samuel 6:15),

6) during the renewal of the covenant under King Asa (2 Chronicles 15:14),

7) to announce the Sabbatical Year and the Year of Jubilee on the Day of Atonement (Leviticus 25:9),

8) in the regular worship services of the Temple (Psalm 98:6; 150:3; 1 Chronicles 16:6),

9) and to announce the beginning and the ending of the Sabbath each week (see Josephus, *The Jewish War* 4.9.12.582).

Israel used the *shofar* as a **call to battle**. When Joshua and the Israelites conquered Jericho, each day for six days the people marched around the city in total silence while seven priests blew ram's horns. On the seventh day, they marched seven times around the city, then the priests blew a final blast of the ram's horn, the people shouted, the walls crumbled, and Israel conquered Jericho. Ehud used the ram's horn for a call to battle in Judges 3:27–30. God instructed Gideon to go into battle with only three hundred men. Gideon directed each man to take a ram's horn in addition to a torch and a clay pitcher and follow his lead. Surrounding the camp of Midian below, Gideon and his men broke the pitchers revealing the torches and blew the ram's horns. God used the sound of three hundred trumpets calling to battle to bewilder the Midianites and God gave a great victory. Centuries later Nehemiah spoke of the *shofar* ready at his side to rally the people to battle if needed.

📖 What does the trumpet sound do to a city according to Amos 3:6a?

If a trumpet is blown in a city, will not the people be afraid

122 FOLLOWING GOD – LIFE PRINCIPLES FOR WORSHIP FROM THE FEASTS OF ISRAEL

📖 What insights about the trumpet sound do you find in Ezekiel 33:1–7?

Watchman was to blow the Trumpets to warn the people

Amos 3:6a speaks of the people of a city trembling at the sound of the *shofar*. Its ominous announcement of approaching danger or of a call to arms set the most serious tone. It was time for action, immediate and wholehearted. Ezekiel 33 speaks of the watchman on the wall **alerting** the city with the *shofar*. If a watchman failed to alert the people of danger, the Lord would hold him guilty for the harm done to the city. If, however, he warned of approaching danger and one failed to respond, then that person must bear responsibility for the consequences in his life. God called Ezekiel as a watchman to trumpet His message of warning so that people could experience deliverance rather than judgment.

📖 The ram's horn not only served as a signal of alarm, but also signaled a new day or new relationships. What do you discover in the following verses?

Leviticus 25:8–12, note verse 9

Sound the trumpets on the 10th day of 7th month on the Day of Atonement.

1 Kings 1:34–39

Sound of trumpets when Solomon was anointed at Zadok

Psalm 47:1–9 (note verse 5)

Sound the trumpet to praise God for the victory

Isaiah 27:13

a call to worship the lord

Matthew 24:30–31

Sound of Trumpet will gather the Lord elect from the 4 winds Jesus's 2nd coming

1 Thessalonians 4:16

The Lord will descend from heaven with a Shout, with voice of Archagel, with trumpet of God and dead in Christ will rise first

God instructed Israel to sound the ram's horn for the year of Jubilee, announcing all Hebrew slaves freed, all debts cleared, all lands returned to their owners, and the land set apart to a year of rest. It signaled a new day and new relationships. The ascendancy of Solomon and his coronation as the new king was announced by Zadok the priest, sounding the *shofar*. That

Did You Know?
THE TRUMPETING STONE

Archaeologists have excavated an eight-feet long stone block known as the "trumpeting stone" in the rubble directly below the southwest corner of the Temple Mount in Jerusalem. On three sides of the stone is the partial Hebrew inscription "to the place of trumpeting" referring to the top of that corner, what some consider the "pinnacle of the Temple." From there the priest blew the *shofar* for the beginning and ending of each Sabbath and each Feast (Josephus, *The Jewish War*, 4.9.12.582). It was the place of public proclamations. Some see this as the setting of Jesus' second temptation in which Satan tempted Him to publicly announce Himself as *"the Son of God"* and Messiah (Matthew 4:5–7).

Put Yourself In Their Shoes
"IN THE DAY OF YOUR GLADNESS"

Numbers 10:10 speaks of sounding the silver trumpets *"in the day of your gladness."* Many consider this to refer to every Sabbath as well as those special occasions of rejoicing. Examples include when David and the people brought the Ark of the Covenant to Jerusalem (1 Chronicles 13:8; 15:24, 28), the dedication of the Temple under Solomon (2 Chronicles 5:12–13), the reforms of Asa to seek the Lord (2 Chronicles 15:10–15), the completion of the foundation for the Second Temple (Ezra 3:10–11), and the dedication of the newly repaired wall of Jerusalem (Nehemiah 12:27, 35).

accepted custom occurred often with a new king (see, for example, 2 Samuel 15:10, 2 Kings 9:13). The psalmist proclaimed *"the LORD Most High"* as the *"great King over all the earth"* who *"has ascended . . . with the sound of the trumpet"* (*shofar*). Psalm 47 praised God for His able victory on behalf of Israel. By way of current application, it is a call to shout for joy and sing praises to Him as our true King. He brings a new day of His victory, His provision, and His protection. Isaiah prophesied the day when a *"great trumpet"* would signal the return of dispersed Israel to the land to worship the Lord. Jesus spoke of *"a great trumpet"* summoning His elect at His return at the end of the tribulation days. When Paul informed the Thessalonian believers about the return of the Lord for His saints, he spoke of the sound of *"the trumpet of God"* summoning the dead in Christ to rise along with the Christians still alive on earth *"to meet the Lord in the air"* to be forever with Him. Each of these instances signals a new day, new relationships, and the fulfillment of the promises of God.

The trumpet sounded as an attention-getting noise to make certain all the people heard, all ears opened, so all could respond. In many instances, it announced a change or a challenge to the people, calling for wholehearted involvement. In every instance, the trumpets called to attention and action. Circumstances and situations change and people must respond. God used the silver trumpets and the *shofar* to direct His people in worship, in daily life, in the battles of life, and in the fulfillment of His promises for His people. In Day Two we will begin looking at how these trumpets were used on the Day of the Feast of Trumpets.

Lesson Six **DAY TWO**

THE FEAST OF TRUMPETS—A DAY OF REMEMBRANCE

The Feast of Trumpets occurred on the first day of Tishri, the seventh or sabbatical month in the religious year and the first month of the civil year. It occurred in conjunction with the New Moon, so it was a day of coming out of darkness into the first light of the month. In order to accurately celebrate this Feast, the Jews carefully looked for that first sliver of light in the New Moon. In later Jewish history, the Sanhedrin met in council requiring the witness of two who had seen the new moon to validate the start of the Feast. At that point, the trumpet would sound to begin the celebration. In order to assure they were correct, the Feast came to be celebrated for two days, counting the forty-eight hours of Tishri 1 and 2 as "one day"—just in case they had made an error in judgment on seeing the new moon.

This Feast also signaled the soon approach of the Day of Atonement (Tishri 10) and thus took on a somber tone calling all to readiness and repentance. In the Feast of Trumpets, God directed His people to use trumpets as part of their worship, emphasizing their relationship with Him. He had a message to give, directions for His people in this yearly event. What can we learn from His instructions? What is the fuller meaning of this Feast for Israel and for the people of God in the New Testament? Let's begin exploring these questions in today's Scriptures.

📖 God first mentions the Feast of Trumpets in Leviticus 23:23–25, the chapter that includes all seven Feasts. What basic instructions did God give concerning this fifth Feast?

_____
_____
_____

📖 In Numbers 29:1–6, God gives more detailed instructions about celebrating the Feast of Trumpets. What additional insights do you receive from reading those verses?

_____
_____
_____

For this Feast day, God called for a five-element celebration—
1) a day as a *"reminder by blowing of trumpets,"*
2) a day of *"rest,"*
3) no *"laborious work,"*
4) specific sacrifices and offerings *"by fire,"*
5) a worshiping assembly or *"holy convocation."*

The Feast of Trumpets was one of the simplest of the seven feasts in that it focused on the blowing of trumpets as a *"reminder."* A day of *"rest"* with *"no laborious work"* allowed the people to give their full attention to the Lord. That included the offering by fire. Numbers 29 gives the specifics of that sacrifice. In addition, they were to have a *"holy convocation"* or assembly. What further details can we find in the Scriptures about each of these elements for this Feast day? Consider each of the following.

The DAY as *"a REMINDER by BLOWING of TRUMPETS"*

📖 Review Leviticus 23:23–25. On what does verse 24 focus during this day? What were the people to do?

_____
_____
_____

What additional insights come to you concerning the reminder mentioned in Numbers 10:10?

_____
_____
_____

In the summary of the seven Feasts in Leviticus 23, God specified the Feast of Trumpets as His appointed day of *"blowing of trumpets"* as *"a reminder."* This reminding is mentioned in Numbers 10:10. In the blowing of the silver trumpets, they called the Lord to remember them and their offerings before Him. It is also a reminder to the people of God, calling them to attention and to action. For the celebration of the day of the Feast of Trumpets, the *shofar* trumpet called them to a *"day of rest,"* to assemble in the *"holy convocation"* for worship and giving various offerings and sacrifices. It also

---

Put Yourself In Their Shoes
ACKNOWLEDGING THE LORD AS KING

Alfred Edersheim has well summed up the significance of the blowing of trumpets—"The object of it [the "blowing of trumpets"] is expressly stated to have been 'for a memorial,' that they might 'be remembered before Jehovah,' it being specially added: 'I am Jehovah your God' [Numbers 10:10]. It was, so to speak, the host of God assembled, waiting for their Leader; the people of God united to proclaim their King. At the blast of the priests' trumpets they ranged themselves, as it were, under His banner and before His throne, and this symbolical confession and proclamation of Him as 'Jehovah their God,' brought them before Him to be 'remembered' and 'saved.' And so every season of 'blowing of trumpets,' . , . was a public acknowledgement of Jehovah as King." (Edersheim, *The Temple, Its Ministries and Services* [Grand Rapids: Wm. B. Erdmans Publishing Company, reprinted 1983], pages 290–291)

spoke of their accountability before the Lord on this beginning of the seventh month, the sabbatical month. It was also the first month of the civil year, and this Feast provided an opportunity to express their surrender anew in light of the start of this new civil year.

📖 When were the trumpets blown according to Numbers 10:10?

___

The Lord directed that the silver trumpets be blown over each of the sacrifices of the day—the regular daily burnt offerings, the offerings of the New Moon, and the specific offerings unique to the Feast of Trumpets, a total of 23 sacrifices on that day. In addition, the priests sounded the trumpets at the beginning of the day and at the close of the day.

📖 Psalm 81 speaks of the blowing of a *shofar* trumpet. Israel used this psalm in their worship times on the day of the Feast of Trumpets. Read Psalm 81 noting verses 1–3. What is the focus in those verses?

___

📖 What is the emphasis in Psalms 81:8–16? What is God's desire in these verses?

___

The focus of Psalm 81 is the Lord Himself and Israel's relationship to Him, singing and shouting *"aloud to God our strength."* God desired it to be a day of celebration. The *shofar* called the people to attention—the day emphasizing their relationship with God, specifically His call to obedience. That included repentance for their failures to obey, remembering they had acted in stubborn disobedience many times in their history. God called them to listen to Him and to put away any foreign god. Those idols were marks of unfaithfulness to their Lord and their covenant promises. He desired to give and to bless, yet too often they would not listen, but walked instead with stubborn hearts, resisting His will to promote their selfish agendas. The Feast of Trumpets served as a yearly reminder to evaluate their relationship with the Lord, to repent of any waywardness, and to prepare their hearts for the upcoming Day of Atonement just ten days away.

The DAY of *"REST"* and NO *"LABORIOUS WORK"*

📖 **First**, consider the day of *"rest."* What would this day entail? Look at God's first words about days of *"rest"* in Exodus 20:8–11 and 23:12. What should mark such a day?

___

> **EXTRA MILE**
> **THE SABBATH REGULATIONS**
>
> For further insight into God's regulations on the Sabbath as a *"sign"* and a day of rest see Exodus 16:22–30 and 31:12–17.

📖 Leviticus 23:24 calls for a day of *"sabbath-rest"* or *"solemn rest,"* literally *shabbathon*, a *sabbatism* or special day of rest with *"no laborious work"* in celebrating the Feast of Trumpets? Why do you think God called His people to a day of *"rest"*? How would this help the people focus their attention on the Lord?

_____

_____

_____

A day of *"rest"* (the Sabbath or a Feast day) meant resting from the usual labors of the week—business, trading, farming, and so forth. For the weekly Sabbath, meals were to be prepared the day before since no fire was to be kindled (see Exodus 16:22–26 and 35:3). They fulfilled the necessary care of family and livestock, but focused on the times of worship centered around the Tabernacle or Temple. On the day of the Feast of Trumpets, the phrase *"no laborious work"* (Hebrew *melakah abodah*) referred to skilled labor, business, and agricultural work, but allowed only necessary light work (Leviticus 23:25; Numbers 29:1). God designed this day as a day of focus on Him and His Word, on seeking Him, worshiping Him together as a family and as a community. He wanted wholehearted involvement, not tired leftovers. It involved the whole day and it involved everyone—men and women, parents and children, slaves and hired servants, as well as foreigners living in the land. Even the livestock rested. God's directions left open the opportunity for undistracted, full participation by everyone.

Did You Know?
SEVEN SPECIAL SABBATH REST DAYS

In celebrating some of the Feasts, God called for a special Sabbath (not necessarily on a Saturday) in which extra care was shown to do no labor. The seven days were (1) the first and (2) seventh days of Unleavened Bread (Nisan 15 and 21), (3) Pentecost Day, (4) the Feast of Trumpets (Tishri 1), (5), the Day of Atonement (Tishri 10), (6) the first and (7) eighth days of Tabernacles (Tishri 15 and 22). Each of these days intensified the people's focus on the Lord and their walk with Him, a 'time-out' to reflect, realign, and rejoice.

THE FEAST OF TRUMPETS— A DAY FOR WORSHIP

Lesson Six   **DAY THREE**

The Lord set aside the first of Tishri for the Feast of Trumpets, a day for remembering the Lord and His work among the people of Israel. They focused this day on remembering His promises, His provision, and His protection of this chosen people. It was also a day for calling on the Lord to remember Israel and their offerings to the Lord. This day set the stage for the Day of Atonement just ten days later. Those ten days came to be known as "the days of awe" in light of the seriousness of the Day of Atonement. We will see more concerning this when we look at the Day of Atonement. In the Feast of Trumpets, the Lord and His people set aside the entire day as a unique day of worship. Today, we continue looking at how they celebrated the day, especially in their offerings and in their times of gathering for worship.

The SACRIFICES and OFFERINGS
📖 List the specific sacrifices for the Feast of Trumpets as given in Numbers 29:1–6. What would this mean to the Lord, according to verse 2?

_____

_____

_____

> *Did You Know?*
> ### FEASTS OF FAMILIES AND KINGS
>
> In 1 Samuel 20:5, 24–25, we find evidence of a New Moon feast held by King Saul for his family and his court. This first of the month feast was considered a civil and religious celebration in Israel as seen in the comment about necessary ritual cleanness (20:26). The feast lasted two days indicating the nature of the New Moon celebrations (20:27). In order to assure they accurately ascertained the precise day of the New Moon, the Jews celebrated the feast for two days. This became common in the years that followed. It is quite possible this is a celebration of the yearly New Moon Feast of Trumpets on Tishri 1, since David also mentions being in Bethlehem with his family for their *"yearly sacrifice"* and celebration of the feast (1 Samuel 20:6, 29).

📖 Why do you think God required burnt offerings and a sin offering in this day of worship? What significance do you see in the burnt offerings being totally consumed before the Lord? What could that mean to the Israelites?

_____
_____
_____

📖 What would the sin offering mean, according to verse 5?

_____
_____

📖 In these offerings, what insights do you see for the follower of Christ today?

_____
_____
_____

On the day of the Feast of Trumpets, the Lord required *"a burnt offering"* consisting of one bull, one ram, and seven one-year-old male lambs accompanied by the grain offerings of flour mixed with olive oil along with the fruit of the vine poured out with each animal sacrifice. The fires of the altar totally consumed the burnt offering. None of the priests or people ate any of this offering. It pictured a worshipful surrender to the Lord, each part of the offering being totally given up, poured out, and consumed on the bronze altar. It is a statement of being consumed with the Lord Himself, of surrender to Him and His will, of yielding all to Him as God.

In addition, they offered a goat for a *"sin offering,"* acknowledging sin and the need for God's forgiveness through the offering of a substitute *"to make atonement,"* or to cover over their sins. God always calls people to deal with sin, to account for their lives in the light of His holiness and righteousness. Where there is sin, any breaking of God's law, there must be a just death. God in His mercy provided for a substitute for His people through these sin offerings. He continually gave them an open door into forgiveness and restored fellowship with Himself. These offerings were in addition to the regular daily burnt offerings (9:00 am and 3:00 pm—see Exodus 29:38–46) and the monthly New Moon burnt offerings for the first day of the month (see Numbers 28:11–14).

The time frame or the calendar significance of these offerings is important to see. Each offering spoke of the relationship between the people and their God. Each offering served to symbolize the setting aside of oneself to the Lord, of consecrating one's life. It also pointed to hallowing their days, a reminder of living holy or set apart to the Lord in their daily life. The daily offerings pictured the necessity of **daily** surrender to the Lord, at the start and end of the day. The New Moon offerings pictured setting aside every **month** to the Lord. The offerings of the Feast of Trumpets pictured setting aside the *year* **from the start.** (The month Tishri, the first month of the civil year was also the first day of the seventh month in the religious year counting from Nisan in the Spring.)

These offerings also exemplified the Old Testament principle of the first representing the whole. As the firstfruits symbolized the whole harvest and the firstborn symbolized the remainder of people and livestock, so the offerings of the New Moon and the Feast of Trumpets set aside the whole month and all the year. Tishri served as the seventh month of the religious calendar **and** the **first** month of the civil calendar, thus this day set apart to the Lord, signaled setting apart the whole year. All of Israel's year, all of Israel's everyday life, all of Israel's people set apart to worship, follow, obey, and rejoice in their Lord.

APPLY — **Is Your Heart Set Apart from the Start ?**—How do you start each day, each week, each month, or even each year? Do you have in place an altar of the heart at which you moment by moment lay your life before the Lord Jesus? Are you walking under the Lordship of Jesus in your home, your job, as well as your ministry involvement? Is every business, financial, or purchase decision governed by surrender to His will? Are your relationships and conversations seasoned with the salt of a life offered first to Jesus and His will? Is every day a day for worship—are you worshiping Him in the way you spend all seven days, all twenty-four hours of the day? Perhaps you need to make a fresh start today. Pause and talk to the Lord about these matters.

The *"HOLY CONVOCATION"* or *"SACRED ASSEMBLY"*

What would the "holy convocation" or "sacred assembly" look like? We have a wonderful picture from the days of Ezra and Nehemiah. How did they celebrate the Feast of Trumpets then? Consider the following scriptures and questions.

📖 What day is noted in Nehemiah 7:73 and 8:2?

_____

_____

📖 What occurred on this first day of the seventh month (Tishri), according to Nehemiah 8:1–12? Consider some of the details of the day, of this *"holy convocation."* First, look at the scene in verses 1–5. Where did they gather? Describe the details of the scene from these verses.

_____

_____

_____

_____

📖 What did they do during this time together? What did they read in this gathering?

_____

_____

_____

_____

Put Yourself In Their Shoes
TOTALLY CONSUMED

The various Feasts and celebrations and the **burnt offerings** connected with each one are an outward picture of God's desire for hearts being totally consumed with Him. The entire burnt offering was devoted to God, none to priest or worshiper. At the **start of each day** the priests offered a burnt offering for the nation (Exodus 29:38–46; Numbers 28:1–8). At the **start of each month** (New Moon), they offered a burnt offering (Numbers 28:11–14). At the **start of each year** (Feast of Trumpets, Tishri 1), they offered a burnt offering (Numbers 29:1–4). God desired a relationship totally consumed with Him and His will from the start and from the heart. He desires the same consuming heart today, everyday—to love Him with all one's heart, soul, mind, and strength (Mark 12:30), and to offer one's body *"a living and holy sacrifice, well-pleasing to God, which is your spiri-*

Did You Know?
ZERUBBABEL AND THE FEASTS OF THE SEVENTH MONTH

Around 537/536 BC, Zerubbabel led the first group of Jews (around 50,000 in number) out of the seventy-year captivity in Babylon to Jerusalem. Ezra 3:1–6 reports the rebuilding of the altar and the celebration of the Feast of Trumpets in the seventh month. During this seventh month, the people gathered in Jerusalem to celebrate the Day of Atonement and the Feast of Tabernacles as well. This occurred after 70 years of no celebrations because of their captivity in Babylon.

📖 How did the people respond to this reading, according to verses 2–3, 5, 6?

_____

_____

_____

📖 What did Ezra and the men in leadership do during this time together, according to verses 7–9?

_____

_____

_____

📖 What happened when the people understood what the Scriptures said? Note what occurred after the Scriptures were read in verses 3, 6, 9–11, 12?

_____

_____

_____

> *Did You Know?*
>
> ## DANIEL'S PROPHECY AND NEHEMIAH'S MISSION
>
> Around 538 BC, in answer to his prayers concerning Jerusalem and the fate of the people of God, Daniel received revelation from God through the angel Gabriel. He recorded that revelation in Daniel 9:24–27. Gabriel spoke of the passing of sixty-nine weeks of years (483 years) at the end of which the Messiah would be *"cut off"* or killed (9:26). Verse 27 speaks of a seventieth *"week"* (seven years) and the *"covenant… for one week"* made by *"the prince who is to come,"* the substitute false Christ or Antichrist (9:26). Many see this *"week"* as the seven year Tribulation period after the rapture of the church. It is also called *"the time of Jacob's trouble"* (Jeremiah 30:7), the last three and one-half years being called *"the Great Tribulation"* (Matthew 24:21; Revelation 7:14) and *"the Day of the Lord"* (1 Thessalonians 5:2–3). Other verses that speak of this end time include Joel 3:12–16, Malachi 4:5, and 2 Thessalonians 1:7–10; 2:3–12. Each of these events is associated with future trumpets. In Babylon, Nehemiah had access to this prophecy and fulfilled part of it in his journey from Babylon/Persia to Jerusalem to rebuild its walls in 445 BC (Nehemiah 1—7).

First, on a historical note, this was a unique time in Israel's history. This observance of the Feast of Trumpets occurred on the first of Tishri in the autumn of the year 445 BC (around mid-September). Nehemiah had just led the people in rebuilding the wall around Jerusalem in 52 days (from the fourth day of the month Ab (mid-July) to the twenty-fifth of Elul (mid-September), only five days before the first of Tishri (Nehemiah 6:15). People came to celebrate the Feast of Trumpets in Jerusalem from many cities and villages throughout Israel.

This *"holy convocation"* within the newly built walls of Jerusalem began early on the morning of Tishri 1. The day of *"rest"* would be focused in a time of Scripture-saturated worship. Ezra the scribe and several Levites and priests stood on a raised wooden platform built for this occasion. Ezra began reading from the Law as the people stood listening attentively. Apparently they had seldom or never celebrated this Feast with such focus, especially those who had recently come from Babylon. Because they were born in Babylon, they spoke the Chaldean language and Hebrew was not as familiar to them. Those who understood Hebrew and who were more skilled in interpreting the Scriptures, helped translate and explain the meaning to the people.

As they began to understand the Law, they recognized how many ways they had failed to keep it. The sense of potential judgment overwhelmed some. Many began to weep. Ezra the scribe, Nehemiah the governor, and several Levites sought to quiet the people, pointing to Scriptures that indicated God desired this to be a Feast of joy. They reminded them that *"this day is holy to our Lord"* and called them to *"eat of the fat, drink of the sweet,"* while sharing with those around them. As the people understood the fuller intention of the Scriptures and God's call in this Feast, they began to rejoice. Their hunger for the Word of God brought about a second day of reading and fresh understanding. They began to prepare for the upcoming Feast of Tabernacles (Tishri 15 to 22) and their rejoicing increased. Obedience to God's call brings a new measure of joy as well as a sense of fulfilling His will in the matter at hand.

How do these Old Testament practices apply to us today? What do we find in the New Testament? We will see in Day Four.

The Feast of Trumpets in New Testament Light

Lesson Six **DAY FOUR**

What do we find about the Feast of Trumpets in the New Testament? There is no record of how Jesus celebrated this Feast during His days on earth, but the mention of trumpets is clearly evident. How are we to see this Old Testament Feast in our daily walk with God? As we look at this Feast and its meaning, it is important to remember two realities associated with this celebration. One is a physical reality of the New Moon as the land comes out of the darkness of no moon into the first light of the new moon. It is a dawning of a new month, a new day so to speak. The second reality is the spiritual application. Each reference related to a trumpet call in the New Testament prefaces the dawning of a new day—at the rapture of the church to reward His followers and at the return of Christ to begin His reign. An exploration of the pages of the New Testament opens up some wonderful insights and applications.

📖 We have seen how trumpets summoned God's people to assembly, to accountability, to war, and to worship. Each year at the Feast of Trumpets as the trumpets sounded, the people gathered before the Lord at the Tabernacle or Temple. There is a future gathering spoken of in the New Testament as well. Read Paul's words of comfort and expectation in 1 Thessalonians 4:13–18? What is the order of the events found in verses 16–17?

_____
_____
_____
_____

📖 What part does a trumpet play?

_____
_____
_____

📖 Why did Paul desire to clarify this event, according to verses 13–15 and verse 18?

_____
_____
_____

> **Word Study**
> **"RAPTURE"**
>
> The words *"caught up"* are a translation of the Greek word *harpazo* used in 1 Thessalonians 4:17 which refers to a sudden snatching away. It means "to seize with force" and was used of a wolf quickly taking a lamb from a flock. This catching up is often referred to as the "rapture" of the church. The English word "rapture" is rooted in the Latin word *raptus*, the Latin translation of the Greek word, *harpazo*.

LESSON SIX – THE FEAST OF TRUMPETS 131

Did You Know?
JEWISH WEDDING CUSTOMS

Many of the Thessalonian Christians came out of a Jewish background. When Paul spoke of the return of the Lord with a shout and a trumpet (*shofar*) (1 Thessalonians 4:16), it is likely that for many of them Jewish wedding customs came to mind. After a bridegroom proposed to a bride, he would promise to go, prepare a place for her, and then come back to receive her to himself (see John 14:1–3). When he returned (often in a torch-lit night procession) with his "'best man," the friend of the bridegroom, the wedding party approached the bride's home with a signal of a *shofar* trumpet and a shout (see Matthew 25:6). The bride knew he had returned. The wedding procession would then go to his newly prepared home for the wedding celebration and life together.

Word Study
"IN A MOMENT, IN THE TWINKLING OF AN EYE"

The Greek word translated *"moment"* is *atomos*, from which we derive the English word "atom," once thought to be the indivisible unit of matter before the discovery of protons, electrons, and neutrons. *Atomos*, which literally means "not to cut" [*a* + *temno*] refers to an uncut or indivisible moment of time. *"Twinkling"* is a translation of *rhipe* meaning rapid movement. It was used of the flapping of a bird's wing, the buzz of a gnat, the rush of a flame, the darting of a bird, or the twinkling of a light. Both terms show the suddenness with which Christ will return and transform the bodies of believers. What a wonderful promise!

📖 What is Paul's confident hope in making these statements, according to the first part of verse 15?

_____

_____

_____

The Lord promised to return for those who belong to Him, those who have placed their faith in Jesus Christ as Lord and Savior. Paul revealed his confident hope in writing *"by the word of the Lord"* the details of these events. Believers at Thessalonica and all who would read these words could know this is a message from the Lord, a word of confident expectation and a word of comfort. They are given to inform, to clarify Christ's return for all believers, and to comfort the hearts of those whose believing friends and family have *"fallen asleep in Jesus,"* those who have died prior to these events. The New Testament often pictures physical death as the body lying down in sleep, ready to be raised by Christ (never as "soul sleep") (see 1 Corinthians 15:20–23; 2 Corinthians 5:8; Philippians 1:23).

The events surrounding the gathering to meet the Lord pictured in 1 Thessalonians 4 begin with the Lord Jesus personally descending *"from heaven with a shout"* or a cry of command, a word used of a military command. Jesus comes as the victorious conqueror, calling His people to come to Him. Believers will hear the voice of the archangel along with *"the trumpet of God,"* implying the *shofar* sound like that which summoned all to Mount Sinai. A bridegroom coming for his bride also used a *shofar*. *"The dead in Christ"* who are present with Christ are the first to receive their resurrection bodies. Then the believers still alive will be *"caught up together with them in the clouds to meet the Lord in the air"* to be forever with Him, the beginning of a new day and new relationships as God fulfills His promises. What occurs next? Many also see this *"trumpet of God"* as the signal to war as Christ reveals Himself as Lord and deals with the nations of the earth during the seven-year tribulation (Revelation 5—19). In addition, Scriptures indicate this as a time in which Christ will reward His followers in preparation for them reigning with Him. We will look at that in Day Five.

📖 What additional insights do you find in 1 Corinthians 15:51–54? What do you discover about the trumpet?

_____

_____

_____

📖 How are believers to live now in light of this coming resurrection according to 1 Corinthians 15:58?

_____

_____

_____

God promises resurrection transformation for all believers. Not every Christian will face death. Those who do are assured that the Lord will resurrect them. Those still alive when the trumpet sounds will be changed. Paul confidently declares that at the sounding of *"the last trumpet,"* in a *"moment,"* even *"in the twinkling of an eye,"* the dead will be raised and those still alive will be changed, each from *"this perishable"* body to the imperishable resurrection body, from mortal to immortal. Death will be swallowed up in the victory Christ promised and gained. Some see Paul's reference to *"the last trumpet"* as an allusion to the Feast of Trumpets. In the Jewish calendar, the term *"the last trumpet"* referred to the specific **day** of the Feast of Trumpets. On the day of the Feast of Trumpets there were one hundred blasts of the trumpet, the last of which being a long blast to gather Israel to prepare for the coming Day of Atonement. Some see this Feast as a prophetic picture of the rapture of the church to assemble before Him in heaven and the call of the Lord to Israel to gather to Him, calling them to repentance and faith in the Messiah.

Because of the promise of this resurrection, every believer should live each day expecting a future with the Lord. First Corinthians 15:58 clearly calls each believer to be faithful following Jesus. *"Be steadfast, immovable, always abounding in the work of the Lord,"* the assignments He has given. Do not stray from the path or the tasks of the Lord. Do not let anyone move you off track. Keep *"abounding"* in the Lord's work. We can be assured our labor in the Lord is not *"in vain,"* or empty. It is not just busy work. It has meaning and significance, eternal significance.

📖 At the rapture of the church all believers will be with the Lord forever. Many see this event as the promised *"day of Christ,"* a time **before** the *"Day of the Lord"* and its focus on judgment. Look first at Philippians 1:9–11. What did Paul pray for these believers? Note the context of Paul's confidence and care in verses 6–8.

_____

_____

_____

Paul prayed, confident in God's *"good work"* in each believer knowing He will perfect that work *"until the day of Christ Jesus."* He prayed that the love of each believer would abound with understanding and discernment so that every choice would be made in light of what matters forever. He prayed they would be *"sincere and blameless"* in every deed *"until the day of Christ,"* that their lives would be characterized by *"the fruit of righteousness which comes through Jesus Christ."*

📖 What do you find about Paul's perspective concerning *"that day"* in 2 Timothy 4:6–8? Note that Paul wrote this about six months before his execution by Roman officials.

_____

_____

_____

As the time of Paul's execution drew near, he wrote to Timothy about the importance of one's life testimony, the advancement of the gospel, and the glory of Jesus Christ. He saw his coming death as his *"departure,"* the Greek word *analusis* being used of a soldier breaking camp or a ship going from one port to another. Paul looked forward to being awarded *"the crown of righteousness"* by *"the righteous Judge"* Jesus Christ *"on that Day."* Paul gave

Did You Know?
"THE LAST TRUMPET" IN THE ROMAN ARMY

In the Roman Army, certain trumpet signals directed marching orders. A certain blast of the trumpet signaled to strike camp, pack tents, and prepare to depart. A second trumpet blast signaled to fall in line. The *"last trumpet"* signaled the soldiers to 'move out.' It is possible Paul alluded to this practice in 1 Corinthians 15:52, referring to the *"last trumpet"* which signals the resurrection of believers moving out to be with the Lord, the *"earthly tent"* of this body changed into the likeness of Jesus' glorious body (cf. 1 Thessalonians 4:16–17; 2 Corinthians 5:1–5; Philippians 3:21).

Doctrine
MILLENNIAL FEASTS

Ezekiel records four Feasts that will be celebrated during the millennial reign of Christ. Each of them celebrates either a remembrance of God's redemptive history or of His ongoing work in the Millennium. First is the Feast of the New Year (Nisan/Abib 1–7) in which the priests cleanse the Millennial Temple (Ezekiel 45:18–20). As a remembrance, the Passover and Unleavened Bread are celebrated (Nisan 14–21; Ezekiel 45:21–24) as is the Feast of Tabernacles (Tishri 15–21; Ezekiel 45:25; Zechariah 14:16–19). Firstfruits, Pentecost, Trumpets, and the Day of Atonement are not celebrated, their prophetic message being fulfilled in what Christ has done.

Did You Know?
THREE TRUMPETS—THREE FEASTS

Ancient Jewish teachings associated three calendar days with three trumpets—the First, the Last, and the Great Trumpet. The First Trumpet refers to the day the trumpet (*shofar*) of the Lord sounded at Mount Sinai for the betrothal between the Lord and Israel (Exodus 19:19; Jeremiah 2:2). That calendar day is the Feast Day of Pentecost. Some consider *"the Last Trumpet"* (*shofar*) a technical term referring to the first day of the civil year, Rosh Hashanah ("head of the year"), the day of the Feast of Trumpets. Many see this as the time of the coming of the Messiah. The day of *"the Great Trumpet"* refers to Yom Kippur, the Day of Atonement, the day of God's fulfillment of redemption when Christ returns to reign on earth (Isaiah 27:12–13; Matthew 24:29–31). Each trumpet calls His people to assemble before Him in worship and to accountability to Him with His evaluation and rewards. At *"the last trumpet"* the redeemed are assembled before Jesus followed by the Judgment Seat of Christ with its rewards or loss of rewards (1 Corinthians 3:10–15; 15:23, 52–58; 2 Corinthians 5:10). At *"the Great Trumpet,"* Jesus will gather all to Himself to judge the nations (sheep and goats) giving rewards to the righteous and banishing the wicked from His presence (Matthew 24:30–31; 25:31–46).

a word of hope to every believer declaring that *"all who have loved His appearing,"* all who belong to Him, who live in the light of His return and their accountability, will receive the *"crown of righteousness."*

📖 Before we conclude today's exploration, consider one other sounding of a trumpet. Jesus speaks of this in Matthew 24:29–31. Give a brief description of what will occur.

_____

_____

_____

📖 What happens next? Review Matthew 25:31–46. What do the righteous receive according to verses 34 and 46b?

_____

_____

_____

📖 What additional insights do you find in Revelation 20:4–6?

_____

_____

_____

In Matthew 24:29–31, Jesus spoke of the days of tribulation after which He, the Son of Man, would return for all to see. This is His Second Coming when He appears to all. He spoke of this coming during His ministry (Matthew 16:27; Luke 21:27) and to the Jewish leaders the night before they crucified Him (see Matthew 26:64; Mark 14:62). When He returns in His Second Coming, He will sound "A GREAT TRUMPET" summoning His elect to Himself just before setting up His millennial kingdom. This trumpet signals a new day, new relationships, and the fulfillment of the promises of God. That new day is the entrance of the kingdom of God in its full earthly manifestation as Jesus begins His millennial reign. At the end of the Great Tribulation when He visibly returns, He summons the nations before Him for judgment. Those who have shown genuine faith in Him are His *"sheep,"* those *"blessed of My Father"* who *"inherit the kingdom prepared for you from the foundation of the world."* These and all believers resurrected from the Great Tribulation will reign with Christ for a thousand years.

Trumpet calls change things—from peace to war, from work to rest, from labor to accounting. **Trumpets celebrate relationships**—the king and his people, the bridegroom and his bride, the Lord and His worshipers. When we look at the trumpets of the Old and New Testaments we see them used to call the people to assemble before the Lord at His Temple for worship, to call all to follow Him to the Promised Land, to announce the return of the bridegroom for his bride, to announce and celebrate the coronation of a king and the beginning of his new reign, to signal readiness for war or to send into battle, to celebrate the offerings and sacrifices, and to signal the Sabbath, the Jubilee, and the beginning of a Feast.

All of these things occur as the Lord Jesus returns. The *"trumpet of the Lord"* calls the church to assemble before the Lord in the clouds to follow Him to the place prepared, to worship Him in His heavenly temple, to rejoice as His bride, to join in the coronation and reign of Jesus as the Messiah King, to signal the beginning of His battle against the unbelieving nations in the Tribulation, and to rejoice over the renewed worship of His people in heaven and on earth. Then, as *"the Great Trumpet"* sounds, the millennial kingdom arises. This will begin the millennial "Sabbath" and "Jubilee." It also begins the worship associated with the millennial Feasts.

How do we answer the call of the Feast of Trumpets today? We will see in Day Five.

ANSWERING THE CALL OF THE FEAST OF TRUMPETS

Lesson Six **DAY FIVE**

Everything about the Feast of Trumpets centers around the Lord—remembering Him and one's relationship with Him, proper worship of Him, and accountability before Him. For centuries the Jews saw this as a time of preparation for the Day of Atonement ten days later. The days leading up to the Day of Atonement took on a somber tone and called for serious reflection and repentance. In fact, it was the only required day of fasting in Israel's calendar. We will look at that day in our next lesson.

The Feast of Trumpets focuses on the call to assemble and rejoice before the Lord. It also spurs individuals to consider one's accountability to the Lord. When we turn to the pages of the New Testament, we find a call to accountability in each case in which the coming of the Lord is mentioned. There is a day of accounting coming. The Feast of Trumpets in the Old Testament has symbolized this for centuries, and its reality is carried on in the New Testament. Today we will look at some of the passages that call us to accountability and to the hopes of reward and rejoicing. They also call us to serious and sober reflection on what we are doing, how our lives are being lived out, how our attitudes, actions, thoughts, and words are being seen by others and, most importantly, by the Lord. We must answer to Him. Consider these passages about our Lord and about our accountability to Him. Consider their application to your life.

MEETING OUR LORD, SAVIOR, AND JUDGE
First of all, look at the following passages concerning the Lord before whom we will stand. Remember, this is not a time of condemnation, but of evaluation. Romans 8:1 makes it clear that there is *"no condemnation to those who are in Christ Jesus."* Review these verses and summarize what you find about our Lord, Savior, and Judge.

John 5:22–30

_____

_____

> **Did You Know?**
> **THE FEAST OF TRUMPETS AND THE RESURRECTION**
>
> Jewish tradition has long said the resurrection of the dead will occur on Rosh Hashanah, the day of the Feast of Trumpets. In light of this, Jewish gravestones are often found with a *shofar* engraved on them.

> **Word Study**
> **"HIS APPEARING"**
>
> Paul speaks of those who *"have loved His appearing"* receiving rewards from Christ. The word for *"appearing"* is the Greek word *epiphaneia*, used in 2 Timothy 1:10 of Christ's first coming and in 1 Timothy 6:14, 2 Timothy 4:1, 8, and Titus 2:13 of His second coming.

Doctrine
JESUS AND THE JUDGMENT

Jesus continually spoke of His return and how He would *"reward each according to his works"* (Matthew 16:27). This reality is presented throughout the Old and New Testaments (see Job 34:10–11; Psalm 62:12; Proverbs 24:12; John 5:29; Romans 2:3–11; 1 Peter 1:17–22). The *"good"* Jesus talks about in John 5:29 is believing in Him as the Son sent by the Father (John 5:24). Not surprisingly, the *"evil"* is a refusal to believe in Jesus as God's son. Doing "good" does not refer to salvation by works (Ephesians 2:8–9), but to evaluation of a person's works as to whether or not they have shown genuine faith in Him. Good works are the evidence of salvation, not the basis of salvation. James 2:14–26 speaks of Abraham and Rahab, who did good works **because** they had genuine faith in God, **not** to become right with God. Their works gave evidence of being justified. This is the point of Paul's words in Romans 2:3–11. When Jesus returns and begins the process of judgment, of rewards, and recompense for deeds done, He will do so on the basis of a relationship with Him, a relationship of genuine faith (see also Matthew 25:31–46).

Acts 10:36–43
_____
_____

Acts 17:30–31
_____
_____

2 Timothy 4:1
_____
_____

2 Timothy 4:8
_____
_____

Matthew 25:31–34, (35–46)
_____
_____

Revelation 20:11–15
_____
_____

Jesus made it clear that the Father had given all judgment into His hands. The specific matter around which judgment begins is what a person does with Jesus. The one who repents of sin, turning to Jesus, believing in Him and receiving Him as Lord and Savior, receives forgiveness of sins and eternal life. The one rejecting Him and the witness of the Father faces condemnation. Jesus is the Judge of the living and the dead and all will one day hear His voice summoning each to stand before Him and be judged or evaluated based on their heart response to the revelation of God. The first judgment comes for believers at the Judgment Seat of Christ in which Jesus *"the righteous Judge"* will reward His followers. We will look at that next. The second will be Jesus' judgment of the nations (the sheep and the goats) in preparation for His kingdom reign on the earth. The third judgment occurs after the millennial reign and is known as the Great White Throne judgment at which Jesus judges all non-believers.

APPLY

Who is Jesus to you?—Is Jesus your Lord and Savior? If so, then you will never face the judgment of condemnation. He is your Lord and King and as such will surely reward your faithful service to Him. If you are not sure about your relationship with the Lord, today is the best day to make sure. *"Examine yourselves as to whether you are in the faith"* (2 Corinthians 13:5). Call on Him to *"search"* your heart and see if there is any wrong or hurtful way in you (Psalm 139:23–24). Trust Him and His full forgiveness and cleansing for any sin (1 John 1:7–9). If you know Him as Lord and Savior, ask Him to confirm His work in your life. Pray and rejoice in the reality of Colossians 1:9–14 for your life and for others who follow Him. That is His will for *every* believer.

The Meaning of our "Day" of Reckoning and Rewards

We have seen that trumpets announce the coming of Christ—both at the rapture of the church and at the Second Coming when He returns to reign on earth. In each case, there is an assembly and a call to accountability. Paul looked forward to *"the Day"* when he would stand before Christ. What further details do we find about this *"day of Christ"*? What happens immediately after all are caught up to be with the Lord? Many see this as *"the day"* of evaluation. What does *"the day"* hold for each believer?

📖 First, look at 1 Corinthians 3:1–8. What is the context of Paul's discussion about rewards for one's work?

_____

_____

_____

📖 Survey 1 Corinthians 3:8–15. According to verses 8 and 10, who will be rewarded?

_____

_____

📖 When will God evaluate each person's work, according to verse 13?

_____

_____

📖 What will God look at when He evaluates each believer according to 1 Corinthians 3:10–13?

_____

_____

_____

📖 Considering verses 12 and 13, what materials stand the test of God's fire? Which ones fail the test?

_____

_____

_____

📖 What are the two options each believer faces according to verses 14–15?

_____

_____

📖 What additional exhortation does Paul give in 1 Corinthians 4:5?

_____

_____

_____

Word Study
BEMA—"THE JUDGMENT SEAT"

In 2 Corinthians 5:10, Paul speaks of every believer standing before the *"Judgment Seat of Christ."* He uses the Greek word *bema*, a term familiar to those in Corinth and in the Roman world. It refers to a raised platform that served as a place for public trials and evaluating legal disputes like those conducted by Gallio in Corinth (Acts 18:12–17) or by Festus in Caesarea (Acts 25:6, 10, 17). Pilate sat on the *bema* or *"tribunal"* during the trial of Jesus (Matthew 27:19; John 19:13) as did Herod in delivering his address in the city of Caesarea (Acts 12:21). At the *bema,* officials also gave rewards for the victors in athletic contests such as the Olympics (cf. 1 Corinthians 9:24–27). At the *Bema* of Christ, He will evaluate each believer and give rewards accordingly (2 Corinthians 5:10; Romans 14:10).

> **Doctrine**
> ## SAINTS REIGN
>
> Psalm 2 prophesies about the coming Messiah and how He will reign over the nations *"with a rod of iron,"* referring to a king's scepter. This lines up with the prophecy in Genesis 49:10 about *"the scepter"* never departing from Judah through whom came David and then the Messiah Jesus, the Son of David. Paul applied this Psalm to Jesus (Acts 13:23, 33). He will rule with the *"rod of iron"* according to Revelation 12:5 and 19:15. Those who believe in Him will also rule with Him with a *"rod of iron"* according to Revelation 2:26–27. Those who follow Christ are destined to *"reign with Him"* over the world (Revelation 1:6; 3:21; 20:4, 6 and 1 Corinthians 6:2).

> *"His lord said to him, 'Well done, good and faithful servant; you were faithful over a few things, I will make you ruler over many things. Enter into the joy of your lord."*
>
> **Matthew 25:21**

In writing to the Corinthians, Paul had to address some matters of immaturity as well as some points of ignorance regarding the ways of God in the church. They were acting like babies, like little children jealously quarreling over who is the best leader, honoring one leader over another, rather than looking to Christ and His work in and through each one. Paul reminded them that God causes the growth of a ministry. We all work together like those working in a field or in constructing a building. Each one—no one is left out—receives his own wages or reward according to the labor assigned and accomplished. Anything we do right is by God-given grace.

We must be diligent and careful. We have a choice of building with *"gold, silver, precious stones,"* those things that last, symbolic of the things of the Spirit, of His leadership and empowering. Or we can build with *"wood, hay, straw,"* very short-lived and symbolic of the temporal, decaying things of the flesh, of earth. God tests *"the quality of each man's work."* That phrase literally reads "will test of **what sort** each man's work is," referring to the **nature** of the work. Does it have the nature of the Spirit or the nature of the flesh or the world? On *"the day,"* that time of evaluation before the Lord, what we have done will become evident—those who have built by grace with the things given by God will receive a reward. Those who have not, will not. Those who have labored in the energy of the flesh, with self-centeredness and selfishness, will see those works *"burned up,"* but *"he himself shall be saved, yet so as through fire."* There will be loss of reward, but never loss of salvation.

This is not a judgment to determine where we will spend eternity or to deal with sin. Christ paid for all sin on the cross, and we are forgiven (John 19:30; Luke 24:47; Ephesians 1:7; Colossians 2:13–14). One's eternity is also settled when a person places faith in Jesus Christ as Lord and Savior. This is an evaluation of how faithfully we have followed and obeyed. The fire of God's evaluation quickly reveals the lasting nature of the things of the Spirit while the things of the flesh become smoke and ashes. God also accurately evaluates our motives, why we did what we did. God will bring that to light. **Now** many receive praise from various sources. *"Then each one's praise will come from God"* (emphasis added), honestly, accurately, thoroughly.

📖 Paul dealt with this issue again with the Corinthian believers. What added insights do you find in 2 Corinthians 5:6–10? Note the context of verses 1–5.

_____
_____
_____
_____

Paul continually kept in mind a view of eternity and continually reminded others. We tend to forget that this life is transitory. Every believer is one heart beat away from *"the earthly tent"* being *"torn down."* Our transfer to heaven to be with the Lord could be moments away. We know from 1 Thessalonians 4:16 that Paul lived ready for *"the trumpet of God"* sounding any moment. Living in light of these realities also brings to mind the future Judgment Seat of Christ. There every believer *"must appear"* to be recompensed for the works he or she has done, the good and the bad. Each will be rewarded for his or her obedience and faithfulness to the Lord. Paul desired to be pleasing to the Lord in his daily walk, an ambition marked by the awareness of our accounting before Christ. Paul lived in the light of the Judgment Seat of Christ and the joy of rewards given by Christ Himself.

📖 Paul also spoke of these matters in Romans 14. What complimentary truths do you find in Romans 14:7–12?

_____
_____
_____

📖 Revelation 19:7–9 speaks of the bride of the Lamb, her preparations and her expectations. What do you discover about this bride in these verses? In what is she clothed? How does she "weave" her clothing?

_____
_____
_____
_____

📖 What additional insights do you glean from Ephesians 2:10?

_____
_____
_____

Each believer belongs to the Lord, those who have died and those still alive. Under His lordship, each and every follower of Christ will *"stand before the judgment seat of God,"* and *"each one of us will give an account of himself to God,"* all we have done, whether good or bad. The Greek word translated *"account"* is *logon,* which emphasizes an accurate account, a clear statement of our words and deeds.

When God sounds His trumpet, calling us to assemble to Him, He will also call us to an accounting before Him. He will reward us in light of that. This is not a time of "paying" for sins. That was taken care of by Christ—He fully paid our sin debt on the cross (John 1:29; Colossians 2:13–14; 1 John 2:2). He will evaluate each of us based on what we have done. Have we walked in the *"good works"* God prepared beforehand for us (Ephesians 2:10) or in our own self-initiated, self-powered, self-glorifying deeds? As the bride of the Lamb, we have woven our royal garments through the "righteous acts" of obedience to our Lord, empowered by His Spirit.

APPLY **Are you looking forward to** *"the Day"*? As believers, we can have a joyous expectation of rewards for faithful obedience to the Lord and His Word or we can have a certain degree of sorrow and regret over the poor choices of *"wood, hay, straw."* Failing to follow the Lord has consequences including the loss of many rewards. However, **today** can be a fresh start of obedience, of getting ready for **"the Day."** Ask the Lord to show you any area over which He is grieved, anywhere you have quenched His Spirit's work in you or through you. Take one simple step of obedience today, then the next step and the next. Trust Him for wisdom, grace, and strength.

Put Yourself In Their Shoes
HOLY AMBITION

Paul said he had as his *"ambition... to be pleasing"* to Christ. The Greek word translated "ambition" is *philotimeomai,* which is made up of two words, *phileo* and *time,* literally translated "love of honor." It speaks of having a love of what is valuable or honorable. Paul used the word **three** times. He valued *"pleasing"* Christ (2 Corinthians 5:10). In 1 Thessalonians 4:11, he stated *"make it your ambition to lead a quiet life and attend to your own business and work with your hands."* That speaks of the value of hard work, being responsible and helpful, easing others in your daily life. In Romans 15:20, Paul spoke of his ambition to preach Christ where He had not been named. He desired to bring the gospel to more people, to give them the message of Christ and His salvation. Paul valued His relation to the Lord, a wholesome relationship with other believers, and the opportunities to touch the lives of non-believers—a holy ambition that fulfills love for God and love for one's neighbors.

Doctrine
"THE DAY OF CHRIST," "THE DAY OF THE LORD" AND "THE DAY OF GOD"

In Scripture, the period in which Christ will gather His church to Himself is referred to as *"the Day of Christ"* (Philippians 1:10), *"the day of Christ Jesus"* (Philippians 1:6), *"the day of our Lord Jesus Christ"* (1 Corinthians 1:8), *"the day"* of revealing each believer's work (1 Corinthians 3:13), *"the day of the Lord Jesus"* (1 Corinthians 5:5), *"the day of our Lord Jesus"* (2 Corinthians 1:14), and *"that Day"* of reward (2 Timothy 1:12, 18; 4:8). Hebrews 10:25 speaks of *"the day drawing near."* It is a day of light and rejoicing. On the other hand, **"the Day of the Lord"** is a day of darkness, gloom, and judgment at the end of this present age (see Isaiah 2:10–21; 13:6–10; Joel 1:15; 2:1–2, 10–11, 31; 3:14; Amos 5:18–20; Obadiah 15; Zephaniah 1:14–18; Zechariah 14:1–4; Malachi 4:1; Acts 2:20; 1 Thessalonians 5:2; 2 Thessalonians 2:2; 2 Peter 3:10). The *"last trumpet"* of 1 Corinthians 15:52 signals *"the day of Christ,"* and *"the Great Trumpet"* signals the return of Christ as part of *"the Day of the Lord"* (Matthew 24:30–31). Then, finally **"the Day of God"** refers to that point when the "day" of sinful man is finished and God establishes *"new heavens and a new earth in which righteousness dwells"* (2 Peter 3:12–13).

Lord, may I be attentive to the trumpet voice of Your Word and Your Spirit day by day. May I be ready for Your return—Your Voice and Your Trumpet calling me to resurrection. May I live in the power You have given for today, to walk in that resurrection newness of life. I pray that I will be a *"bride"* who is making ready my garments of *"righteous acts"* as I worship You, obey Your Word, and look for Your return. Show me ways to comfort, encourage, and equip other believers as we await the trumpet sound. Thank You for Horatio Spafford's testimony and his hymn to You. In the face of deep sorrow, he had great hope—"And Lord, haste the day when the faith shall be sight, The clouds be rolled back as a scroll, The Trump shall resound and the Lord shall descend, 'Even so'—it is well with my soul." Give us wisdom and Your empowering to be the witness to those who do not yet know You—that we may see a great number come to faith in You and join in worship, awaiting the coming of the fullness of Your Kingdom. In Jesus' name, Amen.

The Day of Atonement

SEEING CHRIST'S COMPLETION OF OUR SALVATION

The sixth Feast is known as the Day of Atonement, occurring on the tenth day of Tishri, the second of the fall Feasts, ten days after the Feast of Trumpets. It is a unique Feast in that it is a day of fasting. As the only Fast Day of the seven feasts, it served as a day for humbling oneself before the Lord, a day of serious prayer and reflection, and a day of great hope in the mercy and forgiveness of God.

This Day was also a day with an intense focus on purity and holiness. The High Priest did his work paying attention to minute details of ritual cleanliness. It pictures for us the necessity for holiness in the presence of God. It also unveils for us the rejoicing one could know in His presence when all is as He directs. We were created to experience the joy of His presence, but sin brought separation from His presence and loss of that joy. It would require a work of new creation proportions, a work only God could do. In the New Testament, we see the open door into His presence in the redemption provided by Christ in His new creation work.

Too many today seek various substitutes for the presence of God, substitutes that try to cover guilt, bring peace, or offer some hope, but always a false hope when not connected to Jesus Christ. The substitute satisfactions always fall short—unsatisfactory and temporary.

The Day of Atonement is perhaps the most reflective of the seven Feasts since it calls for an intense searching of the heart and life. It is a time for serious reflection on the words and deeds of the past year, a time to consider how God has seen them, and a time of seeking His mercy. After all, the attention of the people is on the High Priest as he goes before the Mercy Seat seeking the cleansing and forgiveness of God for yet another year. When the day is done, it is also a time of great rejoicing. Sins have been covered for another year, and guilt is carried away into the wilderness, symbolically removed through the scapegoat. We will see the pictures of these realities in the events of the Day of Atonement, especially in the work of Jesus Christ

> **Did You Know?**
>
> **THE DAY OF ATONEMENT— "YOM KIPPUR"**
>
> The Day of Atonement is known in the Hebrew language as *Yom Kippur*, literally, "Day of Covering." It is the **one day** of the year, *Tishri* 10, in which **one man** in all Israel, the high priest, could enter behind the veil into the Holy of Holies and "cover" the sins of the people at the Mercy Seat (the *kapporeth* or covering of the Ark of the Covenant). Though incomplete, that covering of another year's sins opened the way for another year of worship and fellowship with the Lord. This day was fulfilled on **one day** in **one man**—Jesus Christ, our High Priest who brought completion in dealing with our sin, not merely covering it, but removing it, cleansing each believer, giving full forgiveness along with constant access into the presence of God.

fulfilling these pictures. In our exploration of the Day of Atonement, we will also see how Christ fulfills all the hopes and promises of this day for the one who places faith in Him.

The seventh month is the Sabbath of months, the number seven pointing to the attainment of fullness, thus Tishri pictures the attainment of the fullness of months. In light of this and the three Feast days occurring in this month, Tishri is considered the most sacred of months. It culminates in the Feast of Tabernacles, the greatest of the Feasts in joy and celebration. We will see that in our final lesson. For this lesson, the Day of Atonement is our focus with its careful attention on our much-needed redemption and with that, its certain rejoicing in His presence.

Lesson Seven — DAY ONE

HOLY GROUND—HUMBLE GROUND

The Day of Atonement was perhaps the most serious day in the Jewish calendar, certainly the most serious of the seven Feasts. The priests and the people took this day very seriously. Why? What do the Scriptures show us about these matters? Today we will look at the background to this momentous yearly event and begin to discover the fuller teaching of Scripture not only of the Day of Atonement, but also its meaning for us today.

📖 Leviticus 23:26–32 summarizes the events of the Day of Atonement. We will look at the details in Day Two. First, what do you see as unique to this day as found in verses 27, 29, and 32?

_____
_____
_____

The Lord called Israel to observe a Day of Atonement on the tenth day of Tishri, from the evening of the ninth to the evening of the tenth. Like other Feast times, this day included a *"holy convocation"* and a *"sabbath of complete rest."* God required offerings by fire with the focus on making atonement *"before the LORD your God."* The unique aspect of this day is the call to *"humble your souls,"* for each person to *"humble himself"* for the entire day, evening to evening. Humbling one's soul refers to an attitude of humility which included fasting for this one day. So significant was the factor of fasting that in the New Testament account of Paul's Mediterranean voyage to Rome, Acts 27:9 gives the calendar parameters using the term *"the fast"* referring to the Day of Atonement in late September. This day of fasting proved central throughout Israel's history, in Old and New Testament days.

Why this emphasis on humbling one's soul? Perhaps we will gain further insight as we look into the background of this day.

📖 Look at Leviticus 16:1–2. On what incident does verse 1 focus?

_____
_____

Did You Know?
THIS DATE IN ANCIENT HISTORY

Alfred Edersheim notes that according to Jewish tradition the Day of Atonement on *Tishri* 10 coincides with the day Adam sinned and repented, the day Abraham was circumcised, and the day Moses came down from the mountain to atone for the sin of the golden calf incident [*The Temple*, p. 305, n. 1]. The Scriptures show the timing of Moses' descent from Mount Sinai with the second set of stone tablets containing the Ten Commandments to be around Tishri 9. That date coincides very closely with the timeline of Moses' activities—forty days on Mount Sinai (Exodus 32:1, 15; Deuteronomy 9:9–11) from around *Sivan* 6 (the date Israel heard the Ten Commandments on Mount Sinai) to *Tammuz* 16, followed by forty days of prayer (Exodus 32:30–31; Deuteronomy 9:18–20, 25–29), then a second forty days on Mount Sinai (Exodus 34:2, 27–28; Deuteronomy 10:1–5, 10). Those 120 plus days conclude around *Tishri* 7 to 9.

📖 What did the two sons do?

_____

_____

📖 On what did the Lord focus attention in verse 2?

_____

_____

In beginning the discussion and guidelines for the Day of Atonement in Leviticus 16, the incident of the death of two of Aaron's sons takes center stage. Verse one records that they approached the presence of the Lord irreverently and died as a result. Therefore, the Lord carefully cautioned Moses on how Aaron should approach the Lord in the Holy of Holies behind the veil. He could not enter there just any time he wanted to, in any way he chose, but he was required to follow the Lord's directions. If he failed to obey, he would die upon entering the Holy of Holies. There at the Mercy Seat, God would make Himself visible in *"the cloud,"* what theologians often refer to as the *"Shekinah* Glory Cloud." The word *"Shekinah"* is linked to the Hebrew word *shakan* which means to dwell, to settle down, to abide, or to permanently reside. It refers to God's promised, covenant presence, His uniquely and powerfully manifested presence with His people.

What can we learn from the two sons of Aaron who died? What did they do wrong? Why in Leviticus 16:1 did God refocus Moses' and Aaron's attention on this incident? In order to better understand the Day of Atonement and the guidelines God gave for that day, it is important to trace the journey of these two sons, Nadab and Abihu.

📖 What did Nadab and Abihu experience in Exodus 24:1–2, 9–11?

_____

_____

_____

📖 What could this kind of experience mean in the lives of these men?

_____

_____

_____

Put Yourself In Their Shoes
NADAB AND ABIHU

were the two oldest of four sons born to Aaron and Amminadab. Eleazar and Ithamar were the two youngest (Exodus 6:23). All four brothers were chosen as priests along with their father Aaron (Exodus 28:1). The incident of Nadab and Abihu dying when they offered *"strange fire"* in the presence of the Lord is mentioned five times in Scripture (Leviticus 10:1–2; 16:1; Numbers 3:4; 26:61; 1 Chronicles 24:2). Scripture records that neither of them had any children (Numbers 3:4).

As part of the covenant ceremony, the Lord invited Moses to ascend Mount Sinai and bring Aaron and his two oldest sons Nadab and Abihu along with seventy of the elders of Israel to worship the Lord. When they journeyed up the mountain, *"they saw the God of Israel"* with a pavement of clear sapphire under His feet. (Ezekiel 1:26–28 and Revelation 4:6 use similar language about the Presence of the Lord.) There they ate and drank the covenant meal sealing the covenant, and they *"beheld"* God gazing contemplatively, the Hebrew word *chazah* conveying perception, insight, contemplating with pleasure. Apparently this vision of God and something of His majesty proved stunning to these men, especially at this momentous covenant event. Certainly this could prove life-changing for them.

Leviticus 10:1-2

Put Yourself In Their Shoes
A WARNING ABOUT WINE

In Leviticus 10:8–11, after the incident of Nadab and Abihu offering *"strange fire,"* God warned against drinking any wine or strong drink in the Tabernacle, *"so that you may not die."* Coming in the context of this incident, it is possible that wine or strong drink had something to do with Nadab's and Abihu's unholy and presumptuous actions. Moses made a point about being able *"to make a distinction between the holy and the profane and between the unclean and the clean"* and about being able to teach the people the Word of God. These actions take mental and spiritual alertness and discernment. Wine and strong drink impair such alertness and sensitivity to the things of God.

[Handwritten notes in margin:]
- sabbath create
- Passover Lamb
- Feat First Priest
- Peticost
- God writing word on our heart
- Feat trumpy New year God
- Atonement
- How to aposh God
- Tabernacle to dwell with God

In Exodus 28:1 God chose Aaron and his four sons to minister as priests to Him, and He set apart special garments first for Aaron as high priest, then for the four sons as priests assisting their father (Exodus 28:2–43; 39). They were to be anointed with special oil, ordained and consecrated as priests through certain unique sacrifices and offerings with a special seven-day ceremony (Exodus 29; 40:12–15). This valued office and ministry was a great and sacred honor. These would minister to the Lord Himself, and they would be His representatives to the people. Each aspect of setting them apart showed great honor to them as God's chosen priests. This consecration took place according to God's instructions (Leviticus 8) and Aaron and his sons began ministering in the Tabernacle (Leviticus 9). When they had finished the required offerings, God revealed His pleasure as *"the glory of the LORD appeared to all the people"* and *"fire came out from before the LORD and consumed the burnt offering"* and the people worshiped (Leviticus 9:24).

📖 All *seemed* well, but something was not as it should be. Read Leviticus 10:1–7. What did Nadab and Abihu do, according to verse 1?

_____
_____
_____

📖 Where did they do this, according to Leviticus 16:1–2? What additional clues are in Leviticus 10:4 about where they were?

In the Sanuary.
_____
_____

📖 According to Leviticus 10:2, how did God respond?

Fire went out from the Lord and devoured them and they died before the Lord

📖 What explanation did Moses give in verse 3?

By those who come near me, I must be regarded as holy before all people. I must be Glorified.

📖 Why do you think Nadab and Abihu acted in this manner?

Not humbling themselves, pride
_____
_____

Nadab and Abihu took bronze fire pans, placed ordinary burning coals on them, and then placed the special incense on those coals. God saw this as an offering of *"strange fire,"* apparently with coals from a general campfire rather than the blood-soaked coals from the bronze altar. They acted independent of the Lord and, most likely independent of their father, Aaron. When Leviticus 16:1 states they *"approached the presence of the LORD"* and died, we find that they were in front of *"the sanctuary"* or Holy of Holies, perhaps at the veil dividing the Holy Place from the Holy of Holies or even within the veil inside the Holy of Holies at the Mercy Seat. In Leviticus 16:2,

God's caution focuses on being before the Mercy Seat with the penalty being certain death for anyone approaching apart from the Lord's clear guidelines. That is the response Nadab and Abihu received from the Lord for their actions.

Moses saw how they came near the Lord as failing to treat the Lord as holy. Since God promised to dwell in the Holy of Holies at the Mercy Seat, it is likely that the two brothers proudly presumed to enter there with their *"strange fire."* It is clear from God's regulations concerning the incense and proper worship that He would only accept the blood-soaked coals of the bronze altar for burning the special incense. Everything He ordered in the Tabernacle had a specific place and a specific message to convey about Him, about worship, and about the salvation He would give through that place. Moses made it clear that in what they did and in how they did it, Nadab and Abihu did not treat the Lord as holy nor did they honor Him before the people. Apparently this was evident to Aaron as well.

After all they had seen and experienced, why would Nadab and Abihu act this way? Perhaps we have a clue in the Lord's call for the Day of Atonement to be a day of humbling oneself. Nadab and Abihu experienced the blessing of God in their lives, including the privilege of being part of the covenant meal and seeing a stunning view of the Lord on Mount Sinai. It was truly a very holy moment on holy ground. Such blessings and privileges can lead in one of two ways, toward humility or toward pride. Pride can then lead to presumption and even foolishness or folly. Humility on the other hand leads to gratitude and greater surrender and worship, to pliability before the Lord, to being flexible in His hands, ready for Him to lead. It means trusting His mighty hand in one's life. It also leads to honesty and purity before Him, ready to admit where one is wrong or where one is weak or unsure. That kind of honest and repentant heart opens the way for one to receive God's forgiveness and His wisdom and strength. It appears that Nadab and Abihu erred toward pride. Proverbs 16:18 wisely warns, *"Pride goes before destruction, and a haughty spirit before stumbling."*

📖 Look at these verses. What response do you see when Moses or Aaron and the people encountered *"the cloud"* of the Lord's presence?

Exodus 19:9

_____

_____

Exodus 33:9–10

_____

_____

Leviticus 9:23–24

_____

_____

The Lord told Moses He would appear in *"a thick cloud."* That manifestation would reveal the awesomeness of the Lord and the authority He gave to Moses, so the people would believe in Moses and be more likely to follow.

[Handwritten margin notes: Set apart / Glorified / Near Him]

Did You Know?
YOU ARE THE HOLY OF HOLIES

Paul states in 1 Corinthians 6:19–20 that each believer is a *"temple of the Holy Spirit."* The Greek word *naos* translated *"temple,"* specifically refers to the Holy of Holies, the room of God's dwelling in the Tabernacle. Each believer is indwelt by the Spirit of God as Jesus promised in John 14:16–17. Isaiah 57:15 speaks of the reality of God dwelling with the *"humble spirit."* Drawing near to God does not mean we have to journey to Jerusalem or to heaven. He has journeyed to us, to indwell each and every believer. Drawing near means coming to Him in humble prayer, anywhere we are.

Often, when they saw the pillar of cloud descend where the Lord spoke with Moses, the people viewing would worship at their tents. When the Lord manifested His glory to the people as Aaron and the priests began their ministry, especially when His fire consumed the burnt offering, the people *"shouted and fell on their faces."* It was a time of humility and worship.

> 📖 In Leviticus 16:2, what do you think the Lord is emphasizing in His statement, *"for I will appear in the cloud over the mercy seat"*? What attitude or mindset is God calling for on the Day of Atonement?
>
> _____
> _____
> _____

The Lord carefully instructed Moses and Aaron in the procedures for the Day of Atonement, giving them more instruction for this "Feast" than for any other. When He did, He reminded them of the incident of Nadab and Abihu. Before walking them through the procedures for the Day of Atonement, He set the boundaries for approaching the Lord. He emphasized the fact that the Lord Himself would be there visible via *"the cloud over the mercy seat."* It was a statement emphasizing the uniqueness and holiness of the Lord and of this place as well as an experience of the mercy of God that could meet Aaron there. God's holiness, His being uniquely set apart as pure, as unlike any other god or like any sinful person, brought a seriousness to this setting and to this meeting. It also brought a measure of hope in the Lord's mercy. After all, God did provide a way, His way to meet together, and to receive His forgiveness, cleansing, and mercy. All of this called for an attitude of humility. This was holy ground. Aaron and the people should be careful to make it humble ground, coming before the Lord in humility and honesty.

What did this day hold? We will begin to look at that in Day Two.

Lesson Seven — Day Two
"Here's How You Come to Me"—The Elements of the Day of Atonement

When we look at the guidelines the Lord gave Moses for the Day of Atonement, we find Him saying in essence, "Here's how you come to Me and walk with Me." What exactly occurred on the Day of Atonement? A walk through this day will help us see the importance of this day to the Lord and to His people. It will also help us see how it relates to the work of salvation Jesus has accomplished on our behalf and how He wants us to come to Him and walk with Him.

> 📖 Leviticus 23:26–32 gives a summary of the Day of Atonement. Leviticus 16:29–34 also highlights the main points of the day. First, what was the purpose of this day according to Leviticus 16:30, 34 and 23:28?
>
> _____
> _____

📖 What specifics do you find in Leviticus 16:29 and 31? Who is to be involved? What was to be their mindset on this day? What physical action did God require of all the people for this day?

_____
_____
_____
_____

📖 What and who needed to be cleansed, according to verses 32–33?

_____
_____

The Day of Atonement was a day set aside for the people to be cleansed, specifically being cleansed *"from all* [their] *sins before the LORD."* The biblical term as found in Leviticus 23:27 is *Yom Hakippurim,* a plural term literally translated, *"Day of Atonings,"* focusing on the multi-faceted cleansing of this day. The Lord set the standard and knows the hearts of everyone. In His holiness He recognizes anything that does not match with His nature and character, anything that comes short of His glory and holiness. The Lord set aside this same day, the tenth of *Tishri* every year to focus on making atonement *"for the sons of Israel for all their sins."* He emphasized their relationship with the Lord in this day which focused on making atonement *"on* [their] *behalf before the LORD* [their] *God"* [emphasis mine].

To focus attention on the Lord and their relationship, in Leviticus 16:31 and 23:32, God called for *"a sabbath of solemn rest,"* literally *shabbath* (meaning "to cease," therefore "to rest") *shabbathon,* "a sabbath of sabbath," a carefully guarded rest, ceasing all work. No one did any work, none of the people of Israel, nor any foreigners living temporarily in the land, lest they face God's judgment (Leviticus 23:30). The call to *"humble your souls,"* meant not only a serious mindset, but showing a humble attitude by fasting the entire day, from the evening of the ninth to the evening of the tenth of Tishri, a day of honest reflection and humble petition for cleansing from sin. This cleansing included the priests and the people, the Tabernacle and the altar, everything related to their worship and walk in everyday life. *All* needed cleansing. This day covered all of life.

📖 Concerning the procedures for the day, what is the first detail God addresses in Leviticus 16:3?

_____
_____

📖 What is unique in the high priest's dress for this day of ministry according to Leviticus 16:4? What message or meaning do you think these garments convey?

_____
_____
_____
_____

Word Study
"MAKE ATONEMENT"

The Hebrew word translated *"make atonement"* is *kaphar,* which literally means, "to cover." The root word from which it originates refers to covering with bitumen or tar. Interestingly, it is the word used of Noah covering the Ark with pitch or tar thus making it waterproof, a place of safety and salvation because it was covered (Genesis 6:14). A derivative of this word is the Hebrew word for "village" referring to a community *protected* by walls. The covering we must have is the "atonement" provided by Jesus in His death and resurrection (Romans 4:25; 5:9–11). He is our Ark of Salvation, our Wall of Protection, our Atonement covering who forgives and cleanses from sin.

Put Yourself In Their Shoes
HUMBLING YOURSELVES

In the Old Testament, the term *"humble your souls"* or similar terms, usually included fasting from food and sometimes food and drink. This is the implication in the passages referring to the Day of Atonement (Leviticus 16:29, 31; 23:27, 29, 32). Humbling oneself in fasting is also found in Psalm 35:13 and 69:10–11. Isaiah 58:5 speaks of *"a fast, even an acceptable day to the LORD,"* linking humble fasting with pleasing the Lord. The word *"acceptable,"* from the Hebrew word *ratsown,* refers to being a delight or well-pleasing to another. God delighted in His people humbling themselves before Him on the Day of Atonement, admitting their sins and being grateful to Him for forgiveness.

LESSON SEVEN – THE DAY OF ATONEMENT 147

Word Study
MERCY SEAT

The term *"mercy seat"* (Leviticus 16:15) is also translated *"the atonement cover"* or *"propitiatory,"* from the Hebrew word *kapporeth*, which literally means "covering," derived from the verb *kaphar*, to cover. *Kapporeth* is the term used to refer to the *"mercy seat,"* the solid gold lid of the Ark of the Covenant to which were attached two solid gold cherubim. It is considered the "throne of God" (1 Samuel 4:4; 2 Samuel 6:2; Psalm 80:1; 99:1). The Greek equivalent to *kapporeth* is *hilasterion*, found in Romans 3:25, 1 John 2:2, 4:10, and Hebrews 2:17 where it is translated *"propitiation"* referring to Jesus and His sacrifice on the cross. *Hilasterion* can be translated "expiation" or "satisfaction." It is also found in Hebrews 9:5 where it is translated *"mercy seat"* or *"atonement cover."* Jesus **is** our Mercy Seat, the place where the mercy and justice of God meet to pay the penalty for our sins in order to forgive us and bring us into fellowship in His presence.

Did You Know?
THE SCAPEGOAT AND THE TEMPLE

Jewish tradition (as found in the *Mishna* and the Talmud, *Yoma* 39a, b) says that part of the scarlet sash of the scapegoat was torn and tied to the Temple door. When the sacrifices were complete and accepted by God, the scarlet thread that the scapegoat had worn turned white. According to Jewish tradition, that miracle did not take place for approximately forty years before the Temple was destroyed (**30 to 70 AD**). **Jesus died around AD 30**.

📖 Review Leviticus 16:5–28 and Numbers 29:7–11. What animals were selected for sacrifice on this day, according to Leviticus 16:3, 5, and 6 and Numbers 29:8–11?

_____
_____
_____

📖 What unique practice do you find in Leviticus 16:7–9?

_____
_____

📖 Who are the people for whom Aaron must make atonement, according to verses 11 and 15?

_____
_____
_____

📖 What places must be cleansed by blood, according to verses 16, 18–20?

_____
_____
_____

God required the high priest to bring certain offerings and to do so clothed appropriately. One of the first matters upon which God focused was the cleanliness of the high priest. God required a complete bathing and then special white linen garments made for this day—a linen tunic and undergarments, a linen sash and turban. The high priest set aside his normal dress (see Exodus 28:1–43; Leviticus 8:6–19) during the sin offerings and wore these simpler garments focused on purity, holiness, and humility. God required first a sin offering for the high priest and his household before he offered anything for the people. The animals to be offered were a bull as a sin offering for the priest and two goats as sin offerings for the people. Unique to this day was the casting of lots for the two goats. The lot placed on the head of the goat *"for the LORD"* designated that goat to be slain as a sin offering. The other lot *"for Azazel"* or *"for the scapegoat"* designated the goat which would remain alive to be sent away into the wilderness as *"Azazel"* (*"goat of removal"*) or *"the scapegoat."* Each is a picture of Jesus who was slain as our sin offering and who took away our sins.

After the bull and the first goat sin offerings were slain, the high priest applied the blood on the Mercy Seat in the Holy of Holies, in the Holy Place, and at the bronze altar to symbolically cleanse the entire Tabernacle *"because of the impurities of the sons of Israel, and because of their transgressions"* committed over the past year. The worshipers, the priests, and their worship throughout the year were not without defilements and imperfections that must be atoned for and cleansed.

📖 We have seen the second goat known as *"Azazel"* or *"the scapegoat,"* or as some theologians term it, the "escape goat." A literal translation of

"Azazel" is "the goat of removal." How was this seen? What details concerning this second goat of the sin offering do you find in verses 20–22?

_____

_____

_____

The high priest applied the blood of the bull and the first goat, the goat *"for the Lord"* (or *"for Jehovah"*), to atone for himself, his household, and the people, as well as for the holy place, the Tabernacle, and the bronze altar. He then offered the live goat, *"Azazel"* or *"the scapegoat"* in a unique way. This second goat would not be slain at the altar. The high priest placed his hands on the head of the goat confessing the sins of the people, symbolically placing those sins on the goat. Laying hands on a person or animal is a picture of identifying with that one. Aaron the high priest by faith identified the people and their sins with the goat, the goat being then the substitute to bear away those sins. After that, the high priest sent the goat away *"into the wilderness by the hand of a man who stands in readiness."* One of the priests walked the goat out into the barren wilderness, *"to a solitary land"* where he released the *"scapegoat"* or "escape goat," symbolically taking away sin and guilt. The people escaped judgment.

📖 What did the high priest do after the release of the scapegoat? Summarize what he did according to Leviticus 16:23–25.

_____

_____

_____

📖 What significance do you see in the blood of the sin offering being applied first, before the offering of the burnt offerings?

_____

_____

_____

📖 What remained to be done to the bull and the goat of the sin offering according to verse 27?

_____

_____

_____

📖 What did God require of those who helped in these offerings, according to verses 26 and 28? What message does this send to the people who observed these matters?

_____

_____

_____

We have seen the sprinkling of the blood of the sin offerings (bull and goat) and the sending away of the scapegoat. God ordered that the high priest first deal with the sin of the people. Sin must be dealt with before worship can be

---

Word Study
"AZAZEL" AND "NASAH"

The Hebrew word "Azazel" is used only in Leviticus 16 (verses 8, 10, 26) referring to *"the scapegoat"* or as some term it "the escape goat." Some believe the word to be made up of two words translated as "the goat of removal." Alfred Edersheim sees it rooted in a word meaning "wholly to go away" or "wholly to put aside." Leviticus 16:22 uses the Hebrew word "nasah," "to bear, carry, lift," to describe the scapegoat which *"shall bear on itself all their iniquities."* That same word is used in Isaiah 53:4 of the *"Man of sorrows"* who *"bore"* our griefs and in Isaiah 53:12, which states, *"He Himself bore the sin of many."* Isaiah 53 is quoted several times referring to Jesus' life, ministry, and death on the cross (e.g., Matthew 8:17; Luke 22:37; Acts 8:30–35; 1 Peter 2:22–25). Each of these points to the singular truth of the removal of sin and guilt, ultimately fulfilled in Jesus the Lamb of God *"who takes away the sin of the world"* (John 1:29; Hebrews 10:4, 11–18).

> "For on that day the priest shall make atonement for you, to cleanse you, that you may be clean from all your sins before the Lord."
>
> Leviticus 16:30 (NKJV)

Put Yourself In Their Shoes
WE NEED CLEANSING

On the Day of Atonement the priests sacrificed **15** animals. **Five hundred** priests assisted the High Priest. The High Priest sprinkled the blood **43** times. He washed his whole body and changed garments **5** times. He washed his hands and feet an additional **10** times. The emphasis on cleansing filled the day—through the ashes of the Red Heifer, through the water washings, through the clean garments, and through the blood of the sacrificed animals.

---

what it should be. There still remained the burnt offerings and the actual placing of the sin offerings on the altar. After he sent away the scapegoat, the high priest took off the white linen garments, bathed completely and dressed in the beautiful garments of the high priest. In those garments, he offered the burnt offering of a ram for himself and his family and the burnt offering of a ram for the people. In addition, he offered the burnt offerings of a young bull, seven lambs, and the appropriate grain and wine offerings. According to Numbers 29:8–10, he also offered the kid of a goat as an additional sin offering for this day. The burnt offerings totally consumed in the fires of the altar speak of surrender, of worship with a whole heart, the worshiper consumed with the Lord and His will. Having dealt with sin and experiencing the cleansing of sin through the sin offering, the high priest dressed in his glorious apparel could lead the people in worship to the Lord.

After offering the burnt offerings, the high priest took the fat portions of the bull and goat sin offerings and offered those on the bronze altar. Then certain priests took the remaining carcass of the bull and the goat sin offerings outside the camp to a certain clean place and burned them. God required the one who released the scapegoat to bathe his body and wash his clothes before coming back into the camp. The same held true for the one burning the sin offering outside the camp. Everything about this day spoke of cleansing. The physical matters of cleansing symbolized the spiritual, mental, moral, and ethical cleansing of the people. Of greater significance, these offerings pictured the ultimate fulfillment of Jesus Christ as our pure and holy sin offering dying *"outside the camp"* (Hebrews 13:10–13). God desired for His people to be *"a holy nation"* (see Exodus 19:6), every area of life touched by Him, His holiness, and His ways.

What can we learn from the New Testament about the Day of Atonement? How did Jesus relate to this Day? We will explore those questions in Days Three and Four.

Lesson Seven — DAY THREE
JESUS AND THE DAY OF ATONEMENT

We have seen God's order for the Day of Atonement in the Old Testament. How does the Day of Atonement in the Old Testament link to the New Testament and to believers today? The link is found in Jesus Christ, our High Priest. How did Jesus fulfill His role as our High Priest? The author of the book of Hebrews shows how Jesus fulfills this very important role and this *"Day"* and how it applies to every believer. Today we will explore these Scriptures.

📖 The book of Hebrews has much to say about the Tabernacle, the offerings, and the priesthood, as well as the Day of Atonement. First, what does this book say about Jesus and His role as High Priest? Look at each of these verses and give a brief summary of the characteristics about Jesus.

Hebrews 1:1–4

_____

_____

Hebrews 1:6, 8–12

_____

_____

Hebrews 2:9

_____

_____

Hebrews 2:17–18

_____

_____

Hebrews 3:1–2

_____

_____

Hebrews 4:14–16

_____

_____

Hebrews 5:4–10

_____

_____

Hebrews 7:16–17, 24–25

_____

_____

Hebrews 7:26–28

_____

_____

Hebrews 8:1–2

_____

_____

HEBREWS 2:17–18; 3:1–2a

"Therefore, He had to be made like His brethren in all things that He might become a merciful and faithful high priest in things pertaining to God, to make propitiation for the sins of the people. For since He Himself was tempted in that which He has suffered, He is able to come to the aid of those who are tempted. Therefore, holy brethren, partakers of a heavenly calling, consider Jesus, the Apostle and High Priest of our confession. He was faithful to Him who appointed Him…"

The book of Hebrews exalts the Lord Jesus Christ. He is the Son of God, heir of all things, creator and sustainer of all, being the exact image of God, who in His life, death, and resurrection *"purged our sins"* and now reigns enthroned on high having the name above all names. He is forever worthy of worship as God, the righteous one. Jesus is crowned with and worthy of all glory and honor. As the God-Man, He tasted death for everyone after being tempted in all things but never sinning. He lives as *"a merciful and faithful high priest"* forever. He is able *"to make propitiation for the sins of the people"* and daily able to come to the aid of all who are tempted.

> **Put Yourself In Their Shoes**
> ### THE CENTRALITY OF THE TEMPLE
>
> John MacArthur answers the question, why the emphasis on the Temple in the Old Testament. "1) It was the center of worship that called people to correct belief through the generations. 2) It was the symbol of God's presence with His people. 3) It was the symbol of forgiveness and grace, reminding the people of the seriousness of sin and the availability of mercy. 4) It prepared the people for the true Lamb of God, Jesus Christ, who would take away sin. 5) It was a place of prayer. (Cf. 2 Chronicles 7:12–17)" (John MacArthur, *The MacArthur Study Bible*, p. 602, Note on 2 Chronicles 5:1).

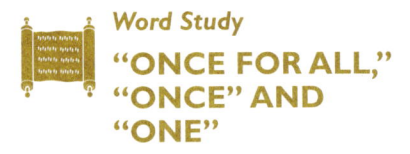

He is our High Priest, faithful to the Father in all things and faithful to His followers in all of life. He has obtained *"eternal salvation"* for all who trust Him. As we come to His *"throne of grace,"* He gives of His mercy and provides well-timed help for our needs. He is *"able to save to the uttermost"* or *"forever"* anyone *"who comes to God through Him."* Jesus is well qualified in character and power—*"holy, innocent, undefiled, separated from sinners and exalted above the heavens"* (7:26). The author of Hebrews makes it clear that his *"main point"* in chapters 1—8 is that *"we have such a High Priest, who is seated at the right hand of the Majesty in the heavens, a Minister of the sanctuary . . . in the true tabernacle"* in heaven. Jesus **is** better than the angels, the better High Priest who brings in a better covenant with a better hope, better promises, and a better inheritance having offered the better sacrifice of Himself (Hebrews 1:4; 7:19, 22; 8:6; 9:15, 23). Hebrews 3:1 states it well, *"consider Jesus"*—observe carefully, perceive clearly, apply accurately, and obey fully. Now let's see how He fulfills the Day of Atonement for any and all believers.

Hebrews 7—10 speaks of the covenants God enacted, the Tabernacle, the priesthood, and the various sacrifices offered. Specifically, certain aspects unique to the Day of Atonement are referred to in Hebrews 9:7, 12–14, 24–26 and 10:1–4. How did Jesus fulfill that Day and the sacrifices required for our sins? A brief overview of that will help us see the bigger picture of the Day of Atonement from the New Testament perspective.

📖 First, what condition existed when Jesus came, according to Hebrews 9:6–9 and 10:1–4? What inadequacies are found there? List what the Law can and cannot do.

_____

_____

First, the Law and the Tabernacle provided a shadow of *"the good things to come,"* of coming realities, specifically the salvation Jesus would bring. Second, all the sacrifices of the Old Testament, in the Tabernacle for 480 years and in the Temple for over 990 years (1 Kings 6:1, 37–38), could not *"make perfect"* the priests or the worshipers. Instead, we see the third reality; all those sacrifices are *"a reminder of sins year by year."* Why? Because, fourthly, it is *"impossible for the blood of bulls and goats to take away sins."* All the sacrifices offered year after year on the Day of Atonement can remind of sin, but can **never remove** that sin.

> **Word Study**
> ### "ONCE FOR ALL," "ONCE" AND "ONE"
>
> The Greek word *hapax* translated *"once,"* appears eight times in the book of Hebrews, twice (9:26, 28) referring to Christ's sacrifice for sin. The Greek word *ephapax* (*epi* + *hapax*), an intensified form of *hapax*, translated literally *"upon once,"* appears three times in reference to Christ offering Himself *"once for all"* and entering *"the holy place once for all"* (Hebrews 7:27; 9:12; 10:10). The word *"one"* from the Greek word *mia* is used of Christ's sacrifice in Hebrews 10:12, 14. Jesus did not need to make many sacrifices or offer Himself often, *"but now **once** at the consummation of the ages He has been manifested to put away sin by the sacrifice of Himself"* (Hebrews 9:26).

📖 Many sacrifices or one? That is one of the central points of the discussion about Jesus and His ministry as High Priest. Look at these verses and summarize what you find.

Hebrews 7:27

_____

_____

Hebrews 9:12

_____

_____

Hebrews 10:10, 12

_____

_____

While the many high priests over the years offered countless sacrifices, Jesus our High Priest offered Himself *"once for all,"* not for His own sins, but for ours. *"Once for all"* He entered the holy place *"through His own blood."* He offered one sacrifice for sins *"for all time."* He did not and would not need to offer Himself ever again. By His offering, He also *"perfected"* or *"completely saved" "for all time"* those who believe in Him. Jesus secured *"eternal redemption"* by His *"once for all"* sacrifice.

What has God done through His Son, the Lord Jesus? In the Old Covenant the substitutionary death of several animals symbolized the death of the covenant parties to an old way and entering into a new way. That death enacted the covenant. In various ceremonies and phases of enacting the Old Covenant, Moses sprinkled the blood of various animals on the Book of the Law, on the Tabernacle, on the priests, and on the people.

The priests began performing their sacred duties, offering the various sacrifices for their own sins and for those of the people, and applying the blood of those sacrifices at the Tabernacle. That service provided a temporary covering for sin, particularly in the work of the Day of Atonement each year, but it could not perfect the consciences of the priests or the worshipers. It reminded of sin year after year, but could never remove sin. It provided a temporal redemption, a provisional salvation.

The need existed for a better covenant, a more perfect Tabernacle, a greater High Priest and a more perfect sacrifice with blood that would remove sin, which would provide eternal redemption. Jesus met that need. He died in our place as our sacrifice, for our sin and lawlessness. As the greater High Priest, He enacted the New Covenant, ultimately presenting Himself and His sacrifice in *"the greater and more perfect tabernacle, not made with hands…not of this creation."* Through His blood He removes our sin, cleanses our consciences forever, and sanctifies us completely. The redemption He provides is eternal. All of our sins and lawless deeds He forgives and forgets, never to remember them again. Now all the redeemed await His return to reveal the fullness of salvation He secured in His death and resurrection. Those who face death do so with an eternal hope, a confidence that all His promises and provision will be fully seen **and experienced** in that day.

📖 Let's summarize what Christ has done to fulfill all the pictures presented in the Day of Atonement. Look at the following verses and fill in the blank as to who Christ is or what He has done.

1. Hebrews 8:1 and 9:11—Jesus is the _____ _____.

2. Ephesians 5:2—Jesus is the _____ and _____ for us (see Hebrews 9:14).

3. Hebrews 9:12—Jesus applied His own _____ in the greater tabernacle.

4. Hebrews 10:20—Jesus was torn as the _____ opening the way for us into the Holy of Holies or the Most Holy Place.

Word Study
"FOR ALL TIME" OR "FOREVER"

Hebrews 10:12 and 14 use the phrase *"for all time"* or *"forever"* referring to Christ's sacrifice and our salvation. It is a translation of the Greek phrase *eis to dienekes*, literally "into the carrying through." *Dienekes* is made up of two Greek words, *dia*, meaning "through" as in our English word "diameter" and *enegko* meaning to bear or carry. Christ carried through to completion His sacrifice for sins, assuring us of our salvation forever. He will carry each of us through into eternity.

Did You Know?
COVENANT DEATH AND COVENANT LIFE, A LEGAL GUARANTEE

Every covenant agreement was a legally binding agreement involving the death of an animal(s) as symbolic of the death of the two parties entering into the covenant relationship. Each agreed to die to an old way of life and enter into a new way. When God entered into covenant with Abram in Genesis 15:9–21, it meant that Abram had a new relationship with a new destiny. Abram no longer walked in the ways of his homeland of Ur, nor in the ways of the Canaanites or the Egyptians. He walked in a new way, following God and His ways (see also Genesis 26:26–33). It is the same with Jesus' New Covenant death. When He died in our place, opening the door to death to the old life and to living with His new life, He did so with legal guarantees. Hebrews 9:17 states that a death causes the covenant to be *"valid"* (ratified, take effect) and *"in force,"* translations of two legal terms, *bebaios* and *ischuo*. Jesus legally guarantees this covenant in His death and resurrection.

Word Study
"WILL, TESTAMENT, COVENANT"

The words "covenant" or "testament," as used in the term Old Testament is a translation of the Hebrew word *beriyth*, meaning *"covenant"* as found in Genesis 15:18. It is closely linked with the idea of cutting (to cut a covenant) because one making the covenant often passed between pieces of a sacrifice cut in two, as in Genesis 15:10–21. Those in a covenant agreement saw it with life and death seriousness. In the New Testament, *"covenant"* is a translation of the Greek word *diatheke*, which means to set in order, to arrange thoroughly. *Diatheke* is the Greek equivalent to he Hebrew word *beriyth*. In our day, a person's "last will and testament," refers to the legal agreement enacted upon his or her death. The covenant or testament or **will** of God was fully enacted by the **death** of Jesus. He has thoroughly arranged our salvation and now **lives** to fulfill all the provisions and promises He made. What a guarantee of security!

EXTRA MILE
JESUS' MINISTRY

We have seen some of the ministry of Jesus and how it contrasted with the Old Covenant ministries. In what other ways is Jesus' ministry different, according to Hebrews, chapters 7, 8, 9, and 10?

---

5. Romans 3:25 and 1 John 2:2—Jesus is the _____ (Greek—*hilasterion*, translated *"Mercy Seat"* in Hebrews 9:5) for our sins.

6. 2 Corinthians 4:6—Jesus is *"the light of the knowledge of the* _____ *of God."* Just as the Glory Cloud shown in the Tabernacle, so Jesus shines in our hearts giving His light, and Colossians 1:27 assures us that *"Christ in you"* is *"the hope of glory,"* the confidence of His glorious presence forever.

7. Colossians 2:16–17—Jesus is the _____ of every *"shadow"* in the Old Covenant, of every Feast, including the Day of Atonement.

Jesus is the High Priest who offered the sacrifice of Himself on the cross and who took His own blood into the greater Tabernacle. His body was the veil torn for us, opening the way into unbroken access to the Holy of Holies and forever fellowship with God. He was also the Mercy Seat, the covering for all our sin and the place where His blood met our law breaking. In coming to Jesus, we receive His life and His light—His *"glory"* (John 17:22, 24)— His glorious presence by His Spirit. He will never leave us. We can walk in fellowship with Him forever. Jesus fulfills every aspect of the Day of Atonement—every picture, every prophecy, every promise. He provides eternal redemption to any who come to Him in repentance and faith, not just covering sin, but removing it and granting forgiveness. All that we see in the Old Covenant is a *"shadow"* of what was to come. Jesus is *"the substance"* in fullest measure, as we see in the Day of Atonement.

There is more to see about the Day of Atonement and its application in the New Testament. We will view that in Day Four. For a more detailed historical view see **The Procedures of the Day of Atonement in New Testament Days** at the end of this lesson.

Interact with the selected verses presented below and on the following pages, **"The Work of Christ in Bringing Salvation."** Carefully consider the verses in each column, **The Old Covenant and its Temporal Ministry** and **The New Covenant and its Eternal Ministry.** Write your insights in the space provided in the chart.

The Work of Christ in Bringing Salvation		
Category	Old Covenant— Temporal Ministry	New Covenant— Eternal Ministry
The Covenant Enacted	Hebrews 9:18–21; 8:7	Hebrews 9:15–17; 8:13
The Tabernacle	Hebrews 9:1–5	Hebrews 8:1–2
		Hebrews 9:11, 24

Category	Old Covenant—Temporal Ministry	New Covenant—Eternal Ministry
The Priesthood	Hebrews 7:23, 27a	Hebrews 7:21–22, 24–25, 26–28
	Hebrews 9:6–7	Hebrews 8:1; 9:11
Services and Sacrifices	9:6, 25	9:12, 26b, 28a
	10:1, 11	10:9a, 12a
	10:5a, 6, 8	10:5b, 7, 9, 10
	10:11a	7:27b; 8:1; 10:12–13
The Blood	9:7; 10:4	9:12, 26b
	9:13, 22a, 23a	9:14, 22b, 23b

> **Doctrine**
>
> ## ISRAEL'S FINAL DAY OF ATONEMENT
>
> In Romans 9—11, Paul deals with unbelieving Israel and salvation by faith. In his discussion, he brings to light the fact that the entire remnant will be saved in the final day. In Romans 11:27, God speaks of *"when I take away their sins,"* an event considered as the final Day of Atonement for the remnant of Israel alive at the end of the Tribulation days. This matches the prophecy found in Zechariah 12:10, in which Israel will behold Him whom they pierced, the Lord Jesus at His second coming. Zechariah 13:8–9 speak of the one-third remnant that will *"call on [His] name"* and receive His salvation. These are the *"sheep"* mentioned in Matthew 25:31–46 who are *"blessed of My Father"* and enter the kingdom. This coincides with the promise of Isaiah 59:20–21 and 27:9 quoted by Paul in Romans 11:26–27 where he assures his readers that *"all Israel,"* will be saved as they call on Jesus as Lord and Savior.

THE WORK OF CHRIST IN BRINGING SALVATION (CONT)		
Category	Old Covenant—Temporal Ministry	New Covenant—Eternal Ministry
Results–1	9:9; 10:1	9:12b, 14; 10:14
Results–2	10:3, 4, 11b	8:12; 9:26b; 10:15–18
Future Expectation	Hebrews 9:27	Hebrews 10:13; 9:28

Lesson Seven — **DAY FOUR**

The Year of Jubilee and the Day of Atonement

The Year of Jubilee occurred every fiftieth year on the Day of Atonement. What did it mean in the days of the Old Testament? How did the New Testament speak of this day? In His life and work, how did Jesus not only fulfill the Day of Atonement, but the Year of Jubilee as well? We will look at how this occurred in today's lesson.

📖 Read Leviticus 25:1–17. What general principles do you find regarding the regular sabbatical year in verses 1–7? What did God hold His people responsible to do? What did He promise to do?

_____
_____
_____

📖 What further guidelines did God provide in Leviticus 25:18–22?

_____
_____
_____

156 FOLLOWING GOD – LIFE PRINCIPLES FOR WORSHIP FROM THE FEASTS OF ISRAEL

God called for a sabbatical year, a year of rest for the land every seventh year. Israel could sow and reap for six years, but on the seventh year there should be no sowing of the field or pruning of the vine. Do not touch the fruit of the field in the seventh year. God assured them of His care and provision so they would *"live securely in the land."* He promised He would *"order My blessing for you"* so that the crop of the sixth year would be more than enough to feed them in the sixth, seventh, and eighth years until the crop of the ninth year. In giving the sabbatical years, the Lord called His people to trust Him. He also had a message of His care in these years and in the fiftieth *"Jubilee"* year.

📖 How were they to determine the *"Jubilee"* year, according to verses 8–10?

_____

_____

📖 What did God command for this year, according to verse 10–12?

_____

_____

_____

God ordered His people to count seven sabbatical periods or forty-nine years after which they were to celebrate a *"jubilee"* year, the fiftieth year, a recognition and celebration of the Sabbath of Sabbath years in the eighth year of the seventh sabbatical season. God called Israel to *"consecrate the fiftieth year,"* setting it apart to God. In that fiftieth year He ordered the priest to sound the *shofar* trumpet on the Day of Atonement *"all through the land."* He called for the trumpet to sound and *"proclaim a release through the land to all its inhabitants."* It is *"a jubilee for you."* We have seen in reviewing the use of trumpets in the lesson on the Feast of Trumpets how the sounding of the ram's horn or *shofar* announced the year of Jubilee. To Israel that signal announced all Hebrew slaves freed to return to their families, as well as all debts cleared, all lands returned to their owners, all inheritances secured, and the land set apart to a year of rest. The *shofar* signaled a new day of freedom, a holy year set apart to the Lord. God also called them to trust Him for their needs in this God-given economy.

By way of New Testament application, every Christian is called to declare to the *"ends of the earth"* (Acts 1:8) the *"release,"* the "Jubilee" salvation Jesus brought by His death and resurrection. The call to place one's personal faith in Him, to trust in Christ wholly and follow Christ fully, should sound from our lives and our lips. He gives forgiveness and freedom, the message the world needs to see and hear through every believer.

📖 What additional regulations concerning land, its use and its price did God give in verses 13–17? Note the general principle given in Leviticus 25:23.

_____

_____

_____

First of all, since the land belongs to the Lord, no one could buy or sell *"permanently."* God chose to give the land to Israel for their use as His 'tenants' in a sense. God gave very clear guidelines on the buying and selling of prop-

---

Word Study
"JUBILEE"

The word "Jubilee" is a translation of the Hebrew word *yobel*, which refers to a ram and, by implication, a ram's horn. The word for *"ram"* (*yobel*) is akin to the Aramaic word *yubil* and much like the English *"Jubilee."* Every fiftieth year on the Day of Atonement, the priest blew the *shofar* signaling the year of *"Jubilee,"* the year of "the ram/ram's horn." Some see in this a reference to the ram caught in the thicket in Genesis 22. Abraham offered up that ram in place of his son Isaac, thus releasing Isaac by the sacrifice of the ram. Jesus is our "jubilee," our release from the debt and enslavement of sin. He is the sacrificial lamb that Abraham prophesied would be provided and seen on Mount Moriah (Genesis 22:8, 14). The **Year of "Jubilee"** is also called *"the Acceptable* [Favorable] *Year of the LORD"* (Isaiah 61:2; Luke 4:19), *"the Year of My Redeemed"* (Isaiah 63:4), and *"the Year of Liberty"* (Ezekiel 46:17), all terms ultimately fulfilled in the work of Christ.

Did You Know?
THE EIGHTH DAY

In Scripture, the eighth day speaks of a new day and new relationships. Jesus arose on the Feast of First Fruits, the day after the Sabbath, an eighth day and the dawning of the new creation through the Second Adam. Pentecost occurred on an eighth day, ushering in the birth of the church. In the year of "Jubilee" is yet another eighth day, the eighth year after the seventh Sabbath year, a new day of freedom. The Feast of Tabernacles concludes with an eighth day, Tishri 22, symbolic of the eternal reign of Christ with new heavens and new earth.

Put Yourself In Their Shoes
"THE JOYFUL SOUND"

Psalm 89:15–16 says, *"Blessed are the people who know the joyful sound! They walk in the light of Your countenance. In Your name they rejoice all day long, and in Your righteousness they are exalted."* The phrase *"the joyful sound"* is literally translated the "blast" or "sound" (Hebrew, *teruah*), referring to "the blast of the trumpet." Many see this as a reference to the shofar trumpet blast of the Feasts and especially of the Year of Jubilee, one of the most joyful sounds because of the release proclaimed throughout the land. In the New Testament, those who know "the joyful sound" of the message of salvation in Christ truly walk in the light of His countenance. They rejoice in the name of Jesus and in the righteousness He gives to every believing heart (Romans 10:4–13). In 1882, Priscilla Owens used the phrase "the joyful sound" in her hymn "Jesus Saves," also declaring "Earth shall keep her Jubilee, Jesus saves!"

Did You Know?
THE LIBERTY BELL

The Liberty Bell located in Philadelphia, Pennsylvania, is inseparably linked to Leviticus 25. Forged in 1753 to commemorate the fiftieth anniversary of William Penn's charter, it honored that fiftieth year (1751) and Penn's work in establishing liberty in the colonies. On the Liberty Bell is the inscription from Leviticus 25:10, **"Proclaim liberty throughout the land to all the inhabitants thereof."** The greater the spiritual freedom experienced by a person, community or nation, the greater the freedom of relationships within that nation because such freedoms are founded not in the freedom to do whatever one wants, but the freedom to do what is right.

---

erty in light of this and as it relates to the year of Jubilee. Every transaction must take into account how many years remained before the next jubilee year at which time it reverted back to the original Hebrew family. The number of years determined the value since the person was actually buying years of crops and not the land itself. These factors guided all negotiations on buying and selling land. Knowing people would be tempted to forego these regulations trying to get a better buy or even being greedy for more gain, God warned them against wronging one another. They must live in the fear and respect of the Lord and His laws and show love to their neighbors. God continually pointed them to right relationships with Him and with one another. (See Leviticus 25:24–55 and 27:16–24 for further guidelines touched by the year of Jubilee.)

📖 The promises of God's salvation through the ages find their connection in Christ, especially as He relates to the *"Year of Jubilee."* Consider first Isaiah 49:8 and 61:1–2. (Note: Isaiah 49:5–13 gives the fuller picture for verse 8.) What did God promise, especially in Isaiah 61:2a? What similarities do you find between Isaiah 49:8 and Isaiah 61:2?

_____
_____
_____
_____

📖 Look at Luke 4:14–21. What connection did Jesus make between the passage in Isaiah and Himself?

_____
_____
_____

Through Isaiah, God spoke of the fullness of salvation He would bring to Israel, times of compassion, of caring for them guiding them to *"springs of water."* Isaiah spoke of the *"favorable time"* or the *"acceptable time"* and connected it to *"the day of salvation."* The *"day of salvation"* is also linked to *"the year of My redeemed"* in Isaiah 63:4b. Many see the passages that speak of the *"favorable"* or *"acceptable time"* as referring to the Lord's greater fulfillment of the *"year of jubilee."* Both Isaiah 49:8 and 61:2 speak of that *"favorable"* time of compassion, freedom, and salvation.

Jesus made this kind of connection as He began His ministry. Soon after Jesus' baptism in the Jordan River and His temptation experiences in the Wilderness, He came to His home town of Nazareth. In the synagogue, when given the scroll of Isaiah, He turned to Isaiah 61 and read verse 1 and the first part of verse 2. Then, Jesus declared, *"Today this Scripture has been fulfilled in your hearing."* Jesus spoke of proclaiming *"liberty to the captives"* and the *"oppressed"* as well as proclaiming *"the acceptable year of the Lord,"* a reference to the *"year of jubilee."* Jesus came to bring the fullness of *"jubilee"* pictured in the Old Testament practices. He sets free not only in the physical and material realm, but in the whole person, delivering from the debt of sin and the sentence of death, giving eternal life.

📖 In the ministry of the apostle Paul, we find him making a connection between these Old Testament passages and Jesus' redemptive work. On what does Paul focus in 2 Corinthians 5:14–21?

📖 What do you discover immediately following 2 Corinthians 5 in 6:1–2? What Old Testament connections does Paul make in those verses?

_____

_____

In 2 Corinthians 5, Paul spoke in terms that easily connect with what we have seen about the work of Jesus as the High Priest in which *"one died for all."* God *"made Him who knew no sin to be sin on our behalf, that we might become the righteousness of God in Him."* All who receive Him and His grace by faith receive this salvation. Paul then relates this to all God has done in bringing *"the acceptable time"* and *"the day of salvation."* Paul joined with the Spirit of God calling his readers to wholeheartedly receive *"the grace of God."* Believers should live in that grace, not by fleshly works, something of which certain Corinthians were guilty.

These verses call anyone who has not yet received Christ as Lord and Savior to do so *"now"* because the *"acceptable time,"* *"the day of salvation,"* and *"the year of jubilee"* all find fulfillment in the work of Jesus Christ. This "day" of *"jubilee"*—sin debts cleared, release from any and all enslavement, all one's spiritual inheritance guaranteed—can find fulfillment in the life of anyone who will believe and receive. Jesus does not give us the inheritance of a "land" like Israel, but of a *"life,"* His life, abundant life (John 10:10; Colossians 3:1–4). By repentance and faith in Jesus, anyone can experience the "jubilee," freedom and life of Jesus.

APPLY — **Are you walking in "Jubilee Freedom"?** We have seen how Jesus fulfilled everything concerning the *"Day of Atonement"* and the *"Year of Jubilee."* He did this on behalf of any willing to believe Him, receive Him, and walk following Him. Are there sin problems plaguing you, any enslavement to wrong habits or to bitterness, anger, and other works of the flesh? Anything enslaving you? Any wrong to which you are still clinging? Listen to His Spirit's *shofar*, His trumpet call—"Freedom is here!" Trust Him to be true to His Word. Call on the Lord to give you His "Jubilee Freedom."

Word Study
"ACCEPTABLE TIME"

The term *"favorable"* or *"acceptable time"* (Isaiah 49:8; 61:2) comes from the Hebrew word *ratsown*, that which is a delight or well-pleasing to another. It is used in Isaiah 49:8, which is quoted in 2 Corinthians 6:2, speaking of *"the acceptable time"* and *"the day of salvation."* In Luke 4:18–19, Jesus read Isaiah 61:1–2a, speaking of *"the favorable/acceptable* [Hebrew, *ratsown*] *year of the Lord."* God is well-pleased with this time of salvation. He is also *"well-pleased"* with His Son, the Savior (Matthew 3:17). Many date the baptism of Jesus around the time of the Day of Atonement in the fall of the year. In His baptism, Jesus focused on His mission identifying with man in order *"to fulfill all righteousness"* (Matthew 3:15). Jesus connected His baptism to His dying, rising, and bringing righteousness to those who would place faith in Him. His baptism pictured His mission of fulfilling the "Day of Atonement," bringing about *"the favorable time"* and *"the day of salvation,"* even the eternal "Jubilee" Year.

ANSWERING THE CALL OF THE DAY OF ATONEMENT

Lesson Seven — **DAY FIVE**

We have seen many truths about the Day of Atonement in both the Old and New Testaments. How are these truths to be applied to our lives?

APPLY — **Right From the Start**—How do we start to answer the Call of the Day of Atonement? We saw in Day One that in Moses' and Aaron's time, the call of the Day of Atonement included a very real call to **humility** and **purity**—to humble oneself before the Lord and pur-

Word Study
"DRAW NEAR"

The Greek word *proserchomai* is found seven times in the book of Hebrews, translated *"draw near," "come(s),"* or *"approach"* (4:16; 7:25; 10:1, 22; 11:6; 12:18, 22). In the society of the day, it was used of one coming before a judge, thus implying a certain humility, honesty, and seriousness, showing honor and respect toward the one approached, never with arrogance or swagger. It was used of coming to a seat at a banquet where one would enjoy a feast, a place of great joy, honor, privilege, and gratitude. In Hebrews, it is used of coming before the Lord's throne of grace (4:16), into His Holy Place, the Holy of Holies (10:22), coming before Him diligently seeking Him in prayer (11:6), each with a humble and honest heart. It speaks of one coming to *"Mount Zion,"* the *"Heavenly Jerusalem,"* and *"Jesus, the mediator of a new covenant"* (12:18, 22–24). The call continues—*"draw near"* to God with confidence in His work on your behalf.

Jesus did not die and rise again only to open the way for us to be in God's Presence, but to continually practice His Presence by His power, making every decision with Him at one's side, every conversation with Him in on it, all of life an interactive offering to Him.

sue the things that make for a holy lifestyle, a life of walking in holy fellowship with the Lord. A show of humility without purity quickly becomes a manipulative way to fulfill one's selfish desires, not biblical humility. Attempts at purity without humility can quickly become legalism or Pharisaism or some other manifestation of pride. Biblical humility with biblical purity is the starting point. Answering the call of the Day of Atonement today starts with answering the call to humility, to honesty before the Lord about ourselves, about our sins, and, as the New Testament brings out, a call to look to Jesus and His provision for forgiveness and cleansing. As we begin today, pause and pray. Humble yourself before the Lord with an expectation of meeting with Him.

The New Testament path to answering the Call of the Day of Atonement is given to us in Hebrews 10:19–25. After walking us through how Jesus fulfilled the Day of Atonement, this passage begins with *"therefore..."* That is our connection point. Look at these verses, one at a time, make the connection, and begin to answer the Call of the Day of Atonement.

📖 Read through Hebrews 10:19–25. What has Jesus done to open the way to God, according to verses 19–21?

_____

_____

_____

Jesus came and died as our High Priest. He gave His own blood to open the way for each believer into the Holy of Holies (Most Holy Place), the place of God's presence. That included Him being torn in body and soul like the veil in the Temple was torn at the moment of His death (Matthew 27:51). He is the *"new and living way"* to the Father. That phrase literally speaks of a "freshly sacrificed and now filled with God's kind of life" way. It is the way of Jesus death and resurrection, a way that is qualitatively new. It means a change, a different way than in the Old Covenant.

Hebrews 10:20 says Jesus *"inaugurated"* (Greek—*egkainizo*) this way through the veil of His flesh. The Greek word *egkainizo* refers to making a qualitatively new way, to entering a new lifestyle. It was used in the Septuagint in Deuteronomy 20:5 of dedicating a new house for a newly married couple, thus a new lifestyle as a family. It was used of Solomon and the people of Israel dedicating the Temple in 1 Kings 8:63—a new day for the priests and the people, a new day of worship in the new Temple. Jesus led the way into a new lifestyle, a lifestyle in the Holy of Holies, always in the presence of God. However, it is not just **in** His Presence, but continually **practicing** His presence by His power, making every decision with Him at one's side, every conversation with Him in on it, all of life an interactive offering to Him.

📖 What is the first command we should follow, according to Hebrews 10:22?

_____

_____

📖 What has God done for our *"hearts"* according to verse 22? First, what hindrances has God dealt with?

160 FOLLOWING GOD – LIFE PRINCIPLES FOR WORSHIP FROM THE FEASTS OF ISRAEL

The Christian life is meant to be a lifestyle of answering God's call to *"draw near."* To do that we must deal with a conscience tainted, stained, turned and twisted by sin and evil. That evil comes first from an inborn "sinful nature" or the "flesh" that selfishly and stubbornly goes after what pleases "self." Then there are the self-will choices we have made against God's will, following the evil temptations of Satan drawing us away from God. Plus, this *"evil age"* (Galatians 1:4), this world 'system' lures us with its lusts (1 John 2:15–17), its deceptive desires. Jesus dealt with all of this. As the high priest sprinkled blood to cleanse the Mercy Seat and the Tabernacle from the contamination of sin, so Jesus has by His blood *"sprinkled clean"* the heart of each believer. He removed the hindrances of an *"evil conscience"* that hides or runs from God. He has washed us clean through His work. Now we can walk in right relationship and open fellowship with God, doing His will, serving *"the living God"* (Hebrews 9:14).

📖 What do we bring before the Lord? With what kind of heart do we come near?

_____

_____

Cleansed by the Lord, we can bring before Him a *"sincere heart,"* literally *"a true heart,"* the Greek word *aletheia* pointing to no deceit, nothing hidden, honest and transparent before the Lord. That heart fully trusts the Lord. Convinced the Lord welcomes us into His fellowship, we are free to speak all that is on our hearts. He calls us to walk with Him in the details of life—the joys and hurts, the certainties and perplexities, the times of provision and the times of need, the victories and the failures (see Hebrews 4:14–16). The word *"confidence"* or *"boldness"* refers to the openness to speak what is on the heart. We have full access to the Lord.

APPLY — **"Draw Near"**—How well are you drawing near? What is distracting you? Jesus has invested His life in giving you full access to the Father. Do you recognize the treasure, the wealth of fellowship into which God invites you? Write one practical step you could take to spend more time with the Lord.

_____

_____

_____

_____

_____

_____

_____

> *"As for me, the nearness of God is my good"*
>
> **Psalm 73:28**

📖 What command and promises do you find in Hebrews 10:23?

_____

_____

We can walk in confidence concerning our salvation. God is faithful to His Word, to all His promises. We walk with certainty and can tell others of that hope. The temptation will come when pressures or opposition arises to veer off the path. The term *"without wavering"* (Greek—*aklines*) is a nautical term used of keeping a ship on course, not blown off course by winds or waves. The world full of doubt and without a true hope will often pull at us to not hope in God, but in some substitute of its making. The devil will tempt us to doubt God, doubt His Word and His motives, as he did with Eve and Adam in the Garden of Eden (Genesis 3:1–7). Our own "flesh" is susceptible to discouragement, especially when circumstances crowd in on us. Let us keep holding firmly to our hope in Jesus. He has indeed defeated evil, secured our forgiveness and cleansing, and guaranteed His glorious presence forever. Hebrews 6:19 affirms this with another nautical term, declaring *"this hope we have as an anchor of the soul, a hope both sure and steadfast and one which enters within the veil,"* the place of God's presence.

APPLY

Confess Your Hope—What is the level of your hope, your confidence in Jesus? Are you telling others how they can trust in Him? How about those who do not yet know Jesus as Lord and Savior? Ask God to show you how to confess your hope to others—to believers and non-believers. Seek opportunities to share your faith in Christ.

📖 What practical applications do you discover in Hebrews 10:24–25?

_____

_____

God never intended our faith walk to be self-contained—"just me and Jesus." He always calls us to love others, to give and live to benefit and serve others. That is the heart and activity of Jesus. Think of God's priority commands—love Him fully and love others purely. We struggle. We are born selfish, and we sin. Jesus came to die in our place, to take the punishment for our sins, to forgive and cleanse us so that He could indwell us. Why? He desires to express His life and love in us and through us. That means loving interaction with the Father and love towards our "neighbor," which includes sharing Christ so that others can place faith in Him and follow in love and obedience. Now He calls us to cooperate with Him as He continues that work in us and through us toward believers and non-believers.

Therefore, *"consider,"* think with intensity, perceive clearly how you might help one another love more effectively. Think of ways to love and encourage others. Think of good deeds to do. Doing *"good deeds"* refers to a wide range of activities. It is the *"good"* of the *"good shepherd"* (John 10:11, 14). These deeds are morally good, truly beautiful in nature, of good or excellent quality, valuable, profitable to others.

Where is the best place to do these good deeds? Any place, but especially in the company of other believers working together in those good deeds. As we come together as believers, we should encourage one another in the things of God and in the deeds in which He leads. Again, temptations will come to not be involved, to not come together to do these *"good deeds."* In the light of *"the day drawing near,"* the day in which God will evaluate our deeds and reward accordingly, let us continually work at ways to encourage one another, especially in helpful, loving deeds.

APPLY — *"Good Deeds"* **Check-Up**—How well are you doing in *"good deeds"*? Ask God to show you some practical deeds to do for others, ideas He gives you, things that He puts on your heart and that match His working in your life. Join Him where you see Him working.

LOOKING BACK AND LOOKING FORWARD. We have seen **the pictures of Christ** in the Day of Atonement in both Old and New Testaments. We read in the Old Testament **the prophetic promises** of the Day of Atonement. Many see a future application of the "Day of Atonement" when all Israel will view the Messiah whom they pierced, begin to mourn, and then call on Him to save them (Zechariah 12:10; 13:1, 8–9). This relates to what Paul states in Romans 11 concerning the day when *"all Israel will be saved,"* the day occurring at the Second Coming of Christ at the end of the seven years of Tribulation (Romans 11:25–27).

When we compare the work of Christ in the New Testament to the pictures and promises in the Old, we also see an immediate personal application especially viewing the Day of Atonement in light of the Feast of Tabernacles. Five days after the Day of Atonement, the Feast of Tabernacles celebrates God's presence with His people. Alfred Edersheim makes a clear personal application for us in these historic events. He notes that before a person or a people can celebrate the goodness God has shown in the harvest (Feast of Tabernacles), he must deal with sin and "be reconciled unto God, for only a people at peace with God might rejoice before Him in the blessing with which He had crowned the year" [*The Temple,* p. 304]. We will see more of this truth in the next lesson on the Feast of Tabernacles.

Considering all we have seen about the Day of Atonement and the work of our Lord and Savior Jesus Christ, pray through this prayer. Consider the ways it applies to your life.

Lord, thank You for coming to earth, facing temptation, then freely giving Your life on the cross to pay for, forgive, and remove our sins (Hebrews 8:12; 10:17–18). Thank You that I can have a cleansed, guilt-free conscience in spite of the evil I have done. I humble myself before You. Sensitize my conscience to see any uncleanness, any attitude or action unholy in Your sight (Leviticus 10:3; 1 Peter 1:14–21). Thank You for Your cleansing and for "Jubilee Freedom" (Leviticus 25:9–13)—my sin debt cleared, my enslavement gone, my inheritance secure. Praise You for making us free in heart to love and serve You and others (Hebrews 9:14; Galatians 5:1). Thank You for ACCESS GRANTED to the Father any day, all day, not just one day a year (Hebrews 10:19–22; Ephesians 2:18). May I draw near more often, with greater intensity. May I maintain a firm grasp on my confession of hope (1 Peter 3:15) and express this faith and hope in witness and in good, loving deeds (Hebrews 10:23–25). May I keep in mind *"the Day drawing near"* when I will stand before You, give an account, and receive

EXTRA MILE

FAITH-HOPE-LOVE IN HEBREWS 11—13

Read through Hebrews 11 and examine your **faith** level. Read Hebrews 12 and examine your **hope**, your confidence in God, His promises, and His work in your life. Read Hebrews 13 and examine your **love** for others and your own love and worship of God.

eternal rewards along with my assignments in reigning with You. May the Life, the tears, the prayers You invested and the price You paid, bring You the rewards You deserve. May You receive the honor and glory You deserve from me through the obedient choices I make and may I grow in grace as You work in and through me. Amen.

THE PROCEDURES FOR THE DAY OF ATONEMENT IN NEW TESTAMENT DAYS

[The following notes are a summary and condensation of material presented by Alfred Edersheim in his work *The Temple: Its Ministry and Services as They Were in the Time of Christ*. (Grand Rapids: Wm. B. Eerdmans Publishing Co., Reprint, 1983), pages 305–329.]

Preparation of the High Priest

The High Priest alone officiated over this day although in New Testament days it is estimated that 500 priests assisted him. Seven days before the Day, he left his home in Jerusalem in order to stay in one of the chambers of the Temple. During that time he guarded himself meticulously to assure his ceremonial purity. A substitute stood ready in case he defiled himself in any way. On the **third day** and the **seventh day,** he was sprinkled for cleansing with the ashes of the Red Heifer (see Numbers 19:1–9, 17–19; Hebrews 9:13). During that week, he practiced each of the priestly functions—the daily sacrifice, the lighting of the lamp (seven–branch lampstand), offering the incense and sprinkling the blood—no mistakes could be made on the Day of Atonement. All night before the Day, the High Priest listened to and expounded the Scriptures so he would not fall asleep. At midnight they began preparations for the bronze altar. It is noteworthy that Jesus did not sleep the night before He went to the Cross, being occupied with bearing our sins, fulfilling the Scriptures and His Father's will.

On the Day of Atonement, the High Priest wore two kinds of garments, the white linen garments and the regular golden garments of the High Priest. He offered three kinds of Offerings—**1)** The Daily Offerings [Morning and Evening Burnt Offerings], **2)** The Burnt Offerings of the Day of Atonement, and **3)** the Sin Offerings of the Day of Atonement. The High Priest personally paid for the sacrifices which he brought for himself and his household. The priests shared in some of the cost of this purchase. The Temple treasury provided for the sacrifices for the people. The first break of morning light began the services.

THE ORDER OF THE DAY
Morning Sacrifice—Burnt Offering

First, the High Priest bathed in a special golden vessel and put on his regular golden garments and offered the first offering, the regular morning sacrifice of a burnt offering (9:00 AM, one-year lamb, grain with olive oil, wine), all totally consumed in the fires of the altar.

Preparation for the Sin Offering—Washing and the White Garments.

After the High Priest offered the morning burnt offering, he washed totally before putting on his particular dress for the Day of Atonement sin offerings—all white—not the typical dress of the High Priest. This consisted of a white linen long tunic with linen undergarments, a white belt or sash, a cap or turban of white, the wearing of which symbolized the perfect purity sought through the washings and sacrifices of the day. Those who stand nearest to God are described as clothed in white (Ezekiel 9:2; Daniel 10:5, 12:6; see also Zechariah 3:3–4). Note that with each change of garment he had to wash his whole body. In all, he washed completely **five times** and washed his hands and feet an additional **ten times.** With this second bath and clothed in his white linen garments he prepared to offer the first sin offering or atonement offering (atoning for sin). This consisted of a bull as a sin offering for the high priest and priesthood. First, the High Priest laid his hands on the head of the animal and prayed, repeating the sacred name of Jehovah/Yahweh three times. Because of repeating that name, the people bowed face down on the ground. The bull would be sacrificed later in the day. The High Priest then asked a blessing of God on the people. Several priests played instruments accompanying this blessing of the people. The name of Jehovah/Yahweh was repeated by the High Priest a total of ten times on this day.

The Drawing of Lots for the Two Goats.

Then the High Priest went to the two goats that faced west toward the Temple with their backs to the people. Using an urn containing two lots (small tablets) with the inscriptions "For Jehovah" and "For Azazel," the High Priest reached into the urn and placed a tablet in each hand as the method of choosing the "scapegoat" (Hebrew—*azazel*). He placed the inscriptions from the urn on the head of the two goats. The Jews considered it a sign for good if the lot for the goat *"for Jehovah"* came up in the right hand of the priest. In New Testament days, the goat "For Jehovah" had a scarlet sash tied around its neck. That goat would be sacrificed. The goat "For Azazel" ("scapegoat") had a piece of scarlet sash tied on its horns. The High Priest turned this goat so that it faced the people. There it waited for the symbolic placing of the sins of the people on it. That scapegoat would carry away those sins to the wilderness. Note the parallel of Jesus being turned around by Pilate to face the people and being presented to be crucified (John 19:1–6, 14–19). Our sins were not placed on Him symbolically but in reality (2 Corinthians 5:21).

The Sacrifice of the Bull as the Sin Offering for the Priests

The High Priest turned back to the bull that stood near the altar. He laid his hands on the bull and confessed the sins of **himself**, his **family**, and the **priesthood**, then the bull was slain, its blood caught in a vessel.

The Golden Incense Censer

The High Priest then filled a censer with burning coals from the bronze altar where the burnt offering had just been offered. He gathered incense into a dish and carried the golden censer and the incense into the Holy Place. He folded back the Veil and entered into the Holy of Holies the first time of the day. He placed the Golden Censer before the Ark of the Covenant (in Moses' day in the Tabernacle, in Solomon's day in the Temple). The High Priest then placed the incense offering on the burning coals and the fragrant cloud of smoke filled the Holy of Holies. He exited the Holy of Holies and prayed outside the veil for God's blessings on the people, then emerged from the Holy Place.

Sprinkling the Blood of the Bull on the Mercy Seat.

The High Priest then took the blood of the bull and entered the Holy of Holies a second time. There he sprinkled blood up **once** upon the Mercy Seat and down **seven times** in front of the Mercy Seat/Ark of the Covenant. Then he placed the basin of blood on a golden stand before the veil.

The Sacrifice of the Goat as the Sin Offering for the People
After this, the High Priest killed the goat set apart "For Jehovah" and entered the Holy of Holies a third time, sprinkling the blood of the goat **once** upon the Mercy Seat and **seven times** down in front as before. He then placed the basin of goat's blood on a second golden stand before the veil.

Sprinkling the Blood on the Veil and the Golden Altar
He then sprinkled the blood of the bull on the Veil, **once upward** and **seven times downward** and repeated that with the blood of the goat. He mixed the two bowls of blood and sprinkled that mix on the **four** horns of the golden altar of incense and **seven times** on the top of that altar, sprinkling blood a total of forty-three times on this day. He then poured the remainder of that blood at the base of the west side of the bronze altar. Thus he completed the atoning work for the Temple (the Holy of Holies, the Veil, and remainder of the Tabernacle/Temple), the priesthood, and the people to be cleansed of defilement and sin (Leviticus 16:15–20). Sin was atoned for or covered. The people had clear access and fellowship with God. There remained the God-given actions that would *"send away"* their sins (Leviticus 16:21–22).

The Sending Away of the Scapegoat for the Sins of the People
The High Priest then dealt with the symbolic freeing of the conscience of guilt and sin through the scapegoat. The High Priest laid his hands on the head of the goat, confessing *"all their sins"* (Leviticus 16:21) and claiming the promise of Leviticus 16:30—*"For on that day, the priest shall make atonement for you, to cleanse you, that you may be clean from all your sins before the LORD."* He led the scapegoat out the eastern gate and across the bridge over the Kidron Valley to the Mount of Olives where he entrusted the scapegoat into the hands of *"a man who stands in readiness"* who then led the goat out into the wilderness and released it. In New Testament days, part of the scarlet cloth was torn off and placed on a rock. Then word was sent back to the Temple that the scapegoat had born their sins away into a solitary place. They were free of them in a sense. This fulfilled Leviticus 16:21–22 until the offering of Jesus Christ, the ultimate fulfillment of all these offerings. Alfred Edersheim calls these sacrifices "preparatory and temporary" (*The Temple: Its Ministry and Services*, page 322). The two goats counted as one and pictured the cleansing from sin *and* the removal of guilt. Sin was not truly blotted out, only taken away some distance, put aside until the work of Christ could be applied, sin paid for, and the conscience truly cleansed. In this scheme of the Day of Atonement, we see the Priests cleansed, the Temple cleansed, and the People cleansed for a time.

The Offering Fires for the Sin Offerings.
After the High Priest sent the scapegoat away, he cut up the bullock and the goat sin offerings, and then set aside the fat portions and inward parts in a container to be burned later on the bronze altar. At this point, he sent the remainder of the carcasses outside the city to the clean place to be burnt on the Mount of Olives where the Temple ashes were placed. Tradition says the High Priest then went into the Court of the Women and read Leviticus 16 and Leviticus 23:27–32 and recited Numbers 29:7–11 from memory. He then prayed in light of these Scriptures.

Washing hands and feet followed, after which the high priest took off the white linen garment, put on his golden garments, and washed his hands and feet once again. He then appeared to the people in his golden garments.

The Other Feast Offerings of the Day of Atonement
As part of the specific offerings of this day, the High Priest in his regular golden garments then offered *"one kid of the goats as a sin offering, besides the sin offering for atonement,"* a sin offering atoning for the services of this day (Numbers 29:11). The priests ate this later that night. After this sin offering, he offered several Burnt Offerings, for the people (consisting of one bull, one ram, and seven lambs) and for himself (one ram). He then took the formerly collected inward parts of the bull and the goat sin offerings and burned them on the bronze altar. This concluded the special offerings of this day, fulfilling Leviticus 16:33–34. There remained to be offered the regular daily offerings.

Evening Sacrifice—Burnt Offering
The High Priest offered the regular Evening Sacrifice (3:00 PM) of a Burnt Offering (a one-year lamb, grain plus olive oil, and wine). He then washed hands and feet.

Final Arrangements
The High Priest then took off the golden garments, bathed again, put on the white linen garments, and washed hands and feet. He then went for a fourth time into the Holy of Holies to retrieve the censer and incense dish. After this, the High Priest washed his hands and feet, took off the white garments, bathed, and put on the golden garments, washed hands and feet again, burned the evening incense on the golden altar of incense and lit the sevenfold golden lampstand. He then washed hands and feet again before taking off his regular golden garments and putting on his ordinary cloths.

The Conclusion of the Day and the Feast
After the High Priest finished his ministry in the Holy Place, he exited the Temple. From there the people escorted him to his house. The day concluded with the Fast ending and everyone enjoying a Feast in the joy that sins were covered once more for the year past. Next year they would repeat this for the year's sin, awaiting the coming of the promised Messiah who would fulfill all the procedures, pictures, and prophecies of this and the other Feasts of the Lord.

Notes

The Feast of Tabernacles

CELEBRATING THE PRESENCE OF CHRIST
IN SALVATION AND IN HIS REIGN

The Feast of Tabernacles is the last of the seven feasts of Israel, occurring from the fifteenth of the seventh month (Tishri) to the twenty-second (around our late September or early October). It is also called *"the Feast of Booths,"* recalling God's deliverance of Israel from Egypt and their journey through the Wilderness to the Promised Land. This Feast is also known as *Sukkot*, the Hebrew word for "tabernacles" or "booths." Their first stop out of Egypt was known as Succoth, a temporary place of rest (Exodus 12:37). This Feast celebrated God's provision of a land of bountiful fruit and a life in a settled place. It is also called *"the Feast of Ingathering"* because it celebrated the final harvests of the year. Leviticus 23:39 speaks of it as *"the Feast of the LORD"* or *"the Feast of Yahweh/Jehovah."*

Trumpets announced every New Moon and every Feast, but this seventh month and the Feast of Tabernacles along with the Day of Atonement were announced with the greatest of Trumpet calls, the Feast of Trumpets, pointing to these as unique Feasts. With the Feast of Tabernacles, we come to the most celebrated, the most joyous of the seven feasts This Feast time is also known as "the Season of Our Joy," emphasizing the rejoicing over God dwelling with His people and His provision of the harvest. Expressions of joy are multiplied since they celebrate the harvest of fruit and grain as well as the spiritual cleansing of the Day of Atonement just five days before. As Passover comes at the height of the first month, Tabernacles comes at the height of the seventh or Sabbath month,—on the fifteenth at full moon,.

This Feast in many ways speaks prophetically and expresses the desires of the godly in the Old Testament—it pictures a time to come when the people of God will rejoice before the Lord in His presence—unhindered, unharmed, with all openness and prosperity, sharing their abundance with one another and with all the nations so that all may know that *"the LORD, He is God."* With this feast coming five days after the Day of Atonement, we see that "a sanctified nation could keep a holy feast of harvest joy unto the

Put Yourself In Their Shoes
THE FULLNESS OF THE SEVENTH MONTH

Alfred Edersheim insightfully notes, "what the seventh day, or Sabbath, was in reference to the week, the seventh month seems to have been in reference to the year. It closed not only the sacred cycle, but also the agricultural or working year. It also marked the change of seasons, the approach of rain and of the winter equinox, and determined alike the commencement and the close of a sabbatical year [Deuteronomy 31:10]." (*The Temple*, p. 271).

Lord, just as in the truest sense it will be 'in that day' when the full meaning of the Feast of Tabernacles shall be really fulfilled" (Alfred Edersheim, *The Temple*, pp. 271–272).

The events of this feast in the Old Testament and in Jesus' day paint a picture for us, a picture of great hope and expectation. The beauty of this picture grows richer and deeper in meaning the longer we look at it. This Feast encompasses a hope that is eternal for us and for all who will accept its message by faith, for the message *is* Christ, the Lord and Savior and the fullness of salvation He promises.

Lesson Eight — Day One

THE GREATEST CELEBRATION

The Feast of Tabernacles is unique in several ways. It is the last of the seven Feasts. It is the culmination of the three observances in the seventh month and the celebration of the greatest harvest of the year. We will see certain characteristics of this Feast as we go through this week's lesson. Ask the Lord to make this Feast come alive to you as we begin to explore the Scriptures.

First, look at Exodus 23:16b. What is the focus of the latter half of that verse?

When u have gathered in the fruit of your labors from the field.

Review Leviticus 23:33–44. Summarize the guidelines found in verses 33–36, 39.

15th day of 7th month Fet Tab for 7 days, holy convocation the 1th day and 8th day, no work offering by fire 7 days, sacred assembly

God called for the people to assemble before Him three times a year. The third gathering was the Feast of Ingathering or Tabernacles. It took place at the end of the year after they gathered in all the produce of the land. This Feast began on *Tishri* 15 and lasted for seven days to *Tishri* 21 with an additional day of celebration on *Tishri* 22, the eighth day. God required a *"holy convocation"* or a *"holy assembly"* on the first day and the eighth day, each of those involving *"no laborious work,"* a day of rest so the people could gather for focused worship unencumbered with daily tasks. Each day also included offerings by fire at the altar of the Tabernacle or Temple.

What unique practice do you find in verses 40–42? Why were the Israelites to do this, according to verse 43?

Gather tree branches to rejoice before the Lord 7 days. to make booths - dwell remind them of deliverance from Egypt

> **Did You Know?**
> **"HOLY CONVOCATIONS"**
>
> God called His people to a *"holy convocation"* or *"holy assembly"* seven times in the Feasts—during the Feast of Unleavened Bread on *Nisan* 15 and 21, on Pentecost Sunday, on the Feast of Trumpets (*Tishri* 1), on the Day of Atonement (*Tishri* 10), and during the Feast of Tabernacles on *Tishri* 15 and 22. In addition, every weekly Sabbath included a *"holy assembly"* of the people.

The Feast began with people gathering various leafy branches to *"rejoice before the LORD your God for seven days."* There is an indication here that during this week the people gathered the branches and carried them around the Tabernacle/Temple, using them to wave in worship and rejoicing before the Lord. They also used them in making temporary booths or tabernacles. The branches included *"the foliage"* or *"the fruit of beautiful trees"* which many have interpreted as the citron tree with its lemon-like fruit. In addition, they carried palm branches (likely the date palm), the branches of *"leafy trees"* which Rabbis declared to be myrtle trees, and willow branches of the brook. These four kinds of branches provided a booth of shade in the day and covering at night. Historians tell us priests and worshipers also placed the willow branches in a canopy arrangement around the altar. God called the people of each generation to make the pilgrimage to Jerusalem and live in those booths for seven days, the eighth day being a day of celebration without booths or branches. This week served as a reminder of their deliverance from Egypt, of God's provision in the Wilderness, and of their entrance into the land of His rich bounty and goodness, a place of permanent abode.

> *Did You Know?*
>
> ### THE DIFFERENT BRANCHES OF TREES
>
> Why four different branches of trees? Alfred Edersheim provides an insightful note. The different branches reminded the people of the various stages of their journey—"the palm branches recalling the valleys and plains, the 'boughs of thick trees,' the bushes on the mountain heights, and the willows those brooks from which God had given His people drink; while the *aethrog* [citron] was to remind them of the fruits of the good land which the Lord had given them" (*The Temple*, p. 275).

📖 Read through the guidelines for this Feast given in Numbers 29:12–39. Note the requirements for the week. How did they spend their time?

Holy convocation, one goat for sin offering burnt offering, 2 rams, 14 lambs, 13 bulls and decease by one daily, grain offering and drink offering

📖 Summarize the various offerings made during the week.

Celebrating the goodness of God and abandence of the Love he gives

📖 What additional offerings are mentioned for this and other feasts in Numbers 29:39?

vowed offering, freewill, burnt, grain, drink offering, Peace offering

God called for setting aside seven days for this Feast, with a special *"holy convocation"* on the first and eighth days. With that He called for a specific set of offerings for each day, the most offerings of any of the feasts. Each day the priests sacrificed one goat as a sin offering, ever acknowledging the need for forgiveness and cleansing. The burnt offering spoke of total yielding to and worship of the Lord as their God. It consisted of two rams daily, fourteen lambs daily, and a varying number of bulls, beginning with thirteen the first day, twelve the second day, decreasing by one each day until the seventh day when they offered seven bulls. On the eighth day, another day of *"holy convocation"* occurred and the priests offered one goat as a sin offering and one bull, one ram, and seven lambs as a burnt offering.

In this seventh month of the religious calendar, a sabbatical month, the number seven is clearly prominent in the calculations of the offerings. In

Hebrew thinking, the number seven speaks of completion, and we see a message of completion in these offerings (70 bulls, 14 rams, and 7 goats for the week, with 14 lambs daily, in addition to the regular burnt offerings of two lambs each of the seven days). A whole people, wholly provided for and wholly devoted to the Lord celebrated each day with great enthusiasm. In addition, each night was highlighted by the unique circumstance of dwelling in makeshift tabernacles or booths. This idea of completion is not only in the numbers offered, but also in the quality of each one. Each must be *"without defect,"* whole, healthy, a holy sacrifice to the Lord. In addition, the people brought personal offerings to fulfill vows, plus freewill offerings, thank offerings, and peace offerings expressing their personal worship and thanksgiving to the Lord. Both priests and people ate these personal offerings in an atmosphere of fellowship and rejoicing.

> *Did You Know?*
> **SACRIFICES AS SIGNS OF COMPLETION**
>
> In the seventh month, seven being a symbol of completion, we see a unique pattern in the sacrifices of the week. Every day the priests offered a burnt offering of a different number of bulls, 2 rams, and 14 lambs, with grain, oil, and wine, and a sin offering of a goat. The number of bulls started at 13 the first day and decreased by one each day until they offered 7 on the last day. On this **seventh** month for **seven** days they sacrificed a total of 70 bulls (10 × 7), 14 rams (2 × 7), 98 lambs (14 × 7) all the sevens focusing on the idea of completion in this Feast. Some note that the *Talmud* emphasizes the focus on the world in that there were seventy bulls offered corresponding to the seventy nations of the world. There is a strong emphasis in this Feast on all the world coming before the Lord.

📖 What additional guidelines do you discover in Deuteronomy 16:13–17? Who is to be involved in this Feast according to verse 14?

u shall rejoice in your feast, u an your daughter your manservant an maidservant an the Levite an stranger, an fatherless and the widow, who are within your gates. Seek the Lord

📖 Deuteronomy 12:5–7 gives general guidelines for the various times of worship at God's chosen place. Read those verses for another description of their times at the Tabernacle/Temple. Record any additional insights.

u shall eat before the Lord and rejoice in all his blessings

📖 What are some of the reasons the Lord gives for this Feast in verses 15–17?

God called every one to come and give to the feast according to what the Lord has given you.

📖 As you read those verses, imagine the scene. What are some of the marks of this Feast? Describe some of the activities the people would be doing.

It was praise and worship, and eating and drinking, fellowship. Celebrating the Lord and his great blessing

A holy week set aside, holy sacrifices offered, a holy assembly gathered to begin and close the celebration; all spoke of the spiritual and material bounty of belonging to their holy Lord in this God-given land. God called His people to *"seek the* L<small>ORD</small>*"* together in these times. They gladly shared in worship times and meal times with one another—husbands and wives, sons and daughters, male and female servants, the priests and Levites serving in the Temple, the stranger or foreigner—even the orphans and widows, those who often suffered greater privation. God called **all** to be involved and *"rejoice in all to which you have put your hand, you and your households, in* which the LORD your God has blessed you" (12:7). Daily worship and fellowship, nightly conversations in the open air at the Temple and among the many booths in nearby fields, on hillsides, streets, and rooftops, all combined to make the city festive because of God's goodness.

God called His people to come before Him not *"empty-handed,"* but with offerings reflecting His abundance and their gratitude. This was not just for the few or the rich, but *"every man."* Each can give something for the Feast and for the ongoing ministry of the Temple *"as he is able, according to the blessing of the LORD your God which He has given you."* The people brought various offerings from their lands and flocks. The bounty of the year included that of the *"threshing floor,"* barley and wheat, the abundance of the grape harvest, plus dates, pomegranates, and the riches of the olive groves gathered in. In God's chosen location, they would celebrate the multiplied blessing of God on the *"produce,"* fruits, vegetables, flocks, inclusive of *"all the work of your hands."* It was a time to be *"altogether joyful"* in the Lord and His provision. This indeed was the most joyous of feasts.

📖 Did this Feast occur regularly as God intended? There are indications that Israel did not follow these directions all the time, but there are also records of how they repented and obeyed His Word. One of those occurred in Ezra's and Nehemiah's day, in the autumn of 445 BC. Read Nehemiah 8:13–18 and summarize what happened.

_____

_____

_____

_____

📖 What characterized this celebration, according to verse 17?

_____

_____

After the people in Jerusalem celebrated the Feast of Trumpets (Nehemiah 8:1–12), they continued the public reading of the Word of God and discovered the Lord's call to celebrate the Feast of Tabernacles. They responded enthusiastically, going to the surrounding countryside and bringing in olive branches, oil tree branches, myrtle and palm branches. They made booths all around Jerusalem—on the flat rooftops, in their courtyards, in the open spaces of the city, and in the outer courts of the Temple area. *"Great gladness"* marked their celebration and their holy assemblies, as does all obedience to the Word of God and the leadership of His Spirit.

The Feast of Tabernacles served as a very special time for the people of Israel. One of the times of greatest celebration occurred in the reign of Solomon. We will explore those events in Day Two.

Put Yourself In Their Shoes
"ALTOGETHER JOYFUL"

In the Feast of Tabernacles, God expressed the desire that His people be *"altogether joyful"* in His presence (Deuteronomy 16:15). David states in Psalm 16:11, *"In Your presence is fullness of joy,"* a verse Peter quoted in Acts 2:28 speaking of Christ's resurrection joy in His Father's presence. Acts records believers in the early church being full of joy. *"Gladness"* marked many in Jerusalem (2:46), even in times of opposition (5:41). Those in Samaria experienced *"great joy"* after placing faith in Christ (8:8). The Ethiopian went on his way *"rejoicing"* after he believed in Jesus (8:39). Acts 13:52 records of those in Antioch of Pisidia, *"the disciples were filled with joy and with the Holy Spirit."* The fruit of the Holy Spirit is "joy" (Galatians 5:22). Jesus spoke of entering *"into the joy of your Lord"* in the future kingdom (Matthew 25:21, 23). Revelation 19:7, speaking of the marriage of the Lamb, states, *"let us be glad and rejoice."* Indeed, Jesus Christ desires His followers to be *"altogether joyful"* with Him forever.

Put Yourself In Their Shoes
A PILGRIM JOURNEY

This third pilgrimage of each year to celebrate the Feast of Tabernacles emphasized the pilgrim mindset of the people of God. Living for a week in tents/booths made of branches reminded them of the past Wilderness Journey and awaiting entrance into the Promised Land. It also spoke of the present Earth journey awaiting the *Parousia*—the New Testament term for the continuous manifested presence of the Lord beginning with the Second Coming of the Lord to establish His reign on earth. It continues for one thousand years and then moves into the eternal realm in the New Heavens and the New Earth (Revelation 20:4–6; 21:1ff.).

Lesson Eight — DAY TWO

THE GREATEST DEDICATION

In 2 Samuel 7 and 1 Chronicles 17, we find the account of King David's desire to build God a house of worship. Nathan the prophet encouraged him to go forward. Then, the Lord spoke to Nathan and said that would not be, but David's son would build a house for the Lord, a temple in Jerusalem. In that encounter, the Lord also established the Davidic covenant, making wonderful promises to David about an enduring house and an everlasting kingdom. Those promises would be fulfilled in the Greater Son of David, the Messiah, the Lord Jesus. God honored the heart of David. His desires and motives spoke of his heart for God. Later, God commissioned David's son Solomon to build a house of worship in Jerusalem. The dedication of that house occurred in 958 BC at the Feast of Tabernacles. Today we will walk through that celebration.

When the people of Israel dwelt in booths or tabernacles/tents in the Wilderness, God dwelt with them in a tent as well. He made the Tabernacle His dwelling place, specifically the Holy of Holies or Most Holy Place. There He manifested His presence in the cloud of glory by day and in the pillar of fire by night (Exodus 25:8; 40:34–38). Solomon finished building the Temple in the eighth month (*Bul*—our late October, 959 BC). Before the priests began ministering there, there had to first be the dedication of the Temple. The calendar choice for that celebration occurred about eleven months later, during the Feast of Tabernacles in the month *Tishri* in 958, a Jubilee year.

> *Did You Know?*
> **GOD'S CHOSEN PLACE**
>
> God instructed Moses and the children of Israel about coming to appear before Him in His chosen place. He mentions this repeatedly in Deuteronomy (12:5–7, 11–14, 17–19, 26; 14:23; 16:2, 6, 11, 15–16). In 2 Chronicles 3:1, we discover that the chosen place is Jerusalem, specifically on Mount Moriah, where Abraham and Isaac worshipped in Genesis 22. It is also *"the place that David had prepared on the threshing floor of Ornan the Jebusite"* (see 1 Chronicles 21:18–28; 22:1). There Solomon built and dedicated the Temple, the house of the Lord (966–959 BC). It is also God's chosen place for the future celebrations of the Feast of Tabernacles in the Millennial Kingdom (Zechariah 14:16–21).

📖 David had made many preparations for the Temple following the detailed directions God had given Him (see 1 Chronicles 28–29, especially 28:19). What final preparations did Solomon make for the use of the Temple, according to 2 Chronicles 5:1?

_____
_____
_____

📖 What did Solomon do as described in 2 Chronicles 5:2–3? Who joined in this time?

_____
_____
_____

📖 When did this occur, according to verse 3? What further time parameters do you find in 2 Chronicles 7:8–10? Note that all journeyed home on *Tishri* 23 after two weeks of celebration.

_____
_____
_____

David had provided much for the building of the Temple, gold, silver, bronze, iron, and detailed instructions for the building. Solomon organized

174 FOLLOWING GOD – LIFE PRINCIPLES FOR WORSHIP FROM THE FEASTS OF ISRAEL

workers in wood and stone and the seven-year process began. When all was finished, Solomon brought all the needed utensils and supplies into the storerooms of the Temple. He called together the elders of Israel and heads of each of the tribes, along with the men and families of Israel, *"a very great assembly."* All these gathered around *"the feast"* of the seventh month, the Feast of Tabernacles. The workers finished the Temple in the eighth month of 959 BC (1 Kings 6:38), and Solomon scheduled the dedication for the seventh month of 958, coinciding with the Feast of Tabernacles *and* a Jubilee Year. The people came together *Tishri* 8–14 for seven days of dedication of the Temple which would have included the Day of Atonement, followed by seven days of the Feast of Tabernacles, concluding with the eighth day, *Tishri* 22. The people returned to their homes on *Tishri* 23, *"joyful and glad of heart for the good that the Lord had done for David, for Solomon, and for His people Israel"* (2 Chronicles 7:10).

📖 In these days of the temple dedication, what did they do first, according to 2 Chronicles 5:4–5?

_____

_____

_____

📖 What else occurred during this ceremony as recorded in 2 Chronicles 5:6?

_____

_____

The first event of this celebration involved the Levites bringing the Ark of the Covenant from the Tabernacle into the Holy of Holies. The Ark served as the centerpiece of the nation, the symbol of its covenant relationship. Israel considered it as the throne of God and the Holy of Holies as His throne room, the place of meeting Him. At the Temple, Solomon and the *"congregation of Israel"* offered countless sheep and oxen, all joyfully participating in worship.

📖 Imagine the scene thus far. What sights and sounds occurred as the priests came out of the Holy of Holies (Most Holy Place), according to 2 Chronicles 5:11–13?

_____

_____

_____

📖 According to 2 Chronicles 5:14, what did the priests do when the Lord manifested His Presence (the *Shekinah* Glory)?

_____

_____

This momentous event involved all the priests. The Levitical singers dressed in spotless white linen stood east of the altar near the entrance with instruments of praise, *"cymbals, harps, and lyres,"* along with 120 priests blowing silver trumpets. The united sound mirrored the united hearts of

> *Put Yourself In Their Shoes*
> ## CAREFUL AND JOYFUL PREPARATIONS
>
> David made careful preparations for his son, Solomon, to build the Temple, receiving the plans and details from the LORD (1 Chronicles 28:19). When David gathered the leaders and people together to give for the building of the Temple, 1 Chronicles 29:9 speaks of their great joy. *"Then the people rejoiced because they had offered so willingly, for they made their offering to the LORD with a whole heart, and King David also rejoiced greatly."*

> "Arise, O Lord, to Your resting place, You and the ark of Your strength. Let Your priests be clothed with righteousness, and let Your saints shout for joy."
>
> Psalm 132:8–9 (NKJV)

the people, one in praising the Lord. What a majestic moment! *"Indeed it came to pass, when the trumpeters and singers were as one, to make one sound to be heard in praising and thanking the L*ORD*, and when they lifted up their voice with the trumpets and cymbals and instruments of music, and praised the L*ORD*, saying: 'For He is good, for His mercy endures forever,' that the house, the house of the L*ORD*, was filled with a cloud,"* the cloud of the glory of the LORD. His magnificent manifested presence filled every eye and heart with wonder. The priests stopped still in awe and worship.

Second Chronicles 6:1 records that in response to these events, Solomon prayed, acknowledging the Lord's Presence, His promise of dwelling in *"the dark cloud"* as He had at Mount Sinai with Moses (Exodus 19:9, 16–20) and in the Tabernacle with Aaron (Leviticus 16:2). The Temple would now be the place to honor God and His presence, to meet with and worship Him. Solomon continued in 2 Chronicles 6, addressing the people about how God had met with David earlier and approved of David's desire for a more permanent dwelling of God among His people (see 1 Chronicles 22:7–9). Though God approved of such a dwelling place, He also declared that David was not the appropriate leader to oversee its construction. However, God promised that David's son, Solomon, would one day lead this building project. In 2 Chronicles 6, Solomon acknowledged God's many promises for the future and for the Temple, and then he prayed.

📖 Read Solomon's prayer of dedication in 1 Kings 8:22–54 (also in 2 Chronicles 6:12–42). To help you grasp his petitions before the Lord, note first his focus on the faithfulness of God (22–26). He acknowledged the greatness of God (27) and the willingness and readiness of God to hear prayer (28–30). To help see the complete picture, note that Solomon then made seven petitions about future needs (31–32, 33–34, 35–36, 37–40, 41–43, 44–45, 46–53). Read this prayer and record any **personal applications** you see to **your** life and **your** needs or to those of **someone** you know.

_____
_____
_____
_____
_____
_____

📖 What final petition did Solomon make in 2 Chronicles 6:41–42?

_____
_____

📖 In that petition, Solomon quoted a portion of Psalm 132. What do you find in Psalm 132 about the Lord's dwelling with His people?

_____
_____
_____

Solomon called on the Lord and the Ark to *"arise … to Your resting place,"* the Holy of Holies, also known as His throne and His footstool. This focused on God dwelling with His people as their King and them experiencing His salvation, rejoicing in His goodness. Psalm 132 recounts the desire of David to have the presence of God and the Ark in Jerusalem, moved from *"the fields of its woods,"* a reference to its temporary location in the countryside of Kiriath Jearim (1 Samuel 7:1–2). Solomon's prayer expressed that desire for the present time in the new Temple as well as the future when the seed of David would be on the throne and the Lord would dwell in Zion, His *"resting place forever."* In that future day, Zion will be marked by abundant provision, joyous salvation, and the crown of David will *"flourish"*—all pictures of the fulfillment of the Feast of Tabernacles in the Messiah's future reign.

📖 What final exhortation and blessing did he speak to the people in 1 Kings 8:54–61? Why did Solomon desire that the Lord answer his request, according to verse 60?

_____

_____

_____

Solomon blessed the Lord for giving rest to His people Israel, according to His promises. His presence with Israel meant His further blessing as the people walked in obedience to Him. Solomon desired that God would answer his prayers so that they would fulfill all His purposes *"as each day may require."* Why? So that *"all the people of the earth may know that the LORD is God; there is no other."* God's presence among His people and the people's obedient worship and testimony of God working among them would lead to other nations calling on the name of the Lord, coming to Him for the salvation He alone can give. The themes of this prayer and this experience during the Feast of Tabernacles point to a wider fulfillment of that Feast when more and more of the nations of the earth rejoice in the LORD as their God.

📖 What occurred when he finished praying, according to 2 Chronicles 7:1–3?

_____

_____

_____

📖 What do you discover in 2 Chronicles 7:4–11? How did the people and priests respond to this obvious work of God?

_____

_____

_____

When Solomon finished praying, the fire of God *"came down from heaven and consumed the burnt offering and the sacrifices; and the glory of the LORD filled the temple."* The priests could do nothing but worship and the people humbly, reverently bowed their faces to the ground in worship and praise. The sacrifices offered to the Lord by Solomon and the people far outnumbered any required offerings—twenty-two thousand bulls and one hundred and twenty thousand sheep sacrificed amidst jubilant worship and

---

Put Yourself In Their Shoes

PICTURES OF THE PEOPLE AND THEIR GOD

The Feast of Tabernacles presents several pictures of the relationship and fellowship of God with His people. **First, a resting people.** The harvest in, the work done, the Feast began with a Day of Rest, a pause after the harvest labors to remember all the Lord had done (Leviticus 23:39; 1 Kings 8:56). **Second, a people walking rightly with God.** In covenant with God, abundant rains and harvests depended upon a right relationship with Him. If they failed to follow, He disciplined them severely. This Feast pictured walking in fellowship with Him (1 Kings 8:35–36). **Third, a rejoicing people.** Sometimes called the Season of Our Joy, this Feast celebrated the goodness and faithfulness of God (Deuteronomy 16:13–15; 1 Kings 8:66). **Fourth, God's refreshing presence** as the people celebrated His presence in worship and fellowship. **Fifth, God's redeeming promise.** As a redeemed people, they could be a light to the nations that they too might come to know Him (1 Kings 8:10–11, 41–43; Isaiah 56:7). **Sixth, God's reigning plan.** The Feast pictured and pointed to a time when the Lord would reign over all the earth in great peace and prosperity, spiritually and materially (Revelation 7:9–17; 20:4–6; Isaiah 44:1–8).

abundant feasting. The Levites played various musical instruments; the priests sounded the many silver trumpets, and all rejoiced in the theme, *"For His mercy endures forever."* The celebration involved a total of fifteen days, and on *Tishri* 23 Solomon sent the people home *"joyful and glad of heart for the good that the Lord had done for David, for Solomon, and for His people Israel."*

This 'Greatest Dedication' focused on the Temple illustrates what life is meant to be—a right relationship with God and with one another, following His Word, pleasing His heart. The heart of any relationships is a loving "presence," being with friends, family, those we love in an honest, caring, righteous fellowship. We see these realities in each of the Feasts, especially in the last two, the Day of Atonement and the Feast of Tabernacles when all have dealt with sin God's way and all rejoice together with the Lord in a harmonious and joyous fellowship.

The fifteen days of continuous Dedication of the Temple, concluding with the Feast of Tabernacles certainly focused the people on the Lord as their awesome God. His majesty and glory were clearly displayed; the people worshiped in wonder, with great feasting, rejoicing, praise and thanksgiving. This was indeed the greatest dedication, a celebration of relationships in right order. Yet, coming in the future is an even greater manifestation of the presence of the Lord and of all things being made right. We will look at some of those in Day Four, but first, we must consider Jesus and *"the Great Day of the Feast"* in Day Three.

Lesson Eight — DAY THREE

Put Yourself In Their Shoes
GOD'S DESIRE GOD'S CALL

When the priests poured the water of Siloam on the altar, the people thought of Isaiah 12:3, drawing *"water from the wells of salvation."* The Scriptures often speak of God pouring forth His Spirit in salvation, bringing great joy. Isaiah speaks of the Spirit being poured upon His people (32:15; 59:21). Isaiah 44:1–6 records God's promise of salvation to His people. In Isaiah 44:3, He assures the thirsty heart, *"For I will pour water on him who is thirsty, and floods on the dry ground; I will pour My Spirit on your descendants, and My blessing on your offspring"* (NKJV). Other passages that speak of God's outpouring of His Spirit and salvation include Isaiah 45:8; Ezekiel 11:19; 36:26–27; 37:14; 39:29; Joel 2:28–29; Zechariah 12:10; John 7:39; 14:16–17, and Acts 1:5–8; 2:1–12, 17–18, 33; 10:44–45.

JESUS AND "THE GREAT DAY" OF THE GREATEST FEAST

The Feast of Tabernacles—the greatest celebration of the seven Feasts, the occasion for the greatest dedication of the Temple in Solomon's day, is also the occasion for one of the greatest days of revelation by Jesus. Jesus said in Matthew 3:15 that He came to *"fulfill all righteousness"* and in Matthew 5:17 that He came to *"fulfill"* the Law and the Prophets. That includes all the Feasts—every picture, prophecy, or promise made in one or all seven of these celebrations. Today we will explore what Jesus thought of the Feast of Tabernacles and how the Father orchestrated His ministry to address and fulfill this all-important Feast.

One of the expectations of the Jews in regard to the Feast of Tabernacles was the coming of the Messiah. Many thought that the Messiah would come during the Feast of Tabernacles and establish His earthly Kingdom. Certain additional ceremonies that developed over the years occupied the scene in Jesus' day and highlighted this expectation. A review of two added Feast of Tabernacles ceremonies will help us better understand how the Jews saw this Feast in the days of Jesus and why Jesus said some of the things He said.

The **first of the two ceremonies** that occurred during the week was the Water Drawing Ceremony. On a physical level, in an arid land it related to the great need and prayer for the winter rains in preparation for the next harvest season. On a spiritual level, this worship time with water pouring focused on the fullness of God's presence among His people in the pouring forth of His Spirit and their drawing *"water from the wells of salvation"* (Isaiah 12:3). Every morning the high priest led a procession of priests and musicians out of the temple to the Pool of Siloam where he drew water from the pool into a golden pitcher. He then marched back through the southern Water Gate of the Temple. At precisely the time of the morning sacrifice, the priests sounded three blasts of the silver trumpets announcing his entrance, and other priests repeated Isaiah 12:3, *"with joy you will draw water from the wells of salvation."*

The high priest came with the procession and poured the water into one of two silver bowls connected to the altar. One bowl received this water, and the other received the daily offerings of wine. Then the priests blew three blasts of the silver trumpets, signaling the Levitical priests to sing the *Hallel* (Psalm 113—118). The people joined in waving palm branches toward the altar and sang Psalm 118:25, *"Save now, I pray* [Hebrew, *yasha annah* or *Hosanna*], *O LORD; O LORD, I pray, send now prosperity."* The word *Hosanna* means *"do save"* or *"save now, I pray"* and refers to His salvation *and* His rule. The plea *"Hosanna"* was so prominent that the liturgical prayers were called *"the Hosannas."* At this point each day, the priests, holding palm branches, marched around the altar once. The palm branches were also called *"Hosannas."*

In Jesus' day, the people connected their rejoicing with palm branches to that pictured in Psalm 118. The branches also served as symbols of victory and freedom from foreign oppression. It was a symbol of the victorious Maccabees who had given Israel religious freedom from the Syrians almost two hundred years earlier. With that, the shout *"Hosanna"* or *"save now"* included the idea of the Messiah King coming to give victory once again, saving Israel from its oppressors and fulfilling the promises of establishing His all-sufficient, glorious reign. On the **seventh** day, *"the great day of the feast,"* also known as "the Day of the Great Hosanna," the priests marched around the altar seven times, again focusing on Isaiah 12:3, joyously drawing water *"from the wells of salvation."* The word *"salvation"* is a translation of the Hebrew word *yeshua,* which is obviously connected to the name *Yeshua* (Joshua) and his great victories (including the remembrance of him marching around Jericho seven times before that victory, Joshua 6:4–5, 15–16). It is translated *"Jesus"* in the New Testament. Revelation 7:9–17 paints a similar future scene of saints holding palm branches celebrating the presence of the Lord in heaven and enjoying His provision of *"living fountains of waters."*

A **second ceremony** occurred each night. To further celebrate the ceremony of drawing water the priests and people joined in the Light Celebration in the Temple every night for six nights. During the Feast of Tabernacles, the people gathered in the Court of the Women at the temple where stood four very tall menorahs with four branches, each holding four large bowls, each bowl containing about ten gallons of olive oil with a linen cloth wick. For the celebration of the light, the sons of priests climbed ladders and lit those giant torches each night illuminating the entire city all night. Instruments played and Levites sang the Songs of Ascent (Psalm 120—134) on the fifteen steps leading from the Nicanor gate into the Court of the Women. As they did this, priests and people celebrated and danced around the court in the light of these four lamps. The rabbis recorded in the *Mishnah*, *Succah* 5:1,

> *Did You Know?*
> ### THE INNER WORKINGS OF THE POOL OF SILOAM
>
> In the early days of Israel, the Gihon Spring rested outside Jerusalem, the City of David, and the people walked there to get water. In order to protect the city's water from enemy hands, King Hezekiah had a 1,700 foot long tunnel dug from the Gihon Spring on the east side to the interior of the city on the south, routing the water from the spring into a pool of Siloam there (2 Kings 20:20; 2 Chronicles 32:30). The water traveled from the underground spring through the new underground tunnel (as much as 60 feet below street level) and out into the pool, providing life giving water to the people. "*Living water*" is any water that is free flowing like a stream or spring, unlike cistern water that can become stagnant, even "dead" with contamination. The picture of the free-flowing "living" waters of Siloam coming from the "innermost" underground of the city matched the thirst-quenching spiritual reality Jesus promised in the work of Jesus and the Spirit, each believer becoming like a 'Pool of Siloam' with flowing *"rivers of living water"* (John 7:37–39; cf., Edersheim, *The Temple*, p. 281).

Did You Know?
PETER AND THE THREE TABERNACLES

In Matthew 16:28, Jesus told His disciples that some of them would not see death until they saw the coming of the Son of Man in His Kingdom. Then, six days later, Peter, James, and John saw the Transfiguration of Jesus on Mount Hermon and the appearance of Moses and Elijah speaking with Him (Matthew 17:1–8; Luke 9:27–36; 2 Peter 1:16–18). Peter quickly spoke of building three tabernacles. Some see this as a reference to the Feast of Tabernacles, just weeks away when Peter said this. In its ultimate fulfillment, that Feast spoke of the Presence of Christ in His earthly millennial Kingdom (Zechariah 14:16). Alfred Edersheim notes, "the Feast of Tabernacles is the only type in the Old Testament which has not yet been fulfilled" (*The Temple*, p. 287).

"If anyone thirsts, let him come to Me and drink."
John 7:37b

"He that hath not beheld the joy of the drawing of water hath never seen joy in his life." The light celebration is spoken of as "the joy of the House of water-pouring," referring to the Temple. This celebration recalled how the light of the *Shekinah* Glory had rested there in Solomon's day and guided the people in Moses' day. This is yet another example of this Feast being the most joyous of the seven. In this atmosphere, Jesus ministered and taught.

Having witnessed these ceremonies for many years, Jesus came to this final season of His ministry before His crucifixion (six months away). Many in Israel expected the Messiah to reveal Himself during this Feast. The events of John 7—9 occurred just before and during this Feast of Tabernacles (John 7:2). What do we discover in that passage and what applications can we see for today?

📖 First of all, what did Jesus face from His brothers in Nazareth, according to John 7:1–9? How did Jesus respond to them?

_____
_____
_____

📖 What did Jesus do, according to John 7:10–13? What did He do in Jerusalem in *"the middle of the Feast,"* according to John 7:14–24?

_____
_____
_____

📖 What main point did Jesus seek to get across in John 7:16–18?

_____
_____

Jesus' brothers knew the traditions that the Messiah would perhaps reveal himself during the Feast of Tabernacles. Whether or not they were suggesting He do this in Jerusalem we do not know, for John 7:5 points out that they did not really believe in Him. They traveled to the Feast, and Jesus chose to go up to the Feast secretly later. He began teaching in the Temple, focusing the listening crowds on the will of God and **His** teaching. If anyone is willing to do the will of God, that person will know whether what Jesus taught is right or not. God will guide the willing heart. Jesus made it clear that all His teaching and all He did were from God, that He genuinely sought the glory of the Father who sent Him. In cooperation with and for the glory of His Father, He had authority to heal, to teach, and to bring salvation to all who would believe in Him.

📖 As the Feast week progressed, the priests and gathered worshipers came to the seventh day, *Tishri* 21, *"the Great Day of the Feast."* During this day, perhaps near the moment when the high priest made his seven circuits around the altar after pouring from the golden pitcher the water from Siloam, Jesus made a loud declaration. What did He say, according to John 7:37–38? To whom did He address His message?

_____
_____

📖 Upon whom did Jesus focus their attention?

_____

_____

📖 What did Jesus promise? What did Jesus require for this promise to be fulfilled in a person's life?

_____

_____

📖 What connections do you see that the people could easily make between the ceremonies of the Feast and the statement of Jesus?

_____

_____

_____

📖 What added information does the apostle John write in John 7:39? How does this relate to the people's thoughts and expectations about the Feast of Tabernacles? For additional insights, you may want to read THE ORDER OF THE FEAST OF TABERNACLES at the end of this final lesson.

_____

_____

On *"the great day of the Feast,"* Jesus cried out in a loud voice drawing attention to Himself and His invitation to experience *"living water."* He issued the invitation to *"any man,"* any *"thirsty"* person willing to admit his or her thirst, the deepest need of the heart. Come to Jesus *"and drink."* He called each one to personal belief in Him. The promise for each one is the experience of His living waters within, not by one's own efforts, religious works, sweat, or merit. The waters are the work of the Holy Spirit who would be given after Jesus had been glorified in His crucifixion, resurrection, ascension, and enthronement. At that point, the Spirit would be poured out in fullness, fulfilling many Old Testament prophecies and the promises of Jesus to His disciples. We discover that fulfillment in Acts 1—2.

When the people heard Jesus' invitation, they would naturally make the connection to all that had been going on during the week. Psalm 118 had been repeatedly sung; the imagery of drawing water from the wells of salvation and the rejoicing with palm branches had been seen over and over. The celebration of light every night spoke of the presence of God in His manifested glory, that *Shekinah* cloud of glory that awed everyone in Moses' and Solomon's days. That light of glory had also led the people in the Pillar of Fire out of Egypt through the Wilderness to the Promised Land. Here was a man promising a fulfillment. Could He actually be the Messiah? Or, is He the Prophet promised by Moses (Deuteronomy 18:15–22)? Many thought the Messiah would manifest Himself during this Feast. Here is a man making those kinds of claims. The day was not over. Conversations focused on all that had occurred. The eighth day remained to be celebrated. What more would occur?

Put Yourself In Their Shoes
LIVING WATER AND STALE WATER

"Living water" referred to running water like that of a spring, a stream, or a river. Cistern water or water in one of the *mikvah* (ritual baptism pools at the Temple) could become stale, even contaminated and impure. God required "running" or "fresh" or "living" water for cleansing of impurities (Leviticus 14:5–7, 48–53). Jesus not only supplies *"living water,"* He is the *"living water."* He promises this to those who believe in Him (John 4:10–11; 7:37–38). Ezekiel 47:1–9 and Zechariah 14:8–9 speak of *"living waters"* flowing in the future millennial kingdom. We also see *"the waters of life"* provided for His people now and in Heaven forever (Revelation 7:17; 21:6; 22:17).

📖 The next day after *"the Great Day,"* the eighth day of the Feast, Jesus made another declaration. What do you find in John 8:12? How would the people view this statement, especially during *this* week? How would this relate to the special ceremonies of the week?

_____

_____

_____

📖 Throughout Israel's history, the people spoke of the Lord leading them from Egypt to Canaan by the Pillar of Fire (Exodus 13:20–22; Numbers 9:15–23). Read Nehemiah 9:19 and note any connections to the reality Jesus sought to convey in His statement.

_____

_____

_____

Doctrine
"MY HOUR" AND "MY DAY"

Jesus often spoke of *"My hour"* or *"My time"* referring to the time or hour of His coming crucifixion and all that would occur then. Jesus spoke of *"My time"* to His mother Mary in John 2:4 and to His brothers in John 7:6, 8. Often those who opposed Jesus sought to arrest or stone Him, but His *"time"* or His *"hour"* had *"not yet come"* (John 7:30; 8:20) Just before His crucifixion, Jesus mentioned that His *"hour"* had indeed come (John 12:23, 27; 13:1; 17:1; Matthew 26:18, 45; Mark 14:41), the time for Him to be *"glorified"* (John 7:39; 12:16, 23; 13:31–32), though He wrestled with intense agony over this *"hour"* (Mark 14:35). When Jesus spoke of His reign, the time of His Kingdom, He referred to it as *"My day"* as in John 8:56. That is *"the day of Christ Jesus"* (Philippians 1:6) or *"the day of Christ"* (1:10). It is *"the day drawing near"* (Hebrews 10:25), *"the day"* of evaluation and rewards for the believer (1 Corinthians 3:13; 2 Timothy 4:8).

Jesus declared *"I am the light of the world; he who follows Me shall not walk in darkness, but shall have the light of life."* What a statement of promise! Jesus made clear His claim to being the light, like that promised in Psalm 118:27. The connection to the Pillar of Fire should be obvious. The children of Israel did not walk in darkness as the light of the Lord led them, showing them *"the way in which they were to go."* He then called people to follow Him exclusively if any wanted to avoid walking in darkness and enjoy walking in *"the light of life."* This would be part of the fulfillment of the joy of this very Feast—a united people rejoicing together in their God, in His goodness, and calling others to join in the celebration of belief in Him, of walking in the light with Him. But not everyone was ready to believe or follow this man and His teachings.

We can summarize the remainder of John 8 with these thoughts. In John 8:13, the Pharisees continued their resistance of Jesus, arguing against His statements and teachings. Jesus clearly revealed God the Father had sent Him, that the Father bore witness of Him, and that those opposing Him did not know the Father. Jesus warned that if they did not believe that He is the "I AM" they would die in their sins, but they continued in their unbelief (John 8:24). However, some did believe Him (John 8:30). Jesus continued pressing the issue of belief in His word, urging them to trust Him. In John 8:51, Jesus promised that anyone who believes Him and keeps His word *"shall never see death."* An expanded translation of that verse literally reads, "if anyone keeps My word, he will absolutely never see death into the age," no death in eternity. The phrase "into the age" is often translated "forever." Jesus did not say a person would not die, but that he or she would never experience eternal death, what Revelation 20:14 refers to as *"the second death,"* judgment forever. Instead, the believer will experience the fullness of God and His will forever. The mention of *"into the age"* can also refer to all God has planned, including Christ's *"day,"* about which Jesus gave a strong declaration in His discussion of Abraham.

As He talked, Jesus stated in John 8:56, *"Abraham rejoiced to see My day, and he saw it and was glad,"* what some see as an allusion to Psalm 118:24 about being *"glad"* in the day when the LORD vindicates and fully sets in place His *"chief cornerstone"* (118:22). When the Jews countered with statements of unbelief, Jesus concluded with *"before Abraham was born, I AM,"* a clear statement to His being God, the Lord, the I AM. How does all this tie together? It is quite probable that the *"day"* Abraham *"saw"* or perceived fits with what occurred on Mount Moriah (modern Jerusalem) in Genesis 22. In this incident in which God provided a sacrificial ram, Abraham named the place *Yahweh/Jehovah Jireh,* translated *"the LORD will provide"* In that encounter, Abraham told Isaac that the LORD would *"provide"* a lamb. Abraham then stated that the Lord *"would be provided,"* or literally, He *"would be seen"* on **that** Mount. The promise is two-fold, relating to Christ being seen in His two comings. The promise proved true first when Jesus was seen as the lamb dying for the sins of the world. At His Second Coming, He will be seen there as the risen reigning Lamb, the King who rules over *"the gate of His enemies"* (Genesis 22:17). The *"gate"* refers to the place of ruling, of power and authority. In His *"day,"* Jesus will first rule over the nations in His millennial kingdom, followed by His eternal rule over new heavens and a new earth, certainly a *"day"* over which Abraham could be *"glad."* In Day Four, we will see more about the kingdom as it relates to the Feast of Tabernacles.

📖 There is more Jesus revealed about Himself as the fulfillment of the symbols found in the Feast of Booths or Tabernacles. A notable event occurred on the eighth day, the day of Sabbath rest and a *"holy assembly."* It is recorded in John 9. Read John 9:1–59 and then look at verses 1–2. What and who caught the attention of Jesus and His disciples? What question did the disciples ask?

_____

_____

_____

📖 According to John 9:5–7, what did Jesus do to bring sight to the man born blind? First, what did Jesus place on the man's eyes?

_____

_____

📖 Where did this clay ointment come from? Describe what occurred moment by moment, step by step.

_____

_____

_____

📖 Where did Jesus send him to wash his eyes? Why do you think He sent him there? What connection could this have to the Feast of these days or to Jesus?

_____

_____

_____

📖 According to John 9:3–5, what statements did Jesus make about Himself in connection with this incident?

_____

_____

LESSON EIGHT – THE FEAST OF THE TABERNACLES

📖 What additional thoughts do you glean from Psalm 118:25–27? This is one of the passages that the priests sang each day during the Water Drawing Ceremony.

___

___

___

It is the eighth day of the Feast, *Tishri 22*, a special day of Sabbath rest. After Jesus left the Temple, He and the disciples passed by a man blind from birth. The rabbis of the day taught that such physical maladies were caused by the person's sin, in this case either the infant before birth or his parents. Jesus denied that and stated that this occurred to clearly manifest or display the works of God. Then Jesus spat on the ground. Out of Jesus' mouth (from within Him) came spittle, which Jesus mixed with dirt to make a clay ointment. He then sent the man to wash in the pool of Siloam, the focal point of the Water-Drawing Ceremony during the Feast of Booths. John notes that Siloam is translated *"sent,"* giving us a connection to Jesus, the one sent by the Father (9:4) to bring living water, light, and salvation. The man washed and came back seeing, healed and rejoicing over the gift of sight. He experienced what Jesus could do as the light of the world; he was no longer walking in darkness physically or spiritually, but knowing *"the light of life"* (8:12).

The daily ceremony of the past seven days focused attention on Isaiah 12:3 about drawing water from the wells of salvation, and Psalm 118:25–27 spoke of God saving now, sending prosperity, and bringing His light. Psalm 118:27 states, *"The Lord is God, and He has given us light."* Jesus, of course, is God, and He gave light to this blind man. Out of His being the Water and the Word of healing came touching the dust of a cursed earth and the blind eyes of a needy man who could do nothing to change his situation. Jesus made the difference. The blind man's obedience to Jesus' command connected him to the change Jesus could make. Jesus displayed the works of God in this man's life, a changed life. The Father sent Jesus to work the works of the Father and to show Himself as *"the light of the world."* Jesus is the fulfillment of every picture in this first century celebration, the living water and the light. Then and now, He brings light and salvation to the trusting, obedient heart.

APPLY **Coming to Jesus**—During the Feast of Tabernacles, Jesus issued an invitation open to anyone—come to Him, believe in Him, and find the life of the Spirit, the living water, clear light and sure sight, spiritual prosperity. God's call to seek Him at the Feasts is His call to seek and see Jesus as the fulfillment of the Feast in every detail. That invitation is **open today** to any who will come to Jesus as Lord and Savior. Have you come to Him—personally, in repentance and faith in Him alone as the I AM, the God of **your** salvation? Do you know someone with whom you can share this invitation for **his or her** salvation? Celebrate the Feast by celebrating your relationship with Jesus and bring others to join with Him by faith and experience the festivities.

We have seen much about the Feast of Tabernacles. There is yet more revealed in Scripture. In Day Four, we will discover "the Greatest Destination," God's plans for the future fulfillment of this Feast in the final works of Jesus Christ.

Put Yourself In Their Shoes
THE TOUCH POINT OF THE TEMPLE

Solomon said in 2 Chronicles 2:6, *"…Who am I then, that I should build Him a temple, except to burn sacrifice before Him?"* The Temple would be for men and women a point of connection with God in worship, never a place to 'contain' or 'constrain' God. However, it would be great in beauty and majesty, for it reflected the God they worshiped, *"for our God is greater than all gods"* (2 Chronicles 2:5). Other verses that address this include Isaiah 66:1; Acts 7:49 and 17:24. Nothing we can buy or bargain with or build can box God in. He is God. We are not. In fact, He has made each of His children His dwelling place, a place of life and light. Each of us should be a place of worship, an expression of the greatness and character of God—every word, every deed, every attitude under the orchestration and fullness of His Spirit (1 Corinthians 6:19–20; 10:31–33; Ephesians 5:18–21).

JESUS AND THE GREATEST DESTINATION

Lesson Eight **DAY FOUR**

At Solomon's dedication of the Temple, he asked a question that at first glance is easily answered, which Solomon does to some extent. His question is *"will God indeed dwell with men on the earth?"* and his immediate thought is *"Behold, heaven and the heaven of heavens cannot contain You. How much less this temple* [literally, *"house"*] *which I have built!"* (2 Chronicles 6:18; 1 Kings 8:27). He answers the question with the obvious answer. No temple could hold God, nor does He need a place to live. However, we need a place to meet with Him.

The Lord has graciously provided a way for us to meet with Him, to know Him, hear Him, and experience His love, mercy, and grace. First, we encounter Him in the Tabernacle/Temple, then ultimately in His Son, the Lord Jesus. Jesus *"died for sins once for all"* to *"bring us to God,"* to a living, personal relationship in which He promises, *"I will never leave you nor forsake you"* (1 Peter 3:18; see also Deuteronomy 31:6, 8; Hebrews 13:5). We meet God in Jesus. His dwelling with His people is a forever reality that the Feast of Tabernacles pictures. What do we discover about this future reality, our future destination, in Scripture?

📖 What promises did God make about His people and especially about the seed of David in 2 Samuel 7:10–12?

_____

_____

_____

📖 What connections to those promises do you find in Luke 1:31–33?

_____

_____

_____

📖 In the celebration of light during the Feast of Tabernacles, one of the passages upon which the people focused was Isaiah 9:1–5, which speaks of those walking in gloom and darkness having a *"great light"* shine upon them. In this celebration, the people thought of the return of the *Shekinah* glory, the intense manifestation of the presence of the Lord when the Messiah would come to establish His reign. Read Isaiah 9:6 and describe the promised Ruler to come.

_____

_____

_____

📖 How do the promises about the seed of David in 2 Samuel 7:10–12 relate to the prophecy found in Isaiah 9:6–7?

_____

_____

_____

Put Yourself In Their Shoes
ISRAEL, THE FEASTS, AND THE CHURCH

Looking Back, Looking Forward—"If the beginning of the harvest [barley (First Fruits)] had pointed back to the birth of Israel in their Exodus from Egypt, and forward to the true Passover-sacrifice in the future; if the corn-harvest [wheat] was connected with the giving of the law on Mount Sinai in the past and the outpouring of the Holy Spirit on the Day of Pentecost; the harvest-thanksgiving of the Feast of Tabernacles reminded Israel, on the one hand, of their dwelling in booths in the wilderness, while, on the other hand, it pointed to the final harvest when Israel's mission should be completed, and all nations gathered unto the Lord. Thus the first of the three great annual feasts spoke, in the presentation of the first sheaf, of the founding of the Church; the second of its harvesting, when the Church in its present state should be presented as two unleavened wave-loaves; while the third pointed forward to the full harvest in the end, when 'in this mountain shall the Lord of Hosts make unto all people a feast of fat things…'" [Alfred Edersheim, *The Temple*, p. 269.]

LESSON EIGHT – THE FEAST OF THE TABERNACLES

📖 What is promised in Isaiah 9:7 that relates to the future? What will this ruler's reign look like?

_____
_____
_____

Through the prophet Isaiah, the Lord promised the *"light"* to come would actually be born *"a Child,"* specifically *"a Son"* upon whose shoulder the government will rest. He will be known as *"Wonderful,"* a term speaking of one indescribable *"Counselor,"* with unmatched wisdom, *"Mighty God,"* His power evident to all, *"Everlasting Father,"* always ruling His people with a father's compassion and care, and *"Prince of Peace,"* in the Hebrew language *Sar Shalom*, one who establishes and maintains peace and well-being throughout His domain. That peace (*shalom*) knows *"no end"* as He forever takes the throne of David. This *"Son"* is the Messiah who rules over His Kingdom, arranging it and stabilizing it with righteous decisions at every turn.

📖 In the Feast of Tabernacles, the people connected the celebration of light to the salvation symbolized in the water pouring ceremony. Isaiah 12:3 and the thoughts of drawing water *"from the wells of salvation"* focused attention on this full salvation God would bring. That verse is in the context of Isaiah 11:1–16 with 12:1–6, also referring to the reign of the Messiah. Read the entire passage, 11:1–16 and 12:1–6. Describe the man of verses 1–5.

_____
_____
_____

📖 Describe the circumstances of Isaiah 11:6–10. What will relationships look like *"in that day"*?

_____
_____
_____

📖 For additional insight look at Isaiah 65:19–25 and Micah 4:1–5 and summarize your insights.

_____
_____
_____
_____

Isaiah 11 speaks of a time after the Lord has returned the remnant to the covenant land of Israel. Though it looked as though the nation and the line of David were cut down by the Babylonian armies and the captivity (605–586 BC), *"a Branch"* would come from the roots and *"a Rod from the stem of Jesse,"* David's father. This refers to the Messiah of the tribe of Judah. Marked by the fullness of the Spirit of the Lord, He would make decisions with supernatural insight. That prophecy began to be fulfilled with the first coming of Jesus Christ, but was not fully realized then. He is yet to show His

---

Put Yourself In Their Shoes
PROMISES FOR TODAY AND TOMORROW

Isaiah 55:1–11 and 56:1–8 begin with the Lord's invitation to *"everyone who thirsts"* to come to Him that *"your soul may live."* Anyone can know the mercy and abundant forgiveness of the Lord. He promised that His word would not return *"void"* or *"empty,"* having no fruit. He will fulfill all His Word. That includes all the promises about the salvation He gives to any believing heart as well as to believing Israel. The Messiah's reign and Israel's restoration will come. Isaiah 55:12–13 promises great joy and peace to His people, including a time when *"instead of the thorn shall come up the cypress tree, and instead of the brier shall come up the myrtle tree,"* a testimony of the Lord's work, a time on earth when the curse of Genesis 3:17 is reversed. The book of Isaiah alone contains over 270 verses related to this Millennial Kingdom. In addition are all the promises made in the other prophets as well as in Psalms and in the historical books, promises made to Israel that cannot be simply applied to the church as a spiritualized Israel. God will be faithful to **all** His promises.

full wisdom and insight in ruling the earth. He will judge with righteousness and equity. The poor and the meek will know His perfect wisdom. The wicked will experience His perfect justice as He faithfully rules.

With Jesus reigning, nations will turn to Him who is both the *"branch"* and *"the root of Jesse."* In Revelation 22:16, Jesus states, *"I am the root and the offspring of David,"* the one before David and after him (see Revelation 5:5). As a result of His rule, the earth will be marked by unusual, even supernatural peace and harmony. The curse reversed, the wolf and lamb, the calf and lion dwell together, harmless even to a little child. Evil will be curtailed. Rejoicing will be the mark of the day as the knowledge of God grows.

During this millennial reign of Christ, one who dies at age 100 will be considered a youth. Those who live less than that will be thought accursed. Regular commerce will prosper and the followers of the Lord will experience unusually blessed lives. Their lifespan will be greatly increased; they will see the Lord's blessing on their descendants and experience clear evidence of quickly answered prayer. Micah adds a description of a time in which Jerusalem will be established as the spiritual and political capital of the nations. The Lord will teach His ways as His word goes forth. The decisions He makes in governing the world will be just and righteous. War will cease and nations will prosper as the Lord of peace reigns.

📖 Isaiah 11:11–16 speaks of God bringing the remnant of His people together once again to a time of greatest unity, victory, and harmony. How will His people respond to Him, according to Isaiah 12:1–4?

___

📖 What occurs because of the presence of God among His people, according to Isaiah 12:5–6?

___

📖 The Feast of Tabernacles will have a reviving, but first there will be many changes in the world and in Israel. Read Zechariah 14:1–15 and give a brief summary of these events.

___

📖 Read Zechariah 14:16–21 and record your insights concerning God's promises about the Feast of Tabernacles in the future.

___

Zechariah 14 describes a great series of battles against Jerusalem in which the Lord Himself will fight for victory in Israel. He will cause a great upheaval at the Mount of Olives and changes in the topography, events that obviously have not yet happened. He will come with His *"holy ones"* amidst these changes. Continuous living waters or free-flowing waters will issue from Jerusalem to the east and the west, unaffected by changes in seasons. In that day, *"the LORD will be king over all the earth,"* with *"no more curse"* on the land. Those who come through the battles to acknowledge and worship *"the King, the LORD of hosts"* will yearly celebrate the Feast of Booths or Tabernacles. Those who fail to honor Him will experience *"no rain,"* the forfeiture of His provision and blessings. His holiness will mark everything *"in that day."* Even simple tools will be inscribed with "HOLY TO THE LORD" acknowledging the vital link of everyone, everything, and every event to the Lord, honoring Him and one's relationship to Him.

Lesson Eight — DAY FIVE

ANSWERING THE CALL OF THE FEAST OF TABERNACLES

Word Study
THE "COMING" OF THE LORD—PAROUSIA

The Greek word *parousia* means "presence," literally phrased "being near or beside." In the first century, *parousia*, the technical term for the official arrival or coming of a king, created an expectancy among the people. It meant certain preparations for his arrival which could include special taxes imposed to provide a gift. The *parousia* often signaled the start of a new era, a change in the calendar of a province, and the striking of new coins in honor of the king's arrival. *Parousia* was also used of the changes brought by a conquering general. To a king or general, people often presented their petitions to right wrongs hoping for a new day of justice. Often translated *"coming"* in the New Testament, it refers to the **coming of the Lord**, pointing to His arrival and presiding *"presence"* in its various stages.

God brought His people through the Wilderness into the Promised Land with His presence and provision—everything they needed to live life as He intended, if they would obey all He said. They did not obey. They did not have the power within.

However, too often they followed their own stubborn will. That is the problem every follower of God faces. As the hymn writer penned, we are all "prone to wander" away from the Lord and His Word, often straying into fruitless, barren wildernesses. The New Testament believer has an advantage. God's presence accompanied the people of Israel. He resided with them. We have His promised presence indwelling, not just with us, but in us. We do not journey to the Temple to celebrate the Feasts. We are the Temple—each believer the personal residence of the Living God by His Holy Spirit.

How well are you practicing God's presence? Paul wrote a good description of one who continually practices His presence, walking in a God-pleasing way. It is found in 2 Corinthians 6:14–18.

📖 According to 2 Corinthians 6:14–16, what are the marks of a personal relationship with Christ?

_____
_____
_____

📖 What are the contrasts, the marks of those who do not know Christ?

_____
_____
_____

📖 What does God promise His children in 2 Corinthians 6:16–18?

_____

_____

_____

📖 According to 2 Corinthians 7:1, what should mark our lives if we take seriously His promises to us?

_____

_____

A follower of Jesus is known as a *"believer,"* one who walks in a trust relationship, believing and obeying the Lord and His Word. Therefore, each believer should be marked by *"righteousness"* rather than *"lawlessness."* He or she should be doing what is right by the power of the Spirit who indwells each one. That also means walking clearly in the *"light,"* not stumbling in the *"darkness"* and walking in harmony with Christ and with one another, not in harmony with the things of *"Belial,"* the devil.

Every believer can experience the presence of the living God and should not be aligning with any kind of lifeless, fruitless idol. God dwells in His people. Each one is a temple. He also walks among us working out His will as our God. Because of His work, every believer should be marked by a separation from the uncleanness of the world and its thinking. God does not call us to a religious system. He made us for a family relationship—Father to son and Father to daughter.

Because of these promises from God Himself, we should be sensitive to any impurity He reveals. He calls us to *"cleanse ourselves"* from any contamination in our thinking or living, any stain or *"defilement of flesh and spirit."* This is not a one-time experience. There is no 'arrival point' while we walk this life. We are ever pursuing, ever seeking, ever growing like a well-rooted tree (Psalm 1:3; Colossians 2:6–7). God calls us to keep maturing in holiness, growing in our walk with Him, walking *"in the fear of God,"* ever mindful that we are accountable to Him and He is available to empower us. There are no excuses for not walking this way.

Think back to what we have seen in the journeys of Israel. God meant life in the land of Canaan to be one of rest in a relationship with Him. As He had given them daily provision, wise leadership and His presence in the Wilderness, so they would experience His presence, provision and leadership in Canaan, but without the wandering, without the Wilderness drudgery. Rather, they could experience a rest in the land, within and without. However, most did not experience that depth of rest because of their stubborn willfulness, following the temptations of the world around them and the "flesh" within them.

God wanted better for His people then. He wants His best for us now. He has not given us a "land," but a "life," *His life* indwelling. Paul spoke of that life experience stating *"for to me, to live is Christ"* in Philippians 1:21 and *"Christ, who is our life"* in Colossians 3:4. To experience His life is to experience the realities of the Seven Feasts. To follow Jesus as Lord is to answer the call of the Feasts.

Put Yourself In Their Shoes
WALKING WITH GOD

The Lord desires to dwell with His people and the Feast of Tabernacles pictures this. Scripture presents this truth in many ways. **1)** He walked with Adam and Eve **in the Garden of Eden** (Genesis 2–3). **2)** He walked with Abraham **in the Covenant Land** (Genesis 17:1–8). **3)** He Tabernacled with Israel **in the Wilderness** (Exodus 25—40; Numbers 9:15–23). **4)** He dwelt with **Israel at the Temple** (2 Chronicles 7:3, 11–14). **5) Jesus, the Word made flesh,** "tabernacled" or *"dwelt among us"* (John 1:1, 14). **6)** He now indwells each believer **as His Temple or Holy of Holies** (Greek—*naos*) (John 14:17; 1 Corinthians 6:19–20). **7)** He promises to dwell among us **in the Millennium** (Numbers 14:21; Revelation 20:4–6; Ezekiel 43:1–9; Zechariah 6:13; Haggai 2:6–9; and in two songs of the Millennium in Isaiah 2:2–5 and 12:1–6). **8)** He will dwell with us and us with Him **in the New Heavens and New Earth** (2 Peter 3:13; Revelation 21:3; 22:1–5).

Put Yourself In Their Shoes
SEVEN FEASTS—SEVEN REALITIES TO EXPERIENCE

The **Feasts** speak of seven historical realities in the life of Israel and today picture seven realities *"in Christ"* for the Christian to **experience** day by day.
1) Passover—Seeing redemption by the blood of a lamb—<u>Remember your redemption by the blood of **the** Lamb.</u>
2) Unleavened Bread—Knowing the purity of "unleavened" living—<u>Live in the purity of Christ's "unleavened" life.</u>
3) First Fruits—Hoping in God's provision, ultimately the provision of Christ's resurrection, a new life now and a future resurrection, made forever whole—<u>Live and reign by Christ's resurrection life.</u> **4) Pentecost**—Living by God's provision, ultimately experiencing the Spirit's promise and provision as a body of believers—<u>Live, fellowship, and witness in the fullness of His Holy Spirit</u>.
5) Trumpets—Knowing God's call to assembly and accountability before Him—<u>Always act accountable to the Lord Jesus Christ</u>. **6) Atonement**—Having confidence in Jesus' *"once for all,"* Atonement for our sin, knowing an eternally secure salvation with sin forgiven and forgotten forever. Come near and live, forgiven, cleansed, free, and eternally secure, in His Presence forever. **7) Tabernacles**—God dwelling with us. Celebrating the fullness of God's life and presence on earth and in eternity—<u>Experience the pleasure of His presence with the fullness of His joy.</u>

At this point, we have journeyed through those Feasts. It is time to consider how well we are experiencing and expressing the fullness of this "life"—all that God desires for us. Think of the Seven Feasts, about what you have seen in these Lessons, *and* about how these truths apply to you today. Consider these questions that overview the Seven Feasts and how they connect with you. How well are you answering the call of the Feasts? As you prayerfully consider each Feast and these questions, ask the Holy Spirit to give you personal insight. Then, record your journal entry and a prayer after each one.

The Passover Feast—For your salvation, have you trusted in the Lord, in the chosen lamb Jesus, the Lamb of God who shed His blood for your sin and died in your place (John 1:29)? Have you followed Him out from under the *"hand of Pharaoh,"* out of the land of *"Egypt,"* clear pictures of the kingdom of darkness? Remember your redemption through the blood of **the** Lamb.

Journal

_____
_____
_____
_____

Prayer

_____
_____
_____
_____

Feast of Unleavened Bread—Are you walking daily in the purity of an "unleavened" life, feasting on His life, experiencing His work in you so that you are walking in *"sincerity and truth"* (1 Corinthians 5:7–8)? Live in the purity of Christ's "unleavened" life.

Journal

_____
_____
_____
_____

Prayer

_____
_____
_____
_____

Feast of Firstfruits—Are you walking daily with a *"living hope"* in Christ, in the promise of resurrection which includes *"an inheritance .... imperishable* *and undefiled,"* one that *"will not fade away"* (1 Peter 1:3–4)? Are you living in His resurrection power day by day, walking in *"newness of life,"* filled and controlled by His Spirit (Romans 6:4–11)? Live and reign by Christ's resurrection life.

Journal

_____
_____
_____
_____

Prayer

_____
_____
_____
_____

> **Did You Know?**
> **GOD'S CALL TO SEEK HIM**
>
> God called His people to seek Him in the Feasts times—"…*You shall seek* **the** L<small>ORD</small> *at the place which the* L<small>ORD</small> *your God shall choose…*" (Deuteronomy 12:5) God called His people to seek Him in time of spiritual and moral decline—"…*It is time to seek the* L<small>ORD</small> *until He comes to rain righteousness on you.*" (Hosea 10:12) God calls all to seek Him wherever each may be—"…*He made from one, every nation of mankind to live on all the face of the earth, …that they should seek God…*" Acts 17:26, 27

Feast of Pentecost—Are you experiencing the fullness of His Spirit, walking in His power and the provision of *"everything pertaining to life and godliness"* (Ephesians 5:18–21; 2 Peter 1:3)? Are you fulfilling your part in building up the Body of Christ, loving one another, walking in the oneness of the Spirit, and being a witness of Him (1 Corinthians 12:4–7, 12–27; Ephesians 2:22; 4:1–7, 12–16; Acts 1:8; 4:31)? Live, fellowship, and witness in the fullness of His Holy Spirit.

Journal

_____
_____
_____
_____

Prayer

_____
_____
_____
_____

Feast of Trumpets—Are you living ready to **answer** the trumpet call, to **assemble** before the Lord, to give an **account** to the Lord, and to receive **all** the rewards He has for you (Romans 14:7–12; 1 Corinthians 3:10–15; 4:2–5; 2 Corinthians 5:9–10)? Are you walking by faith, sensitive to the leadership of His Spirit, and obedient to His Word day by day (Romans 14:16–19, 23; 2 Corinthians 5:7)? Always act accountable to the Lord Jesus Christ.

Journal

_____
_____

Prayer

Day of Atonement—Are you walking daily in the assurance of an eternally secure salvation, with forgiveness of sins, the reality of a cleansed conscience, and the joy of confident, humble prayer and whole-hearted worship (Hebrews 10:18–25)? Are you declaring to others the "Jubilee" redemption freedom Jesus gives (Leviticus 25:9–10; Luke 4:18–19)? Come near and live, forgiven, cleansed, free, and eternally secure, in His forever presence.

Journal

Prayer

Feast of Tabernacles—Are you practicing the presence of the Lord in all of your daily life? Are you walking *with* Him, enjoying His presence, following His leadership, experiencing His provision, and expressing His righteous life in your relationships every day in every place (2 Corinthians 2:14–17; 6:14–18; 7:1)? Is your heart prepared for His return and your entry into the coming kingdom (Acts 1:11; 4:21; Philippians 3:20–21)? Experience the pleasure of His presence with the fullness of His joy.

Journal

Prayer

> Lord, thank You for Your promised Presence fulfilled in the coming of Your Son, our Lord Jesus, the Messiah. Thank You, Lord Jesus, for "tabernacling" among us, revealing the Father's glory, *"full of grace and truth"* (John 1:14). Thank You for all You endured to bring the fullness of salvation to me, to now indwell me moment by moment, to give me daily guidance, to empower me to live as You desire. Forgive me for those stubborn stands I take to do "my" will instead of Your will. Thank You for Your patience and mercy toward me. Thank You for the promises of Your Return, Your *parousia*, when Your presence will be manifested throughout the earth, when Your reign will be clearly revealed for all to experience. Thank You that You include all Your children in the promise of reigning with You. May I have wisdom for this day to live under Your Lordship, investing my time as You will, giving my life away to help others know and grow in You, so they too may rejoice in Your daily presence, in the confident expectation of Your return, and in our resurrection and reigning with You. In Jesus' name, I pray this. Amen.

The Order of Events in the Feast of Tabernacles/Booths In New Testament Days

Beginning the Feast.
The Feast of Tabernacles began on the fifteenth of *Tishri,* but people began arriving in Jerusalem on the fourteenth. They gathered branches of date palms, olive trees, myrtle, and other leafy limbs for use in the worship times and to build their booths for the Feast. The **first day**, the fifteenth, was a special Sabbath which included a *"holy convocation"* or *"assembly,"* the sixth such special Sabbath of the annual Feasts.

Daily Water Pouring Ceremony.
On the morning of the fifteenth, while the priests made final preparations for the morning sacrifice, the high priest left the Temple accompanied by musicians playing flutes. They walked in procession to the Pool of Siloam, the pool that gathered the water from the Gihon Spring through Hezekiah's tunnel. There he filled a golden pitcher with water (over two pints) and carried it back to the Temple, timing his entrance through the Water Gate at the threefold blast (short—long—short) of the priests' silver trumpets. At the same time another procession entered into the city carrying willow branches gathered at a nearby brook. They brought the willow branches to the Temple and placed them in a canopy arrangement around the altar.

The high priest with the pitcher of water came into the Temple area as the priests placed the morning sacrifice on the altar. At the altar were two silver basins, one for the daily wine offerings and the other for the water. The priests poured the wine and the water from Siloam into the two vessels at the same time. The Temple music began and the Levites sang the *Hallel* (Psalms 113—118). When the choir sang *"Give thanks to the LORD, for He is good; for His lovingkindness is everlasting"* (Psalm 118:1), the worshipers took palm branches and shook them toward the altar. At the close when they sang *"Save*

Did You Know?
THE COMING KINGDOM, A TIME OF PERFECT REST

God spoke to His people of "the Promised Land" where they could find the rest of Canaan after their Wilderness wanderings (Deuteronomy 12:9–10; Joshua 21:43–45). However, Joshua could not lead them into the full rest God desired for them. Jesus could. Because of His death and resurrection every believer receives His "promised life," the *"abundant life"* in which we discover the rest of Christ, rest from the wayward world wanderings (Matthew 11:28–30; 16:24; John 14:27; 16:33; Romans 12:2; Galatians 1:3–4; 6:14; Hebrews 4:8–10). Ultimately, Jesus will bring the fullness of His promised Lordship. At His return, every believer will experience the rest of His coming and His Kingdom. We will experience the fullness of His reign, an inner rest and an external order of peace in contrast to the present weariness of the world kingdoms (Isaiah 9:5–7; Matthew 16:26–28). In that rest, all who belong to Jesus will live forever, serving and reigning with Him in the Kingdom and in eternity (Revelation 20:6; 22:3–5).

now, I pray [Hosanna], O LORD; O LORD, I pray, send now prosperity" (Psalm 118:25), the worshipers repeated the waving of the palm branches. (A similar scene of rejoicing in the Lord's salvation and in the waters of life is pictured in Revelation 7:9–17.) The pouring out of water signified the Lord pouring out His salvation from the heavens through the Messiah, the Son of David, whom they believed would come one day. They believed that day would also be marked by the outpouring of the Holy Spirit, accompanied by great joy in His all-sufficient salvation and reign (Isaiah 12:3–6). Their prayers also sought the Lord for the needed rains for the upcoming agriculture season.

Daily Feast Offerings and the Ceremony of the Priests.

The first day included the most burnt offerings (13 bulls, 2 rams, 14 lambs), plus a goat for a sin offering along with grain and wine offerings. This continued each day with one less bull offered each day until the last day when seven were offered. At the close of these Feast offerings, the priests holding palm branches marched in procession around the altar once on the first day as well as on the second through the sixth days. They sang Psalm 118:25, *"O LORD, do save, we beseech Thee [Hosanna]; O LORD, we beseech Thee, do send prosperity!"* The phrase *"do save"* is often translated *"Hosanna,"* meaning *"save now, I pray."* On the seventh day, *"the great day of the Feast,"* they marched around the altar seven times, symbolic of the march around Jericho when the walls fell and the people rejoiced to enter the Promised Land with its abundance and blessings.

Sabbatical Year.

According to Deuteronomy 31:10–13, during a sabbatical year the priests publicly read the entire Law of Moses (Genesis through Deuteronomy) on the first day of the Feast as it was in Nehemiah's day (Nehemiah 8:14–18, first day and daily).

Light Ceremony Each Night.

At the end of each day, beginning on the first day, the worshipers went into the Court of the Women where there were four very large lampstands or menorahs over seventy feet high each with four branches and four large golden bowls on top, each capable of holding about ten gallons along with a linen wick made from worn priestly garments. Four youths from priests' families climbed ladders and poured oil into the bowls, which were then lit to give light to the whole Temple area and the surrounding city. Then the Chasidim ("pious ones" zealous for the ways of Judaism) and men of Deed danced, holding flaming torches and singing hymns of praise. The Levites with various instruments accompanied them (harps, lutes, cymbals, trumpets, etc.) As morning broke, two priests with trumpets gave a threefold blast while standing on the **fifteenth** Temple step leading up to the place of sacrifice. Then they went to the **tenth** step and another threefold blast, then another at the **bottom** step. Then they walked across the Court of the Women (a square space of about one and a half acre) to the Beautiful Gate at the east entrance to the Temple. At the Gate they turned to face west toward the Holy Place in worship of the Lord and to declare their loyalty, never turning their backs on their God.

This ceremony of the Light symbolized the *Shekinah* Glory that had once filled the sky in the Pillar of Fire and filled the Tabernacle in Moses' day. The Lord also manifested His Glory in the Temple in Solomon's day. This ceremony also spoke of the prophesied light of the Messiah (Isaiah 9:3–7) that would come to those walking in darkness (Isaiah 9:2).

Seventh Day—The Great Day of the Feast.

On the **seventh day** of the Feast there were extra festivities. The people called this day *"the Great Day of the Feast"* or the Day of the Great Hosanna. On this day the priests went to Siloam and returned, pouring the water, then offering the festive sacrifices. At the close of those offerings, they marched around the altar **seven times**. The Levites sang the *Hallel*; the people worshiped with the palm branches, and three times the priests played a threefold blast on the trumpets (long note–quavering note–long note). Then, in Jesus' day, perhaps as they were repeating Psalm 118:25—*"O LORD, do save [now], we beseech Thee; O LORD, we beseech Thee, do send prosperity"*—Jesus cried out, *"If anyone thirsts, let him come to Me and drink."*

The cry of the worshipers included the cry for rains for the next year as the winter season approached. Jesus brought this day to a new height focused not on temporal rains, but on Himself as the source of eternal life and the life-changing refreshing *"living water"* of His Spirit. On this day with the festivities at their height, Jesus declared Himself the fulfillment of all the priests and people had pictured. He alone would give the living waters of salvation (John 7:37–39).

The Eighth Day—Tishri 22.

The Lord called for another day of rest and a *"holy convocation"* or *"holy assembly"* on the eighth day, the day of the completion of the Feast of Tabernacles. This was the seventh special *"holy convocation"* or *"assembly"* of the year. On this day, Jesus declared to the people and to the man born blind, *"I am the light of the world"* (John 8:12 and 9:5), fulfilling the symbolism of the Light Ceremony. He is that light, the *"glory as of the only begotten of the Father"* (John 1:14) and that Pillar of Fire which Israel followed in leaving Egypt and entering Canaan. Anyone who would follow Him *"shall not walk in darkness, but have the light of life"* (John 8:12).

Jesus Seen in the Feast.

All that the priests and people did during this most joyous of Feasts was a shadow of the coming Messiah. Jesus was the substance. He is the Messiah or Christ ("Anointed One") sent from the Father to bring the promised salvation. He gives the *"living waters"* of salvation and He is *"the light"* to darkened hearts in a darkened world. Just as the blind man received sight when he obeyed Jesus by faith, so can anyone receive the salvation He offers—*"if anyone thirsts, let him come to Me and drink"* (John 7:37).

THE BIRTH OF CHRIST AND THE FEAST OF TABERNACLES

Christ *"Tabernacled Among Us and We Beheld His Glory"*—John 1:14
Possible Connections between the Messiah and the Feast of Tabernacles

To the Jewish people in Jesus' day **The Feast of Tabernacles** was the most joyous, marked by the greatest festivities of all the Feasts. They celebrated the cleansing of the Day of Atonement, the abundance of the harvests, and their expectation for the **reign of Yahweh** over all the nations in the coming days. During this Feast, people spoke of, sang about, and looked for the coming of the Messiah, the son of David to bring His Kingdom. Everyday they sang the "Hosannas" ("save now, I pray") of Psalm 118:25, praying for the coming of a king-like Messiah/Savior, worshiping and waving palm branches, symbols of a victorious Israel.

The celebrations of the week, including the daily water pouring ceremony, the nightly light festival, and the many different offerings pointed to the coming of Israel's greatest day, the rule of Yahweh as King with His Messiah clearly revealed. Some associate the promises of Zechariah 2:10–11; 3:8–9; 8:1–23; 9:9–17; 10:1–12 and 14:1–21 with the expectation of Yahweh's hand of deliverance and the establishment of His rule over the world. Zechariah's imagery of *"the stone"* (3:9) and *"cornerstone"* (10:4) may be linked to the singing of Psalm 118 everyday of the Feast of Tabernacles as they looked for their king and *"chief cornerstone."*

Jesus began His ministry in the Fall, when He was *"about thirty years of age"* (Luke 3:23), perhaps just after His birthday. His words in John 7—9 point to Him as Lord, the source of *"living water"* and the *"light of the world,"* for all the nations. These words pictured many of the prophecies about the Lord's reign, the wonders of His Kingdom, and the glorious manifestation of His Presence "tabernacling" among us. Jesus, *"the Word"* who is God, *"became flesh and dwelt* [tabernacled] *among us,"* revealing Himself as Messiah and King (John 1:1–18, 29, 41, 49–50; 18:37). The call to us is to believe, worship, and obey Him as Lord and God (John 20:28–31).

In Luke 2:10, the angel announced to the shepherds the birth of the Savior, the Messiah and Lord. The angel spoke of *"great joy"* coming *"to all the people,"* words often associated with the Feast of Tabernacles which was called "the season of our joy" and the feast for all the nations. The possibility of Jesus' birth at the beginning of the Feast of Tabernacles certainly fits the symbolism of this Feast. Consider these truths.

Date	Events Leading to Christ's Birth	Scripture
Around the end of May and beginning of June (Ninth and Tenth weeks of the Religious Year), Zacharias served in the Temple by his Division. Jewish Calendar Month—*Sivan*	**Zacharias** served as a priest in the Division of Abijah, the **Eighth** of 24 Divisions of the Priesthood. The first Division came to the Temple the first week of Nisan (first month in the religious calendar). The others followed in the weeks after. **All** came during Passover and Pentecost weeks (the Eighth Division in the ninth and tenth weeks).	1 Chronicles 24:1–3, 10, 19
During the Ninth week (around fourth week of May into the first week of June) Jewish Calendar Month—*Sivan*	Priests chosen by lot offered incense in the Temple. So many served in the priesthood, this was a once in a lifetime opportunity for any priest. Zacharias was chosen and entered the Holy Place to offer incense and several prayers. This included praying for the coming of the Messiah and His forerunner "Elijah."	Luke 1:5; 8–10 Malachi 4:5; Matthew 17:10–13
One of the days of his week of service (end of May, early June). Probably one of the seven days of early *Sivan*	The Angel Gabriel appeared at the right of the Altar of Incense announcing the coming conception and birth of John (the Baptist) to Zacharias and Elizabeth. He would *"go before Him* [the Lord] *in the spirit and power of Elijah."*	Luke 1:11–22 Malachi 4:5–6; Matthew 3:2; 11:14; Mark 1:4; 9:12
In the first half of June. Month *Sivan*	Zacharias finished his service at the Temple and returned to his home in the hill country of Judah (Judea).	Luke 1:23, 39

Date	Events Leading to Christ's Birth	Scripture
Around the third week of June / *Tammuz* through November, *Bul* / *Marchesvan*	After a necessary time of separation for ritual purity, Elizabeth conceived a child and stayed secluded for five months (late June to November).	Leviticus 12:5; 15:19, 24–25 Luke 1:24–25
Six Months Passed—Late June to Early December. *Tammuz* to *Kislev*—The Angel Gabriel came mid- to late December	In the Sixth Month of Elizabeth's pregnancy (December), the Angel Gabriel came to Nazareth to Mary and announced the coming conception by the Holy Spirit and the Birth of the Messiah Jesus through her as a virgin.	Luke 1:26–38
During late *Kislev/Chislev* or early *Tebeth* (mid- to late December).	Mary conceived the infant Messiah Jesus in her womb by the Holy Spirit.	Matthew 1:18–23 Luke 1:39–45
Tebeth, Shebat, Adar—the first 3 months of Mary's pregnancy—Mid- or late December to mid-March.	Mary traveled to the hill country of Judah to the home of Zacharias and Elizabeth who was in the late sixth month of her pregnancy. Mary stayed there three months (Tebeth, Shebat, Adar/ December to mid-March) and then returned to her home in Nazareth.	Luke 1:39–57
The ninth month of Elizabeth's pregnancy would come in the month *Nisan*. Passover is *Nisan* 14. Some date John's birth on this date. Late March.	John would have been born in the Spring, likely during the week of Passover. In modern observances of Passover a chair is left empty for "Elijah" to come and join the celebration. Counting from late June, Passover occurs at the fortieth week of gestation (late March).	Matthew 17:10–13
Nisan through *Elul* (six months)—Late March through Early September.	Mary experienced the fourth through the eighth months of her pregnancy in Nazareth.	Luke 1:56; 2:4–6
During Late *Elul* and/or Early *Tishri*—The month of September	Mary and Joseph traveled to Bethlehem to be registered in the tax census of Caesar Augustus. The journey (likely in a caravan with other travelers) covered about 80 miles and would have taken a minimum of four days, but likely closer to a week or more due to Mary's pregnancy.	Matthew 1:24–25 Luke 2:1–5
Possibly on *Tishri* 15, the beginning day of the **Feast of Tabernacles**. Approximately, between September 20 and 30. Shepherds would be keeping their flocks in the field at night during this time of year.	The statement, *"while they were there* [Bethlehem], *the days were completed for her to be delivered"* indicates Mary and Joseph were in town at least a few **days** before Mary delivered her firstborn Son, Jesus (Luke 2:6). It is of interest to note that if *Tishri* 15 is the birth date of Jesus, it points to a forty week gestation period from *Tebeth* /Mid-December to Tishri 15/Late September.	Luke 2:6–7 Luke 2:8–20 Galatians 4:4 (*"the fullness of time"*— Greek, *chronos*, precise, measured time)

THE BIRTH OF CHRIST AND THE FEAST OF TABERNACLES (cont)

CHRIST *"TABERNACLED AMONG US AND WE BEHELD HIS GLORY"*—**JOHN 1:14**

POSSIBLE CONNECTIONS BETWEEN THE MESSIAH AND THE FEAST OF TABERNACLES

DATE	EVENTS LEADING TO CHRIST'S BIRTH	SCRIPTURE
Possibly *Tishri* 22, the eighth day of the Feast of Tabernacles, the seventh special Sabbath in the year. Between late September and early October.	Eight days after Jesus birth, He was circumcised in Bethlehem. Joseph gave Him the name "**JESUS**" … *"for He will save His people from their sins"* (Matthew 1:21).	Leviticus 12:3 Matthew 1:25 Luke 2:21 Genesis 3:15 Galatians 4:4–7
"In the fullness of time"—Galatians 4:4	The most important fact about Jesus' birth is not *when* He was born, but *why* He was born—He was *"born of a woman"* to *"redeem"* us, so we *"might receive the adoption as sons"* becoming *"heirs through God,"* celebrating the "Feast" of knowing Jesus **every day**.	Genesis 3:15 with Galatians 4:4–11; 5:1–25
Possibly on *Bul / Marchesvan* 24, forty days after Mary gave birth to Jesus. Approximately between late October and November 10	Mary was ceremonially unclean for forty days after giving birth to her son. After *"her purification,"* the Law of Moses required an offering of a lamb and a turtledove or pigeon, or two turtledoves or pigeons if poor (the offering of Joseph and Mary). The Law of Moses also required the dedication of the firstborn son as *"holy to the LORD,"* set apart to Him. Mary and Joseph traveled to Jerusalem (5 or 6 miles from Bethlehem) and fulfilled these offerings and the dedication of **Jesus**, her first born.	Luke 2:22–24 Exodus 13:2, 12, 15; 22:29; Leviticus 12:2–8; 27:26; Numbers 3:13; 8:17; Deuteronomy 18:4
Possibly 12 to 18 (or 24) months after the Birth of Jesus, the *"young Child"* Jesus was in a *"house"* in Bethlehem with Mary and Joseph (Matthew 2:11, 16). Soon after, Herod slew the male children 2 years and under.	The *"wise men from the East"* came to Jerusalem then Bethlehem to *"worship"* the newborn *"King of the Jews."* These *magi* could have had some rabbinical connection and Scripture information due to the Jews' historical sojourn in Babylon. They also interpreted changes in star movements as indicating the birth of a king and the beginning of a new era. Indeed, it was! They **worshiped** as should we!	Matthew 2:1–12, 16

THE SIGNIFICANCE OF SACRED GATHERINGS IN THE FEASTS
WITH THE VARIOUS SOLEMN ASSEMBLIES IN ISRAEL'S HISTORY
AND THE NOTABLE SACRED GATHERINGS IN THE NEW TESTAMENT

The three seasonal Feast pilgrimages brought the people of God together *nationally* around the worship of God and adherence to His Word (Deuteronomy 16:1–17).

The **three seasons** occurred in the first month (Nisan/Abib, very early Spring), in the third month (Sivan, late Spring), and in the seventh month (Tishri, early Autumn). In the seasonal pilgrimages to the Tabernacle or Temple to observe the various Feasts, the people gathered for **Seven Sacred Gatherings**, also called *"holy convocations"* or *"sacred assemblies,"* times of public gathering to worship and hear the Word of God. Those occurring during the **first** season of the Feasts Gatherings were the first and seventh days of Unleavened Bread. During the **second** season it was on the first Day of Pentecost. During the **third** season of Feasts in the seventh month, four special Sabbaths occurred, the Day of Trumpets, the Day of Atonement, and the first and eighth days of Tabernacles/Booths.

These Feasts were given **by the Lord** as *"My feasts,"* *"the feasts of the LORD,"* at *"their appointed times"* to **focus** on *Him* and His Word more fervently, to **worship** Him through various offerings, all to **celebrate** the covenant relationship with Him personally and nationally (Leviticus 23:2, 4).

WHEN?	THE SEVEN ANNUAL SACRED GATHERINGS *"HOLY CONVOCATIONS"* OR *"SACRED ASSEMBLIES"*	SCRIPTURE
Every Sabbath	The Seventh Day of **every week** was to be a day of *"complete rest."* They celebrated a *"holy convocation"* together as the people of God.	Leviticus 23:3
Nisan 15 *First* Gathering	On the *Seventh Day* of Unleavened Bread, Israel celebrated the **second** *"holy convocation"* of the year.	Leviticus 23:8
Nisan 21 *Second* Gathering	On the *Seventh Day* of Unleavened Bread, Israel celebrated the **second** *"holy convocation"* of the year.	Leviticus 23:8
Sivan 6 (?) *Third* Gathering	On the *First Day* of the Pentecost Celebration, Israel celebrated the **third** *"holy convocation"* of the year.	Leviticus 23:21
Tishri 1 *Fourth* Gathering	On the *Day* of the Feast of Trumpets, Israel celebrated the **fourth** *"holy convocation"* of the year.	Leviticus 23:24–25
Tishri 10 *Fifth* Gathering	*The Day* of Atonement was the **fifth** *"holy convocation"* of the year. This included the only required fast of the year, **fasting** from evening on the ninth of Tishri to evening on the tenth of Tishri	Leviticus 23:27–32
Tishri 15 *Sixth* Gathering	On the *First Day* of the Feast of Tabernacles/Booths, Israel celebrated the **sixth** *"holy convocation"* of the year.	Leviticus 23:35
Tishri 22 *Seventh* Gathering	On the *Eighth Day* of the Feast of Tabernacles/ Booths, Israel celebrated the **seventh** *"holy convocation"* of the year—the seventh gathering during the seventh Feast in the seventh month.	Leviticus 23:36
	SIGNIFICANT *"HOLY CONVOCATIONS"* / *"SACRED ASSEMBLIES"* DURING THE FEASTS IN ISRAEL'S HISTORY	
958 BC	Solomon and the people celebrated the dedication of the newly built Temple in Jerusalem during the seventh month before and during the Feast of Tabernacles. They concluded on *"the eighth day"* with the *"sacred assembly"* after seven days of dedicating the altar and seven days of the Feast of **Tabernacles**.	2 Chronicles 5:3; 7:8–10

BONUS CHARTS 199

THE SIGNIFICANCE OF SACRED GATHERINGS IN THE FEASTS (CONT)
with the Various Solemn Assemblies in Israel's History and The Notable Sacred Gatherings in the New Testament

When?	Significant "Holy Convocations" / "Sacred Assemblies" during the Feasts in Israel's History (continued)	Scripture
897 BC	In the third month (Pentecost season), Asa called the people to seek the Lord (likely during the Feast of **Weeks/Pentecost** celebration). Judah rejoiced as the Lord gave them peace all around.	2 Chronicles 15:9 15 (note verse 10)
715 BC	The **Passover** assembly of Hezekiah's day led to national revival. Under a special provision of God's law, it occurred in the second month. This Feast made such an impact that they prolonged it for an additional seven days.	2 Chronicles 30:1–27; 31:1 (note 30:23)
621 BC	After the Solemn Assembly of 622 BC under Josiah, the **Passover** assembly of 621 BC was more noteworthy than any since Samuel's day.	2 Chronicles 35:1–19
537 BC	The newly-returned exiles from Babylon rebuilt the Temple altar and celebrated the Feasts of **Trumpets**, **Atonement**, and **Tabernacles**.	Ezra 3:1–7
516 BC	The dedication of the rebuilt Temple and the **Passover** assembly of Zerubbabel led to a renewal in Jerusalem.	Ezra 6:15–22
445 BC	Beginning with the gathering for the Feast of **Trumpets** and including the gatherings of the Feast of **Tabernacles**, God brought a national revival to Israel in Ezra's and Nehemiah's day.	Nehemiah 7:73; 8:1–18
	**Special Calls to a "Solemn Assembly" or "Sacred Assembly" in Israel's History**	

From time to time, especially in times of spiritual and moral decline, God called for a special *"solemn assembly"* or *"sacred assembly"* to gather the people to deal with their sin, with points of disobedience, and to *"cry out to the LORD"* and *"return to Me"* (e.g., Joel 1:14, 2:12). Certain holy convocations sparked times of national renewal as God's people returned to Him in repentance and renewed obedience to His Word as in the days of Hezekiah or as in the days of Ezra and Nehemiah. These times led to **personal** and **corporate confession** of sins as well as personal and corporate **restoration**.

Observations about the various times of Solemn Assembly—
1) There was often a time of spiritual and moral decline and/or threats from the enemies of God and His people. In every case, the people recognized an obvious need they were unable to deal with apart from the Lord and His power and wisdom.
2) At times, the occasion was the sin and rebellion of the people of God. With that, God sometimes allowed or brought a measure of judgment in some form (natural calamity, foreign army, etc.).
3) God raised up and used a burdened leader (a prophet, a king, a priest) willing to obey His call and gather the people.
4) The leader called other leaders such as priests, kings, and officials to be involved and follow the Lord and His Word.
5) The primary focus was always on the Lord and their covenant relationship with Him. Circumstances were secondary.
6) God required the people to repent and put away sin, rebellion, and disobedience. Confession, forgiveness, and cleansing marked the meetings.
7) As the people responded with repentance and obedience, they rejoiced as God showed abundant mercy, readily forgiving and restoring His people.

Around 1065 BC	The prophet Samuel gathered Israel at Mizpah for a solemn assembly to pray, fast, and confess their sins. God gave victory over the Philistines.	1 Samuel 7:5–6, 7–14
1000 BC	King David gathered the people for a worship assembly to bring the Ark of the Covenant to Jerusalem. The People rejoiced as they followed the Word of God and worshiped Him.	1 Chronicles 15:1–29; 16:1–36, 43; 2 Samual 6:12–15

THE SIGNIFICANCE OF SACRED GATHERINGS IN THE FEASTS (CONT)
WITH THE VARIOUS SOLEMN ASSEMBLIES IN ISRAEL'S HISTORY
AND THE NOTABLE SACRED GATHERINGS IN THE NEW TESTAMENT

WHEN?	SPECIAL CALLS TO A "SOLEMN ASSEMBLY" OR "SACRED ASSEMBLY" IN ISRAEL'S HISTORY (CONTINUED)	SCRIPTURE
Around 850 BC	King Jehoshaphat called for a solemn assembly to deal with the unprovoked threat of three armies coming against Judah. God gave a great victory to Judah.	2 Chronicles 20:3–30
835 BC	Jehoida the priest called the people and king together to make a covenant to renew their obedience to the Lord. They obeyed, ridding the land of evil.	2 Chronicles 23:16–21
Around 835–800 BC	After a plague of locusts, the prophet Joel called the people to *"proclaim a solemn assembly"* to *"call on the Lord"* for His deliverance. A *"return to the LORD your God"* would be accompanied by His merciful blessing (2:12–14).	Joel 1—2 (note 1:14; 2:1, 12–17)
622 BC	King Josiah called all to a solemn assembly to renew their covenant with the Lord and rid the land of any abominations.	2 Chronicles 34:29–33
458 BC (Spring)	Ezra the priest called for a fast to seek the Lord for His protection on the journey from Babylon to Jerusalem.	Ezra 8:21–23
458 BC (Winter)	Ezra the priest led the people in a solemn assembly to repent of disobedience and to put right their hearts, lives, and homes.	Ezra 9:5–15; 10:1–15
	GOD'S CALL TO NEVER MISUSE THE SOLEMN ASSEMBLY	
739 BC	Through the prophet Isaiah, God called His people to stop their empty rituals of Sabbaths, Feasts, and solemn assemblies. He would not hear their prayers.	Isaiah 1:10–15
739 BC	Through the prophet Isaiah, God called His people to confess their sins, cease from evil, and do good. He offered the people forgiveness and restoration if they obeyed, or, if not, judgment.	Isaiah 1:16–20
	NOTABLE SACRED GATHERINGS IN THE NEW TESTAMENT	
AD 30	After Jesus' Ascension, 120 believers gathered in the Upper Room and had extended times of prayer over the next ten days prior to **Pentecost**.	Acts 1:11–26
AD 30	The Upper Room gathering of the 120 believers included focused seeking of God about His choice of spiritual leadership (*"they prayed"*).	Acts 1:24–25
Pentecost AD 30	On the Day of **Pentecost** Feast, the 120 believers were gathered in prayer at the Temple at 9:00 AM, the hour of prayer. The Father poured out the Holy Spirit on them that morning. After Peter preached, 3,000 believers were added to the newly-birthed church.	Acts 2:1–15
AD 31 or 32	The believers gathered to pray over their call to spread the message of Jesus in light of the prohibitions of the Jewish officials. They **prayed** together *"with one accord"* and *"the place where they were assembled together was shaken;"* they were filled with the Holy Spirit afresh, and went out speaking the Word of God with boldness.	Acts 4:23–31
AD 37 or 38?	King Herod Agrippa I, after beheading James the brother of John, arrested Peter and put him in prison during the Feast of **Unleavened Bread**. Many would be gathered for this Feast and for times of worship. The church gathered and offered fervent prayer. God miraculously released Peter.	Acts 12:1–19
AD 95	**Jesus Christ** called the **Seven Churches** in Asia to hear, repent, and obey His Word. These words would have been heard in a **local church gathering** with the intent of leading the people to prayer, seeking the Lord, and returning to Him in repentance and renewed obedience.	Revelation 2:1–29; 3:1–22
Ongoing	The ongoing observance of the **Lord's Supper** is one of the ways God designed for the church to have regular times of **coming together** for prayer, reflection, heart examining, needed repentance, and restoration. It is a time of remembrance and proclaiming of the Lord's death, reflection on one's walk with Him and with others, and readiness for the Lord's return… *"until He comes."* Jesus commanded, *"Do this in remembrance of Me."* It is always meant to be a heart to heart meeting *with* **Him** in the joy of a covenant relationship.	1 Corinthians 11:23–32; Matthew 26:26–28; Mark 14:22–24; Luke 22:17–20

A LOOK AT THE FEAST OF DEDICATION AND ITS RELATION TO JESUS CHRIST

In **John 10:22–39**, two months after the Feast of Tabernacles in John 7—9, **Jesus** was in Jerusalem during the **Feast of Dedication.** This feast, also known as the Feast of Lights or *Hanukkah* (Hebrew for "dedication"), lasted eight days (Chislev/Kislev 25 to Tebeth 2—mid-December). It was modeled after the Feast of Tabernacles in its length, in its use of light, in its celebration with palm branches and "joy and gladness," and in its expectation of a Messiah to come (1 Maccabees 4:52–59; 2 Maccabees 10:6–9; Josephus, *Jewish Antiquities*, xii.7.6–7)

In the year 167 BC, the Seleucids under Antiochus IV Epiphanes controlled Jerusalem. That year, they erected an idol-altar on top of the Temple altar and on Kislev 25 sacrificed a sow in honor of Zeus thus defiling the altar (1 Maccabees 1:54, 59). They continued to profane the Temple for the next three years. The priest Judas Maccabeus led a revolt against them and in 164 BC, recaptured Jerusalem, cleansed the Temple, and called for an eight-day **Dedication** of a newly placed altar. That dedication began on Kislev 25, coinciding with the anniversary of the defilement of 167 BC. The annual "Feast of *Dedication*" recalled the "days of the dedication of the altar" (1 Maccabees 4:59). What connection did Jesus have with this Feast or any of its history? When the priest Judas Maccabeus led the revolt that finally led to victory over the oppressive Seleucids and the cleansing of the Temple in 164 BC, the priests at that first Dedication asked questions about how the old altar was to be treated since it had been defiled. They agreed it must not be used. Worship must be with a new altar properly dedicated to the one true God. They pulled down the old altar and took the stones and stored them "until there should come a prophet to show what should be done with them" (1 Maccabees 4:44–46). Could Jesus be that prophet? Could He lead Israel even better than Judas Maccabeus had?

When **Jesus** walked in the Temple at the **Feast of Dedication** (about four months before His crucifixion), several Jews surrounded Him, questioning Him, *"How long will You keep us in suspense? If You are the Christ, tell us plainly"* (John 10:24). Perhaps they wanted a final answer concerning the ancient stones. They certainly wanted freedom from the Roman oppressors like the freedom Judas Maccabeus had brought. Was Jesus the expected prophet and *"the Christ"* or Messiah who would bring the Kingdom? Moses had predicted a *"prophet like me"* to come (Deuteronomy 18:15). The people of Jesus' day believed that prophet and the one mentioned in 1 Maccabees 4:46 would be one and the same. The Feast of Dedication focused on deliverance from an oppressive ungodly foreign power. In Jesus' day, the Jews had hopes the Messiah would come and deliver them from the oppressive, ungodly Roman rule.

Jesus spoke once again about the evidence of His works, of His oneness with the Father, and of how His sheep hear His Voice (John 10:25–30). The questioners would not believe what Jesus said about Himself, about being one with the Father, in spite of the fact that He could point to numerous miracles as evidence of the Father's work in and through Him. Instead, in their unbelief, they sought to kill Him (John 10:31). What was at the heart of their unbelief? It was about worship *their* way.

The Feast of Dedication spoke of the cleansing, consecration, and reuse of the Temple, with the return to worship God's way. In 164 BC, Judas Maccabeus secured the Temple so that true worship could resume. They renewed true worship, putting away the uncleanness of a foreign ruler.

Could Jesus bring about a more glorious day, including answering the questions concerning the stones of the old altar? Actually, those stones no longer mattered. Jesus Himself was the new "Temple" that would be destroyed and raised again (John 2:19). Jesus had made that statement in the context of cleansing the Temple, promising to raise up the temple of Himself in three days. The old Temple had been cleansed. Now Jesus cleansed the Temple in Jerusalem, but for a far greater reason—to prepare for **Himself** being the **Dedicated** Sacrifice to die on a Roman cross, the altar of God's choice for the sacrifice that would take away the sins of the world (John 1:29, 35). Jesus was leading the people to know the Father and experience true worship through the risen Son (John 10:38).

In the Jerusalem Temple, Jesus had spoken of being the Good Shepherd who lays down His life for the sheep, confident He would rise again. His sheep hear His voice, follow Him in truth, and know they are eternally secure (John 10:1–19, 25–30). While most of the people could not see it, **Jesus** was and is the fulfillment of all the symbolism of the **Feast of Dedication**, all that this feast pointed to or stood for—freedom from oppression and uncleanness, living in the light, rejoicing in pure worship, experiencing the salvation and victory of God. [See also, C. E. Garrad, "Dedication, Feast of" in *Hastings Dictionary of the New Testament: Christ and the Gospels* (Grand Rapids: Baker Book House, 1906, 1973), p. 437]

THE FEASTS OF THE LORD AND THE FULFILLMENT OF PROPHECY
The Life and Work of the Lord Jesus Christ
Prophesied and Seen in the Feasts

Although God instituted each Feast to celebrate or commemorate a harvest season, a holy assembly, or a historical event in the life of Israel, the greater significance is in how each Feast pictures and points to various manifestations of the life and work of Jesus Christ. The first four Feasts picture what has already occurred. The last three picture what is yet to occur. The present time is one of sowing and harvesting in the fields of the world, awaiting the fulfillment of God's times, seasons, and epochs (Acts 1:6–8). The Feasts serve as a prophetic **calendar** of **Christ** and His redemptive work, of God's activity in and through Israel and among the nations. Each Feast relates to prophecies about the Christ/ the Messiah Jesus, some emphasizing the fullness of His work of salvation, and others pointing to His coming reign on earth and in eternity (1 Peter 1:10–12).

Feast / Promise	Fulfillment in Christ	Scripture
Passover—Christ is *"our Passover,"* the Lamb, our substitute.	**The Crucifixion of Jesus Christ**. Christ is *"our Passover"* who was sacrificed for sinners. Jesus is *"the Lamb of God who takes away the sin of the world."*	Isaiah 50:4–7; 53:1–12 John 1:29, 36 1 Corinthians 5:7–8
Feast of Unleavened Bread—Christ continues to work in removing "leaven" from believer's lives. One day the presence of **all** evil will be removed.	**The Burial of the Sinless Savior Jesus Christ**. Jesus was buried during the Feast of Unleavened Bread having lived "unleavened" in all His life—motives, words, deeds. He revealed internal and external purity, *"without blemish and without spot,"* throughout His life and even in His death. He was tempted in every way, *"yet without sin"* in any way. In His burial, His body did not undergo decay or corruption.	Matthew 27:57–66 John 19:31–42 1 Peter 1:19; 2:22–23 Hebrews 2:17–18; 4:15–16 Acts 2:24, 27, 31 1 Corinthians 5:7–8
Feast of First Fruits Christ is the first fruits of the resurrection, the promise and hope of the resurrection to come.	**The Bodily Resurrection of Jesus Christ**. Jesus arose from the dead on the third day, the day after the Sabbath, on the Day of the Feast of First Fruits. He showed Himself to many followers. Jesus is the *"firstfruits of those who have fallen asleep… Christ the firstfruits"* of the Resurrection.	Matthew 28:1–8; Mark 16; Luke 24 John 20:11–31; 21 1 Corinthians 15:4–8, 20, 23
Feast of Pentecost or Weeks—Rains pour forth, then the harvest, so Christ poured forth His *"living water,"* the Spirit who]brings life.	**The Promised Pouring Out of the Holy Spirit**. The Lord promised the pouring out of His Spirit through Joel 2:28–29. The fulfillment of the promise of Jesus that the Father would send the Holy Spirit occurred on Pentecost Sunday. These Spirit-indwelt believers made up the early church, the visible and verbal witnesses of the resurrected Christ.	Joel 2:28–32 Luke 24:49 John 7:37–39; 14:16–17, 26; 15:26 Acts 1:8; 2:1–4, 16, 18, 33, 38–39
Prophecies and Promises Yet to Be Fulfilled		
Feast of Trumpets Believers will assemble before Christ to give an account and receive from Him the rewards due. All will give an account to Him.	**The Calling of Israel and the world to Assembly and Accountability before the Lord**. This is yet to occur in conjunction with the "seventieth week of Daniel," a 'week' of seven years, also known as *"the time of Jacob's trouble."* Some see this occurring after the *"last trumpet"* call and the rapture of the church when Christ returns for His Bride. This is likely the time of the Judgment Seat of Christ.	Daniel 9:27; 12:1 Jeremiah 30:7; 32:37. Isaiah 26:20–21 1 Corinthians 15:51–54, 58 1 Thess. 4:13–18
Day of Atonement Christ is the atonement sacrifice who takes away sin forever. One day all believers will rejoice together as the Redeemed.	**The Return of Christ Jesus to Complete His Redemption Promises**. This occurs at "the Second Coming of Christ." Israel's experience of the Atonement will occur when they see Him whom they pierced and by faith cry out to Him for salvation. Many see this occurring at the end of the Seven-year Tribulation period. It is the time when *"all Israel will be saved"*—all that view Him in that day.	Isaiah 27:9; 59:20–21 Ezekiel 36:16–38 Zechariah 12:10–14; 13:1–6, 8–9 Romans 11:26–27
Feast of Tabernacles or Booths—Christ will live and reign on earth. Believers will serve Him and reign forever.	**The Reign of Christ Jesus on Earth and in Eternity**. When Jesus Christ returns to earth, He will bring about the fulfillment of the Millennial Kingdom followed by the New Heavens and New Earth (see Isaiah 65:17–25; 66:22–23 with Revelation 19–22).	Daniel 2:44 Ezekiel 37:14–28 Zechariah 14:6–9, 16–21 2 Peter 3:10–13 Revelation 21:1–27

FEAST TIMES RECORDED IN SCRIPTURE

When?	What Feast Occurred and Who Was Involved	Scripture
Feast Times in the Old Testament		
1445 BC	The first **Passover** occurred in Egypt led by Moses.	Exodus 12:1–21
1445 BC	Led by Moses, the people carried and ate **Unleavened Bread** as they left Egypt, then during those first days traveling through the land, through the Red Sea, and into the Wilderness.	Exodus 12:15–20, 37–41; 13:17–22; 14–15
1445 BC	The first date associated with **Pentecost** coincides with the giving of the Law at Mount Sinai, fifty days after crossing the Red Sea. The LORD commanded Moses to *"consecrate"* the people for this special gathering at Mount Sinai (Exodus 19:10–11). They obediently prepared to meet God.	Exodus 19–20
1444 BC	The children of Israel kept the **Passover** at Mount Sinai one year after leaving Egypt.	Numbers 9:1–5
1405 BC	The people celebrated the first **Passover** in the land of Canaan at Gilgal after crossing the Jordan River led by Joshua.	Joshua 5:10–12
1405 BC	After Passover, the people ate **Unleavened Bread** in Canaan at Gilgal.	Joshua 5:11–12
1107 BC	Elkanah and his wives Hannah and Peninnah went to worship yearly (Deuteronomy 16:1–17, note verse 16) at the Tabernacle site at Shiloh. The Feast of **Tabernacles** is likely the Feast time noted in 1 Samuel 1:9.	1 Samuel 1–18
1102 BC	The Lord blessed Hannah with a son Samuel, born around 1105 BC. After weaning him, she brought him to live in Shiloh with Eli. This occurred during one of the Feast times, likely the Feast of **Tabernacles**.	1 Samuel 1:19–28; 2:1–11
958 BC	Solomon and the people celebrated the dedication of the newly built Temple in Jerusalem during the seventh month Tishri for seven days (8–14) **before** the Feast of **Tabernacles**, then, seven more days **during** the Feast. They concluded on *"the eighth day"* with the *"sacred assembly."*	2 Chronicles 5:3; 7:8–10
931 BC	When Jeroboam I became king of the divided northern kingdom of Israel, he installed false priests, false gods (two calves of gold), two false worship centers (Dan and Bethel), and instituted a **false feast** one month after the Feast of Tabernacles (on the fifteenth of the eighth month).	1 Kings 12:25–33
897 BC	In the third month (**Pentecost** season), Asa called the people to seek the Lord (likely during the Feast of **Weeks/Pentecost** celebration). Judah rejoiced as the Lord gave them peace all around.	2 Chronicles 15:9–15 (note verse 10)
715 BC	The **Passover** assembly of Hezekiah's day led to national revival. Under a special provision of God's law, it occurred in the second month. This Feast made such an impact that they prolonged it for an additional seven days.	2 Chronicles 30:1–27; 31:1 (note 30:23)
622 BC	Upon rediscovering the Law, Josiah led in a sacred assembly and began cleansing the land of idolatry (2 Kings 22—23:25). The **Passover** of 622 BC conformed to the Law more fully than any since the days of the Judges.	2 Kings 23:21–23; 2 Chronicles 35:1–19
537 BC	Jeshua the High Priest and Zerubbabel led the newly-returned exiles in rebuilding the Temple altar, then celebrated the Feasts of the seventh month (**Trumpets**, Day of **Atonement**, and the Feast of **Tabernacles**).	Ezra 3:1–7
516 BC	The dedication of the rebuilt Temple and the celebration of **Passover** and **Unleavened Bread** under Zerubbabel brought renewal in Jerusalem.	Ezra 6:15–22

FEAST TIMES RECORDED IN SCRIPTURE (CONT)

When?	What Feast Occurred and Who Was Involved	Scripture
473 BC	Mordecai and Esther established the yearly Feast of **Purim** (Adar 14–15).	Esther 9:18–32
445 BC	Beginning with the gathering for the Feast of **Trumpets** and including the gatherings for the Feast of **Tabernacles**, God brought a national revival to Israel in Ezra's and Nehemiah's day.	Nehemiah 7:73; 8:1–18
Feast Times in the Life and Ministry of Jesus		
4, 3 BC?	The Birth of Jesus could have occurred during the Feast of **Tabernacles** according to the chronology beginning with Zacharias' service in the Temple as part of the eighth course or division of Abijah.	Luke 1:5–10, 24, 26–27, 39–40, 56; 2:1–20
Every year	Every year Joseph and Mary took the family to Jerusalem to celebrate the Feast of the **Passover**. At the age of twelve, Jesus celebrated the Passover and stayed three additional days *after* the Feast of **Unleavened Bread**.	Luke 2:41–51
27 AD	In His first year of ministry, Jesus came to Jerusalem for **Passover** and cleansed the Temple because of the religious corruption there.	John 2:13–25; 4:45
28 AD	Jesus went to Jerusalem to a Feast, perhaps **Purim** or **Passover** in the Spring of the second year of His ministry or **Tabernacles** in the Autumn.	John 5:1–47
29 AD	Jesus fed the 5,000 shortly before the Feast of the **Passover** in His third year of ministry.	John 6:4
29 AD	Jesus went up to the Feast of **Tabernacles** where He proclaimed He could give *"living water."* He also declared, *"I am the Light of the world."*	John 7:2 (see chapters 7—9)
29 AD	Jesus was in Jerusalem during the Feast of **Dedication** (Hanukkah).	John 10:22–39
30 AD	After three and a half years of ministry, Jesus was crucified at the Feast of **Passover** as our Passover Lamb. The events of this Passover Season are covered from John 11:55 through John 19.30	John 1:29, 36; 11:55–57; 12–18; 19:1–30
30 AD	Jesus was buried during the Feast of **Unleavened Bread**	John 19:3142
30 AD	Jesus arose on the Sunday (*"the first day of the week"*) on which the Jews were celebrating the Feast of **First Fruits**.	1 Corinthians 15:4–5, 20; John 20:1–23
30 AD	Jesus Ascension occurred ten days before **Pentecost** in preparation for the sending and pouring out of His Holy Spirit by the Father on that Feast day.	Luke 24:49–53; Acts 1:4–11
Feast Times in the New Testament		
AD 30	The 120 gathered for prayer in the Upper Room after Jesus' Ascension and had extended times of prayer over the next ten days prior to **Pentecost**.	Acts 1:11–25
Pentecost AD 30	On the Day of **Pentecost** Feast, the 120 were gathered in prayer at the Temple at 9:00 AM, the hour of prayer. The Father poured out the Holy Spirit on them that morning and the Church was birthed.	Acts 2:1–15
AD 34 ?	The Ethiopian Eunuch came to Jerusalem to worship, likely during one of the three Feast "seasons" (Passover, Pentecost, or Tabernacles).	Acts 8:27
AD 37 or 38 ?	King Herod Agrippa I, after beheading James the brother of John, arrested Peter and put him in prison during the Feast of **Unleavened Bread**. Many would be gathered for this Feast and for times of worship. The church gathered and offered fervent prayer. God miraculously released Peter.	Acts 12:1–19

When?	What Feast Occurred and Who Was Involved	Scripture
AD 57	Paul, on his way to Jerusalem, had a detour. He chose to stay in Philippi during the Days of **Unleavened Bread** before resuming his journey.	Acts 19:6
AD 57	Paul journeyed from Corinth to Jerusalem hoping to participate in the Feast of **Pentecost** (Acts 20:3—21:15).	Acts 20:16; 1 Corinthians 16:8
AD 57	It is likely Paul arrived in Jerusalem in time to celebrate **Pentecost**. Paul was in the Temple during this season when many Jews from all over the region and the Roman Empire would have been in Jerusalem for the Feast. The Temple riot occurred in this time frame, during which Paul had opportunity to give to many his testimony about Jesus as Messiah.	Acts 21:15–40; 22:1–30; 23:1–35
AD 60	When considering traveling in the shipping lanes in October, Paul mentions *"the Fast,"* a calendar term referring to the Day of **Atonement**.	Acts 27:9
Ongoing	**Personally**, God calls each Christian to *"keep the feast"* of **Passover** / **Unleavened Bread** by trusting *"Christ our Passover"* and walking in *"sincerity and truth,"* living by the power of His *"unleavened"* life.	1 Corinthians 5:7–8
Ongoing	God calls Christians to come together as a church for the observance of the Lord's Supper. This is part of celebrating our **Passover** in Christ.	1 Corinthians 11:18a, 23–32
Feast Times in the Millennium and Eternity		
1000 years	A *new* **Feast of the New Year** will focus on holiness and cleansing from sin during the first seven days of the first month (Abib/Nisan) each year.	Ezekiel 45:18–20
1000 years	The Feast of **Passover** and **Unleavened Bread** will be celebrated, Nisan 14 and 15–21.	Ezekiel 45:21–24
1000 years	The Feast of **Tabernacles** / **Booths** will be celebrated in the seventh month, Tishri 15–21.	Ezekiel 45:25; Zechariah 14:16–19
Eternity	God will *"dwell"* **forever** with His people in the New Jerusalem with New Heavens and a New Earth, **every Feast fulfilled** through **Jesus Christ**!	Revelation 21; 2 Peter 3:13

An Account of The Feast of Purim

Covenant and Chastening

The people of Israel entered into a covenant relationship with the Lord God at Mount Sinai, a covenant based on faithfulness to His Word. After years of idolatry, rebellion, and disobedience to the Word of God, God in faithfulness chastened them, scattering them among the nations (Leviticus 26:39; Deuteronomy 4:29–31; 28:63–67; Nehemiah 1:8–9). In 605 BC, they went into Babylonian Captivity for seventy years. During that time, the Temple in Jerusalem was also destroyed (586 BC). In 539 BC, Cyrus the Persian conquered the Babylonians and further established the Persian Kingdom. With that, he issued orders that all the exiles who desired to return to Israel could do so and if they desired to rebuild their Temple, he would finance the undertaking. In 538 BC, Zerubbabel led around 50,000 Jews back to Jerusalem and they began working on the Temple. It was completed in 516 BC (Ezra 1—4:1–5; 4:24—6:22).

Deceit and Danger

Israel remained under the control of the Persian Empire for over 200 more years. During that time, God continued to be faithful to the Jews throughout the empire, but there were trials and threats along the way. One of those came in the reign of Ahasuerus (Xerxes I, 486–465 BC). The *Book of Esther* tells the story of this threat and the roles of Esther and Mordecai.

Esther, a Jewess and the daughter of Mordecai's uncle, became Queen in 479 BC (Esther 2:7, 16). The king promoted Haman, an Agagite, to a place of honor in the palace. From that position, Haman sought a way to destroy the Jews, the people of Esther and Mordecai. His animosity can likely be traced back to the conflict between the Amalekites and Israel. The descendants of Amalek, the son of Esau, attacked Israel when they left Egypt (Exodus 17:8–16). God cursed them and later ordered Saul to eliminate them (1 Samuel 15:2–3), but Saul left their king Agag alive. The prophet Samuel promptly executed him (1 Samuel 15:2–3, 11, 26, 32–33). Haman was a descendant of Agag and apparently remembered the 550-year-old conflict with King Saul, of the tribe of Benjamin. Mordecai was also of the tribe of Benjamin. He continually refused to bow to Haman in their daily traffic around the palace. Haman's hatred for Mordecai and the Jews intensified and soon became apparent.

With power, Haman saw his opportunity to carry out his hatred by eliminating the Jews in the Persian Kingdom (from India to Ethiopia—1:1, 3:6). In Nisan (March), 474 BC, Haman began working his plot against the Jews, arranging for their destruction on Adar 13, 473 BC (February), having determined the exact date by casting the **lot** (the Persian word is *Pur,* plural *Purim*). The king sealed the decree and couriers carried the message throughout the kingdom (3:7–15). When Mordecai heard, he immediately called upon Esther to intercede before the king for her people—she was in place *"for such a time as this"* (4:14). She called for three days of fasting before seeking an audience with the king, knowing she could perish if uninvited. She moved forward in faith—*"if I perish, I perish"*—and on the third day called the king and Haman to a banquet (4:13–16; 5:1–7).

Judgment and Reward

Haman rejoiced in the favor he enjoyed, but was seething over Mordecai's failure to show him honor. He plotted to have Mordecai hanged on the gallows (5:9–14). Big doors turn on small hinges. That night, the king could not sleep and commanded one of his servants to read the detailed chronicles of the king. In the reading, an incident surfaced from five years before in which Mordecai had helped foil an assassination plot on the king. The king wanted to reward him. About the time Haman came into the court, the king requested advice on how to honor one whom the king favored. Haman spoke of how one should be honored and the king gave orders for Haman to do so for Mordecai. Mortified, Haman carried out the request, but questioned his future (6:1–13).

At the banquet, Queen Esther revealed the plot hatched by *"this wicked Haman."* He was taken out and hanged on the gallows *"he had prepared for Mordecai"* (7:1–10). The king appointed Mordecai in place of Haman. In the month Sivan (May), Queen Esther and Mordecai composed and issued a counter-decree in which the Jews could defend their lives and property from any attacks (8:1–14). When Adar 13 came, the Jews dealt with those who *"sought their harm"* and overcame them but took no plunder from anyone (9:1–17).

The Jews rejoiced greatly on Adar 15. That year, Mordecai established a yearly celebration, Adar 14–15, known as *"days of Purim"* (lots) as *"days of feasting and joy, of sending presents to one another and gifts to the poor"* (9:20–28). Queen Esther issued a decree confirming this **yearly Feast of Purim throughout the kingdom** (9:29–32). Second to King Ahaseurus, Mordecai continued *"seeking the good of his people and speaking peace to all his countrymen,"* a faithful picture of all Christ will do in fulfilling His covenant promises to His people forever (10:3).

While Purim is celebrated annually, there is no other mention of this Feast in Scripture.

Notes